PARENT–CHILD RELATIONS
History, Theory, Research, and Context

Phyllis Heath
Central Michigan University

PEARSON

Merrill
Prentice Hall

Upper Saddle River, New Jersey
Columbus, Ohio

Library of Congress Cataloging-in-Publication Data

Heath, Phyllis.
  Parent-child relations : history, theory, research, and context / Phyllis Heath.— 1st ed.
    p. cm.
  ISBN 0-13-048842-9
  1. Child rearing—United States. 2. Parent and child—United States.
I. Title.

  HQ769.H473 2005
  649′. 1′0973—dc22

2003027138

Vice President and Executive Publisher: Jeffery W. Johnston
Publisher: Kevin M. Davis
Acquisitions Editor: Julie Peters
Associate Editor: Martha Flynn
Editorial Assistant: Autumn Benson
Production Coordination and Text Design: *The GTS Companies*/York, PA Campus
Production Editor: Linda Hillis Bayma

Design Coordinator: Diane C. Lorenzo
Photo Coordinator: Cynthia Cassidy
Cover Designer: Bryan Huber
Cover image: Getty One
Production Manager: Laura Messerly
Director of Marketing: Ann Castel Davis
Marketing Manager: Autumn Purdy
Marketing Coordinator: Tyra Poole

Photo Credits: James Carroll/PH College, pp. 150, 220; Scott Cunningham/Merrill, pp. 224, 237, 306; George Dodson/PH College, p. 168; Dorling Kindersley Media Library, p. 127; Laima Druskis/PH College, pp. 35, 61, 90, 156, 185, 277; Larry Fleming/PH College, p. 268; Neil Goldstein/PH College, p. 58; Eugene Gordon/PH College, p. 32; David Grossman/PH College, p. 233; Jo Hall/Merrill, p. 106; Charles Hangar, pp. 100, 180; Phyllis Heath, pp. xxii, 133, 144; Michal Heron/PH College, pp. 33, 147, 167, 207, 211, 221; Martin Lueders, Insight Photos/U.S. Census Bureau, p. 36; Anthony Magnacca/Merrill, pp. 69, 118, 135, 187; JoLynne McDonald, p. 282; L. Morris Nantz/PH College, p. 8; PCA International, Inc., p. 172; Pearson Learning, p. 97; Mike Peters/Silver Burdett Ginn, p. 295; PH College, pp. 176, 254; Roy Ramsey/PH College, pp. 19, 235; Barbara Schwartz/Merrill, pp. 114, 195, 239; Rhoda Sidney/PH College, p. 273; Silver Burdett Ginn, pp. 109, 230, 300; Skjold/PH College, p. 163; Teri Stratford/PH College, p. 209; UN/DPI Photo/John Isaac, p. 56; courtesy of U.S. Census Bureau, p. 161; courtesy of USDA Natural Resources Conservation Service, p. 131; Anne Vega/Merrill, pp. 15, 24, 50, 78, 83, 260, 284; Todd Yarrington/Merrill, p. 280; Shirley Zeiberg/PH College, pp. 43, 76, 116, 198, 202.

This book was set in Optima by *The GTS Companies*/York, PA Campus. It was printed and bound by R.R. Donnelley & Sons Company. The cover was printed by Phoenix Color Corp.

Pearson Education Ltd.
Pearson Education Singapore Pte. Ltd.
Pearson Education Canada, Ltd.
Pearson Education—Japan

Pearson Education Australia Pty. Limited
Pearson Education North Asia Ltd.
Pearson Educación de Mexico, S.A. de C.V.
Pearson Education Malaysia Pte. Ltd.

10 9 8 7 6 5 4 3 2 1
ISBN: 0-13-048842-9

To my children, Ken, Todd, and Kelly; to my mother, Grace Heath; and in loving memory of my father, James Heath, and my brothers, Wade and Harvey.

About the Author

Phyllis Heath is a professor in the Department of Human Environment Studies at Central Michigan University. She has also taught courses for Michigan State University in Okinawa, Japan. She was educated at the University of North Carolina at Asheville (where she earned a BA in Psychology), the University of North Carolina at Charlotte (where she earned a MA in Human Development and Learning) and the University of North Carolina at Greensboro (where she earned a PhD in Human Development and Learning). Her research has focused on the ways in which parent–child relationships impact the development of children and adolescents. This research has included the impact of parenting patterns on children's social competence, factors influencing parenting patterns (such as gender role ideology and locus of control), and more recently, the links between parenting patterns and adolescent depression. She is presently researching parenting patterns of indigenous people. She lives in Mt. Pleasant, Michigan.

Preface

This book was written to acquaint undergraduate students with the study of parent–child relations in the following major areas:

- The history of childrearing in the United States as well as philosophical and theoretical perspectives that have guided child socialization practices in this country.
- Variations in childrearing patterns, including the childrearing practices of ethnic majority and ethnic minority parents in the United States as well as childrearing practices in other countries.
- Coverage of parent–child relations at each of the following developmental stages: infancy and toddlerhood, preschool and middle childhood, early to late adolescence, and early to late adulthood.
- Challenges faced by parents and children when the special needs of the child, the family dynamics, or the experience of grief and loss place children at developmental risk.
- Child socialization strategies for guiding children to become increasingly more competent and to have higher self-esteem as well as parenting skills for preventing and responding to problem behaviors.

Contextual Approach to Parenting

The contextual approach to parenting, which is a distinctive feature of the book, is emphasized by the inclusion of both historical and cultural approaches to understanding parent–child relations. Historically, we will examine how those relationships have changed during the past century as well as ways in which more recent changes in the family (such as the rising rates of grandparent primary caregivers) have altered caregiver–child relationships. We will also explore parent–child relationships in various ethnic groups within the United States and compare those to the lives of parents and children in selected cultures throughout the world. Theory and research in human development and family relations have been interwoven with presentations of historical, cultural, and structural variations in the family; this focus is the basis for most of the chapters in the text.

A discussion drawing attention to how cultural beliefs affect parent–child relations is presented early in the text. Because the cultural approach is a central theme of this book, it is essential to understand that there are important differences and similarities in parent–child relationships across cultures. A discussion of the variations in families due to marital status, sexual orientation, and the care of children by adults other than parents is presented early in the text as well. The purpose of addressing the similarities and differences in various family arrangements is to heighten understanding of the commitment to the care of children that exists in families regardless of the conditions that have brought them together. The early presentations of cultural and structural variations in families are not meant to stand alone but rather to set the stage for discussions throughout the text that will focus on parents and children in the various settings in which their development occurs. That approach allows students to see how culture and family variations, as well as age and gender, are related to parent–child interactions at each stage of life.

Parenting Strategies

Another distinctive feature of this textbook is the in-depth coverage of parenting strategies. An overview of contemporary parenting strategies is presented in the final chapter, chapter 11, which includes a variety of techniques. Abundant figures in that chapter help explain each technique, and sufficient examples are provided to enhance students' understanding of how to use each of them. Furthermore, the strategies contained in the final chapter support information covered in previous chapters and provide guidance for parents as well as for professionals working with children and their parents or other caregivers. This approach to the presentation of child socialization strategies allows students to integrate theory, research, and technique. The first part of chapter 11 contains strategies designed to prevent misbehavior, to promote the child's self-esteem, and to enhance effective parent–child communication. The second part of that chapter focuses on methods used for providing consequences for behavior and for resolving parent–child conflict.

Supplements to This Text

The *Instructor's Manual* includes learning objectives, key chapter concepts, audiovisual suggestions, and a Test Bank containing a variety of test items in multiple-choice, true/false, and essay formats. The Companion Website at www.prenhall.com/heath includes learning objectives, a list of key concepts to help students focus on the chapter's big ideas, a self-test module with multiple-choice and essay practice items, chapter glossary, and Web links.

ACKNOWLEDGMENTS

Preparing a textbook is an enormous undertaking that involves an entire network of individuals, and I have many people to thank for their contributions. I wish to thank Christina Tawney, my original editor at Merrill/Prentice Hall, who recruited me to write the book; it was her enthusiasm over my new ideas for a parent–child relations textbook that persuaded me to take on the project. Kevin Davis and Martha Flynn, who took over as editors when Christina left for maternity leave and decided to stay home with her new baby, have supported the book wholeheartedly and have provided me with the resources I requested to ensure that the book is as good as I could make it.

The review process for the book was long and rigorous, and the reviewers were indispensable for the numerous comments and recommendations for improvement they provided. I am very grateful for the time and care spent by the reviewers to give me detailed, well-informed reviews: Susan Bowers, Northern Illinois University; Lane Brigham, Nicholls State University; Martha Bristor, Michigan State University; Patricia Cantor, Plymouth State College; Rena Hallam, University of Kentucky; Arminta Jacobson, University of North Texas; Celeste Matthews, Winona State University; Jacob Mayala, St. Cloud State University; and Sandra J. Wanner, University of Mary Hardin-Baylor.

Following the expert reviews, the book was copyedited by Cheryl Uppling, whose painstaking attention to detail was invaluable. The production editor for the book was John Probst, who was exemplary in his competence and professionalism. The photo researcher was Cynthia Cassidy, who came up with a wonderful selection of photographs, as you will see.

I also want to thank my colleagues at Central Michigan University who shared my enthusiasm for the book, supported my taking a sabbatical leave to begin the project, and were interested in my progress along the way. Finally, I want to thank my parents, James and Grace Heath, who provided me with the model of loving, caring parents that set me on the course of a career that has focused on the study of parent–child relations. Many thanks, all of you.

Discover the Companion Website Accompanying This Book

THE PRENTICE HALL COMPANION WEBSITE: A VIRTUAL LEARNING ENVIRONMENT

Technology is a constantly growing and changing aspect of our field that is creating a need for content and resources. To address this emerging need, Prentice Hall has developed an on-line learning environment for students and professors alike—Companion Websites—to support our textbooks.

In creating a Companion Website, our goal is to build on and enhance what the textbook already offers. For this reason, the content for each user-friendly Web site is organized by chapter and provides the professor and student with a variety of meaningful resources.

For the Professor—

Every Companion Website integrates **Syllabus Manager**™, an on-line syllabus creation and management utility.

- **Syllabus Manager**™ provides you, the instructor, with an easy, step-by-step process to create and revise syllabi, with direct links into Companion Website and other on-line content without having to learn HTML.

- Students may log on to your syllabus during any study session. All they need to know is the Web address for the Companion Website and the password you've assigned to your syllabus.

- After you have created a syllabus using **Syllabus Manager**™, students may enter the syllabus for their course section from any point in the Companion Website.

- Clicking on a date, the student is shown the list of activities for the assignment. The activities for each assignment are linked directly to actual content, saving time for students.

- Adding assignments consists of clicking on the desired due date, then filling in the details of the assignment—name of the assignment, instructions, and whether it is a one-time or repeating assignment.

- In addition, links to other activities can be created easily. If the activity is on-line, a URL can be entered in the space provided, and it will be linked automatically in the final syllabus.

- Your completed syllabus is hosted on our servers, allowing convenient updates from any computer on the Internet. Changes you make to your syllabus are immediately available to your students at their next log-on.

Common Companion Website features for students include:

For the Student—

- *Learning Objectives*—Outline key concepts from the text.
- *Key Concepts*—Help students focus on the chapter's big ideas.
- *Interactive Self-Tests*—Complete with hints and automatic grading that provide immediate feedback for students.

  After students submit their answers for the interactive self-tests, the Companion Website **Results Reporter** computes a percentage grade, provides a graphic representation of how many questions were answered correctly and incorrectly, and gives a question-by-question analysis of the self-test. Students are given the option to send their self-test to up to four e-mail addresses (professor, teaching assistant, study partner, etc.).
- *Chapter Glossary*—Defines key terms identified in text.
- *Web Links*—Links to www sites that relate to chapter content.
- *Message Board*—Virtual bulletin board to post or respond to questions or comments from a national audience.

To take advantage of the many available resources, please visit the *Parent–Child Relations: History, Theory, Research, and Context* Companion Website at

www.prenhall.com/heath

Educator Learning Center:
An Invaluable On-Line Resource

Merrill Education and the Association for Supervision and Curriculum Development (ASCD) invite you to take advantage of a new on-line resource, one that provides access to the top research and proven strategies associated with ASCD and Merrill— the Educator Learning Center. At **www.EducatorLearningCenter.com** you will find resources that will enhance your students' understanding of course topics and of current educational issues, in addition to being invaluable for further research.

How the Educator Learning Center Will Help Your Students Become Better Teachers

With the combined resources of Merrill Education and ASCD, you and your students will find a wealth of tools and materials to better prepare them for the classroom.

Research

- More than 600 articles from the ASCD journal *Educational Leadership* discuss everyday issues faced by practicing teachers.
- A direct link on the site to Research Navigator™ gives students access to many of the leading education journals as well as extensive content detailing the research process.
- Excerpts from Merrill Education texts give your students insights on important topics of instructional methods, diverse populations, assessment, classroom management, technology, and refining classroom practice.

Classroom Practice

- Hundreds of lesson plans and teaching strategies are categorized by content area and age range.
- Case studies and classroom video footage provide virtual field experience for student reflection.
- Computer simulations and other electronic tools keep your students abreast of today's classrooms and current technologies.

Look into the Value of Educator Learning Center Yourself

A four-month subscription to Educator Learning Center is $25 but is **FREE** when used in conjunction with this text. To obtain free passcodes for your students, simply contact your Merrill/Prenctice Hall sales representative, and your representative will give you a special ISBN to give your bookstore when ordering your textbooks. To preview the value of this website to you and your students, please go to **www.EducatorLearningCenter.com** and click on "Demo."

Brief Contents

Contents

Chapter 6
Parent–Adolescent Interactions   145

Chapter 11
Child Socialization Strategies and Techniques   281

Note: Every effort has been made to provide accurate and current Internet information in this book. However, the Internet and information posted on it are constantly changing, and it is inevitable that some of the Internet addresses listed in this textbook will change.

1

Historical and Theoretical Influences of Childrearing

From the beginning of the 20th century to the present, American parents' relationships with their children have undergone considerable change. The way in which parents view children has changed dramatically, and the parental role has undergone considerable redefinition. Child socialization practices of American parents have been scrutinized, criticized, and discussed in writings that have gained increasing public attention. Recommendations for better ways to rear children have been offered by varied sources, including psychologists, educators, and other well-known authorities. In that climate, scientists began to study the interaction patterns of children and their parents or other caregivers, and the findings of those studies have been widely disseminated. Based on those publications, public policy related to the care and protection of children has changed significantly. All these modifications in the way Americans interact with their children and in how they perceive their roles as parents have not changed overnight. Furthermore, the changes in American childrearing practices have not been uniform. As will be discussed in future chapters, Americans differ in the degree to which they accept professional advice and alter their childrearing practices. Those differences can be traced to influences such as the culture in which parents are rearing their children and the parents' educational level as well as a variety of other sources.

AUTOCRATIC PARENTING: A TRADITION OF HARSH, STRICT CHILDREARING

At the beginning of the 20th century, the autocratic approach was the prevailing belief guiding early American childrearing. Children were told what to do and expected to respond accordingly without expressing their opinions regarding parental demands. The autocratic approach to child socialization was influenced by two primary sources: the Hobbesian perspective of childrearing that was prevalent throughout Europe for many centuries (Aries, 1962), as well as Calvinist doctrine that influenced the childrearing beliefs of the early Puritans in the United States (Kagan, 1978).

The Hobbesian View: The Willful Child

Thomas Hobbes, who expressed the view that the child's will needs to be tamed, proposed that parental authority when strictly applied upholds both a religious mandate and a cultural tradition. It is from Hobbes that we obtained the view of the home as "a man's castle," based on his belief that the family was a miniature monarchy and that the rights and consequences of paternal (he did not mention maternal) and despotic domain were the same. Hobbes equated the status of children with that of household servants, both of whom were expected to have unquestioned obedience to the "master of the house" (Hobbes, 1994). Few questioned the justification for parental authority until the 20th century, and even Rousseau, who (in the 1700s) romanticized the child and recommended that parents consider the nature of the child in their socialization goals, argued in favor of despotic rule in the family (Baumrind, 1996).

Puritan Beliefs: The Sinful Child

Autocratic parenting views based on Hobbes' idea of the willful child found easy acceptance among early American Puritans whose religious beliefs were shaped by the doctrine of John Calvin. Because Calvinist doctrine emphasized the inherent sinfulness of the child, early American parents believed that to be the cause of children's willfulness. Firm discipline that included a strong belief in corporal punishment rather than parental affection was thought to be necessary for children's development (Kagan, 1978). Parents, therefore, expected strict obedience and submission from their children, not independence or assertiveness. Children who were considered to be disobedient received "correction," which often took the form of a brutal beating (Cleverley & Phillips, 1986).

Thinking Critically

As we begin the study of ways in which to raise children, take a moment to consider your own views regarding the essential nature of the child. What influences in your life have contributed to your view of the child? How do you think the two views discussed previously regarding the nature of children influence the childrearing approaches that parents use in bringing up their children?

THE QUESTIONING OF AUTOCRATIC PARENTING

The autocratic approach to child socialization began to be questioned early in the 20th century as the views of early childhood educators and psychologists began to influence childrearing practices in the United States and Europe. As will be shown in the following discussion, autocratic child socialization was challenged from a variety of different perspectives, and those challenges altered Americans' view of the nature of children, the role of the parent, and the appropriate way to bring up children.

The Legacy of G. Stanley Hall: The Child Study Movement

The first of the theorists who influenced American childrearing patterns was G. Stanley Hall, who received the first PhD in psychology in the United States and who began the Child Study Movement in the late 1800s. The goal of the Child Study Movement, according to Hall, was to develop a science of psychology and education that respected the true nature and needs of the child. Hall believed that Americans were slowly awakening to a recognition that "children are not like adults, with all the faculties of maturity on a reduced scale, but unique and very different creatures" (p. 88). Hall believed that "the child's senses, instincts, views of truth, credulity, emotions, and feelings toward objects have very little in common with ours . . ." (Hall, 1965, p. 89).

Sigmund Freud: An Emphasis on Children's Natural Instincts

The next theorist to influence both European and American childrearing beliefs was the Austrian-born founder of psychoanalysis, Sigmund Freud. Freud's view of the nature of the child reflected the philosophical perspective of the French philosopher Jean-Jacques Rousseau—that children are basically good and that under optimal conditions their innate talents would emerge (Synnott, 1988). Reflections of Rousseau's philosophy can be seen in Freud's emphasis on children's innate drives and in his view of the mother as the prototype for all future relationships (Freud, 1931/1961). The beliefs of G. Stanley Hall, that children are different from adults and have with their own instincts, also are reflected in Freudian theory. Freud developed the Theory of Psychosexual Development to explain the ways in which the focus of children's sexual energy corresponds to their stage of development (Brill, 1938). Based on that theory, Freud was the first contemporary theorist to propose that parental acceptance of the child's natural instincts should accompany parental attempts to socialize the child to conform to societal norms (Baumrind, 1996).

American parents, who were influenced by Freud during the 1930s, 1940s, and 1950s, rejected the autocratic approach to childrearing in favor of a more relaxed approach to child socialization. Freud's views of childrearing arose in direct opposition to the autocratic childrearing approach, and followers of Freud portrayed the child as psychologically fragile and in danger of being made chronically anxious by parental restrictions and demands (Baumrind, 1996). The lenient parenting pattern that developed as a result of Freudian influence reflected Freud's beliefs that (a) early influences are very important for children's development, and (b) harsh parenting methods are detrimental to children's well-being (Freud, 1931/1961).

❦ ❦

Thinking Critically

As we began the 20th century, autocratic parenting practices bolstered by fundamental religious beliefs were firmly in place. Then a few decades later, Freud recommended that parents should be less strict with their children but did not address the issue of how parents were to maintain control over their children. Before reading further, how influential do you think Freudian theory was in altering the childrearing behaviors of the typical American parent? Explain your answer.

❦ ❦

Although the acceptance of Freudian beliefs regarding childrearing loosened the grip of harsh, autocratic parenting in the United States, it did not sufficiently address the issue of limits, boundaries, and guidelines. Since American parents with their Hobbesian–Calvinist legacy still understood discipline from the perspective of autocracy and punitive discipline, not being harsh with children was interpreted as not interfering with children's natural inclinations, thereby not providing limits and guidelines for children. Consequently, most American parents were not influenced by Freudian views of childrearing owing to concerns that they were being asked to relinquish control of their children. Those parents who believed that Freud's advice was a better approach than the familiar autocratic parenting practices tended to develop a lenient childrearing pattern whereby they did not provide sufficient guidelines for their children.

Watson: The Dangers of Parental Affection

Although the study of family socialization during the 1930s and 1940s reflected Freud's view of lenient parenting, this child socialization pattern was never widespread in the United States (Baumrind, 1996). Its reception among better educated parents, however, opened the door to acceptance of psychological theory as a source of information regarding how to rear children. It was in this climate that behaviorist views espoused by the American psychologist John Watson found easy acceptance. The philosophy of the British philosopher John Locke (who adopted an environmentalist stance on development) provided the foundation for Watson's research in behaviorism as well as for his views on childrearing. Locke's suggestion that children's minds are blank slates at birth, to be molded by their caretakers, is easily recognized in Watson's childrearing recommendations. On the other hand, Locke's philosophy, that parents *should* show affection for their children was not incorporated into Watson's theory of how parents should rear their children (Kagan, 1978). As we shall see, Watson was strongly opposed to parental expressions of affection for their children.

Watson recommended that parents use a scientific approach to the rearing of children, but he did not provide scientific evidence to support his views of childrearing. Instead, Watson's childrearing advice was based on his fervent personal belief that parents should ignore their natural inclinations to be nurturing and responsive to their children. His first recommendation was that parents should disregard their natural inclinations to respond to their crying infants and should feed their infants according to a strict schedule. His second recommendation was that parents ought to ignore their natural impulses to be affectionate with their children to avoid spoiling them. Those two suggestions, though not supported by research evidence, found widespread acceptance in the American culture at a time when the new psychological theorizing was highly valued (Cohen, 1979; Kagan, 1978).

Watson's conviction about the harmful effects of parental affection for children was demonstrated in his interactions with his own children. His children have reported that they not only received little affection from their parents but that they were not even allowed to be affectionate with each other. An example of Watson's attitude that children were not supposed to get much affection is seen in his early notes that when his baby son cried upon the departure of his parents, the nurse was told to let the baby "cry it out" (Cohen, 1979). Watson's own parental behaviors reflected his position that physical affection and expressions of love impeded good development.

Watson's "Evidence" for His Childrearing Beliefs.   Because Watson had such a tremendous effect on child socialization patterns in the United States, it is instructive to examine the foundations for his beliefs. To begin, Watson believed that he had "scientific evidence" showing that children should get little affection. We are now going to examine that so-called evidence. Interestingly, Freud's ideas influenced Watson's beliefs regarding childrearing. Watson thought that Freud had shown that many children were hopelessly **fixated** on their mother or their father and in their most secret unconscious dreams "wished to be seduced" by them. Watson believed the fixations of children resulted from too much infant hugging, kissing, and coddling and concluded that too much parental love harms children (Cohen, 1979). According to Freud, a **fixation** is a weakness that obstructs the process of development (Brill, 1938). Although Watson claimed to be influenced by Freud's view of fixations, his theory contradicted, rather than supported, Freudian theory. For example, unlike Freud, Watson minimized the importance of children's instincts. Because Watson gave no consideration to the child's contributions to parent–child interactions beyond those of simple reflexes, he believed the parent was extremely important in molding the child's personality. His devaluing of parental responsiveness is actually a departure from Freudian theory since Freud enjoined parents not to be overly strict (Cohen, 1979).

The Influence of the Media on Americans' Acceptance of Watson's Views.   As a uniquely American theory, Watson's "scientific approach to the rearing of children" gained acceptance among American academics as well as Americans at large. The way in which Watson's ideas came to affect so many American parents can be traced to the methods he used to disseminate his controversial views. After having been forced to resign from Johns Hopkins University and at the time unable to obtain a university position, Watson was still a well-recognized "parenting expert." Throughout 1926 and 1927, he addressed teachers' groups and medical groups on his theories. Then in 1928, he began to organize his ideas more formally for a set of six articles that appeared in *McCall's* Magazine (read by many young mothers) that later came out in a book under the title, *The Psychological Care of the Infant and Child* (Watson & Watson, 1928). In magazine articles that were published in *Ladies' Home Journal* and *McCall's,* Watson consistently reminded mothers to put their babies on a strict feeding schedule and not to spoil their infants by being responsive. The popularity of Watson's beliefs regarding how parents should rear their children was, therefore, due to his views being broadcast on the radio and published in easily accessible popular magazines at the time. Because Watson's admonitions about parental responsiveness and recommendations regarding scheduled care found their way into the American popular media, they had a much more widespread influence on American childrearing than did Freud's concerns regarding the detrimental effects of harsh parenting on children. In Watson's articles in popular magazines and in his radio broadcasts (before television was available), he said that parenthood is a science and that parents should treat childrearing as an experiment. Given the newfound allegiance to science at the time, the linking of parenting with science was a very persuasive message to American parents (Cohen, 1979).

Thinking Critically

Which group of parents do you think Watson influenced by publishing his ideas in popular magazines that he would not have reached if he had published those ideas in academic journals?

Watson's Ridicule of the Childrearing Practices of His Time.   Even though Watson's extreme views were immensely popular at the time, he had his share of dissenters. Those who spoke out against his radical position, however, were not as influential or as well recognized as the founder of the American Behaviorist Movement who had already been hailed as a parenting expert because of his work on the desensitization of children's fears. An example of an objection to Watson's childrearing advice is evident in one mother's response to one of his lectures, "that she was glad she had her children before she had ever heard of John B. Watson and his blasted behaviorism because, that way, she had been able to enjoy them" (p. 210). Instead of respecting that mother's position, her remarks were used by Watson in subsequent lectures to show how parents had used their children selfishly as a means of enjoying themselves (Cohen, 1979).

That criticism of American mothers was expanded in a chapter titled "The Dangers of Too Much Mother Love" in his well-known book, wherein he suggested that the reason mothers indulged in baby loving was sexual and that children should not be hugged, kissed, or allowed to sit on the parent's lap. Not only did Watson object to parents showing affection to their children, he frowned also on parental supervision and monitoring of young children. He noted that parents were always keeping an eye on their children, never giving them any freedom. He suggested that if parents could not restrain themselves from watching their children they might use a periscope to observe them, so at least the children would not know they were being watched (Cohen, 1979).

Thinking Critically

How do you feel about the fact that Watson had such a strong influence on mothers whom he consistently criticized for their natural loving behaviors toward their children? How do you think mothers today would react to that type of criticism?

The Impact of Watson's Views on American Childrearing.   Although there is no question that Watson's views were extreme, the impact of his beliefs on American childrearing and the American child was not negligible. Parents in the 1930s, 1940s, and 1950s were eager for new knowledge, and science seemed to have limitless potential. Given the enthusiasm for scientific discovery that existed during that period of American history, it was plausible to assume that a psychological theory would offer a way of rearing perfect children. As the recognized American authority on childrearing, Watson was constantly asked for interviews and articles on the subject of childrearing. The U.S. Department of Health even adopted some of Watson's ideas and disseminated them in their pamphlets for parents (Cohen, 1979).

The views of Watson established such a stronghold on parenting patterns, during the 1930s, 1940s, and 1950s, that we still see his influence on childrearing in the United States today. Concerns regarding the spoiling of children, practices of scheduling infant feeding, and beliefs that parents should let their babies "cry it out," unfortunately, are still considered by some American parents to be the appropriate way to socialize their children. Although there is no doubt that Watson made valuable contributions to the field of psychology, he has been described by contemporary writers as a dogmatist who went beyond his data to popularize his views regarding children's development. There is a consensus among many contemporary psychologists that the extreme nature of his unbridled environmentalism, as it was translated into popular childrearing advice, is regrettable (Cohen, 1979).

CHALLENGES TO SCHEDULED CARE

Although John Watson's views held center stage in American childrearing beliefs throughout the 1930s, 1940s, and 1950s, other theories that were developed during that period contributed to alternative perspectives regarding the appropriate way to rear children. The development of Attachment Theory by John Bowlby (Bowlby, 1958,

1969) and studies of infant attachment by Bowlby's colleague Mary Ainsworth (Ainsworth, 1973) seriously challenged Watson's recommendation that parents not express affection toward their children. Additionally, the theories of Piaget and Vygotsky contradicted the view of children as passive learners. During the second half of the 20th century, theorists such as Erik Erikson and Lev Vygotsky continued to emphasize the importance of parental respect for children's feelings, an appreciation of children's cognitive abilities, and the growth-producing effect of parental support for their children. The most recent trends in theory development focusing on parent–child relationships come from Family Systems Theory and Urie Bronfenbrenner's Ecological Theory. Those theoretical approaches have drawn attention to the role of context as an influence of childrearing behaviors and children's development. In addition to continued theory development that has called attention to the need for parents to incorporate an understanding of children into their childrearing patterns, a number of early childhood educators have spoken out in favor of better childrearing practices.

Attachment Theory: The Importance of Parental Responsiveness

Attachment theory, which was developed by the British psychiatrist John Bowlby in the early 1940s (Bowlby, 1958, 1969), is in common with the theories of Freud and the views of G. Stanley Hall in that its philosophical foundation came from Rousseau's belief that children have natural instincts that should be considered when one is socializing them. Respect for the natural instincts of children served as the foundation for studies of interactions between mothers and infants by Bowlby's colleague Mary Ainsworth. According to Ainsworth (1973), emotionally available caregivers contribute to the development of **attachment**, which is the "affectional tie that one person forms to another specific person, binding them together in space and enduring over time" (p. 33). Ainsworth's perspective emphasizes that (a) socialization

Responsiveness to the infant's cues is a key factor in the promotion of secure attachment.

begins with personal attachment; (b) the infant is born helpless, requiring care, and (c) parents should respond to the feelings evoked by the child (Elkin & Handel, 1989). Studies of infant attachment during the 1940s awakened the scientific community to how essential parental responsiveness is for the healthy development of infants. Those studies documented the following: (a) that infants, whose caregivers are emotionally and physically available to them, develop **secure attachment**; (b) that having a secure attachment to a parent promotes the infant's exploration of the environment; (c) that the sensitive responsiveness of the caregiver in stressful situations provides reassurance, comfort, and protection for the infant; and (d) that the sensitive responsiveness of the caregiver provides for the child an internalized working model of parental availability (Ainsworth, Blehar, Waters, & Wall, 1978).

Rene Spitz: The Harmful Effects of Unresponsive Caregiving

Scholars in the areas of developmental psychology were beginning to see the importance of parental responsiveness to infants in the 1940s based on Ainsworth's attachment studies when the French psychologist Rene Spitz provided further strong evidence in the mid-1940s of the crucial importance of parental responsiveness. In his studies of institutionalized infants and children in Europe, Spitz provided indisputable data demonstrating that the responsiveness of the caregiver to infants' cries and other gestures of communication are crucial to infant development. In dramatic film footage that shocked the world, Spitz revealed that infants and children in orphanages who were provided scheduled rather than responsive care showed pained expressions of grief and in many cases became listless and apathetic. Many of those infants and children lost weight and became ill and some of them died (Spitz, 1954). Concern for the development of children growing up in orphanages led to the appointment by the World Health Organization (WHO) of other researchers to study orphaned children in countries around the world. Those social scientists reported findings similar to those of Spitz and his colleagues and concluded that children who receive minimal maternal care exhibit delayed development in many areas (Bowlby, 1951).

The Change in Public Policy from Institutionalization to Foster Care

Although the views of Watson (that parents should not be responsive to their children) were still basic to American parenting styles, the studies of Bowlby, Ainsworth, and Spitz as well as findings from other researchers around the world brought about a change in public policy regarding the institutionalization of children in the United States. Prior to the publication of those studies of orphaned children, American children placed for adoption were typically kept in orphanages until they were around 3 months of age so parents could be assured of adopting a "normal, healthy child." After being confronted with evidence that scheduled care rather than responsive care puts normal children at risk for incurring developmental delays, a significant change in adoption placement policy occurred in the United States during the 1950s. That change resulted in infants and children being placed in foster care until they could be adopted so that they might receive responsive rather than scheduled care (Jones, 1993).

Thinking Critically

Considering the scientific evidence of Ainsworth and Spitz, and the change in public policy based on findings of the harmful effects of scheduled care in orphanages, do you think that unresponsive parenting among American parents is a thing of the past? If not, why not?

Erikson: The Resolution of Psychosocial Crises

In the early 1960s, Erik Erikson, a follower of Freud, developed the theory of psychosocial development that emphasizes that individuals achieve psychosocial maturity by resolving the psychosocial crises that emerge at each developmental level. According to Erikson, the quality of the parent–child relationship impacts the individual's ability to resolve psychosocial crises related to each stage of development (see Figure 1.1). For example, the psychosocial crisis of infancy is the development of trust versus mistrust. According to Erikson, by being consistently responsive to their infants' needs during that stage of development, parents contribute to the infant's development of a **sense of trust**. In turn, being effective in promoting their infants' sense of trust contributes to feelings of satisfaction for parents and those feelings of parental competence promote adults' psychosocial development (Goldhaber, 2000). The crises of children and adults at different stages of development will be discussed more fully in chapters 3 to 8, which focus on the influence of the parent–child relationship on an individual's development.

Benjamin Spock: Limits Within the Context of Warmth and Affection

During the 1930s, 1940s, and 1950s, the theories of Freud and Erikson emphasized the importance of parental understanding of children's natural instincts. Bowlby's Attachment Theory focused attention on the role of the parent in promoting infant attachment. Researchers using Attachment Theory provided strong evidence refuting the use of scheduled care and demonstrating the importance of responsive care for children's development. It was only after Benjamin Spock's views related to childrearing became well-known, however, that autocratic and unresponsive parenting approaches were challenged in the American public domain. Not only did Spock question autocratic and unresponsive childrearing approaches, he challenged also the lenient approach to parenting adopted by those parents who were influenced by the views of Freud.

Similar to the ways that Watson's views on child socialization became well-known via the popular media, Spock's message regarding childrearing reached large numbers of American mothers who sought childrearing advice from popular magazines and other readily available reading material. Beginning in the 1940s and continuing to the 1970s, Spock's beliefs regarding how parents should rear their children were widely disseminated. During that period of time, in addition to publishing several

Stage 1: Infants—Trust versus Mistrust
The task of the infant is to learn to trust the environment. Successful resolution of this stage is the development of a sense of trust that contributes to the development of hope. Unsuccessful resolution of this stage results in general mistrust and a failure in the development of mutuality between the infant and the parent.

Stage 2: Toddlers—Autonomy versus Shame and Doubt
The task of toddlers is to learn to do things for themselves and on their own. Successful resolution of this stage results in a sense of autonomy that results in a basic strength of will. Unsuccessful resolution of this stage results in the development of a sense of shame and doubt that leads to compulsion and impulsivity.

Stage 3: Preschoolers—Initiative versus Guilt
The task of the preschooler is to take the initiative in play and playful encounters. Preschoolers develop initiative by thinking of and carrying out multifaceted plans. Successful resolution of this stage contributes to a sense of initiative that results in the strength of virtue. Unsuccessful resolution of this stage contributes to a sense of guilt and results in feelings of inhibition.

Stage 4: School-age Children—Industry versus Inferiority
The task of school-age children is to learn to be productive by learning the skills and acquiring the knowledge valued by the culture in which they live. The successful resolution of this stage is a sense of industry that results in the strength of competence. The unsuccessful resolution of this stage contributes to the development of a sense of inferiority that results in inertia.

Stage 5: Adolescence—Identity versus Identity Confusion
The task of adolescents is to come to terms with who they are and with who they are becoming. The successful resolution of this stage leads to a basic sense of identity with the accompanying strength of fidelity. The unsuccessful resolution of this stage results in the development of a sense of confusion that is demonstrated by repudiation of the roles of society.

Stage 6: Young Adulthood—Intimacy versus Isolation
The goal of young adults is to join with others in a shared experience. The successful resolution of this stage is the development of a sense of intimacy and the basic strength that derives from the development of a sense of intimacy is love. The unsuccessful resolution of this stage results in a sense of isolation and accompanying self-absorption.

Stage 7: Adulthood—Generativity versus Stagnation
The goal of individuals in this stage is to be able to determine the significance of their efforts beyond their own generation. Resolution of this stage results in the development of a sense of generativity and the basic strength that emerges is care. Unsuccessful resolution of this stage results in a sense of stagnation that contributes to rejection.

Stage 8: Old Age—Ego Integrity versus Despair
The goal of this stage is to maintain a sense of integrity and avoid a sense of despair during a period in the life span characterized by loss of biological and psychological competence and loss of social status. Individuals who are able to evaluate their past life and establish a sense of integrity during this stage demonstrate the basic strength of wisdom. Those who do not demonstrate the acquisition of wisdom show disdain for themselves and for others.

FIGURE 1.1   Erikson's Stages of Psychosocial Development

Source: Adapted from *Theories of Human Development* by D. Goldhaber, 2000, Mountain View, CA: Mayfield.

popular books on childrearing, Spock contributed numerous articles to two popular magazines, *Ladies' Home Journal* and *Redbook.* In those publications, Spock emphasized that children need limits within the context of warmth and affection. He repeatedly emphasized the need for parents to provide their children with firm and consistent but also loving guidance (Spock, 1946, 1985).

The publication of Spock's childrearing advice in popular magazines established him as the new American parenting expert, the role previously held by John Watson (who had earlier gained acceptance as a parent expert through publications in *McCall's* as well as in radio broadcasts). Spock's advice to parents (that they should be warm and responsive to their children) reflects Freud's position (that children need to experience the love of their parents), a point overlooked by Watson who drew on other aspects of Freud's theory. Spock's recommendations also reflect insights regarding the importance of parental responsiveness to children, which was demonstrated by the attachment studies of Bowlby and Ainsworth. Spock did not agree, however, with the lenient style of parenting that had become popular among those American parents who believed they were following the recommendations of Freud. By emphasizing the important role of parental limits coupled with parental responsiveness, Spock more accurately represented Freud's theoretical perspective (that parents should be neither overly strict nor overly lenient).

Thinking Critically

At the turn of the 20th century, the autocratic pattern of parenting was the prevailing approach for rearing children, but by midcentury a host of psychologists and educators had challenged the autocratic approach. Furthermore, there has continued to be increasing information regarding the dangers of autocratic parenting and the rewards of the expression of warmth and responsiveness toward children. Based on the many voices that have called for the abolishment of autocratic parenting practices across many decades, why do you think the autocratic pattern of childrearing still exists in America today?

B. F. Skinner: Reinforcement as a Consequence of Appropriate Behavior

During the same era of the 20th century that the theories of Freud, Adler, Erikson, and Bowlby, and the views of Spock, were influencing childrearing patterns in Europe and in the United States, B. F. Skinner, developed his Principles of Operant Conditioning. The operant conditioning paradigm suggests that different response contingencies influence behavioral performance. Thus, how one responds to a behavior determines whether that behavior will or will not be repeated. Like his behaviorist predecessor John Watson, Skinner was influenced by Locke's view of the child as a passive learner. Locke's contribution to Skinner's theory is demonstrated by Skinner's emphasis on the role of the environment in promoting and maintaining children's behaviors. Skinner, who drew also on Darwin's classical conditioning experiments, called attention to the role of consequences in promoting, maintaining, and decreasing certain behaviors of children. Skinner stressed that in order for parents to be effective in their childrearing efforts they should have a basic understanding of the role of contingencies in affecting behavior. A **contingency** refers to the relation between a behavior and the events that follow the behavior. According to Skinner, behavior changes occur when certain consequences are contingent on the performance of desired behavior (Goldhaber, 2000; Skinner, 1950).

The Importance of Parental Social Approval.   The significance of Skinner's Theory of Operant Conditioning in terms of its effect on American childrearing behaviors is that it called attention to the fact that (a) the reinforcement of appropriate behavior is more effective than is the punishment of inappropriate behavior, and (b) if parents use punishment they should avoid corporal punishment and other forms of punishment that humiliate or belittle the child. In his studies of the effect of reinforcement on children's behavior, Skinner provided scientific evidence that parental social approval is the most effective type of reinforcement used by parents. By highlighting the value of parents using social approval to promote appropriate behaviors in children, Skinner's Theory of Operant Conditioning more accurately reflects the philosophy of John Locke than does Watson's Theory of Radical Behaviorism because it was Locke who said that parents should show affection for their children (Kagan, 1978). Another difference between Skinner's views of childrearing and those of Watson is that Skinner provided scientific evidence of the effectiveness of his reinforcement techniques for producing desirable behavior and lessening undesirable behavior in children.

Thinking Critically

Although John Locke influenced the theories of John Watson as well as those of B. F. Skinner, Watson's theory had a negative impact on American childrearing and Skinner's theory offered positive advice for parents. The differences in their theories reflect the differences in their view of the child. Based on Skinner's childrearing advice, what do you think was his view of the child?

The Social Learning Theorists: Imitation and Modeling

The behaviorist emphasis on the role of the environment in shaping children's development began to wane in the 1960s as behaviorist views were considered alongside those of theorists who were emphasizing children's needs and the perspective that children are active participants in their own development. In that intellectual climate, Social Learning Theory evolved from Skinner's Principles of Operant Conditioning. The basic premise of Social Learning Theory, developed by Bandura and Walters (1963), is that children do not have to be directly reinforced or punished to learn a behavior. Instead, children learn through vicarious reinforcement or punishment that involves two interrelated strategies: imitation and modeling. As observed by Bandura and Walters, children select the persons in their environment to serve as models for their own behavior based on four criteria: (a) their warmth and availability to the child, (b) their perceived prestige, (c) their similarity to the child, and (d) their competence or power. According to Bandura (1986), children have a natural tendency to imitate, and they choose the models whose behaviors they will emulate based on attributes previously explained. Moreover, the models for children's behavior can promote certain desired behaviors by understanding the circumstances that increase imitative behavior. The ways in which parents might promote their children's imitation of desired behaviors are outlined in chapter 11.

There are two ways in which the social learning theorists drew attention to what the child brings to the learning environment. First, by noting children's natural tendency to imitate, the social learning theorists (unlike Watson and Skinner) acknowledged the natural instincts of the child. Second, when they pointed out the fact that children learn behaviors that they sometimes perform later, the social learning theorists emphasized the role of children's memory for specific events. By linking children's natural tendency to imitate and remember behaviors that they might or might not perform later (depending on other environmental influences), the social learning theorists de-emphasized the role of the environment and escalated the role of the child (Bandura & Walters, 1963). That direction toward a greater understanding of the nature of the child fit well into the other theorizing of the latter part of the 20th century.

RESPECTING AND ATTENDING TO CHILDREN'S ENTHUSIASM FOR LEARNING

In addition to the influences discussed so far, American childrearing patterns during the 20th century were influenced as well by European educators who speculated on how children learn. Some of the pioneers of early Education who influenced childrearing patterns in the United States and Europe included Friedrich Froebel, Marie Montessori, and Caroline Pratt. Their views that children have an inborn drive to learn that is expressed in their need to be actively engaged in the learning process led to modifications in school curricula and influenced the cognitive theories of Jean Piaget and Lev Vygotsky.

Friedrich Froebel: Play and the Playthings of a Child

Friedrich Froebel was a pioneer of child study who believed that everything a child does is significant and of educational importance. Influenced by the French philosopher René Descartes who said "I think, therefore, I am," Froebel's view of the child

The enthusiasm these youngsters are demonstrating in their play reflects the views of Froebel, Pratt, and Montessori.

was that a child has an inborn drive to learn, which is expressed in the child's strong interest in being consistently engaged in activities that promote learning. According to Froebel, "Everyone who observes with any attention even the first stage of the child's life is met therein (frequently as well as definitely) by the requirement of fostering the child's impulse to activity, but he is also met by the perception of how little is done to satisfy the requirement generally" (p. 16). The belief of Froebel was that all genuine human education and true human training is connected with the quiet fostering in the child of the instinct for activity with the thoughtful development of the child to satisfy that instinct. Froebel believed that parental love manifests itself by means of nourishing and developing the child's impulse to be engaged in creative activity (Froebel, 1909).

Caroline Pratt: Children's Play Is Their Work

Influenced by the views of Froebel, Caroline Pratt published a treatise in 1948, which grew out of her observations of children and was aptly titled: *I Learn from Children*. As a dramatic departure from the early Puritan belief that children who played were being mischievous, Pratt emphasized just the opposite—that childhood's work is learning and that it is in play that children get their work done. Not only did Pratt elevate children's play to an esteemed position, she emphasized as well the importance of truly seeing children. She believed that to see a child one must be willing to do so from the child's own horizons almost from the day the child is born, "to see how the child's circle of interests widens outward like a stone thrown into a pond" (p. 8). Pratt called attention to the need to observe the urge of the child to learn, an urge that is immediate, practical, and within the scope of the child's learning ability (Pratt, 1970).

❦ ❦

Thinking Critically

How do you think the responses of early American parents influenced by Hobbesian philosophy and Calvinist religious doctrine would compare to the responses of parents influenced by Froebel and Pratt when their toddlers seem to want to "get into everything" and when their highly energetic preschoolers want to be continuously engaged in play?

❦ ❦

Maria Montessori: Children Have Absorbent Minds

Maria Montessori, who became the first woman physician in Italy in 1892, was a pioneer in early childhood education, who challenged European and American parents to allow their children the freedom to explore and learn. Montessori drew on the ideas of Rousseau and Froebel as well as on her own observations of children, at different stages in life in several different cultures, in her development of the Montessori Method of Early Childhood Education. The Montessori Method, which was described in Montessori's first publication in 1909, might be summed up as follows: (a) all children have absorbent minds, (b) all children want to learn, (c) all children pass through several stages of development, (d) all children want to be independent, and (e) all children pass through sensitive periods of development (Britton, 1992). A sensitive period of development is a genetically determined timetable during which certain developmental changes occur when normal environmental conditions are present, such as the onset of puberty during adolescence, the development of infant attachment, or the early development of language.

The Absorbent Mind.   Based on her observations of children, Montessori concluded that the young child's process of learning is active rather than passive and that the child has an **absorbent mind**, which unconsciously soaks up information from the environment resulting in the child's learning at a rapid pace. According to Montessori, the child's capacity to learn at a rapid rate lasts for the first 6 years of life, more or less. Based on the young child's ability to learn so quickly, every early experience of the child is vitally important. During the ages from 3 to 6, while the child's mind is still absorbent, consciousness begins and parents will be asked endless questions of *why* and *how*. Therefore, the young child's inborn energies and drives require a say in what experiences they encounter—rather like a blueprint. Montessori believed that the parent's role is to help their children's personality develop during their first 6 years and outlined three golden rules for parents: (a) allow freedom within limits, (b) respect the individuality of the child, and (c) resist imposing their own will and personality on the child. Accordingly, Montessori recommended that parents give their young children as much freedom as possible emphasizing that it is only with that freedom that children are able to develop to their full potential (Britton, 1992).

Thinking Critically

Consider a situation in which the parent asks a young child to pick up her toys before coming to lunch and the child responds by asking why. How do you think the autocratic parent would respond to the child's question? How do you think a parent who is influenced by Montessori would answer the child's question?

Jean Piaget: Children Are Active Participants in Their Own Development

We now turn our attention to the contributions of the Swiss psychologist Jean Piaget, who began to influence European views of the child in the 1930s and 1940s. Piaget's view of infants and children is that they are cognitively capable human beings with inborn reflexes that are very quickly altered by their active engagement of the environment. According to that perspective, children (through their active engagement of people and objects in their environment) construct their own cognitive structures (Elkind, 1976). Piaget's view of children as active participants in the development of their own mental structures reflect those of Montessori, although Piaget provided more detail regarding what happens as children's minds take in and adapt to information from the environment. Piaget's theory of how children learn extended beyond the first 6 years that were the focus of Montessori. Piaget theorized that there are four major age-related stages of cognitive development from infancy through adolescence. As will be demonstrated in later chapters, each of the stages in Piaget's theory has features that permit certain types of knowing and understanding (see Figure 1.2) (Piaget & Inhelder, 1969).

Lev Vygotsky: Guided Participation

Following in the tradition of Froebel and Montessori, Lev Vygotsky developed an alternative theory of children as active participants in the learning process. The views of Lev Vygotsky, a psychologist from the former Soviet Union, have provided valuable insights regarding ways for parents to guide their children. A primary contribution of Vygotsky's theory is that it addresses the issue of the role of context in child socialization. Vygotsky (1978) was particularly interested in understanding the cognitive competencies that developed among the culturally diverse peoples of the previous Soviet Union, such as the advanced use of tools in an agricultural community and the use of abstract language among people who had never received formal education. His Sociocultural Theory that emerged from that interest in the mid-1920s challenged autocratic parenting, emphasized the need for parents to guide their children's learning experience, and provided a model for studying variations in childrearing in diverse cultures.

The Sensorimotor Stage (from Birth up to the Age of 18 to 24 Months)
This stage consists of a six-step sequence of knowledge construction whereby infants depend on their senses of smell, hearing, touch, and taste to construct concepts of objects, space, and causality. The acquisitions associated with each period of the six-step sequence are specified in chapter 3.

The Preoperational Stage (from 2 to 6 or 7 Years of Age)
This stage can be divided into two phases. Between the ages of 2 and 4 years, the child displays an egocentric use of language and a heavy reliance on perception in problem solving. Between the ages of about 5 to around 7 years, social speech and intuitive thinking emerge.

The Concrete Operational Stage (from 6 or 7 to 11 to 13 Years of Age)
The ability to perform logical operations is reflected in the school-age child's interest in conservation and classification tasks. Development of the ability to conserve matter, volume, length, time, distance, and speed coincides with the development of the ability to understand reversibility and compensation. The development of the ability to classify coincides with the development of the ability to recognize defining properties of objects.

The Formal Operations Stage (Begins from 11 to 13 Years of Age and Is Evident Throughout Adulthood)
The transition to formal operations during adolescence allows the person to consider what is abstract and not immediately present. Thus concrete operations focus on "what is" and formal operations focus on "what if."

FIGURE 1.2   Piaget's Stages of Cognitive Development
Source: Adapted from *Comparing Theories of Child Development,* 5th ed., by R. M. Thomas, 2000, Belmont, CA: Wadsworth/Thomson Learning.

The sociocultural perspective of Vygotsky drew attention to the ways in which competencies come about as a result of interactions between novices and more skilled members of a society acting as tutors or mentors. According to that perspective, the implicit goal of the tutor or mentor is to provide the instruction and necessary support to assist the beginner in acquiring the knowledge and capabilities valued by that person's culture. The best way to accomplish that goal is through **guided participation** wherein the teacher engages the learner in joint activities providing instruction as well as direct involvement in the learning process. In describing the best ways for parents and teachers to guide children's learning, Vygotsky pointed out that there is a **zone of proximal development** between the child's ability to perform a skill independently and the child's capability of performing that same skill with the guidance and assistance of a more capable individual. Vygotsky's theory provides a model of parent–child interactions that emphasizes the important role of the parent in working closely with the child as a partner in the child's learning. Vygotsky pointed out that one cannot measure a child's capability simply by that child's performance of a previously accomplished skill but rather by what the child is capable of accomplishing with the assistance of a more capable person, such as a parent, older sibling, teacher, or coach.

Through guided participation, this mother is scaffolding the learning experience of her daughter.

Thinking Critically

In traditional cultures, children work with their parents and other older relatives in many activities that benefit the entire family, such as tending farm animals, preparing meals, and taking care of younger children. From the perspective of Vygotsky, how might the performance of those shared tasks contribute to children's cognitive development?

The Parent Education Movement Based on Democratic Parent–Child Relationships

While other theorists were focusing increasing attention on understanding how children think and feel, Alfred Adler developed the Social Discipline Theory. Adler's theory, based on democratic relationships between parents and their children, provided the foundation for the Parent Education Movement in the United States that was led by Rudolf Dreikurs. The basic premise of the Social Discipline Theory is the recognition of the equal worth of everyone in a group. As applied to families, all members of a household are allowed to raise issues, and other family members are expected to respect issues raised by any member. According to the democratic approach, although parents and children are not equal in terms of responsibility or privilege, both parents and children have equal worth. The attitude of equal worth is played out in valuing the needs and desires of each family member (Dreikurs, 1972; Dreikurs & Grey, 1968, 1970). In articulating his conception of democratic parent–child relationships, Adler provided specific guidelines for incorporating limits and warmth into the rearing of children. Those guidelines are outlined in chapter 11, Child Socialization Strategies and Techniques.

THE ROLE OF CONTEXT IN CHILD SOCIALIZATION

After decades of theorizing on what constitutes the nature of the child and how best to bring up children, it has become clear that differences in childrearing patterns are not based simply on variations in individual belief systems. It is now recognized that diversity in child socialization patterns is linked to differences in family context, variation in cultural beliefs, and many other contextual influences. Two contemporary theories emphasize the role of context in child socialization and provide models for understanding the ways in which child socialization patterns are shaped by the various contexts in which families interact with each other, with their communities, and with the institutions within their society. Those theories are the Ecological Theory proposed by Urie Bronfenbrenner (1979, 1989) and the Family Systems Theory (Minuchin, 1974).

Ecological Theory: A Model for Examining the Various Contexts of Development

Urie Bronfenbrenner's Ecological Theory represents a model for studying people in their diverse social environments and draws attention to the assorted contexts that impact the socialization process and the ongoing development of the individual. Bronfenbrenner's theory has drawn attention to the fact that whereas parental behaviors influence the development of children, there are multiple influences on parental childrearing behaviors, including the parents' family of origin, the community in which the family lives, and the culture in which the family is a part. Bronfenbrenner recently added the context of the chronosystem to his model, which highlights the influence of time on the various interacting systems that affect a person's development. Time might be considered as the time within a person's life, the influence of time on interactions within the family, and the effect of time on the childrearing beliefs within a culture. The contexts of development, according to Bronfenbrenner (1979, 1989), are described in Figure 1.3.

Thinking Critically

Which one of the various systems in Bronfenbrenner's Ecological Theory represents the changes that have taken place in the ways that parents rear their children from the beginning to the end of the 20th century?

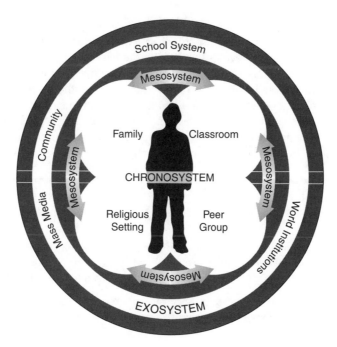

FIGURE 1.3   Bronfenbrenner's Ecological Model

Source: From *The Developing Person Through the Life Span*, 5/e, page 7, by Kathleen Stassen Berger and Ross A. Thompson. © 2001 by Worth Publishers. Used with permission.

Family Systems Theory: A Look at the Dynamics in the Family System

Families are dynamic systems, characterized by stability and change. Whereas family stability contributes to a sense of shared history and a certain degree of predictability, the changes in the family system challenge members to adapt to those changes and to continuously redefine their roles in relation to each other. When children undergo physical, cognitive, and social–emotional development, those changes contribute to alterations in their behavior that impact other family members' behaviors. The resulting imbalance or disequilibrium in the family system challenges all family members to adjust to those changes, thereby contributing to the reestablishment of family equilibrium (Minuchin, 1974). Parents are undergoing development as well and some of the impact on the dynamics of the family system is related to challenges associated with the parents' stages of development (Steinberg & Steinberg, 1994). For example, the developmental challenges of adolescents are quite different from the developmental challenges of their parents.

In addition to alterations in the family system brought about by the developmental changes of family members, there are normative and nonnormative events that provoke changes in parents, children, and the family system. Examples of normative events are the births of children, the deaths of older family members, or children starting school or going to college. Examples of nonnormative events are winning the lottery, the unexpected death of a family member, or learning that a family member has a serious illness. By and large, the events that impact the life of one person in a family affect the lives of all family members, and the behavior of each person in the family has an influence on the behaviors of all other family members. Furthermore, the behaviors of all family members contribute to ongoing alterations in the family system, which in turn impact the lives of the persons who participate in that system. The stability of the family is thereby enhanced if its members are capable of adapting their expectations and behaviors to meet the changing needs of all family members (Beevar & Beevar, 1988).

Thinking Critically

Consider an example of disequilibrium that occurred in your family and was brought about by a normative or nonnormative event. In what ways did you, your parents, and other family members adapt to the resulting family imbalance, thereby reestablishing equilibrium in the family?

SUMMARY

In glancing back over the past 100 years, it is possible to discern that American parents' understanding of the inherent nature of the child has increased substantially, which has altered their beliefs regarding their role in promoting their children's development. In this chapter, we have traced the philosophical and theoretical influences of contemporary American beliefs regarding how parents should socialize their children. An advantage of examining the roots of childrearing practices is that it challenges students to take a closer look at their own beliefs regarding child socialization. The examination of historical changes in the way parents have thought it best to rear their children calls attention to the fact that childrearing beliefs vary historically and are influenced by the "experts of the time." That realization prepares students to be open-minded regarding the varying childrearing patterns in diverse family structures and in different cultures. As will be discussed in future chapters, the degree to which parents are willing to consider more sympathetic views of the child and to adopt more democratic patterns of childrearing are related to a number of factors, such as the parents' age (Kemp, Sibley, & Pond, 1990), educational level (Hoff-Ginsberg & Tardif, 1995), and cultural beliefs (Fuligni, Tseng, & Lam, 1999).

KEY TERMS

- absorbent mind
- attachment
- contingency
- fixation

- guided participation
- secure attachment
- sense of trust
- zone of proximal development

2

Parenting Patterns in Cultural–Structural Context

Now that we have taken a historical look at the ways in which various philosophers and theorists have contributed to the evolution of childrearing patterns in the United States, we turn our attention to the role of context in contemporary parent–child relations. We will begin by looking at the current patterns of childrearing in the United States and contrast those to parenting patterns in cultures outside the United States. Next, we will consider the ways in which cultural norms and belief systems contribute to different parenting styles within the various cultures in American society. We then will consider other contextual influences of childrearing, including family structure, religiosity, and socioeconomic level. Throughout all of these discussions we will be examining the ways in which the lives of parents and children are shaped by the parent–child relationships in which they participate.

CHILD SOCIALIZATION PATTERNS OF AMERICAN PARENTS

Studies of childrearing patterns in the United States during the past several decades have resulted in the identification of five distinct parenting styles: **authoritative, authoritarian, permissive** (Baumrind, 1967), **indulgent**, and **indifferent** (Maccoby & Martin, 1983). There are two dimensions that distinguish among those parenting patterns: accepting versus rejecting and demanding versus undemanding. That is, parents differ in the degree to which they demonstrate acceptance or rejection of their children and differ as well in the demands and expectations they have of their children. As will be pointed out in the upcoming dialogue, each of those parenting patterns contributes to differing outcomes for children.

Authoritative Parents

The authoritative parenting pattern describes an approach to childrearing wherein parents are controlling and demanding but also nurturing and communicative with their children. In her 1968 article, Baumrind stated that authoritative parents direct their children's activities but in a rational, issue-oriented manner. Authoritative parents display firm control at many points of divergence but do not hem their children in with restrictions. An important trait of authoritative parents is that they recognize their children's individual interests and unique personalities. They, therefore, set standards for their children regarding expectations for future conduct but do not expect unquestioned obedience. On the contrary, authoritative parents are willing to explain to their children the reasons for expected behavior. They also are willing to discuss with their children the behavioral guidelines they have set (Baumrind, 1971, 1991a; Steinberg & Levine, 1997). Authoritative parents believe in rational discipline accomplished through parent–child interactions that are friendly as well as tutorial and disciplining. Integration of the needs of the child with those of other family members is, therefore, a high value for authoritative parents (Baumrind, 1996).

Children of Authoritative Parents.   Studies of children from authoritative families have demonstrated that those children have more positive outcomes than do children reared by parents who have authoritarian, permissive, indulgent, or indifferent parenting styles. Children from authoritative families have high levels of achievement motivation (Dornbusch, Ritter, Liederman, Roberts, & Fraleigh, 1987; Steinberg, 1996) and tend to be cooperative with peers, siblings, and adults (Denham, Renwick, & Holt, 1991). Specifically, the authoritative parenting style has been linked to general psychosocial maturity (Mantzipoulos & Oh-Hwang, 1998), reasoning ability, empathy, altruism, and school achievement (Aunola, Stattin, & Nurmi, 2000). Furthermore, children whose parents have an authoritative parenting style are less likely to exhibit behavior problems in comparison with children of parents who use authoritarian, permissive, or indifferent parenting styles (Baumrind, 1991b). Finally, children of authoritative parents have the highest levels of self-actualization when compared to children of parents who have adopted other styles of child socialization (Carton & Dominguez, 1997). Self-actualization refers to the experience of heightened aesthetic, creative, philosophical, and spiritual understanding (Maslow, 1970).

The encouragement of children's participation in decision making by authoritative parents appears to provide children with the experience needed to engage in thoughtful and responsible behavior. Although some of the competencies promoted by authoritative parenting (e.g., independent thinking) might not be considered as desirable in traditional cultures, authoritative parenting has emerged as the most effective parenting style for the socialization of American children and adolescents (Steinberg, Mounts, Lamborn, & Dornbusch, 1991). Furthermore, the advantages of the authoritative parenting style for American children's development have been found to outweigh factors such as socioeconomic status and ethnic group membership. As a case in point, Mantzipoulos and Oh-Hwang (1998) examined gender, intellectual ability, and parenting practices in a group of 344 Korean American adolescents and 214 European American adolescents. Differences in parenting styles across those two groups were predictive of psychosocial maturity regardless of ethnic group membership. Moreover, compared to all other parenting styles, authoritative parenting was related to significantly higher levels of psychosocial maturity.

Thinking Critically

Consider the parent–child interactions of a family with whom you are familiar (your own or those of friends or relatives) and see if you can identify a family that fits the authoritative pattern. If so, what are the lives of the children like? See if you can identify some of the positive outcomes of authoritative parenting in those families.

Authoritarian Parents

Authoritarian-oriented beliefs and attitudes are firmly grounded in early American childrearing patterns in the United States. The choice to use an authoritarian parenting approach stems from the view of the child as willful, and parents who are authoritarian tend to favor punitive, forceful measures to curb what they believe to be their children's willful nature. Those parents place value on (a) keeping children in their place, (b) restricting children's autonomy, and (c) assigning household responsibilities in order to instill respect for work. A principal goal of authoritarian parents is to obtain obedience from their children, and forceful means (including physical punishment) are frequently used to obtain their children's compliance to rules (Baumrind, 1967). In addition to the goal of obedience, a secondary goal of authoritarian parents is to emphasize respect for parents, which is demonstrated by their insistence on children's unquestioning acceptance of their parents' word for what is right or wrong. In authoritarian families, rules are set by the parent without discussion with the child and a child's questioning of the rules is likely to gain the response of "Because I said so." Children reared by authoritarian parents are not encouraged to think for themselves but are expected to look to their parents for approval and answers to problems. Furthermore, authoritarian parents discourage their children from freely expressing their feelings (Baumrind, 1967, 1971, 1980; Steinberg, 1996).

Children of Authoritarian Parents.   The authoritarian style of rearing children is not considered to be conducive to positive outcomes for children. Because such parents intimidate their children rather than promote their feelings of self-worth, Alice Miller (1990) labeled authoritarian beliefs as "the **poisonous pedagogy**," charging that such beliefs promote child socialization behaviors that rob children of their human spirit and inhibit their normal emotional development. Children whose parents are authoritarian tend to be dependent, passive, and conforming, less self-assured, less creative, and less socially adept than are other children. In comparison to children of authoritative parents, children of authoritarian parents have been found to have lower psychosocial maturity (Mantzipoulos & Oh-Hwang, 1998) and lower achievement (Aunola et al., 2000). Additionally, children from authoritarian families are more at risk for behavior problems such as substance abuse, crime, and delinquency than are children from authoritative or permissive families (Baumrind, 1991a).

Thinking Critically

Consider the lives of children you know or have known whose parents are authoritarian. Are you able to identify some of negative consequences of authoritarian parenting in the lives of those children? If so, what are they?

Permissive Parents

In sharp contrast to the authoritarian parenting style is the permissive parenting style. Basically, permissive parents are noncontrolling and nondemanding. They are not very well organized or effective in running their households, and they engage less in independence training of their children. An example of permissive parents' lack of demandingness is seen in their giving their children few household responsibilities. Instead of expecting compliance to usual behavioral standards, they by and large allow their children to regulate their own behavior. The lax parenting style of permissive parents reflects their evaluations of their parenting capabilities. Permissive parents tend to be self-effacing individuals who are insecure in their abilities to influence their children (Baumrind, 1968).

Children of Permissive Parents.   Children of permissive parents tend to lack impulse control and to be more immature, less self-reliant, less socially responsible, and less independent in comparison to children of authoritative parents. They are also less happy than children whose parents are authoritative or authoritarian (Baumrind, 1971, 1973, 1991a). Additionally, they have lower academic achievement than do children from authoritative families (e.g., Dornbusch et al., 1987; Paulson,

Thinking Critically

Based on children's academic performance, they are typically considered by others to be smart or not so smart. The previous discussion, however, suggests that we look not only at the child's abilities but also at the pattern of childrearing in the child's home. In light of what you have just learned about the effects of childrearing patterns on children's academic performance, what would you recommend to parents regarding ways to promote their children's academic achievement?

Marchant, & Rothlisberg, 1998). Although children of permissive parents have lower academic performance when compared to children of authoritative parents, they have higher grades in comparison to children of authoritarian parents (Dornbusch et al., 1987). The association between the higher academic achievement scores of children of permissive parents in comparison to children of authoritarian parents emphasizes the link between parental responsiveness and children's achievement.

Indulgent Parents

The indulgent approach to child socialization represents an extremely lax parenting pattern wherein parents do not exercise control over their children. The pattern of indulgent parenting emphasizes high responsiveness and low demandingness. In comparison to parents with other childrearing patterns, indulgent parents are highest in involvement with their children and lowest in strictness with their children. They have few clear expectations for their children, and they seldom set limits for them or provide consequences for their actions. Their emphasis instead is on responsiveness, believing that children need love that is virtually unconditional. Indulgent parents view discipline and control as being potentially damaging to children's developing creativity. Therefore, although they provide their children with love, they do not provide them with limits and guidelines but grant them instead the freedom to do as they please (Lamborn, Mounts, Steinberg, & Dornbusch, 1991; Maccoby & Martin, 1983; Steinberg, 1996).

Children of Indulgent Parents.   Children of indulgent parents are likely to be irresponsible and immature. They are more likely than other adolescents to conform to their peers and more likely than children whose parents are authoritative or permissive to be involved in risk behaviors such as crime and delinquency (Baumrind, 1991a; Lamborn et al., 1991; Steinberg, 1996, 2000). In spite of the fact that their indulgent parents have provided them with responsive care and have promoted their autonomy, their parents have not required the kind of responsibility from them that is associated with healthy development.

Thinking Critically

Everyone seems to know a child or children whose parents are indulgent and have noticed the negative effects of that style of parenting. If you have observed such a relationship and its effects, what are the behaviors of the parent that you would consider indulgent and what examples of negative outcomes have you observed in the child's or children's behaviors?

Indifferent Parents

Indifferent parents have either rejected their children or for various reasons do not expend the necessary time and energy required of the parenting role. They seem uninvolved and even uninterested in their children's development. Their goal appears to be to minimize the amount of time and emotion devoted to childrearing. Thus, they require little of their children, rarely bother to discipline them or provide clear guidelines regarding expected behavior, and express little love or concern for their children. In their study of indifferent parents, researchers have found that such parents tend to have life problems and stressors that limit their availability to their children (Maccoby & Martin, 1983; Steinberg, 1996). Although the indifferent pattern of parenting is nonnormative for parents of young to preadolescent children, it is a common childrearing pattern of parents of American adolescents. In a study by Lamborn, et al. (1991) of over 4,000 American adolescents between the ages of 14 and 18 from several different ethnic groups, the indifferent parenting pattern was the most prevalent of all the patterns identified.

Children of Indifferent Parents.   A general lack of involvement by parents characterized by a lack of affection and/or high levels of criticism and hostility provides the basis for the development of childhood aggressiveness and antisocial behavior problems. As early as preschool, low parental involvement is associated with children's noncompliance. Over time and with ongoing parental difficulties, noncompliance evolves into a behavior pattern characterized by peer rejection, poor academic performance, delinquency, and a dependence syndrome related to alcohol or other drugs (Maccoby & Martin, 1983; Steinberg, 1996). Adolescent children of indifferent parents tend to have (a) higher rates of delinquency, (b) earlier sexual involvement, and (c) a greater likelihood of using drugs and alcohol. The problem behaviors seen in children of indifferent parents might be partly explained by their tendency toward impulsivity and to some extent by their parents' lack of monitoring of their activities (Jacob, 1997).

Thinking Critically

Of all the childrearing patterns discussed thus far, the indifferent pattern has been associated with the most negative outcomes for children. Generally, we become aware of the high-risk behaviors of the child and are then able to link the child's behaviors to a lack of sufficient involvement of parents. What are some examples you are aware of that demonstrate the ways in which indifferent parents impact their children's lives?

Children of Parents with Inconsistent Parenting Styles

Although both parents in a family tend to have fairly consistent parenting styles, inconsistency between parents in their socialization patterns is linked to negative outcomes for children. For example, researchers have found that children who perceive inconsistency between their parents' childrearing styles are lower in self-esteem, self-control, and school performance compared with those children who perceive both parents as authoritarian as well as those children who perceive both parents as permissive (Brand, Crous, & Hanekom, 1990). Inconsistent parenting has been found to be related as well to children's and adolescents' deviant peer affiliations (Brody, Ge, & Conger, 2001) and externalizing behaviors (Lindahl & Malik, 1999).

CULTURAL VARIATIONS IN PARENTING PATTERNS

In the foregoing discussion, we learned that in studies of American child socialization patterns the authoritative parenting style has been associated most often with positive outcomes for children. It is important to point out, however, that almost all research focused on child socialization patterns has taken place in the United States and that most of that research has focused on European American parents. When we look outside that relatively narrow focus, the most striking finding is how rare authoritative parenting is in other cultural groups. In both non-Western families as well as in American ethnic minority families, we frequently see a style of child socialization that although often labeled as authoritarian actually falls somewhere between authoritarian and authoritative. Not only does the style of child socialization in those families not fit into the classifications discussed thus far, their childrearing approach has other culturally valued traditions that are not found in the childrearing styles of European American parents.

Before continuing, it is important to distinguish between **society** and **culture** and to provide descriptions of **the West, industrialized societies**, and **traditional cultures**. *Society* refers to a group of people who live and interact with each other because they share a common geographical area. A society might include a variety of customs, religions, family traditions, and economic practices and is therefore different from a culture. Members of a *culture* share a common way of life, although members of a society might not. For example, American society encompasses many diverse cultures such as the African American culture, the Native American culture, the Latino American culture, and the Asian American culture. Members of all those cultures share the common characteristic of being American, are subject to the same laws, and are educated in similar schools. They differ, however, in various customs and beliefs that are related to their unique cultures (Arnett, 2001).

The West includes majority cultures in the United States, Canada, Western Europe, Australia, and New Zealand. Those societies are all industrialized, which means that they have highly developed economies, have passed through a period of industrialization, and now have economies that are based primarily on services such as banking, sales, accounting, and information (computer-related companies). The majority cultures in the West also have representative democracies and share to some extent a common cultural history. In each of those countries, there are cultural groups that do not share the characteristics of the majority culture. Those groups are referred to as traditional due to their maintenance of a way of life based on stable traditions passed down from one generation to the next. Traditional cultures focus more on group success than on individual success. An example of the stable values of a traditional culture within a Western society is reflected in the following words of a Canadian Cree woman:

> Life was challenging with its physical and emotional demands and discipline but culturally and spiritually rewarding with good values grounded in Cree ways. Values like sharing, interconnectedness among relatives, land, plants, and animal life was an unspoken understanding. . . . I remember the many responsibilities we had as children in our family where we were expected to actively participate in the following work. I have chopped and hauled firewood; hauled water from the lake to our dwellings; helped my mother, sisters and aunts prepare hides for tanning; preserve and cook food; make clothes; tend our vegetable garden, look after the younger siblings, among many other chores. (Goduka & Kunnie, 2004, p. 14)

In contrast to traditional cultures found in ethnic minority groups in Western societies, there are traditional cultures outside the West that represent the majority culture in a society. The majority culture of the highly industrialized country of Japan, for example, is considered to be traditional based on its stable traditions that are preserved across generations (Arnett, 2001).

Child Socialization in Non-Western Societies

American scholars studying non-Western parents have consistently attempted to apply Baumrind's original categorizations of parenting styles (authoritative, permissive, and authoritarian) to the approaches non-Western families use in the rearing of

In traditional cultures, family life includes adults and children sharing tasks.

The closeness of non-Western families is supported by many family get-togethers.

their children. The result has been the labeling of non-Western families as authoritarian because they are typically higher on demandingness than are those parents who fall into the authoritative pattern. Scholars usually acknowledge, however, that the style they identify as authoritarian among non-Western parents does not have the negative effects typically seen in children of Western parents who are authoritarian. What is not addressed in those comparisons is the possibility that the higher demandingness coupled with higher responsiveness of the non-Western parenting pattern places it outside the original parenting categories identified by Baumrind (1967, 1971).

The Parental Role in Non-Western Societies. A key point in understanding child socialization patterns in non-Western societies is that independence in those societies is not the overriding issue that it is for Western parents and their children. Outside the West, explanation and discussion of parental directives is an extremely rare approach and compliance of children is expected without explanation or question. Examples include Asian societies such as China, Japan, Vietnam, and South Korea. In those societies, the role of the parent carries more authority than does the role of the parent in the West (Alwin, 1988; Fuligni, et al., 1999; Whiting & Edwards, 1988). The finding that authoritative parenting is rare outside the West does not mean that the child socialization pattern of non-Western parents is authoritarian. Arnett (2001) emphasizes that although non-Western parents adopt a more noncompromising stance on authority than is seen in the West, their demandingness is most likely to be accompanied by a closeness to children that is rarely observed in Western families.

Based on their high levels of closeness to their children, Arnett suggests that non-Western parents come closer to the authoritative style than to the authoritarian style. An example of parent–child closeness in non-Western societies is demonstrated by the cultural norm of **amae** in Japan that emphasizes close, affectionate mother–child relationships as the foundation for parenting (Hsai & Scanzoni, 1996). Another example of parent–child intimacy in non-Western families is seen in the findings of

Shek and Chen (1999) who studied Hong Kong Chinese parents' perceptions of the ideal child and found that those parents included "maintaining good parent–child relationships" as being one of their primary goals of childrearing. Although social scientists appear to have misapplied the authoritarian pattern to non-Western families, Baumrind (1987) recognized the difficulty of fitting traditional cultures into her previously identified parenting patterns. In response to that dilemma, she conceptualized the **traditional parenting style** to describe the pattern of parenting usually found in traditional cultures—high in responsiveness accompanied by a type of demandingness that does not encourage discussion or debate.

Thinking Critically

Similar to the authoritative parenting style, the traditional parenting style has a high level of demandingness as well as high levels of responsiveness toward children. If these are the similarities between the two styles, what distinguishes these patterns from each other?

Parent–Child Relations in U.S. Ethnic Minority Families

With the exception of Native Americans, all Americans trace their cultural origins to various countries with different beliefs and values. Therefore, each ethnic group in the United States has its own set of values related to differing cultural beliefs. As ethnic minority populations in the United States have steadily increased because of immigration and higher reproductive rates in some ethnic groups, there has been a growing recognition and appreciation of the diversity in American families. An example of the increased focus on the diversity of American families is that researchers have begun to make greater efforts to include ethnic minority parents in studies of childrearing patterns and their effects on children. Attempts to distinguish the parenting styles of American ethnic minority parents parallel efforts to demarcate non-Western parenting styles. As in studies of non-Western parenting patterns, the style of child socialization seen in many American ethnic minority families has been most often labeled as authoritarian. It has been recently argued, however, that the labeling of U.S. ethnic minority parenting patterns as authoritarian is a misapplication of the authoritarian style (Chao, 1994). It appears that the traditional childrearing pattern conceptualized by Baumrind in 1987 might more appropriately describe the childrearing approaches found among American ethnic minority families as well as the child socialization patterns seen in non-Western cultures. According to Baumrind, traditional families are characterized by high demandingness as well as high responsiveness and by a strong belief system that has been consistent across generations. Those characteristics are common in U.S. ethnic minority families.

This scene depicts the family closeness found in many U.S. ethnic minority families.

In addition to belief systems that originated in their countries of origin and are consistent across generations, the circumstances associated with being members of ethnic minority cultures also have influenced the childrearing patterns of those parents. Family scholars have pointed out that an important component of child socialization in ethnic minority families is **racial socialization**, which acts as a buffer against negative racial messages in the environment (Peters, 1985; Stevenson, 1994, 1995). Racial socialization includes providing a home that is rich in racial culture and socializing children to be proud of their racial heritage. An example of the benefit of racial socialization for American ethnic minority children is that children whose parents provide racial socialization have higher levels of factual knowledge and better problem-solving skills (O'Brien-Caughu, O'Campo, & Randolph, 2002). Racial socialization contributes also to racial identity, which has been linked to the development of competencies among African American adolescents (Arroyo & Zigler, 1995). Moreover, Taylor, Chatters, Tucker, and Lewis (1990) suggested that African American parents might have felt it necessary to be stricter with their children because they have had to prepare them for coping with the realities of racism and discrimination. The argument here is that protective factors unique to nonmajority American populations should be contemplated when assessing the effectiveness of parenting patterns in American ethnic minority cultures.

Another factor to consider in attempts to discern the parenting patterns of ethnic minority parents is that each U.S. ethnic group is influenced to some degree by the cultural values of the other U.S. ethnic groups. The values that impact the childrearing patterns of all American parents regardless of ethnic group membership are those of the European American ethnic group, because those values have been promoted in the social, educational, and political systems of the United States. An example of the effect of European American values is the finding that third-generation Americans tend to have values more similar to those of mainstream America than to those of their ethnic group of origin (Chen & Lan, 1998).

Traditional Cultures and Extended Family Relations

An examination of child socialization patterns in non-Western families and American ethnic-minority families is not complete without an acknowledgment of the vital role of other family members in supporting the childrearing efforts of parents. Throughout the world, the responsibilities of parents in traditional cultures are extended to grandparents and other family members. In comparison to the launching of adolescents in contemporary American society, young men generally continue to live with their parents in traditional cultures and, when they marry, their wives move into their parents' homes with them. That family arrangement has remained remarkably resilient to globalization influences and is currently the typical pattern in cultures of India and China as well as in traditional cultures in other parts of Asia and some cultures in Africa (Logan & Bian, 1999; Schlegel & Barry, 1991).

The effect of the presence of grandparents in the home is reflected in findings of Schlegel and Barry (1991) that children in traditional cultures often are closer to their grandparents than they are to their parents. Similar patterns of closeness have been observed in Asian American families where grandparents typically live in an adult child's house or nearby. In those family arrangements, children and adolescents report that they receive high levels of support and nurturing from their grandparents (Fuligni et al., 1999). Mexican American children also are likely to have grandparents living

The presence of a grandparent in the home is not unusual in ethnic minority families in the United States.

in their household, and relationships with grandparents are highly valued in the Mexican American culture. The pattern of grandparent involvement is seen likewise in the African American family, which has a tradition of extended family households (Fuller-Thomson, Minkler, & Driver, 1997; Kivett, 1991; Wilson, 1989).

Several studies of African American households have described the mutual support, shared financial resources, and communal parenting responsibilities in those extended families (McAdoo, 1995; Taylor, 1997). Most African American families have a large network of extended family and upward mobility does not seem to erase the African American family's sense of reciprocal family obligation. The extended family network in the African American community therefore appears to be a cultural rather than a financial phenomenon. One of the clearest examples of the importance of extended families in that community is the role of the African American grandmother. African American grandmothers often assume some child care responsibilities and in low-income, single-parent families they frequently become **surrogate parents** (Burton & Dilworth-Anderson, 1991; Corcoran, 1999). Surrogate parents are individuals who have taken on the role and responsibilities of the parents.

THE INFLUENCE OF SOCIOECONOMIC STATUS ON PARENTING PATTERNS

Because American parents are ethnically diverse, their parenting patterns fluctuate considerably across those cultural contexts. Variations in Americans' socioeconomic status further alter their child socialization patterns. Although every cultural group contains a social hierarchy that provides a **developmental niche** for children, a family's **socioeconomic status (SES)** influences the settings in which children live and the childrearing patterns their parents adopt (Hoff-Ginsberg & Tardif, 1995). The term *socioeconomic status* refers to social class, which includes educational level, income level, and occupational status.

In a comprehensive review of the research focused on the influence of SES on parenting patterns, Hoff-Ginsberg and Tardif (1995) point to two significant findings. First, SES distinguishes between a parent-centered and a child-centered approach to child socialization. Second, family SES correlates with differences in verbal and nonverbal interactions between parents and children. The link between SES and child versus parent orientation shows a tendency of higher SES parents to adopt a child-centered approach to parenting, which seeks to understand children's feelings and motivation and to use reasoning and negotiation to solve problems. By contrast, the childrearing behaviors of lower SES parents reflect a more parent-centered approach that emphasizes children's obedience and conformity to parental rules without discussion or explanation.

The relationship between SES and verbal interactions between parents and children is demonstrated in findings that parents with higher levels of SES talk more with their children and elicit more speech from them than do parents with lower levels of SES. The profound impact of the differences in verbal interactions between high and low SES parents was documented in a study by Hart and Risley (1995) who found that professional parents speak about three times as much to their children than do low-income parents. Those researchers also reported that children in lower SES families hear mostly negative parental comments; whereas children in higher SES families hear mostly positive ones.

THE INFLUENCE OF RELIGIOSITY ON PARENTING PATTERNS

Imbedded in cultural influences on childrearing patterns is the influence of religiosity. As in the past, **religiosity** continues to influence parenting styles in contemporary America, although the authority of religion in the daily lives of families today is somewhat weaker than in past generations. Religiosity refers to the extent to which religious beliefs manifest themselves in a person's daily life. In the case of parent–child relationships, religiosity refers to whether and how often parents provide religion to children at home (prayers at meals, family devotions), how much the family's social activities include the church and its members, and whether religious beliefs affect the way parents interact with their children (Gunnoe, Hetherington, & Reiss, 1999). In contrast to the historical association between authoritarian childrearing behaviors and fundamental religious beliefs, a number of contemporary researchers have examined the influence of religiosity on childrearing patterns today and provide a more positive picture. Recent studies of parental values and family functioning have indicated that religiosity might be a better predictor of authoritative than authoritarian parenting (Brody, Stoneman, Flor, & McCrary, 1997; Gunnoe et al., 1999). In their study of mothers, fathers, and adolescents, Gunnoe et al. (1999) found that religiosity is associated positively with authoritative parenting for both parents and that mothers' religiosity is negatively related to authoritarian parenting.

Religiosity has been linked as well with positive family functioning. For example, Brody et al. (1997) reported that parental religiosity serves to organize family interactions in African American families that are economically disadvantaged by promoting higher quality parent–child relationships and by reducing coercive and inconsistent discipline. Moreover, more cooperative parent–child relationships have been reported among those African American Head Start parents who are highly religious (Strayhorn, Weidman, & Larson, 1990). Finally, Stinnett and DeFrain (1989), who examined the traits of over 3,000 strong families for over a decade, reported that spiritual wellness or an ethical value system is one of the qualities found in healthy families.

THE INFLUENCE OF FAMILY STRUCTURE ON CHILD SOCIALIZATION PATTERNS

Just as it is helpful to examine the ways in which culture, SES, and religiosity influence patterns of child socialization, it is useful to understand the relation of family structure to childrearing patterns. The first step toward that understanding is to realize that not all children are reared in families with two married heterosexual parents.

It is important to acknowledge that large numbers of children are raised by parents who are not married, parents who are not heterosexual, or adults who are not the children's biological or adoptive parents. The next step is to emphasize that in all family structures parents are making efforts to provide nurturing guidance for their children. Nevertheless, societal and intergenerational family support varies depending on family structure, and the presence or absence of societal and family support impacts the relationships within various family structures.

Families Affected by Parental Divorce

At some time before reaching adulthood, about half of today's children in the United States will go through a marital dissolution of their parents, which is typically upsetting to them as well as to their parents (Kitson, 1990; Owusu-Bempah, 1995; Wallerstein, 1989). In addition to the stress of coping with their parents' divorce, children have the additional stress of making a transition from living in a household headed by two parents to living in a household headed by only one.

Divorced Single-Parent Families.   When parents divorce, the structure of the family system is altered in such a way that parents and children become members of various family subsystems, and the roles of parents and children are modified. Those changes in family structure and family roles following divorce alter family interaction patterns that in turn impact the lives of parents and children in those families (Beevar & Beevar, 1988; Rosenberg & Guttman, 2001). In a recent investigation of the alteration in the family structure following divorce, Rosenberg and Guttman (2001) studied mothers and children from divorced and two-parent families and found that the majority of children of divorced parents, and about half of the divorced mothers, included the father as a member of the family system. Their results also revealed that both the children as well as the mothers in the divorced family group perceived their postdivorce family subsystem as less hierarchical in comparison to children and mothers in the control group.

Besides the difference in family stability, the other primary difference between families that are headed by married parents and those headed by single parents is gender related. The gender difference is due to the greater likelihood that divorced mothers will maintain custody of their children following divorce combined with the much lower income level of mother-headed households. Based on statistics related to family incomes, women heads of households can expect to have financial difficulties. The situation for father-headed households is somewhat different. Men who gain custody of their children are more likely than are custodial mothers or noncustodial fathers to have significantly higher incomes (Holden & Smock, 1991; U.S. Bureau of the Census, 1999).

Although there are similarities in mother-headed and father-headed families, researchers have shown more interest in studying differences in how divorced single fathers and single divorced mothers handle their children. The findings show that as fathers make the transition from the married-parent household to the single-parent household, they become less authoritarian and thereby less strict with their children, more concerned with the quality of care their children receive, and more protective toward their children. Single divorced mothers, on the other hand, have been found to rely more on authoritarian patterns of interacting with their children following divorce (Hetherington & Clingempeel, 1992).

Before we jump to the hasty conclusion that single custodial fathers are more competent parents than are single custodial mothers, it is important to remember that single custodial fathers tend to have stronger work histories and higher status jobs than do single custodial mothers. Furthermore, fathers who gain custody of their children are a very small minority group of better educated men with higher incomes in comparison to men who do not gain custody of their children. Father-headed households constitute only 17% of all single-parent families (U.S. Bureau of the Census, 1999). Because single custodial fathers do not suffer financially in the same way as do single custodial mothers, it would be biased to lump all single custodial mothers together and compare that large sample of single custodial mothers to the much smaller, select group of better educated, higher salaried, single custodial fathers.

When examining the childrearing patterns of divorced parents, it is important to consider the context in which they occur. Research findings showing that single mothers become more authoritarian and single fathers become more authoritative following divorce might reflect necessary alterations of the role from married to single parent. Single mothers might find it necessary to establish greater authority following divorce, and single fathers might find that they need to increase their responsiveness toward their children. It is valuable to remember as well that the patterns of child socialization are related to the stress levels of parents. Because the demographic evidence reveals that single custodial mothers and their children are more likely to live in poverty than are single custodial fathers and their children (U.S. Bureau of the Census, 1999), it would be instructive to consider how single parenthood interacts with stresses related to financial difficulty when examining the childrearing patterns of single mothers. For example, Kahn, Wise, Kennedy, and Kawachi (2000) found that income inequality is associated with poorer mental and physical health in women with young children and that those associations are most pronounced in women with low income.

Children's Adjustment Following Parental Divorce.   As is the case for their parents, most children and adolescents experience emotional adjustments for 1 to 2 years during the period leading up to, and immediately following, parental separation and divorce. That is typically the period during which family conflict intensifies, legal battles are fought, and relationships with residential and nonresidential parents are renegotiated (Owusu-Bempah, 1995). In addition to the transitions related to their adjustment to parental divorce and restructuring of the family system, many children experience considerable distancing from their noncustodial parent if the custodial or noncustodial parent makes a geographical relocation. To continue satisfactory relationships with both parents in the postdivorce family, children must have easy access to them. The relocation of either parent has a direct and immediate impact on the physical contact between children and their nonresident parent. Because most children of divorced parents are in the custody of their mothers, the residential moves by mothers or fathers are likely to impact the children's access to the father. Furthermore, increased distance between parents and children is related to decreased contact with children, with some nonresident parents becoming considerably less involved in their children's lives following geographical separation from them (Stewart, 1999). Those compound alterations in children's lives are stressful, require considerable adjustment, and are likely to have a detrimental effect on their ongoing development.

In spite of the many adjustments in family system and lifestyle that are required of children whose parents divorce, the adjustment of children and adolescents in postdivorce families is only marginally lower than for children in continuously intact two-parent families (Amato, 2000; Demo & Acock, 1996). Most important to children's postdivorce adjustment are economic resources, positive nurturing relationships with both parents, and low levels of parental and family conflict (Demo, 1992; Gindes, 1998; McLanahan & Sandefur, 1994). Furthermore, research findings suggest that in families where single parents use an authoritative parenting pattern, their children have better developmental outcomes. Family scholars who have compared the childrearing styles of single-parent families headed by mothers, stepfamilies involving previously divorced custodial mothers, and nondivorced parents have shown that authoritative childrearing methods are associated with positive adjustments of children in all three family types (Hetherington & Clingempeel, 1992).

Stepfamilies.   The stepfamily would seem to be a reasonably good solution for reestablishing the family system following divorce. The stepfamily has two adults present to provide parental guidance and care and one of those adults is the children's biological or adoptive parent. Furthermore, stepfamilies typically do not suffer the obvious economic disadvantages of mother-headed, single-parent households. Nevertheless, there are a number of challenges for parents and children in stepfamily households. In the case of remarriage, there are several factors that act as stressors for stepfamilies. First, remarriage represents still another transition in the lives of parents and children who have already undergone adjustments related to parental divorce and the restructuring of their family system. Second, the role of stepparent in the family is not clearly defined. Third, members of stepfamilies are subjected to prejudices and stereotypes related to societal views of the stepfamily. Fourth, stepfamily members must establish and maintain interaction patterns that meet the needs of all family members.

Problems Associated with Multiple Transitions.   Most children of divorced parents will live in a single-parent family for about 5 years, and a small majority of children who have experienced divorce will end up living in a stepfamily. Since over one third of stepfamilies end in divorce, many children endure the extra trauma of seeing their parents' subsequent marriages break up (Zinsmeister, 1996). Therefore, when the single-parent family is reconfigured from the intact family into the stepfamily, both parents and children who have already had major life adjustments related to the divorce face more disruptions associated with changes in many life routines. When children experience multiple life transitions, they are at greater risk for developmental difficulties. Across samples, across gender, and across measures of adjustment, children who have experienced multiple parental transitions have been found to have the most behavior problems, and children of mothers who experienced no partner change (i.e., married mothers who remained married or single mothers who remained single) have been found to have the fewest behavior problems (Kurdek, Fine, & Sinclair, 1994, 1995).

Negative and Stigmatizing Beliefs About Stepfamilies.   American culture continues to view any family form that does not conform to the traditional, politically correct, family pattern as problematic. In spite of their growing numbers, negative and stigmatizing beliefs about stepfamilies are still pervasive in our society. The level and forms of that stigmatization differ according to religion and sociocultural environment. The stigmatization of stepfamilies includes negative stereotypes, myths that depict stepfamilies as pathogenic, and attitudes that blame them for the social, emotional, and relational problems of their members. The belief of the inferiority of stepfamilies is so pervasive that the term *stepchild* is used to denote a state of inferiority and neglect and the stepfamily is often referred to as *a broken home* and *a problematic family* (Berger, 2000).

Lack of Clarity of the Role of Stepparent.   The challenge of assuming the role of stepparent is that stepfamily members frequently do not agree on what role the stepparent should play. Beyond a general consensus that in comparison to stepparents parents are expected to exhibit more warmth toward their children and to more carefully monitor their children's behavior, there is little consistency in perceptions of the content of the stepparent role. Furthermore, stepparents are less certain about their role in the stepfamily than are other members. Some stepfathers deal with the issue of role confusion and stepparent identity by assuming a parent role. In contrast, most stepmothers and many stepfathers (especially nonresidential ones) see themselves as a friend to their stepchildren or in some role between a friend and a parent (Erera-Weatherly, 1996).

Stepfamily Relationships and Children's Well-Being.   Most studies of stepfamily relationships and processes have focused on stepfathers' relationships with children because most stepfamily households consist of the mother, her children from a previous marriage, and a stepfather. Those findings suggest that stepchildren tend to reject stepparents who engage in discipline and control early in the relationship (Bray & Kelly, 1998; Ganong, Coleman, & Fine, 1999). In contrast, the expression of mutual affection more often characterizes stepparent–stepchild relationships when stepfathers initially engage in supportive behaviors with stepchildren (Bray & Kelly, 1998; Hetherington & Clingempeel, 1992). Moreover, stepparents who make efforts to maintain close relationship with stepchildren have closer bonds with them in comparison to stepparents who do not make those efforts. The most effective relationship-building strategies for stepparents are dyadic activities chosen by the stepchildren. When stepchildren recognize that their stepparents are trying to do things with them that the stepchildren like, they generally respond with their own affinity-seeking efforts (Ganong et al., 1999). Although there are multiple challenges in stepfamilies, and children in stepfamilies are at greater risk for problems than are children in first-married families (Kurdek et al., 1994, 1995), many stepfamilies provide a positive environment for children. Furthermore, researchers have noted that the differences between stepchildren and children living in first-marriage families are small. Most stepchildren do well in school and do not have emotional or behavioral problems (Coleman, Ganong, & Fine, 2000).

Parents Who Are Widowed

In some families, a parent's death results in a widowed parent taking on the role of sole parent. For many, the alteration in marital status and family structure comes without warning, as when a parent dies in a sudden accident or other tragic event. Although many children lose their parents without forewarning, others experience the loss of their parents as a result of a terminal illness, which provides a warning that a single-parent household is a part of the family's future. In the case of terminal illness, the surviving parent has time to begin planning for a future as a single parent. The stress-filled months leading up to the death of a spouse and parent take their toll, however, on all family members. Furthermore, widowed single parents must simultaneously deal with their own grief related to the loss of a spouse, assist their children's grief associated with the loss of a parent, and assume the responsibilities of a solo parent (Raveis, Siegel, & Karus, 1999). How family members cope with death and ways to assist children through the grieving process will be covered in chapter 10, Loss and Grief in Parent–Child Relationships.

Adolescent Single Parents

Although pregnancy and parenthood impact the ongoing development of many adolescents, that discussion will be covered in chapter 6, Parent–Adolescent Interactions. The discussion of adolescent parents that is presented in the following section

This adolescent mother is beginning her parenting career with many disadvantages and will require more extended family and social support than will the typical adult parent.

is intended to show how those young parents fit into the overall context of contemporary parenting in the United States. In focusing on the context of parent–child relations when parents are adolescents, it is important to emphasize that in comparison to older parents, adolescent parents must typically depend on their parents for financial, practical, and emotional assistance. Because of their youth, both adolescent fathers and mothers are less likely to be married (DeJong & Cottrell, 1999), are probably living with one or both of their parents, and their children are most often in the custody of their mothers (SmithBattle, 1996). We, therefore, cannot talk about the parent–adolescent household as we do when discussing other single parents who are older, have more experience, usually more education, jobs with regular incomes, and separate households.

Factors That Distinguish Between Adolescent and Young Adult Parents.   There are many factors that distinguish adolescent parents from young adult parents. Taken together, those factors make adolescent parenthood especially problematic. First of all, adolescent parents are likely to have poor nutritional habits and a lifestyle that does not contribute to healthy prenatal development. In comparison to older pregnant females, pregnant teens are less likely to gain adequate weight during pregnancy, less likely to get prenatal care, less likely to receive adequate nutrition, and more likely to smoke and to ingest unhealthy substances. They are, therefore, more likely to have risk conditions such as anemia and pregnancy-related high blood pressure during pregnancy, and more likely to give birth to preterm, underweight infants, who are at greater risk for birth defects or early death (Cohen, 1995; Shiono, Rauh, Park, Lederman, & Zuskar, 1997). Furthermore, the children who are born to teenage mothers are at a developmental disadvantage when compared to children born to older mothers. Whereas differences are indistinguishable during infancy, they begin to emerge during preschool. Young children of parents who were teenagers when they were born are more aggressive and less controlled in comparison to other preschoolers (Chase-Lansdale, Mott, & Brooks-Gunn, 1991).

Adolescent Mothers.   Earlier studies demonstrated that adolescent mothers have more troublesome relationships with their children than do older parents and are more likely than are older mothers to be abusive toward their children (Zuravin, 1988). It is important, however, to bear in mind the variability that exists in that group of young mothers and to consider the context in which young single parenthood occurs. First, although adolescent mothers tend to have problematic relationships with their children, they are not less competent parents by virtue of their youth. When adolescent mothers have been compared with older mothers, they have been found to have comparable parenting skills in a number of areas (Kemp et al., 1990; Lamb & Elster, 1985; Roosa, Fitzgerald, & Carlson, 1982). The factors that place teenage parents and their children more at risk for developmental problems appear to be related to the difficulties those young parents face in attempting to take on the role of early parenthood. Adolescent mothers have several common sources of stress including lower incomes, lower levels of support, interrupted educational experiences, and a lower quality of life (Chase-Lansdale, Brooks-Gunn, & Paikoff, 1991; Zuravin & DiBlasio, 1992). Furthermore, the role of the adolescent mother must be reorganized to accommodate the role of parenthood, and the requirements of those two roles might conflict. For example, body image is a common concern of adolescent females and is likely to influence the choice of whether to breast-feed or to bottle-feed. Other developmental tasks of adolescent mothers that might conflict with the demands of motherhood include the development of a self-identity, the need for peer acceptance, the desire for relationships with romantic partners, and the struggle for independence (Leitch, 1998).

Thinking Critically

Perhaps you had not thought about the adolescent mother in terms of conflicting roles of being a parent and being an adolescent. How do you think their parents might respond to adolescent mothers' conflicting developmental needs?

Adolescent Fathers.   Since most adolescent parents do not marry and adolescent mothers typically retain custody of their children, where does that leave adolescent fathers? In the case of adolescent fathers, there are some who do not acknowledge their role in impregnating an adolescent girl; however, the stereotype of adolescent boys as uncaring, unfeeling, uninvolved, and immature does not describe all adolescent fathers (Furstenberg, Brooks-Gunn, & Chase-Lansdale, 1989). On the contrary, studies of adolescent fathers have found them to be frightened, withdrawn, confused, and guilty about their role in contributing to the pregnancy (Christmon, 1990a, 1990b). A primary challenge for those young males is that they typically experience a lack of clarity regarding their role as fathers. Because fathers are expected to provide financial support for their children and adolescent fathers are usually not working in full-time jobs, they often have diminished roles as fathers. The problems that adolescent fathers experience by virtue of their socioeconomic status, their educational level, and lifestyle experiences are comparable to those experienced by adolescent mothers (Cervera & Videka-Sherman, 1989). Furthermore, there is evidence that early fatherhood has long-term consequences for young males. Drawing on the 1993 report of a longitudinal study of over 4,000 youth between the ages of 14 and 21, Nock (1998) examined the socioeconomic consequences of premarital fatherhood. The findings from that investigation were that men who have children before marriage leave school earlier, have lower wages, work fewer hours per week, and are more likely to live in poverty in comparison to those who do not have children before marriage.

Single Parents Who Are Not Divorced, Widowed, or Adolescents

There was an increase in births to unmarried adult females (ages 20 to 34) during the 1990s, with the largest increase occurring for those females in their early 20s. The increase of births for that age group suggests that adults in contemporary America are freer to take on single parenthood even when they have no immediate plans to marry and might not be in committed relationships. Furthermore, a small (but increasing) number of single adult women are financially capable individuals. Recent census data indicates that 8.3% of never-married women in managerial or professional positions fit that description (U.S. Bureau of the Census, 1999). Single young adults in well-paying careers who choose to become parents differ considerably from other single parents. Besides being better off financially than adolescent parents, divorced custodial mothers, or divorced noncustodial fathers, unmarried young adults in professional careers are not simultaneously coping with single parenting and the stresses of losing a spouse through divorce or death. Next, single parenthood for that group represents more of a choice of single parenthood in comparison to single parenthood that results from divorce, death of a spouse, or an unplanned pregnancy. Although there are unique challenges to be found in the unmarried young adult parent–child relationship, those challenges must be considered alongside advantages related to maturity, higher income, and a high level of commitment to parenthood as reflected by the deliberate choice to become a single parent.

Gay and Lesbian Parents

Families headed by gay fathers are relatively rare but families headed by lesbian mothers occur more frequently than many people realize because such families often are indistinguishable from those headed by heterosexual couples. Moreover, researchers have found few differences in the way that heterosexual and homosexual parents rear their children (Bigner, 1996; Patterson, 1992). Furthermore, families formed by gay or lesbian parents have many characteristics in common with stepfamilies created by heterosexual parents. That is especially true of lesbian mothers who frequently have custody of their children from a former heterosexual marriage. The similarities between heterosexual stepfamilies and gay or lesbian stepfamilies include the following: (a) Both families are created after the disruption of previous families; (b) both families are formed by the joining of an additional family member; and (c) in both families there are nonresidential family members (Erera & Fredrickson, 1999; Visher, 1994).

The Loss Associated with Previous Family Disruption.   Although all stepfamilies are founded on the basis of the disruption of previous families, this loss sets gay or lesbian stepfamilies apart from heterosexual stepfamilies. Although studies of heterosexual stepfamilies have dealt with the issue of loss associated with family disruption (Hetherington & Clingempeel, 1992; Owusu-Bempah, 1995; Wallerstein, 1989), the literature on gay or lesbian stepfamilies does not address the loss issue. It is likely that the issue of loss is overlooked by family scholars because the gay or lesbian stepfamily is perceived as a cohabiting couple rather than as a family (Erera & Fredrickson, 1999). By and large, the gay or lesbian stepfamily is not accorded the status of family owing to the parent's and stepparent's sexual orientation.

Family Roles.　In reality, both gay or lesbian and heterosexual stepfamilies are family systems created by the same circumstances and composed of the same family roles. The birth or adoptive parent and children are joined by a stepparent. Sometimes the stepparent brings to the new family system his or her birth children as well. Both the joining stepparent and the "absorbing" family have their own family connections, rituals, and habits. In the beginning stages, stepfamilies are composed of two distinct subsystems: the absorbing or "veteran" family members and the "newcomer(s)." In addition to the two residential parents and the children and stepchildren, heterosexual and gay or lesbian stepfamilies generally include nonresident members. The nonresidential members are the noncustodial birth or adoptive parent and at times an additional stepparent (the spouse of the noncustodial parent). In some lesbian stepfamilies the nonresidential parent is an inaccessible or an unknown donor. Although seemingly nonexistent, children might develop fantasies and idealize the nonresidential birth father, viewing him as a "parent in the shadows," or a ghost member of the family (Hare, 1994).

Shared Parental Responsibilities.　In both heterosexual and gay or lesbian stepfamilies, residential parents might share parental responsibilities and authority with the nonresidential parents. That interdependence sometimes leads to conflict in situations where the residential and nonresidential parents have different goals or priorities. Lesbian mothers, however, tend to have more congenial relations with their previous husbands than do heterosexual mothers (Hare, 1994). Additionally, research has demonstrated that lesbian mothers are likely to "adopt" male friends as male role models for their children and usually have more men participating in the lives of their children in comparison to single, heterosexual mothers. Although lesbian mothers generally have more cooperative relations with their exspouses, in many cases the noncustodial birth parent attempts to prevent the lesbian birth mother from having custody of her children or even from having visitation rights. Such conflicts suggest that, similar to other stepfamilies, visitation and custody are issues related to mutual antagonism, tension, and competitiveness between the gay or lesbian parents and their previous partners. Gay or lesbian parents, however, tend to be additionally vulnerable in this type of conflict because of societal discrimination (Shapiro, 1996).

The Gay or Lesbian Stepfamily as a Unique Family Form.　Even though heterosexual and gay or lesbian stepfamilies share a number of characteristics and face similar challenges, parents and children in gay or lesbian stepfamilies are confronted with a number of challenges that are unique to their family form. Those challenges include societal prejudices related to the sexual orientation of the residential parents, a lack of or diminished intergenerational support of their lifestyle, and a denial of basic civil rights.

Societal Prejudice Related to Their Sexual Orientation.   The main differences between gay or lesbian parents and heterosexual parents are that gay or lesbian parents are confronted with prejudices related to their sexual orientation whereas the sexual orientation of nongay parents is not questioned. An example of the prejudices that gay parents confront is exemplified by a parent who reported that her 9-year-old son came home and told her that his friend's father had said to him that his mother would burn in hell "because she loves women and that is against the rule of nature" (Shapiro, 1996, p. 504). An aspect of the prejudice that gay men and lesbian women face is related specifically to gay or lesbian parenthood. The prejudices toward gay people create an image of homosexuality as incompatible with family and of gay and lesbian as "antifamily." As noted by a lesbian mother: "Ten years ago . . . when I would say I have a daughter, people would sigh and say 'and we thought you were gay, but obviously you are not . . . you are a mother'" (Shapiro, 1996, p. 504). Even though gay and lesbian parenthood is more acceptable today than it was 10 years ago, many people still believe that homosexuality and parenthood are mutually exclusive (Berger, 2000).

Lack of or Diminished Intergenerational Support.   In most families, intergenerational relationships are important sources of support for parents and that familial support extends the childrearing efforts of parents. Whereas heterosexual parents are usually able to take intergenerational support for granted, that is not the case for gay or lesbian parents. Rather than being able to benefit from parental support, gay or lesbian parents tend to experience moderate to strong parental disapproval of their homosexual lifestyle, which might create stress in their relationships with their partners and/or impact the lives of their children (Berger, 2000). An example of the effect of diminished parental support for gay or lesbian parents is evident in the following statement made by a biological parent in a lesbian stepfamily composed of herself, her partner, and her adolescent son. The statement was made in response to the question, "To what extent do you and your partner experience parental support of your family?" The names used in the quote are fictitious.

> Well, my own parents do not support my lifestyle and are no longer involved in my life. Therefore, it means a lot to me that Barbara's parents welcome Tommy (the son) and me in their home. Since Tommy and I don't have contact with my parents, that gives us a family. They are nice to Tommy and always remember to give him a present at Christmas. When referring to their grandchildren, however, they don't mention Tommy which means they don't consider Tommy as one of the grandchildren. That hurts because he really wants to be included as a part of the family. (Anonymous)

Denial of Basic Civil Rights.   The basic civil rights that extend to other family forms generally do not support gay and lesbian parents and their children. On the contrary, there is currently increasing legal scrutiny of lesbians and gay men and their children. For example, the Defense of Marriage Act was recently passed to prohibit the recognition of interstate same-sex marriages. Lesbians and gay parents also are frequently denied custody of and visitation with their children and are often denied the opportunity to adopt or become foster parents (Shapiro, 1996). The effects of societal prejudices, lack of family support, and not having legal recognition of their family structure are that gay and lesbian parents must establish protective boundaries around their family when confronted with those challenges (LaSala, 2002).

Children of Gay or Lesbian Parents.   Despite the lack of societal, family, and legal support of their lifestyle, the vast majority of social science research has demonstrated that the sexual orientation of gay or lesbian parents affects neither their ability to parent nor the outcomes among their children. In a review of the research findings focusing on that topic, Fredrickson (1999) reported that a parent's sexual orientation is not related to the child's emotional health, interpersonal relationships, social adjustment, gender identity, or sexual orientation. Those findings indicate that gay and lesbian parents generally find creative and healthy ways for responding to the challenges they face. One explanation for the positive adjustment of children in gay and lesbian families is that both lesbian women and gay men are more likely than are heterosexual men and women to form **egalitarian relationships** based on the principle of equality of partners. That structure differs considerably from the structure of heterosexual relationships whereby gender is used as a determinant for dividing household responsibilities. In those families, household responsibilities are generally shared, reflecting the egalitarian principle. Many studies have documented the positive effects of egalitarian parental relationships and have shown also that children are better adjusted when parents divide the child care responsibilities equally (e.g., Kurdek, 1993; Patterson, 1995). Another explanation for the positive adaptation of children in gay or lesbian stepfamilies might be due to findings that the gay or lesbian community is often a vital source of support for gay or lesbian parents (Hare, 1994).

Thinking Critically

As you can see, children in the United States are being reared in a variety of family structures. Nevertheless, there are stereotypes and prejudices about which family type is considered to be "normal and appropriate." How do you think negative beliefs concerning varied family structures affect the lives of parents and children who are living in those family arrangements?

Surrogate Parents

Most children in the United States are being reared by one or more of their parents with or without the support of extended family members. Many other children, within and outside the United States have grandparents living within the household or nearby who are involved in their lives. There are a lot of children in the United States, however, who are being reared by persons who have stepped into the parental role to ensure that children have homes in which to live and caring adults to guide

After rearing their own children, and at a time when many of their contemporaries have retired, these grandparents have taken on the responsibilities of rearing their grandchildren.

and protect them. An increasing number of children are reared by their grandparents or by other relatives (Fuller-Thomson et al., 1997), and growing numbers of children are cared for or reared by foster parents (Roche, 2000).

Grandparents Rearing Their Grandchildren.   In the United States, grandmothers often assume some child care responsibilities or become the primary parent in low-income, single-parent families (Burton & Dilworth-Anderson, 1991; Fuller-Thomson et al., 1997). In previous research, grandparent caregivers have most often been African American females living in the inner city, raising their daughters' children. That picture of the grandparent in the role of primary caregiver of grandchildren has recently shifted. In the late 1990s, 13% of African American children, 6.5% of Hispanic American children, and 4.1% of European American children were being raised by their grandparents (U.S. Bureau of the Census, 1999). Circumstances resulting in grandparents becoming surrogate parents include parental death, parental physical or mental illness, parental substance abuse, parental imprisonment, or parental abuse and/or neglect of children (Karp, 1996; Takas, 1995).

Although grandparents provide a tremendous service to their grandchildren who might otherwise be placed in foster care, taking on the caregiver role as older adults places many of those grandparents at risk for jeopardizing their own physical or psychological health (Minkler & Roe, 1991). As with any family system, however, the success of the grandchild–grandparent household can be viewed in terms of stresses and resources. Although stressors in the family contribute to a grandparent taking on the role of caregiver, the availability of a grandparent to step in when parents cannot fulfill their parental responsibilities represents a family resource. First of all, grandparents who choose to provide a home for their grandchildren provide one of the most positive resources necessary for the optimum development of children—the availability of caring adults. In research of at-risk children, it has been documented that the presence in one's life of at least one adult the child can depend on to be emotionally supportive promotes resilience in the face of other hardships (Baldwin, Baldwin, & Cole, 1990; Werner & Smith, 1989). Furthermore, being able to provide a home for children whose parents are unavailable (for whatever reason) alleviates concerns of grandparents regarding their grandchildren's welfare and for many grandparents contributes to satisfaction derived from stabilizing the life of a child (Waldrup & Weber, 2001). Nevertheless, grandparents who are raising grandchildren are often in need of varied kinds of assistance because they differ in levels of financial security, health problems, employment issues, and family conflict.

Formal Support for Grandparents Raising Their Grandchildren. It is important to remember that taking on the responsibility of caregiver of one's grandchildren is not as simple as transferring residences. **Kinship caregivers** (grandparents, aunts, uncles, or other family members who assume parental responsibilities for the children of relatives) face a host of legal problems. In recognition of the legal vulnerability associated with kinship caregiving, local support groups, statewide coalitions, policymakers, and legislators have begun to seek solutions to those difficulties. Some examples of recent developments include (a) legal authority to make caregiving decisions, (b) financial support for kinship care, (c) resolution of housing problems, and (d) options for permanent care (Takas, 1995). Although recent trends indicate challenging times ahead for families in crisis, policymakers, legislators, and service providers continue to focus on the needs of kinship caregivers and to develop creative solutions to their legal problems (Karp, 1996).

Informal Support for Grandparents Raising Grandchildren. A potential source of support for the grandparent–grandchildren household is from the extended family system. Based on their study of grandparents who are rearing their grandchildren, Waldrup and Weber (2001) identified several ways in which family members sometimes assist those grandparents. First of all, family members might provide emotional assistance such as advice and encouragement. Second, they might offer practical help, such as transportation and financial assistance. Grandparents benefit as well from respite care whether it is provided by family members, friends, or coworkers, or by a social service agency. In the case of grandparents caring for their grandchildren, respite care refers to the temporary care of those children to provide grandparents with the opportunity to relax, to take care of errands, or to participate in leisurely activities. The ways in which family, friends, and coworkers might offer assistance to grandparents who are raising their grandchildren are exemplified in the following anecdote from a 50-year-old grandmother, who is raising her two grandchildren and a nephew, in response to the question, "How do you cope with the situation?"

> I have faith. I have lots of faith. My family supports each other. People that I work with are wonderful. They are just marvelous. They work with me; they support me and say, "Sarah, is there anything that I can do to help you, and stuff like that." It makes a difference— 100% difference. . . . (Waldrup & Weber, 2001, p. 467)

Foster Parents.   Each year, thousands of children are taken from their biological families and placed in foster care. The number of children placed in foster care at the end of 1999 was over 550,000, which was approximately twice as many as were in foster care a decade earlier (Roche, 2000). The rise in foster care placement coincides with an increase of reported cases of child abuse and neglect in the United States. Unfortunately, predictions are that the numbers of children placed in foster care will continue to grow in the next decade (Baum, Crase, & Crase, 2001; Carney, 1997). Not only has the number of children needing foster care become overwhelming, it has become problematic to find families capable of meeting the complex emotional, behavioral, psychological, and medical needs of those children (Baum et al., 2001; Pasztor & Wynne, 1995). Foster children have been found to have up to seven times more emotional adjustment problems, developmental delays, and acute and chronic health problems than a comparative group of children living in poverty (Rosenfeld et al., 1997).

Problems Associated with Finding Foster Parents for Children.   Due to the vast need for foster care placement of children and adolescents, one of the primary challenges of foster care professionals includes finding individuals who are willing to become foster care providers. Findings of Baum et al. (2001) indicate that "awareness of the need for foster care" is the most influential factor in helping individuals make the decision of whether or not to become foster parents. That finding emphasizes the importance of educating the community regarding the crucial need for foster homes. Other motivations that individuals have given for wanting to become foster parents vary but "enjoying and wanting to help children" is a common response.

One of the major concerns for placing children in foster care is the risk that the placement will not be successful (Baum et al., 2001; Stone & Stone, 1983). Foster home breakdowns or the unplanned removal of children from foster homes can be traumatic for children and may interfere with the child's later formation of intimate relationships (Rosenfeld et al., 1997). To lessen the likelihood that those breakdowns will occur, Daly and Dowd (1992) call for a "harm-free, effective environment," that is free from abuse and neglect and in compliance with legal licensing guidelines. Daly and Dowd emphasize that effective foster parents provide care that promotes spiritual, emotional, intellectual, and physical development. Ways to meet the goals

Thinking Critically

In consideration of children's varied living arrangements, how do you think others (teachers, other professionals, friends, and acquaintances) can be thoughtful and considerate in discussing family life, sending notes home, or writing about children and their families so that all children can take pride in themselves and their family life?

of effective foster care have been suggested by Morrisette (1996), who stresses that two important attributes of effective foster parents are emotional stability and a genuine liking for children. Morrisette points out that it is important for foster parents to show respect for the children in their care as well as to set clear limits and follow through with consequences.

THE INFLUENCE OF FAMILIES OF ORIGIN ON CHILDREARING PATTERNS

Closely linked to the effect of family structure on childrearing is the influence of the family of origin. Although adults might not acknowledge the relation between their child socialization patterns and the childrearing behaviors of their parents, the research of Patterson and Capaldi (1991) confirms that parents draw on their own childhood experiences in rearing their children. In chapter 1, we focused on the growth-producing effects of children's attachments to their parents. In that discussion, it was emphasized that secure attachment promotes (among other things) the infant's internalization of a working model of parental availability (Ainsworth et al., 1978). From their own experiences as children, adults also internalize a working model that influences how they view their own children and how they interact with them.

In an effort to relate parents' childhood experiences with their own parents to their parenting patterns, Grusec, Hastings and Mammone (1994) conducted interviews with parents and discovered that the quality of attachment to their own parents predicted the way in which those parents interacted with their children. Parents who had a continuously secure attachment to their own parents were emotionally supportive and responsive to their children while setting clear and consistent limits. Parents with an insecure dismissive attachment to their own parents tended to emphasize their own independence and were likely to remain cool and remote from their children. Basically, those parents were less likely to help or support their children emotionally. Parents who had an insecure preoccupied attachment to their own parents exhibited a confusing and inconsistent pattern of behavior toward their children. Whereas those parents were warm and gentle with their children sometimes, they were angry and forceful with them at other times. Furthermore, they harbored negative thoughts about their children and in difficult childrearing situations tended to blame the problems on the child's personality.

❧ SUMMARY

In this chapter, a foundation has been established for discussing the parent–child relationships to be covered in the upcoming chapters. The contemporary parenting styles of American parents have been distinguished and consideration has been given to the traditional parenting pattern found in non-Western societies and ethnic minority cultures within the United States. Research findings demonstrating the impact of parenting patterns on children's outcome have been presented as well. In those discussions, we considered the ways in which cultural norms and belief systems contribute to different parenting styles within the various cultures in American society and throughout the world. We then considered other contextual influences of childrearing, including family structure, religiosity, and socioeconomic level. Throughout all those discussions, we contemplated the ways in which the lives of parents and children are shaped by the parent–child relations in which they participate. As we have seen, parenting patterns reflect parental belief systems that are shaped and altered according to cultural norms, age, marital status, socioeconomic status, religiosity, and parents' families of origin.

❦ KEY TERMS

- amae
- authoritarian parenting style
- authoritative parenting style
- culture
- developmental niche
- egalitarian relationship
- indifferent parenting style
- indulgent parenting style
- industrialized societies
- kinship caregivers
- nonindustrialized societies
- permissive parenting style
- poisonous pedagogy
- racial socialization
- religiosity
- society
- socioeconomic status (SES)
- surrogate parents
- traditional culture
- traditional parenting style
- the West

3

Becoming Parents and Parenting Infants and Toddlers

To quote what the king told Alice in Lewis Carroll's *Through the Looking Glass,* let us "begin at the beginning" (Tripp, 1970). This chapter is about beginnings, with all the excitement and trepidation that accompany new adventures. The first beginning is the momentous decision to become parents; next there is the anticipation of parenthood. Then, the arrival of a child confers onto adults the adult role of parent and in marriages or committed partnerships extends the couple relationship into a family. Those alterations in adult roles and responsibilities as well as changes in family definition set into motion numerous changes and new beginnings for the child, for the parents, for the immediate and extended family, and for the community.

To appreciate the impact of those various beginnings on the lives of children and their parents, we will start by examining the ways in which expectant parents can take steps to optimize the chances of giving birth to healthy, full-term babies. Next, we will focus on the experience of birth as a universal occurrence that differentially impacts parents according to the nature of the birth or births (in the case of multiple births) and the resources available to the parents. Following the discussion of the birth, we will take a look at the important transition to parenthood. Then we will consider the ways in which parents' interactions with their infants and toddlers impact their children's social–emotional, physical, and cognitive development. Finally, we will take a look at the various ways in which parents coordinate their parental responsibilities with their occupational demands.

OPTIMIZING THE CHANCES OF HAVING HEALTHY BABIES

Although birth is a significant event in all families and the arrival of infants is usually a joyous occasion, the circumstances surrounding babies coming into the world vary considerably. Geographical location, socioeconomic conditions, and the behaviors of expectant parents all contribute to the health and survival of newborns. Complications of pregnancy that contribute to birth defects, premature births, or low-birth-weight infants are sometimes beyond the control of parents. For the majority of

The scene captures the feelings of joyful anticipation of birth and motherhood.

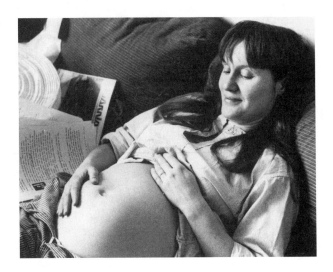

pregnancies, however, there are steps that parents can take to increase the likelihood that their babies will be carried to full term, have a healthy weight, and have a lower risk of birth defects. Those include avoiding **teratogens** and seeking early prenatal care. Teratogens are agents and conditions, including malnutrition, viruses, drugs, chemicals, and stressors that can interfere with prenatal development and contribute to birth defects or death (Conley & Bennett, 2001).

Maintaining a Nutritious Diet

It is imperative that women have a nutritious diet throughout their pregnancies because maternal malnutrition is correlated with low birth weight. Low birth weight has been linked with inadequate nutrition that results from fasting or starvation (even for 1 day) or the lack of specific nutrients, including vitamin A, folic acid, iron, magnesium, calcium, and zinc. Depending on her eating habits, the pregnant woman's maintenance of a healthy diet might require the inclusion of certain foods and drinks as well as the limiting of other foods and drinks. In addition to eating nutritious foods, it is important that pregnant women avoid substances that decrease nutrient absorption, such as tobacco, alcohol, and diuretics (Luke, 1993).

Avoiding Harmful Substances

One of the most commonly used substances that compromises the health of the mother during pregnancy and affects the health of the developing fetus is prenatal exposure to nicotine. Despite abundant adverse publicity, tobacco use occurs in about 25% of all pregnancies in the United States. Several reports have established that maternal smoking during pregnancy adversely affects prenatal and postnatal growth and increases the risk of fetal mortality, low birth weight, and infant mortality.

Furthermore, cognitive deficits and behavior problems of children and adolescents have been traced to their prenatal nicotine exposure (Ernst, Moolchan, & Robinson, 2001). The use of caffeine during pregnancy should be monitored as well. Some research indicates that the probability of premature delivery is somewhat higher among mothers who consume higher levels of caffeine (Jacobson, Fein, Jacobson, Schwartz, & Dowler, 1985) and lower among women who do not consume caffeine (Eskenazi, Stapleton, Kharrazi, & Chee, 1999). Profound birth defects, fetal death, low birth weight, and infant mortality have also been consistently related to the use of legal and illegal drugs. See Figure 3.1 for a list of teratogens that negatively impact prenatal development.

Getting Early Prenatal Care

In addition to eating nutritious foods and avoiding substances that decrease nutrient absorption and inflict harm on the developing fetus, it is very important for pregnant women to receive prenatal care early in their pregnancies and to continue prenatal care throughout their pregnancies. In a review of the research on the link between prenatal care and the health and size of the newborn, Abel (1997) reported that (a) women without prenatal care were three times more likely to have low-birth-weight infants than were women with early and adequate care; and that (b) mothers who are younger, less educated, unmarried, economically disadvantaged, and/or from a minority group were less likely to receive adequate prenatal care and more likely to give birth to low-birth-weight infants.

What This Means for Parents and Professionals Working with Parents. Individuals need to be informed about the importance of adequate nutrition, early prenatal care, and the avoidance of harmful substances during pregnancy. It is important, however, that information of such vital importance to the health and survival of infants be disseminated early and from a variety of professionals who have access to adolescents and adults before and during pregnancy. One might consider prenatal care as a concept that occurs before pregnancy from a host of caring individuals, such as parents, teachers, and physicians. For example, physicians might routinely inquire about the smoking habits of their adolescent and young adult patients and warn them about the harmful effects of smoking on their future pregnancies. Once a pregnancy has occurred, it is important that the expectant parent be made aware of the importance of early prenatal care. Furthermore, family members, the community, and society should work together to ensure access to prenatal care for all pregnant women.

Poverty as a Risk Factor for Low-Birth-Weight Infants

Lack of prenatal care and poor diets during pregnancy are two of the leading causes of preterm deliveries and those two factors are primarily associated with poverty. Furthermore, all of the risk factors for low birth weight correlate with poverty. Compared with women of higher socioeconomic status, poor women are more likely to be ill,

---

Diseases
Most viruses
Virtually all sexually transmitted diseases
Rubella measles—one of the first diseases identified as a teratogen
Pediatric AIDS
Mothers who are HIV positive

Many other maternal conditions
RH-negative blood (a recessive genetic trait, not a disease)
Infection
Bacterial vaginosis—a minor vaginal infection, which is easily cured with standard antibiotics
Minor infections—such as gum disease in a pregnant woman

Many widely used medicinal drugs used to treat real or potential problems
These include tetracycline, anticoagulants, bromides, anticonvulsants, phenobarbital, retinoic acid (a common treatment for acne, found in Accutane), and most hormones.

Nonprescription drugs
These include aspirin, antacids, and diet pills

Psychoactive drugs
These include beer and wine, liquor, cigarettes and smokeless tobacco, heroin and methadone, LSD, marijuana, heroin, cocaine in any form, inhalants, and antidepressant pills. Babies born to narcotics addicts are not only more likely to be premature or to have low birth weight, but they are themselves addicted and suffer withdrawal symptoms labeled *neonatal abstinence syndrome*, including tremors, restlessness, hyperactive reflexes, high-pitched cries, vomiting, fevers, sweating, rapid respirations, seizures, and sometimes death.

Nicotine
Every psychoactive drug slows growth but tobacco is the most prevalent culprit. Cigarettes are implicated in 25% of all low-birth-weight births in the United States and in 50% of low-birth-weight births in Europe (where more people smoke).

Alcohol
The numerous effects of alcohol consumption by pregnant women have been collectively labeled as *fetal alcohol syndrome* (FAS). Not only are the children afflicted with FAS more likely to be born dead, those who survive their births will display facial and skull deformities characteristic of that syndrome.

FIGURE 3.1 Common Teratogens

Source: Adapted from *The Developing Person Through the Life Span*, 5th ed., by Kathleen Stassen Berger and Ross A. Thompson, 2001, New York: Worth Publishers.

malnourished, teenaged, and stressed. Moreover, if they are working during their pregnancies, their jobs frequently consist of physically stressful work, which has been associated with preterm deliveries and low-birth-weight infants (Ceron-Mireles, Harlow, & Sanchez-Carrillo, 1996). Furthermore, mothers who are poor often receive late or inadequate prenatal care, breathe polluted air, live in overcrowded conditions,

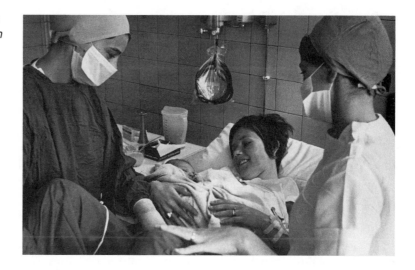

The joy of having given birth to a healthy baby is shown in the face of this new mother.

move from place to place, and ingest unhealthy substances from psychoactive drugs to spoiled food (Shiono et al., 1997). Poverty is part of the reason for differences in birth weight and infant survival between nations; and within the United States, ethnic and historical differences in birth weight and infant mortality have been found to be associated with differences in socioeconomic levels (U.S. Bureau of the Census, 1992, 1996, 1998, 1999).

BIRTH AND NEWBORNS

Birth is a significant event in the lives of families everywhere whether it is the first baby born to a married couple, the birth of a baby to unmarried teenage parents, or the birth of a child who has one or more siblings. The primary goal of expectant parents is to have full-term, healthy babies and most parents get that wish because the majority of babies are carried to full gestational term and are born healthy (Munch & Levick, 2001). In the United States, most of those babies are born in hospitals and taken home by their birth or adoptive parents after a brief 2-day hospital stay (Lubic, 1997). The arrival of a new baby (or new babies in the case of twins or other multiple births) is an occasion in which the parents, siblings, and extended family members usually rejoice. The feeling of elation that accompanies the birth of an infant is summed up in the following description by a new father whose wife had been in labor for a number of hours before having a Caesarian birth:

> 1:56 a.m. A few minutes later we hear a tiny, muffled cry. Dr. L. asks me if I want to see our baby. I expect to see him holding the child in his arms, but as I emerge from our side of the curtain, I see one of the doctors still pulling the baby out. I don't have the stomach for scenes like this on TV, but here I can't look away. At first, all that's visible is the head, but then the whole body comes out. Dr. L. says, "You have a daughter." Then someone asks

her name. As I say "Dayna," I'm filled with a sense of bliss. Before any of this happened, people told me how life-changing it was to have a child. Only now do I understand. Dayna has only been here for a few minutes, but she's already the most precious thing to us in the world. (Beatty, 2000)

When Infants Are Born Early and/or Small

In all societies, there are individuals who have been trained in various ways to assist in the delivery of newborns. There is a major difference, however, in the survival rates of infants born in industrialized and nonindustrialized countries. In some places in the world, hospitals are not available and even in many places where hospitals are available they might not have the advanced medical technology and trained medical staff to meet the needs of at-risk babies. Without the assistance of medical technology, parents in nonindustrialized countries whose babies are considered to be at risk are more likely to suffer the loss of their infants shortly after birth than are parents of at-risk newborns born in industrialized countries (UNICEF, 1998).

Although parents who live in industrialized countries have greater access to medical care for their at-risk newborns, most traditional cultures also have infant care designed to maximize infant survival. Typical features of infant care in traditional cultures include intensive physical nurturance of the infant, breast-feeding on demand, immediate response to the crying of infants, close parent–infant body contact, keeping the baby beside the mother at night, and consistent care by parents, siblings, and other relatives. Those caregiving behaviors have been found to be beneficial for normal weight infants and particularly important for the survival of at-risk infants (Levine et al., 1994; Morelli, Rogoff, Oppenheim, & Goldsmith, 1992). Furthermore, the skin-to-skin contact so common to many traditional cultures has recently been found to increase the chances of survival of preterm and low-birth-weight babies in intensive care units of modern hospitals throughout the world (Feldman, Weller, & Sirota, 2002).

Taking a lesson from the traditional cultural practice of holding infants skin to skin, a procedure known as **kangaroo care** is used in many infant intensive care units to promote survival of at-risk infants. Although kangaroo care is practiced in intensive care units of hospitals, it is not the medical professionals who use kangaroo care; instead, they teach parents of at-risk infants the way to hold their infants skin to skin. The infant (wearing only a diaper) is placed on the parent's bare chest (skin to skin). The infant's head is then turned to the side so that the baby is against the parent's heart and any tubes or wires that are attached to the baby are taped to the parent's clothing. The advantages of using kangaroo care are impressive. Preterm infants whose parents use kangaroo care cry less, sleep for longer periods, gain more weight, have more coordinated breathing and heartbeat patterns, and need less supplemental oxygen in comparison to preterm infants who do not receive kangaroo care. Kangaroo care of preterm infants also has been found to promote infants' self-regulation, sleep–wake cyclicity, arousal modulation, and sustained exploration (Feldman et al., 2002). The following quote is from the author's son Kenneth who practiced kangaroo care with his newborn twin son

Gabriel who weighed in at 4.5 pounds (1 pound lighter than his twin sister Josephine) and had to be placed in intensive care. (Note: The hospital in which the twins were born did not teach kangaroo care to parents of at-risk infants but the author taught her son and daughter-in-law about the procedure during the pregnancy because there was a good chance that the babies would be premature and have lower birth weight.)

> At first, we had both the babies in the room. Then the doctor said they would have to take Gabriel to intensive care and I said I was going with him. I stayed there with him holding him skin to skin as much as possible, even with all the tubes. By the way, Mom, you forgot to tell me that the baby would grab my chest hair. I also talked with him in a soothing voice because I knew he would recognize my voice from my talking to him before birth. Then, when he would sleep, I would lay my head next to his so he could hear me breathing. We developed a special bond between us because of this experience, which I wouldn't trade for the world.

Thinking Critically

Were you surprised to learn that the skin-to-skin holding of preterm infants (kangaroo care) promotes their ability to survive? How do you account for the fact that parents in traditional societies instinctively provide that type of care, whereas parents in industrialized societies have to be taught to hold their preterm infants in that fashion?

The Challenges of Parenting Low-Birth-Weight Infants. The primary challenges accompanying the births of full-term healthy babies are whether to breast-feed or bottle-feed them and how to rearrange family life so that parents can fit the care of the new baby, or babies, into their other family and occupational responsibilities. In comparison to the experiences of parents of full-term, healthy newborns, the parents of babies who receive intensive medical care and/or intensive physical care anxiously watch their newborns' struggles for survival. Although preterm infants are more at risk for not surviving during their first days or weeks of life, most of those infants survive and are later free from even minor problems. Furthermore, the majority of preterm infants show normal development. Other babies who are born prematurely have physical and cognitive exceptionalities that will require specialized care. For example, by the end of the first year only 10% of prematurely born infants display significant developmental challenges and only 5% are seriously disabled. By the age of 6, however, 38% of children who were born prematurely have mild problems that call for special education interventions (Hack, Klein, & Taylor, 1995; Herrgard, Luoma, Tuppurainen, Karjalainen, & Martikainen, 1993). The challenges of parenting children with special needs are discussed in chapter 9.

When At-Risk Newborns Do Not Survive.   The greatest concern for parents of at-risk newborns is that their babies will not survive. In a study of mothers of high-risk infants, DeMier, Hynan, and Hatfield (2002) found that the baby's birth weight, length of hospital stay, and postnatal complications are significant predictors of anxiety and distress of parents. The joy that accompanies the birth of a newborn is tragically overturned when a baby dies, and the relative rarity of that event makes the loss even harder for parents to accept. Whether the death is a stillbirth or occurs shortly after the baby is born, the loss of a child within hours or days of that child's new life is particularly heartbreaking. The impact of a newborn's death on parents is considerable, and they go through the same stages of grief and mourning as experienced when an older family member dies. Moreover, the merciless combination of the first dawning of life and an unnaturally early death makes the loss of a child incredibly difficult to cope with and the depression of parents whose infants die is a traumatic experience (Brockington, 1992; Murphy, Johnson, Gupta, & Das, 1998). Parents' experience of loss and grief following the death of a child, and ways in which parents cope with that loss, are discussed in chapter 10.

THE TRANSITION TO PARENTHOOD: A MAJOR DEVELOPMENTAL MILESTONE

After having accomplished a successful pregnancy and experienced the birth of one's children or after having completed the adoption process, new parents then engage in a process of welcoming their children into their homes and lives. At this point, parents take on the responsibilities that come with the highly significant role of parent. Whether one becomes a parent during adolescence or during adulthood, the transition to parenthood is a major developmental milestone, accompanied by the opportunities and demands for personal reorganization and growth that characterize such major changes. The level of satisfaction parents experience during the transition to parenthood is related to (a) whether the pregnancy was planned (in situations where parenthood results from the birth of a child), (b) the level of support parents receive from spouses, partners, and/or extended family, and (c) the availability and access to medical care (Clinton & Kelber, 1993; Monahan, 2001).

Support for New Parents

Although there are many unmarried adolescent parents today, and there has been an increase in single parenthood among women over 20 years of age, most new parents are in marriages or committed relationships. Whether married or single, however, new parents benefit from the support of family members and the community in making the transition to parenthood. For parents sharing the same household, the primary sources of support tend to come from each other, although extended family members are typically involved in helping individuals to make the transition to parenthood. The relative support of new parents by extended family members varies, however, across families and across cultures. In the United States, the nuclear family arrangement typically limits the involvement of extended family members and leaves the parental couple more reliant on each other for support in their new roles. That the couple might benefit from greater assistance from family and/or the community is evident from the consensus of a number of studies that have shown that new parents' satisfaction with their relationship declines during the first 9 months postpartum (Belsky & Kelly, 1994; Kluwer, Heesink, & van de Vliert, 2002; Kurdek, 1993).

One of the reasons that new parenthood might take a toll on the relationship of new parents is that the transition to parenthood has a segregating influence on husbands' and wives' division of household labor. Motherhood generally involves an increase in the time women invest in domestic work and a decrease in the time they spend in paid employment; whereas new fathers usually spend more time at work. There is evidence, however, that the division of household labor and child care following the arrival of children typically violates the couples' expectations (especially the expectations of mothers) (Belsky & Kelly, 1994; Kluwer et al., 2002; Kurdek, 1993). An indication that new parents might require additional support from others during those early months of adjustment to parenthood is further indicated by findings that new mothers often turn to their own parents for advice and help in childrearing. In addition, mothers in the United States frequently receive informational support from community-based programs. Such support is usually in the form of prenatal classes, hospital visitations, and programs educating new parents on how to cope with the transition to parenthood. In contrast to the pattern in the United States wherein new parents rely primarily on each other for support, new mothers in Asian cultures tend to receive considerable support primarily from extended family members. In many Asian cultures, a common cultural expectation is that after childbirth, a new mother will need assistance with day-to-day activities for a prolonged period of time. Consequently, family members often perform many helpful activities for new mothers, including assistance in child care, social reinforcement, physical comfort, appreciation, and giving advice (Hyun, Lee, & Yoo, 2002).

What This Means for Parents and Professionals Working with Parents. The findings that the division of child care and household responsibilities following the birth or adoption of children usually violates the anticipations of many parents (especially mothers) and contributes to less satisfaction with their relationship with each other emphasizes the need for family and community support of new parents. There are numerous opportunities for family member and friends to support the childrearing efforts of those parents and the types of support provided by extended family members in Asian cultures are excellent examples of ways in which family members and friends might offer assistance.

Thinking Critically

Consider young parents whom you have observed at home with their infants or toddlers. What examples of support for each other's childrearing efforts were you able to discern between those two parents and what examples of family members and friends supporting the new parents' efforts have you observed?

THE ROLE OF PARENTS IN INFANT/TODDLER SOCIAL–EMOTIONAL, PHYSICAL, AND COGNITIVE DEVELOPMENT

As parents and children begin their lives together as a family, parents embark on another new challenge—that of providing an environment in which their babies will grow into healthy, happy children. The care that parents provide for their children impacts their children's social–emotional, cognitive, and physical development. We will now examine the ways in which parents influence the development of their infants and toddlers in each of those domains. The role that parents play in the development of children beyond the infant–toddler stages will be covered in forthcoming chapters.

The Promotion of Social–Emotional Development

There are several important aspects of social–emotional development during infancy that set the stage for positive social development in later stages of life. Furthermore, the relationships that parents establish with their infants provide the basis for those future developments. As will be emphasized in the forthcoming discussion, parents who are consistently sensitive and responsive to their infants contribute to the development of infant trust and attachment that in turn promotes parent–infant synchrony and is later expressed in toddler autonomy and exploratory behavior.

Infant Trust and Attachment.   Probably the most important goal of parenting infants is to promote infants' sense of trust. You might recall from chapter 1 that Erik Erikson theorized that the quality of parent–infant interactions influences whether infants develop a sense of trust or a sense of mistrust (Goldhaber, 2000). The process by which a sense of trust is achieved by infants depends on whether or not they experience **contingent responsiveness** from their parents and other caregivers and whether or not parents and other caregivers provide consistent care of the infant. The way a parent provides contingent responsiveness to the infant is to allow the infant to be actively engaged in the roles of elicitor as well as receiver of parental attention. As elicitors of parental attention, infants play an active role in being able to provide the signals, such as crying and smiling, that guide their parents in understanding when and how to care for them. The parental role in that exchange is to help infants learn to trust that their needs will be met, which is accomplished when parents are consistently responsive to their communication attempts (Erikson, 1963, 1982).

The infant's development of a sense of trust parallels the infant's development of secure attachment. As a reminder, Ainsworth (1973) described secure attachment as the "affectional tie that one person forms to another specific person, binding them together in space and enduring over time" (p. 33). Parents of securely attached infants have been described as more sensitive, more contingently responsive, more consistent, more likely to hold their infants, less intrusive, less tense, and less irritable. The beneficial short-term and long-term outcomes for securely attached infants are impressive. Short-term benefits are that securely attached infants are more responsive than are insecure infants in face-to-face play. Furthermore, they have more varied means of communication, cry less, and quiet more easily when picked up (Ainsworth et al., 1978; Isabella & Belsky, 1991). Long-term outcomes are that securely attached infants tend to become toddlers who demonstrate more exploratory behavior than do infants who do not demonstrate secure attachment (Ainsworth, 1973), and they tend to become children who are competent in a wide array of social and cognitive skills (Belsky & Cassidy, 1995; Fagot, 1997).

Demand Feeding: An Example of Responsive Caregiving. An illustration of child care in which parental responsiveness to infants has developmental implications can be observed in how and when parents feed their infants. Whether to feed the baby on demand is an important decision for parents ranking alongside the choice to breast-feed or bottle-feed, which will be discussed later in the chapter. Throughout the world and all through history, babies have been fed when they cried to be fed. As noted by Nelson (1998) "Crying is inborn attachment behavior which, according to attachment theorists John Bowlby and Margaret Ainsworth, is primarily an appeal for the protective presence of a parent. Infant crying triggers corresponding caretaking behavior in the parents. These reciprocal behaviors help establish and maintain the parent–child attachment bond." Because the cry of the infant is a natural, inborn behavior of the infant, the natural response of the parent to feed the hungry baby is an appropriate one. Unfortunately, as discussed in chapter 1, John Watson instructed American parents not to respond to their crying infants and to schedule the feeding of their infants (Cohen, 1979). Although Watson did not have research evidence that supported those recommendations, his views gained wide acceptance in the United States.

In contrast to the lack of research evidence supporting the scheduled feeding of infants, there is ample research evidence supporting demand feeding. The primary evidence supporting demand feeding comes from the research findings of Ainsworth and her colleagues who demonstrated the importance of responsive parental care in the role of infant attachment. Responsive caregiving of the infant is related to parental sensitivity whereby the parent accurately reads the baby's cues and responds accordingly. In their classic 1969 study, linking parental responsiveness to infant attachment, Ainsworth and Bell reported relationships between mothers' feeding styles during the first 3 months of their infants' lives and the patterns of attachment behavior exhibited by their infants at age 12 months.

The infants in that study were divided into two groups consisting of (a) those whose mothers had responded to their cries as signals to feed them or to pick them up and comfort them and (b) those whose mothers had been designated as insensitive to infant crying. Among the group of infants whose mothers were designated as sensitive, all the infants were classified as securely attached at 12 months of age. In contrast, the majority of the infants whose feeding was not in response to their crying were classified as having resistant or avoidant attachment. The relation between responsive caregiving and infant attachment has been demonstrated in numerous studies that have supported the findings of Ainsworth and colleagues (e.g., Sagi, van Ijzendoorn, Aviezer, Donnell, & Mayseless, 1994; Thompson & Lamb, 1983; van Ijzendoorn, 1995).

The Relation of Responsive Caregiving to Parental Sensitivity.   Because secure attachment is so closely linked to parental sensitivity, the development of secure attachment is more a function of the parent–infant dyad than of the infant. Accordingly, infant attachment can change direction when family life circumstances, childrearing arrangements, or parental sensitivity changes (Thompson & Lamb, 1983). An example of parental sensitivity being compromised by the caregiving context was reported in a study by Sagi et al. (1994). Those researchers demonstrated that, in family-based and communal kibbutzim, parental sensitivity might be overridden by a childrearing arrangement in which infants have to sleep away from home. In a similar vein, the stresses of family problems might overburden potentially sensitive parents. Davies and Cummings (1994) suggested that unresolved marital conflict might have a profound negative effect on children's emotional security even when the bond of the mother is close and her interaction style toward the child is sensitive. To promote secure infant attachment, it is important, therefore, to assess family context as well as parental sensitivity because the accumulation of stresses and risk factors must be considered alongside parental sensitivity.

A Cross-Cultural Perspective of Parental Sensitivity.   Parental sensitivity to infants is a global phenomenon and can be seen in parent–infant interactions throughout the world. Two of the ways that parents demonstrate sensitivity to their infants in many cultures is by infant carrying and cosleeping. In some cultures such as Bali and many African cultures, parents maintain physical closeness to their infants by continuously carrying them while promoting responsiveness to them, and by practicing cosleeping (Ainsworth, 1967; Ball, Hooker, & Kelly, 1999; Bril, 1986; Morelli et al., 1992). Whereas, in U.S. families, parents usually have their babies sleep in bassinettes or cribs in a separate room from them, parents in the rest of the world allow their babies to sleep in the same room with them and often in the same bed. Studies of the effects of infant carrying and cosleeping have been positively related to the physical and social–emotional development of infants. Infant carrying by Ugandan mothers was found by Ainsworth (1967) to be correlated with secure attachment as well as advanced gross motor development. An advantage of cosleeping is that it is beneficial for helping to regulate the infant's physiological functioning and for promoting closeness to the parents (Feldman et al., 2002; Morelli et al., 1992).

What This Means for Parents and Professionals Working with Parents. The importance of parental sensitivity to their infants, which is demonstrated by parents maintaining close proximity to their babies and being consistently responsive to them, cannot be overemphasized. When parents provide a consistency of care of their infants by being reliably available to them and not ignoring their cries and other bids for attention, babies learn to trust that their needs will be met. When interaction with a parent inspires trust and security, the infant develops secure attachment to the parent and gains confidence in engaging and exploring the world.

Parental Responsiveness and the Development of Affective Synchrony. In addition to promoting infant trust and attachment, parental responsiveness contributes to **affective synchrony** between parent and child. The synchrony of parents and their infants and toddlers is seen in the matched emotional states of parents and children and in babies' monitoring of their parents' facial expressions and whereabouts. During those frequent visual encounters, the sensitive parent smiles at the baby; the baby smiles back, then continues playing. Infants and toddlers who look for their caregivers and do not see them typically become distressed, stop playing, and make an active attempt to locate and gain the attention of the caregiver (Ainsworth, 1973). A clear example of a baby monitoring a parent's whereabouts can be seen in the toddler who while busy at play periodically glances in the direction of the parent to confirm the parent's presence (Lieberman, 1993).

What Parental Responsiveness also means is that infants and toddlers reflect the emotional states of their parents, parents are in the position to affect their babies' moods. Parents who smile, laugh, and show joy and pleasure when interacting with

This young parent is showing support for the toddler's strong urge to become increasingly independent.

their babies are more likely to have babies who laugh and smile a great deal also. Furthermore, those infants and toddlers are more likely to respond more favorably to their parents and to other people in their environment. On the other hand, parents who display moodiness, anger, or impatience with their infants and toddlers can expect their babies to mimic those behaviors. Parents should, therefore, be mindful of the feelings they display in front of, and toward, their infants and toddlers.

TODDLER AUTONOMY AND EXPLORATORY BEHAVIOR

Consistent parental responsiveness also plays a vital role as well in the development of toddlers' autonomy and exploratory behavior. According to Erikson (1963, 1982), infants who learn to trust their parents become more autonomous during toddlerhood than do infants who have not developed a sense that they can trust that their parents will be consistently available to them (see Figure 1.1, chapter 1). During Erikson's Autonomy versus Shame and Doubt Stage of psychosocial development, toddlers experience a conflict between their need for assistance from parents and their desire to function independently. During that time, toddlers are motivated toward autonomy in feeding and dressing themselves and become amenable to toilet training (another expression of autonomy). Toddlers also express a strong desire to climb up on things as well as an interest in many other activities that often require parental assistance but that toddlers are motivated to attempt on their own. According to Erikson (1963, 1982), the healthy self-differentiation of the toddler lays the foundation for feelings of self-worth and autonomy and prevents unhealthy dependency on others at later stages of psychosocial development.

Alongside their consistent attempts to do things for themselves and on their own, toddlers show heightened exploratory behavior whereby they are highly motivated to manipulate a variety of objects to see how they feel, how they fit together, how they bounce, roll, and so on (Johnson, Gallagher, & Montagne, 1994). As toddlers become more autonomous and demonstrate increased exploratory behavior, they begin to establish personal boundaries that distinguish their role in the family as more independent of parents than the role they played in the parent–infant relationship. It has been demonstrated that when parents are highly supportive of their toddlers' drives to explore objects and to try out new things, their toddlers become bolder and more competent individuals (Deater-Deckard, 2002).

Autonomy and Independent Toileting

An important developmental milestone in terms of the development of autonomy occurs when toddlers become independent in their toileting. As with other developmental accomplishments of toddlerhood, it is important that parents not push toddlers to achieve toilet training before they are ready nor hold them back when they are ready. Assessing readiness is, therefore, one of the key aspects of successful toilet training. The average age of readiness for toilet training is 22 months, although some toddlers will not be ready at that time and others might be ready slightly earlier. Physical readiness depends on the maturation of the toddler's bladder and sphincter muscles and that maturation varies from one toddler to another (Edwards & Liu, 2002).

Other considerations of successful toilet training include taking preliminary steps to prepare toddlers for toilet training, being ready and willing to devote the necessary time to the training process, and being patient with toddlers as they attempt to accomplish that important goal. Three ways to assess whether a toddler is ready for toilet training is by determining (a) if the toddler is staying dryer for longer periods of time (especially overnight), (b) if the toddler is expressing discomfort with wet diapers, and (c) if the toddler is showing an interest in using the toilet (Edwards & Liu, 2002). After parents have determined that their toddlers are psychologically and physiologically ready to be toilet trained, the child-oriented method of Spock and Rothenberg (1985) is a recommended approach for helping toddlers to achieve that developmental task. That method of toilet training consists of using gentle reminders, modeling, and positive guidance to help children achieve independent toileting.

What This Means for Parents and Professionals Working with Parents. Parents should respond to their toddlers' autonomy needs by being patient with their quest for greater independence and by providing assistance as they are attempting new tasks without taking them over. Parents might remember that, although toddlers often overestimate their abilities and frequently require adult backing, they nevertheless need to continually challenge themselves to become increasingly more self-sufficient. Therefore, even though it takes longer to allow toddlers to attempt autonomous activities (such as feeding themselves and climbing stairs), it is important for parents to take the time and provide the required assistance, whenever possible. Because, with each endeavor to do things for themselves, toddlers become progressively more autonomous, and more and more confident of their capabilities.

In assisting their toddlers to become independent in their toileting, parents should be patient and not punitive. In the case of wet pants, a parent might respond to the mishap with a friendly statement that recognizes the accident but does not condemn the child. For example, the parent might say to the child, "Oh, we don't like wet pants do we?" That type of response to the child's failure to stay dry is not punitive and sends the important message that the parent is there to assist the toddler in the achievement of toilet training. As a partner in the toddler's efforts to accomplish independent toileting, it is imperative that parents not pressure the child to go to the toilet but to make potty visits a natural part of a day in which a number of other interesting activities are taking place.

THE PROMOTION OF PHYSICAL DEVELOPMENT

At the same time that parents are influencing the social–emotional development of their infants and toddlers, they are contributing to their youngsters' physical development. Parents affect the physical development of their infants and toddlers by the decisions they make regarding their nutrition, their health care, and the experiences they provide to support their developing motor abilities.

Meeting the Nutritional Needs of Infants and Toddlers

Just as nutrition plays a crucial role in prenatal development, it plays a major part in the physical development of the infant and toddler. The choices parents make regarding breast-feeding or bottle-feeding, when to wean their infants, the introduction of their infants to solid foods, and the type of food chosen for their infants and toddlers will have a significant impact on their children's health and development.

Breast-Feeding in Comparison to Bottle-Feeding.   The first choice parents must make related to meeting the nutritional needs of their infants is whether to breast-feed or bottle-feed them. Although there are advantages and disadvantages associated with each choice, the advantages of breast-feeding outweigh those of bottle-feeding. To begin, human milk is more nutritious for humans than is cow's milk. As Lieberman (1987) puts it, breast milk is "species specific" and even "infant specific." Human breast milk is always sterile and at body temperature; it contains more iron, vitamin C, and vitamin A than does cow's or goat's milk; and it provides antibodies to protect the infant against any disease the mother is immunized against through vaccination or having had the illness herself. Furthermore, the specific fats and sugars in breast milk make it more digestible than any prepared baby formula, resulting in breast-fed babies having fewer allergies and stomachaches than bottle-fed babies. Also, breast-feeding decreases the frequency of almost every common infectious disease, especially diarrhea which is one of the primary causes of infant death in developing countries (Grant, 1986; Isolauri, Sutas, Salo, Isosonppi, & Kaila, 1998).

Based on the benefits of breast milk, doctors worldwide recommend breast-feeding for all babies unless the mother is an active drug user (including alcohol and tobacco), HIV positive, or severely malnourished. More specifically, the World Health Organization (WHO) recommends that infants be fed exclusively on breast milk for at least the first 4 to 6 months of life. At that point, they recommend that other foods be added, especially cereal and fruit because breast milk does not have adequate iron, vitamin D, or vitamin K for older babies (Lawrence, 1998). Along with the recommendation of the WHO, the American Academy of Pediatrics (AAP), the Canadian Paediatric Society, and the American Dietetic Association all strongly encourage breast-feeding (Boyle & Morris, 1999).

Weaning and the Introduction to Solid Foods.   The shift from liquid to solid foods involves the process of weaning. The decisions parents make regarding the timing of weaning and the choice of solid foods provided after weaning are extremely important to the health and growth of their infants. The AAP recommends that breast-feeding continue for at least 12 months, with exclusive breast-feeding for the first 6 months and the gradual introduction of iron-enriched solid food in the second half of the first year. For babies who are weaned before 12 months of age, the AAP recommends iron-supplemented infant formula rather than cow's milk (Boyle & Morris, 1999; Committee on Nutrition, American Academy of Pediatrics, 1993). After they have weaned their infants, it is imperative that parents provide an adequate amount of protein and iron to meet the infant's growth requirements since the most rapid growth of the entire life span occurs in the first 3 years. Furthermore, the lack of adequate sources of those nutrients can lead to malnutrition. In countries where there is a high rate of malnutrition among children, the WHO recommends that breast-feeding continue to age 2 or older (Lawrence, 1998).

The Problems Associated with Infant Underfeeding.   The primary cause of malnutrition in developing countries is early cessation of breastfeeding. In many of those countries, breast-feeding used to continue for at least 2 years, as recommended by the WHO. Now, it is stopped much earlier in favor of bottle-feeding, usually with powdered formulas that are very often overdiluted with unsafe water (Berger, 2001). Even in wealthy countries, isolated cases of severe protein–calorie malnutrition during infancy still occur. Usually, that happens due to parental emotional or physical stress or the debilitating effects of parental drug addiction, that are so overwhelming that parents either ignore their infants' feeding needs or prepare food improperly. The long-term effects of malnutrition during infancy have been well documented. Longitudinal research on children in Kenya, Egypt, Jamaica, Indonesia, Barbados, Europe, and North America reveals that children who are underfed in infancy tend to display impaired learning abilities (especially in their ability to concentrate) and impairment in their language skills through childhood and adolescence (Pollitt et al., 1996).

Thinking Critically

Given the distressing effects of malnutrition during infancy, to what extent do you think the community should be involved in providing expectant and new parents with information regarding the recommendations of the AAP and the WHO regarding breast-feeding, timing of weaning, and the choice of nutritious foods after infants are weaned?

HEALTH CARE FOR INFANTS AND TODDLERS

To ensure the healthy development of their infants, it is important for parents to provide for their health care. When parents access available health care for their infants and toddlers, they allow medical professionals to determine if their babies are growing and developing according to expected rates and to respond to health problems such as ear infections that periodically rise during infancy. One of the most important aspects of health care that parents need to be certain that their babies receive is

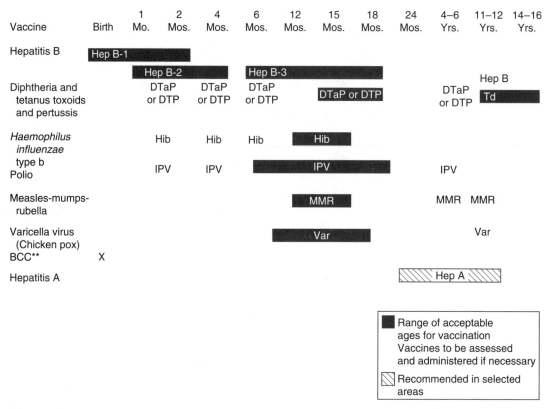

FIGURE 3.2 Recommended Childhood Immunization Schedule, United States, 2000

immunization against communicable diseases. Today, deadly childhood epidemics are rare and an infant's chance of dying from infectious disease in North America, Western Europe, Japan, or Australia is less than 1 in 500, down from 1 in 20 fifty years ago. The single most important cause of the dramatic improvement in child survival is immunization. Worldwide, immunization has reached more children every decade, and currently more than 90% of all infants in the world are immunized against the childhood diseases diptheria, pertussis, tetanus, measles, polio, and mumps (Baker, 2000; UNICEF, 1995). In industrialized nations, many infants are immunized against hepatitis B, *"Haemophilus influenzae"* type B, rubella, and chicken pox as well. See Figure 3.2 for a list of recommended immunizations during the first 2 years of life.

What This Means to Parents and Professionals Working with Parents.   Parental attentiveness to the infant and toddler's nutrition and health needs cannot be overemphasized. Because growth and development (including brain development) proceeds more rapidly during the first 3 years (particularly the first year) than during any other stage of development after the birth of an individual, parents' decisions revolving around infant feeding and infant health care have critical implications for the health, growth, and development of the infant and toddler.

ASSISTING INFANT/TODDLERS IN THE DEVELOPMENT OF SELF-REGULATION

Besides providing for the nutritional and other health needs of their infants and toddlers, parents play an important role in supporting their babies' development of **self-regulation** (Weinberg, Tronick, & Cohn, 1999). Kopp (1982) has described stages children go through in their development of self-regulation. In the first 3 months, infants begin to regulate arousal and sleep cycles as well as the amount of stimulation they receive. From 3 to approximately 9 months, their self-regulation efforts are focused on sensory and motor activities as they use motor skills to gain parental attention and to participate in social interaction. From 9 to 18 months, infants' development of self-regulation includes an awareness of social demands as they learn to comply with parental requests.

Self-Regulation and Infant/Toddler Sleep Patterns

A principal focus of self-regulation for infants relates to the adjustment of their bodies to regular wake and sleep patterns. How much and when a newborn sleeps is an issue of concern for parents. Infants spend much of their first 2 weeks sleeping (an average of 16 to 20 hours in each 24-hour period) although there is much variability from one baby to another. As infants get older, they tend to sleep for longer periods of time and remain awake for more extended intervals. By 6 months, many babies begin sleeping through the night but all infants are not aware that this is how they are to behave (Bamford et al., 1990). It is not until age 3 or 4 months that infants sleep more at night than during the day; however, waking up during the night is common during infancy and early childhood (Anders, 1994; Gaylor, Goodlin-Jones, & Anders, 2001).

By the time of their second birthday, although wake and sleep patterns have been established for some time, toddlers often resist going to bed or taking a nap. That behavior might be an expression of their developing autonomy needs, a reluctance to separate from the parents, or a fear of the dark. Toddlers whose parents handle that phase of bedtime resistance with kindness and understanding are better able to make the transition than are those whose parents are unsympathetic to their children's feelings. According to Bigner (1998), American parents are perhaps the only parents in the world who expect their children to develop self-regulated behavior early in life with little guidance from their parents. As noted by Bigner, American parents are likely to simply place an infant or toddler in a crib and close the door, whereas parents in many other cultures typically sing a short, soft lullaby to their infant or rock the infant to sleep.

What This Means for Parents and Professionals Working with Parents. It is recommended that parents prepare their infants and toddlers for bedtime by means of regular rituals (such as rocking or bathing) designed to assist the child in relaxing and settling down. Those rituals might include the telling or reading of a story. Besides providing a calming and reassuring ritual to assist toddlers in making the transition to going to bed, it is important that parents attend to how much time the child is sleeping during the day. Although infants should not be roused from their sleep, toddlers and young children who sleep for as many as 6 hours during the day might have trouble sleeping through the night. In those cases, parents might alleviate that problem by waking a child earlier and earlier from a long daytime nap.

The Promotion of Infants' and Toddlers' Motor Skills

In addition to providing nutritious food, adequate health care, and relevant experiences to support infants' and toddlers' development of self-regulation, it is important that parents provide the optimal environment to encourage their babies' gross and

Just as it is important to promote the toddler's first steps, it is also important that parents assist their toddlers in achieving other gross motor skills such as climbing.

fine motor skills development. The advance of **gross motor skills** includes the development of large muscle groups involved in the movement of the body and the arms and legs, resulting in the infant/toddler's ability to turn over, sit up, crawl, walk, and climb. **Fine motor skills** development contributes to greater dexterity in the use of fingers and hands (Berger, 2001). Although all infants develop the same motor skills in the same sequence, there is variation in the timing of motor skill accomplishment and that variation can be attributed to ethnic membership, geographic location, and patterns of child care (Berenthal & Clifton, 1998).

What This Means for Parents and Professionals Working with Parents. The first step toward promoting their infants' and toddlers' fine and gross motor skills development is for parents to provide a clean, safe environment in which their babies can freely move about. For example, when infants begin to turn over (which typically occurs at about 3 months), it is very important that they not be placed on elevated surfaces without sides. A quick, unexpected turn can land the infant on the floor and might result in head or bodily injury. Furthermore, as infants and toddlers become increasingly more ambulatory (creeping, crawling, and walking), their household environments should be "baby-proofed," to remove hazardous materials such as cleaning products, poisonous plants, and small objects on which an infant or toddler can choke. Electrical plugs should be covered as well and low cabinets should have closures that are childproof.

While taking care to remove hazardous objects and continuously monitoring their infants and toddlers to ensure their safety, parents should provide a variety of safe, interesting objects for their babies to manipulate. Parents also need to be alert to cues provided by their infants and toddlers regarding readiness to attempt mastery of certain motor skills. For example, when a toddler shows a strong interest in stair climbing that curiosity reflects the child's readiness to master the next step in gross motor skill development. An example of readiness in the area of fine motor skill development is the baby's attempt to grab the spoon when being fed. In fact, the best example of an early fine motor skill is successful grabbing (McCarty & Ashmead, 1999). When parents are aware that attempts to climb stairs or to grab the feeding spoon are actually demonstrations of motor skill readiness, they can assist their babies in reaching those goals, thereby promoting the advancement of their motor skills.

At the time that toddlers begin to show an interest in stair climbing, they certainly cannot be left to climb stairs alone, but parents might climb behind them while steadying them and encouraging them as they climb each step. Similarly, when babies are attempting to master self-feeding, parents can support that goal by being tolerant of the necessary messiness that accompanies those early feeding attempts. Other ways to assist the baby in self-feeding is by providing small pieces of cut-up food which can be easily picked up. Of course, the parent should supplement the infant's early feeding efforts with a second spoon until the infant's mastery of that goal has been sufficiently refined to the point that the food in the baby's spoon actually reaches the baby's mouth.

This mother understands the toddler's readiness to learn and is providing intellectual stimulation for the child.

THE PROMOTION OF COGNITIVE DEVELOPMENT

Parents play an important role not only in supporting the social–emotional and physical development of their infants and toddlers but also in the promotion of their cognitive development. The interactions that parents have with them and the objects they provide for them to interact with sustain their babies' ability to think and reason. Furthermore, the verbal exchanges that parents have with their infants and toddlers during those interactions promote their language development (Moerk, 2000).

Insights from Piaget.   As you might recall from reading chapter 1, Jean Piaget theorized that children are active participants in the development of their own cognitive abilities. Although Piaget's Theory of Cognitive Development covers the stages from infancy through adolescence, the exemplification of the person's participation in the development of cognition is most noticeable during infancy. Piaget referred to the intelligence of infants as **sensorimotor intelligence** based on the view that infants think exclusively with their senses and motor skills during that stage of development. According to Piaget, infants develop through six substages of cognition during the stage of sensorimotor development (see Figure 3.2) wherein advances in cognition occur as a result of their active engagement of the objects in their environment. Infants' lively engagement of objects in their environment involves a process whereby they are continuously comparing new information about objects to what they already know about those objects, while simultaneously altering their level of understanding to take in new information (Piaget & Inhelder, 1969).

What This Means for Parents and Professionals Working with Parents.   It is important for parents to recognize that their infants' and toddlers' curiosity about objects in their environment and their strong interest in looking, listening, touching, biting, and

I. Primary Circular Reactions
During the first two stages, infants are focused on their responses to their own bodies:

Stage One (birth to 1 month)	*Reflexes:* Sucking, grasping, staring, and listening.
Stage Two (1–4 months)	*The first acquired adaptations:* Assimilation and co-ordination of reflexes—Example: sucking a pacifier differently than sucking a nipple.

II. Secondary Circular Reactions
During the next two stages, infants demonstrate responsiveness to people and to objects:

Stage Three (4–8 months)	*Making interesting things last:* Infants actively respond to people and objects.
Stage Four (8–12 months)	*New adaptation and anticipation:* Infants' responsiveness to people and objects becomes more deliberate and more purposeful.

III. Tertiary Circular Reactions
During the last two stages, infants demonstrate creativity, first with objects, then with ideas:

Stage Five (12–18 months)	*New means through active experimentation:* During this stage, the actions of infants, referred to as "little scientists", reflect their ability to experiment and to be creative.
Stage Six (18–24 months)	*New means through mental combinations:* During this stage, the infant's ability to consider before doing enables the child to achieve a goal without resorting to trial-and-error experiments.

FIGURE 3.3   Piaget's Stages of Sensorimotor Intelligence
Source: Adapted from *The Developing Person Through the Life Span,* 5th ed., by Kathleen Stassen Berger and Ross A. Thompson, 2001, New York: Worth Publishers.

tasting is normal and necessary for their cognitive advancement. In the discussion that focused on ways in which parents promote their infants' and toddlers' fine motor skills, it was recommended that parents provide their babies with a variety of toys and other objects to be manipulated. The same toys and other objects that promote the development of fine and gross motor skills contribute to advances in cognition. It is very important, however, for parents to be mindful regarding distinguishing between safe and unsafe objects since infants and toddlers indiscriminately pick up and put any small object into the mouth and tug on a number of objects (such as plants) that can be toppled over.

Insights from Vygotsky.   As discussed in chapter 1, Lev Vygotsky also viewed children's intellectual development as a product of their active exploration of the environment but placed greater emphasis than did Piaget on the role of parents, older siblings, or other adults in aiding that process (guided participation). You might recall from reading chapter 1 that Vygotsky proposed the existence of a zone of proximal development, which is the distance between what a child can accomplish independently and what the child can achieve with the assistance of a more competent person (usually a parent, an older sibling, or a teacher) (Rogoff, 1990).

What This Means for Parents and Professionals Working with Parents. Following Vygotsky's views, parents should be actively engaged with guiding and instructing their infants and toddlers as they interact with the persons and objects in their environment. For example, if a toddler is attempting to put an object into a container, the parent is in the position to help the child figure out how to reach that goal sooner by using language to instruct the toddler and by demonstrating the procedure. Whether following the views of Piaget or Vygotsky, however, parents should be aware of the importance of providing infants and toddlers with a safe, stimulating environment in which their natural curiosity is respected and their active exploration of objects is supported.

Thinking Critically

Drawing on the views of Piaget, consider how a parent might design an activity for a toddler with the goal of promoting the toddler's cognitive development. Then, utilizing Vygotsky's idea of guided participation, how might the parent alter the design of that activity?

"ALIEN GENIUSES": THE BRAIN DEVELOPMENT OF THE INFANT–TODDLER

For decades, scholars have focused on the development of the child's mind as an explanation for children's cognitive abilities. That focus has been guided by the theories of Piaget and Vygotsky who emphasized that children are active participants in the development of their own intellect. The new brain research takes the idea of the child as an active participant in cognitive development a step further by demonstrating that babies and young children participate in the building of their own brains. The research that links the development of the infant's brain to emerging cognitive abilities emphasizes that everything the baby sees, hears, tastes, touches, and smells influences the way the brain connections get hooked up. After birth, as experience floods in from all the senses, the baby's brain cells are continuously attempting to make connections to each other (Gopnik, Meltzoff, & Kuhl, 1999).

Not only is the baby's brain busily building itself based on an abundance of experience, there is neurological evidence that the brain of the baby is much busier than the brain of older children and adults. By 3 months, the brain areas involved in seeing, hearing, and touch are burning an increasing amount of glucose and that energy consumption reaches adult levels by the time the child is 2-years-old. Astoundingly, by the time the child is 3-years-old, the child's brain is actually twice as active as an adult brain and remains at twice the level of an adult's until the child reaches the age of 9 or 10. Although the activity of the child's brain begins to decline at about 9 or 10 years of age, it does not decline to adult levels until around 18 years of age. The result is that babies' and young children's brains are more active, more connected, and more flexible than are adult brains. Therefore, from the perspective of neurological science, infants and young children are alien geniuses (Gopnik et al., 1999).

THE PERCEPTUAL PREFERENCES OF INFANTS

An important first step for parents in their efforts to promote infant cognition is to be aware of the perceptual capabilities their newborns bring into the world because those capabilities provide the foundation for infant cognitive development. Infants' perceptual skills of hearing, smell, and touch are very keen at birth and their visual perception is clearest at a range of about 10 to 20 inches, the distance between the baby held in the parent's arms and the face of the parent holding the infant (Haith, 1993; Morrongiello, Fenwick, & Chance, 1998). Furthermore, infants show clear perceptual preferences, examples of which are seen in the infant's visual preferences, which include (a) the human face; (b) dynamic, moving patterns over static ones (Kaufmann & Kaufmann, 1980; Teller, 1997); (c) sharp-contrast in comparison to low-contrast objects; and (d) primary colors rather than softer pastels (Bornstein & Lamb, 1992; Maurer & Maurer, 1988). Through their perceptual abilities, infants learn to distinguish between colors, shapes, smells, sounds, and a variety of tactile differences.

The Importance of Infant Perceptual Preferences

It is clear that infants' perceptual preferences guide them in seeking the information they need to know about their environment. An obvious example is the infant's fondness for looking at the human face, which dominates over any other visual preference (Dannemiller & Stephens, 1988; Valenza, Simion, & Cassia, 1996). Infants spend more time gazing at the human face than gazing at any other object, and parents spend a great deal of time looking at their infants' faces (**mutual gazing**). The mutual gazing of parents and infants has been found to be a central aspect of the infant–parent interactive process. It has been demonstrated that when either the parent or the infant looks at the other, the probability of infant–parent interaction is increased. By contrast, when either the parent or the baby looks away, the behavior in which they are engaged is likely to subside (Stern, Beebe, Jaffe, & Bennett, 1977; Weinberg & Tronick, 1996). It has been suggested that the gaze of the parent or infant acts as a magnet for the other and that the mutual gazing of parents and infants then spreads to interactive behaviors between infants and parents such as turn-taking vocalizations, mutual touching, and mutual imitation. Thus, mutual gazing appears to provide a context for promoting and sustaining a complex set of parent–infant interactive behaviors (Weinberg & Tronick, 1996).

In addition to understanding the infant's preference for the human face, it is instructive to take into account the role of the infant's other perceptual preferences. The infant's irresistible allure for sharp contrasts, such as stripes, checkerboards, corners, and other highly contrasting objects, helps babies learn where objects begin and end. The infant's fascination with moving objects provides even more information that helps babies distinguish between objects. Through observing movement, babies learn how different objects characteristically move and how they are likely to move in the future. For example, when a parent rolls a ball to a baby, the baby quickly learns to roll the ball back. With more experience with the ball, the baby discovers that it will bounce when dropped on a hard surface. Similarly, infants' keen hearing abilities coupled with their experience with sounds help them to learn which sounds are associated with particular objects or events. For example, they learn that the opening of the front door or the sound of the car pulling into the driveway signals the arrival of a family member or visitor. Finally, babies' preference for the sound of the human voice and their fascination for the human face have tremendous importance for infants' development of social relationships as well as for their development of language (Gopnik et al., 1999).

What This Means for Parents and Professionals Working with Parents.   Based on the neurological as well as the psychological evidence, it is apparent that nature has designed parents to teach babies what they need to learn as much as it has designed babies' brains to rapidly learn from their experiences. In fact, it is the normal, spontaneous interactions between parents and infants that are the most beneficial. Accordingly, the parental actions that nurture babies are the same actions that give infants the information they need; and the nurturing care that parents are naturally motivated to provide their infants is spontaneous, automatic, and unpremeditated. The scientific evidence suggests, therefore, that parents should do just what they normally are inclined to do when they are with their babies—talk, play, make funny faces, and (most important) pay attention to their babies' interests (Gopnik et al., 1999).

Knowing that infants show a preference for the human face, and that their clearest focus is in the range between the caregiver's arms and the caregiver's face, informs parents of the consequence of having frequent face-to-face interactions with their infants while holding them in their arms. The understanding that infants prefer dynamic, moving patterns over static ones influences parents to provide their infants with objects that move such as mobiles. Parents seem to intuitively understand that they must keep in mind the infant's 10- to 20-inch range of optimum visual focus when hanging a mobile. Parental awareness of their babies' preference for dynamic,

This young mother is playing an important role in assisting her child's language development by engaging the child in a face-to-face verbal exchange.

moving patterns can be observed in parent–infant playful interactions. For example, instead of calling the baby's attention to a ball, the parent is more likely to pick up the ball and roll it toward the baby, thereby capitalizing on the baby's high level of attraction to moving objects. Finally, the knowledge that babies prefer sharp-contrast in comparison to low-contrast objects and are more attracted to primary colors than to softer pastels is increasingly reflected in parents' selection of their babies' toys and in the choices they make when painting and/or furnishing the bedrooms of their infants and toddlers.

PARENT–INFANT/TODDLER VERBAL INTERACTIONS

In addition to being aware of their infants' perceptual capabilities, parents also appear to be conscious of the critical role they play in their infants' development of language. There are several ways in which infants' predisposition to learn language is matched by parents' motivation to promote their infants' language capabilities. First, the hearing of infants is extremely well developed at birth, and it has been demonstrated that babies hear and begin to recognize voices even before birth (DeCasper & Fifer, 1980; Morrongiello et al., 1998). Their pronounced hearing ability at birth provides infants with the capability of being able to immediately benefit from verbal exchanges. Second, for young infants the sound of the human voice (whether it comes from a parent, a sibling or a stranger) evokes special interest and curiosity. Third, parents, grandparents, older siblings, and others use a special language called **parentese** when talking to babies that is intended to gain and maintain the attention of infants. Parentese is a form of adult-to-infant speech that is seen in all language communities throughout the world and infants prefer listening to parentese more than ordinary speech. Parentese differs from other normal speech in a variety of ways. In comparison to ordinary language, it is higher pitched, has more low-to-high fluctuations, has a simpler, more concrete vocabulary, and its sentence length is shorter. Also, parentese contains more questions, instructions, and repetitions and has fewer past tenses and pronouns than does the speech directed to older children and adults (Fernald, 1993; Jaffe, Beebe, Feldstein, Crown, & Jasnow, 2001).

Parentese gains the attention of the infant and prompts the infant to attempt a response. Long before babies utter their first words, they have learned to vocalize through cooing and then **babbling** in response to parentese. Babbling consists of the repetitition of certain syllables such as da-da, or ma-ma, and those sounds have come to symbolize the terms used for mother and father throughout the world. At the same time that infants are learning the sounds of their particular language, they are simultaneously developing the ability to use **linguistic turn taking**. In response to their infants need to learn turn taking, parents typically provide very brief pauses when speaking to their infants in order to allow their babies' the opportunity to respond. Interestingly, infants spontaneously provide the same pauses for parents to respond to their utterances. The importance of live language in comparison to recorded language (as heard on the radio or television) is that live language is interactive and children are afforded the opportunity to play an active role in a verbal exchange (Jaffe et al., 2001).

What This Means for Parents and Professionals Working with Parents.   The valuable role parents play in promoting the language development of their infants cannot be overemphasized. By talking to infants often in the special language of parentese and building in brief pauses to allow infants the opportunity to respond, parents provide the ideal conditions for language development to occur. Furthermore, the most verbal babies—first to speak, first to utter sentences, first to use abstract vocabulary— are raised by baby-talking parents (Bruer, 1999). When using parentese to speak with their babies, it is helpful if they clearly pronounce words such as *Mama* and *Dada*, and it is beneficial as well for infants to be able to see their mouths as they form those words. Singing to their infants is another way that parents promote their infant's language development, given that singing has some of the same features of parentese (rhythmic and higher pitched).

THE ROLE OF PARENT–INFANT PLAY

Now, we will turn our attention to the highly important role of parent–infant play in the development of **parent–infant synchrony** and infant cognition. The development of parent–infant synchrony depends on the abilities of the parent and the infant to accurately read and respond to cues provided by the other person. Even though the large majority of parents accurately read infant cues and respond accordingly, there are two main impediments to the initiation and repair of parent–infant synchrony: either the parent ignores the infant's invitation to interact or the parent overstimulates the baby who wants to pause and rest (Isabella & Belsky, 1991). One of the benefits of parent–infant synchrony is that those interactions contribute to the development of infant self-control. According to Feldman, Greenbaums, and Yirmiya (1999), maternal synchrony with infant affect at 3 months (mother leads, infant follows) and mutual synchrony (both infant and parent leads and follows) are each related to higher levels of infant self-control at 2 years of age.

Although parents interact with their babies as they feed and comfort them throughout the day and those interactions contribute to parent–infant synchrony, there are many occasions when infants do not require feeding, comforting, or soothing. During those times, infants exhibit a motivational state referred to as quiet alert that provides the optimum level of alertness for parent–infant/toddler play. Interactive play between parents and their infants and toddlers is sometimes initiated by parents and at other times initiated by babies. In either case, it is important that the parent and the baby each play a role in interactive play whereby each participant initiates and responds to each other's behaviors, thus promoting the development of parent–infant synchrony (Feldman et al., 1999).

What This Means to Parents and Professional Working with Parents.   When engaging in interactive play with their infants, parents should respond not only to their babies' gestures that are designed to draw out responses of parents but should respond also to their babies' signals that they are feeling overstimulated and need a short break. The gesture from infants or toddlers that signals their need for a brief pause in the play activity is seen when babies turn their heads away—the first gesture for "No." After those brief pauses, babies will turn back to look at the parent usually with a smile to indicate they are ready to continue playing. It is important for parent–infant/toddler play to occur simply for the joy of it, and play can be introduced into bathing, dressing and a variety of everyday caregiving activities. Making a game out of giving the baby a bath or playing peek-a-boo as the baby's head comes out from under the shirt during dressing makes those activities more enjoyable for babies and their parents and at the same times increases infants' and toddlers' overall sense of predictability. Furthermore, gaining a sense of predictability regarding what is likely to happen in certain situations promotes infant self-control.

THE CARE OF INFANTS AND TODDLERS WHEN PARENTS WORK

A primary challenge facing parents of infants and toddlers is how to rearrange family life to fit the care of their children into the other family and occupational responsibilities of the parents. There are a variety of different ways that parents coordinate the care of their infants and toddlers with parental occupations. For parents who are married or living with their partners, one parent sometimes works while the other parent provides child care at least in the early weeks or months after the arrival of a child or children. In other two-parent households, both parents work but they coordinate schedules in such a way that each parent takes care of the child, or children, while the other parent is working. Also, grandparents are frequently called-on sources of child care for married or single parents. Although working parents are sometimes able to rely on each other or their own parents to care for their children, most American parents place their children in child care centers while they work.

Tag-Team Parenting: When Both Parents Work and Care for Their Children

Nonoverlapping shift patterns of employment that allow parents to practice **tag-team parenting** are preferred by some dual-earner families for a variety of reasons. For example, in her study of nurses who work the night shift, Garey (1995, 1999) indicated that the night shift was selected specifically to allow those mothers to stay at home with their children during the day. Besides saving on child care costs, parents who coordinate child care with nonstandard shift work are more likely than are other parents to share other household responsibilities. In dual-earner families, in which one spouse or partner works a nonday shift, fathers tend to contribute more in household labor when the mother is unavailable (Presser, 1994). Additionally, infants and toddlers in those families are given the opportunity to be cared for exclusively by their fathers, an arrangement that is not practiced in any of the other child care arrangements. Furthermore, mothers who rely on their spouses to care for their children while they work often have acknowledged that father solo care is beneficial for the fathers as well as for the children. The drawbacks for families of parents who have different shifts for working and parenting is that each parent is responsible for all the child care while the other parent is working and parents have less time to spend with each other (Hattery, 2001).

Grandparent Care

Although noncustodial grandparents no longer constitute the primary source of nonparental care for children in the United States, they continue to be frequently called-upon sources of child care on a regular basis. There are several factors influencing the likelihood that grandparents will take on the role of caregiver of their grandchildren in order to assist working parents. Those factors include the age of the grandchildren, the age, marital status, ethnicity, socioeconomic status, educational level, and gender, of the grandparents, as well as whether grandparents have coresident children. Of those various factors, the age of the grandchildren plays the most important role in influencing grandparent care with 9% of all grandparents providing extensive care to grandchildren who are under 5 years of age. In comparison to grandparents who do not provide extensive care for their grandchildren, grandparents who provide extensive care are significantly younger, and are more likely to be married, African American, and female. Grandparents providing extensive child care also are more likely to have lower incomes, less likely to have graduated from high school, and more likely to have coresident children. The clearest advantage of grandparent child care for working parents is the knowledge that their children are being cared for by a caregiver who has a close relationship with the children. The closeness of the relationship to the grandparent is an advantage for the child as well, who does not experience disruptions in the attachments they form with their care-givers. Furthermore, grandparents who provide extensive care for their grandchildren report that they have closer relationships to their grandchildren than do grandparents who do not provide extensive care of their grandchildren (Fuller-Thomson & Minkler, 2001).

Center-Based Child Care

As stated earlier, the majority of working American parents place their infants and toddlers in center-based child care. More than half of all infants and toddlers in the United States spend at least 20 hours each week being cared for in child care centers. Although the typical age of a baby's first placement in a child care center is 33 months, the age of first placement varies by family income, the marital status and educational level of parents, family size, and the presence or absence of nonparental adults in the household (Singer, Fuller, Keiley, & Wolf, 1998).

Factors Influencing Infant–Toddler Placement in Center-Based Care. A primary factor influencing placement in center-based child care is family income, and there is a skewed picture of the effect of income on the selection of center-based care. Both high-income families and impoverished families are more likely to place their infants and toddlers in center-based child care than are working-class families. Parents with high incomes can afford the private costs and many low income and working poor families receive subsidies that offset the cost. Working-class families, on the other hand, are least likely to use child care centers inasmuch as they cannot afford the private fees and do not receive child care subsidies. In addition to cost, family size and composition affect whether infants and toddlers are placed in child care centers. Infants and toddlers from smaller families, particularly single-parent families, are more likely to be placed in center-based child care. Also, the presence of a kin member or nonparent adult in the family lessens the likelihood of center placement. Finally, the parents' level of education influences their choice of whether or not to use center-based child care. Better educated parents are more likely to place children in center-based care than are parents with less education (Singer et al., 1998).

Assessing the Quality of Center-Based Care. Evidence is mounting that certain features of child care settings are associated with positive outcomes in children and it is precisely those features that reflect the quality of those programs. First among those findings is that center care, family child care, nor father care compromises mother–infant attachment so long as the infant or toddler does not simultaneously experience inattentive mothering while in poor-quality child care. Also, infants and toddlers in higher quality child care settings are more securely attached to their caregivers than are infants and toddlers in poor or minimally adequate care. In addition to earlier concerns regarding the impact of child care placement on infant–mother attachment (which has been laid to rest), traditional assessments of child care quality focused on caregiver–child ratio and the safety of the environment (and those features continue to be important). What is missing in those evaluations is reflected in the new directions for studying child care quality. The contemporary assessments of child care quality emphasize the importance of relationships, continuity, culture, and context (Love, Raikes, Paulsell, & Kisker, 2000).

In assessing quality in terms of relationships, it is important to identify child care programs that address the developmental levels of the children involved. Because a major task of infants and toddlers is to establish secure relationships with their caregivers during the first 2 years, definitions of quality of infant–toddler programs should take into account the nature of those relationships. To assess quality of care in relation to continuity, it should be emphasized that to form relationships, infants and toddlers need to experience a consistency of care. Therefore, frequently entering into new child care arrangements or having to get used to the repeated turnover of child care providers is likely to be detrimental to the developing relationships of infants and toddlers. Evaluating child care quality in terms of culture emphasizes the need to understand the role of **cultural congruence** on children's development. For example, children's development is more likely to be enhanced by caregivers who can speak their language and who look and act in ways that are somewhat familiar. Finally, an assessment of quality child care in terms of context emphasizes such contextual features as the type of setting, staff stability, structural features of the program (such as group composition), staff qualifications, child turnover, and parent involvement (Love et al., 2000).

❊ SUMMARY

This chapter focused on the preparation for and transition to parenthood, the role of parents in promoting the development of their infants and toddlers, and the challenges of coordinating occupational demands with parental responsibilities. We began the chapter by considering ways in which parents might optimize their chances for having healthy, full-term babies. The focus of that discussion was the nutritional needs of pregnant mothers, the harmful effects of teratogens on the unborn child, and the importance of early prenatal care. Next, there was a discussion of the experience of birth as a universal occurrence that differentially impacts parents according to the nature of the birth and the resources of the family and community. We then looked at the ways in which parents, grandparents and the community work together to accommodate the arrival of babies into the family. Much of the remainder of the chapter was devoted to an exploration of the ways in which parent–child interactions promote the social–emotional, physical, and cognitive development of infants and toddlers. Throughout that discussion, we were consistently reminded of the central role that parents play in promoting the health and well-being of their babies. Following the discussion of the ways in which parents impact the development of their infants and toddlers, we explored the varied ways in which working parents arrange for the care of their children, and provided guidelines for parents to consider in assessing quality child care.

✾ KEY TERMS

- affective synchrony
- babbling
- contingent responsiveness
- cultural congruence
- fetal alcohol syndrome
- fine motor skills
- gross motor skills
- kangaroo care
- linguistic turn taking

- mutual gazing
- neonatal abstinence syndrome
- parentese
- parent–infant synchrony
- self-regulation
- sensorimotor intelligence
- tag-team parenting
- teratogens

4

Parent–Preschooler Interactions

Children are entitled in their otherness, as anyone is; and when we reach them, as we sometimes do, it is generally on a point of sheer delight, to us so astonishing, but to them so natural.

—Alastaire Reid (Tripp, 1970)

Sheer delight, exuberance, curiosity, and magical thinking are all ways that describe how preschool children engage and react to their world (Leach, 1997). Because preschoolers require assistance, guidance, and care from their caregivers, parents have numerous opportunities to join them in their lively adventures. Furthermore, the level of support that preschool children receive as they enthusiastically challenge themselves, the environment, and their parents, affects their social–emotional, physical, and cognitive development.

THE PARENTAL ROLE IN PROMOTING PRESCHOOLERS' SOCIAL–EMOTIONAL DEVELOPMENT

Consider how different a 2-year-old is from a 6-year-old, emotionally and socially. Whereas the 2-year-old is still vacillating between dependence and self-determination and cannot be left alone even for a few minutes, the 6-year-old has both the confidence and the competence to be relatively independent. By the time a child leaves the preschool years, that child can be trusted to do many things alone and is proud of the ability to do so. The 6-year-old child also shows affection toward family members without the dependency or exaggerated self-assertion of the 2-year-old. Let's take a look at how that transformation occurs.

Early Attachment and Parent–Preschooler Relationships

First of all, the attachment preschoolers have with their parents has a profound impact on their social–emotional development. It has been demonstrated through longitudinal studies that preschoolers who were securely attached as babies show more elaborate make-believe play and greater enthusiasm, flexibility, and persistence in problem solving. Such children have been found to be high in self-esteem, socially competent, cooperative, popular, and empathic. In contrast, preschoolers with avoidant attachment have been viewed as isolated and disconnected, and preschoolers with resistant attachment have been described as disruptive and difficult (Bar-Haim, Sutton, & Fox, 2000; Frankel & Bates, 1990).

Although secure attachment during infancy is generally related to positive development during preschool, continuity of responsive caregiving determines whether securely attached infants continue to be securely attached during preschool (Bar-Haim et al., 2000; Lamb, Thompson, Gardner, Charnov, & Connell, 1985; Landry, Smith, & Swank, 2001). When parents respond sensitively to their infants and continue to respond sensitively to their young children, more favorable social–emotional development is likely to occur. In contrast, at any point of children's development when parents react insensitively over a prolonged period of time, increased risk of maladjustment can be predicted (Landry et al., 2001; Thompson, 1988).

Securely attached preschoolers not only have parents who have continued to be responsive to their needs, but they also have parents who have adjusted their responsiveness to the developmental needs of their preschoolers. During infancy, parental responsiveness related to secure attachment consists of responding to the needs of the infant in feeding, soothing, and play (Ainsworth, 1973). During preschool, parental responsiveness related to secure attachment includes positive parental mood, enjoyment of the child, and providing a relaxed home atmosphere (Stevenson-Hinde & Shouldice, 1995). Furthermore, parents of securely attached preschoolers are significantly more warm and accepting as well as less controlling of their young children in comparison to parents of insecurely attached preschoolers (Barnett, Kidwell, & Leung, 1998).

Just as parental responsiveness toward preschoolers is expressed differently than is parental responsiveness toward infants and toddlers, the behaviors of securely attached preschoolers are different from those of securely attached infants and toddlers. As noted in chapter 3, securely attached infants show more exploratory behavior than do infants who are not securely attached. Securely attached preschoolers, on the other hand, have moved beyond exploratory behavior to demonstrate competence in a wide array of social and cognitive skills (Belsky & Cassidy, 1995; Fagot, 1997). Attachment security during preschool has been shown to also be a reliable predictor of early conscience development (Laible & Thompson, 2000) and of the development of a positive view of the self (Verschueren, Alfons, & Schoefs, 1996).

What This Means for Parents and Professionals Working With Parents. Anyone who reviews the research related to the behaviors of securely attached infants who become securely attached preschoolers is struck by the importance of parental responsiveness to the feelings and needs of children. It might be reassuring for parents to know that when they consistently respond to their children's questions, laugh with them, play with them, show affection for them, and comfort them, they are sustaining their children's attachment. If parents are informed of the many benefits that spring from attachment, they might be inclined to relax more with their children and to participate more in playful activities with them.

Promoting the Young Child's Sense of Initiative

According to Erik Erikson (1963), a crucial aspect of self during the preschool years comes from the achievement of a **sense of initiative**, which is primarily defined by the skills that demonstrate independence. Young children jump at almost any opportunity to show that "I can do it." Their sense of initiative is stimulated by their drive to discover their personal abilities as reflected by their seemingly endless energy and curiosity about the environment. Preschoolers are more likely to develop a sense of initiative when parents and other caregivers support their adventurous nature by encouraging their curiosity and allowing them to be active. In contrast, if parents and other caregivers react to young children's exuberance and curiosity by inhibiting their activities and emphasizing that they should feel guilty for many of their normal behaviors, they contribute to preschoolers' **sense of guilt**. Essentially, the young child feels guilty about behaviors that significant others label as wrong or bad. The outcomes for children related to the development of a sense of initiative versus a sense of guilt set them either on a road whereby they discover and feel good about their personal abilities or on one whereby they begin to believe that it is wrong to want to discover their physical and social environments (Thomas, 1992).

What This Means for Parents and Professionals Working With Parents. For young children, the world cannot be adequately understood and appreciated simply through observation. They must experience it by taking the initiative in becoming physically and psychologically involved in it. How young children discover the many things they need to know is by doing things and asking questions with the intent of gathering as much information as they can about the world in which they live. To find out the properties of sand, for example, children must be able to put their hands in it, to sift it, to make piles out of it, or to mix water with it to make a sand castle or a fort. *To discover* usually means *to enjoy* as seen in children's delight at discovering the properties of water, by jumping in it, splashing in it, and running through a water sprinkler. To be consistently engaged in learning, children need to have parents and caregivers who are patient with them and who will provide them with opportunities for experimenting and trying out their new skills.

Parental Contributions to Preschoolers' Self-Esteem

Closely tied to the preschooler's development of a sense of initiative is their development of **self-esteem**, which refers to judgments of their worth and feelings associated with those judgments. The self-esteem of young children is in its early developing stage and as such is not as well defined or as stable as that of older children and adults. During those early years, children make judgments about themselves based on how well others like them (social acceptance). Their self-evaluations are linked as well to how good they are at accomplishing the tasks they attempt to master (competence). They have difficulty, however, in discriminating their competence at different activities, and when asked how well they can perform some activity they typically overestimate their ability and underestimate task difficulty. Preschoolers' overranking of their abilities reflects a high self-esteem, a quality that is highly adaptive at that age because it encourages them to persist at tasks during a period in which many new skills must be mastered (Harter, 1990, 1999).

Preschoolers' tendency to evaluate themselves highly does not mean they are unaware of the judgments of others. Throughout the early years, children become increasingly conscious of what others think, and they begin to evaluate their own behaviors using those standards. Although most young children have high self-esteem, by age 4 some children give up when faced with challenges, concluding that they will not be able to accomplish the task or having been discouraged after failure. When nonpersisting preschoolers are asked why they have given up, they frequently report that their parents would be mad at them or punish them for making mistakes (Heyman, Dweck, & Cain, 1992). Children as young as 2 or 3 years of age respond with disappointment or guilt when they fail at a task, such as not being able to tie their shoes, or when they have an accident, perhaps spilling their juice (Butler, 1998). When older preschoolers experience failure or have an accident, they typically spontaneously confess and attempt to make reparations. Furthermore, young children often demonstrate more guilt feelings for those mishaps than is warranted (Cole, Michel, & Teti, 1994).

What This Means for Parents and Professionals Working With Parents.   The knowledge that young children routinely overestimate their abilities and tend to feel disappointed and guilty when they fail at a task or cause an accident provides parents with direction regarding their role in promoting preschoolers' self-concept. Although preschoolers are highly interested in taking initiative in demonstrating what they can do, they need parental backup and parental encouragement. Parental backup consists of allowing the child to attempt a new skill while assisting the child to be successful in mastering that skill. Preschoolers need parents to provide assistance without taking over and to increasingly withdraw assistance as the preschooler becomes more adept. By and large, parents of preschoolers should back up when needed and back off when no longer needed. In addition to assisting their young children to meet their goals, it is essential that parents consistently encourage them in the process of accomplishing what they attempt to master. Parents encourage their children when they attend to children's feelings about their accomplishments and when they emphasize the progress children are making as they are engaged in an activity. Finally, parents promote their young children's self-esteem when they send a clear message to them that they are valued. Outlined in Figure 4.1 are several suggested ways in which a parent might help a child feel valuable, thereby boosting the child's self-esteem.

Promoting Preschoolers' Self-Reliance

As children master a variety of activities, learn responsible ways to behave, and develop a positive self-image, they become increasingly more self-reliant. **Self-reliance** in young children refers to the ability to behave in ways that are considered by parents

1. Build a positive relationship
Parents should send clear messages to their children that they want to be with them by (a) arranging times to be fully available, (b) listening without being judgmental, and (c) expressing some of your own thoughts and feelings because mutual sharing helps children feel valued.

2. Nurture success
Parents should (a) be reasonable in expectations, (b) provide assistance to their young children when they are attempting to do things that they cannot do alone, (c) accentuate the positive in their children's work or behavior by using the language of encouragement, and (d) display their young children's artwork and other symbols of success in highly visible areas to promote their children's sense of pride in their accomplishments.

3. Foster the freedom to choose
Parents should provide children with a sense of responsibility and control over their own lives by giving them choices and manageable responsibilities, including involving them in the choice of when and in what order a task will be done.

4. Acknowledge emotions
Parents should accept their children's strong feelings and suggest constructive ways to handle them. Parents also should offer sympathy and support to their young children when their negative emotions reflect an affront to their self-esteem.

5. Prevent damage to the child's developing self-esteem
Parents should adopt a warm, rational approach to childrearing.

FIGURE 4.1 Recommended Ways to Foster Children's Self-Esteem
Source: Adapted from *The Construction of the Self: A Developmental Perspective*, by S. Harter, 1999, New York: Guilford Press.

and other caregivers to be acceptable. There are a number of ways in which parents might encourage young children's self-reliance. Mauro and Harris (2000) studied the influence of parents on their young children's self-control and self-regulatory behavior by comparing parents' childrearing patterns to their children's ability to delay gratification. The findings from that study show that young children whose parents use an authoritative parenting approach are better able to delay gratification than are children of permissive parents.

What This Means for Parents and Professionals Working With Parents. Parents should expect their young children to become increasingly more self-reliant and not continually do things for them that they can do for themselves. On the other hand, when encouraging children to perform self-help and simple household responsibilities, parents need to keep in mind that young children (a) will take longer to perform those tasks, (b) will need assistance along the way, and (c) will require parental patience with their less-than-perfect performance. For example, in picking up toys after play, preschool children cannot be expected to clean up afterward efficiently, quickly, or completely. A positive way to promote the picking up of toys is to help the child with the job while showing the child how to do certain things and continually making favorable comments regarding the child's performance. Those behaviors of parents serve as reinforcement and encouragement to young children, motivate them to try to do a good job, and help them feel proud of the level of performance they are currently capable of demonstrating.

Helping Young Children Discover Their Personal Boundaries

Children's consistent expression of their sense of initiative through active discovery contributes to their learning about **personal boundaries**, that is, what they might or might not do, and what they can and cannot accomplish. Children's personal boundaries are revealed as they (a) make errors in judgment, (b) fail to accomplish goals, and (c) have conflicts with parents and other caregivers when boundaries and limits are not adhered to. In discovering their limitations during those early years, it is beneficial for children to learn that errors can occur and that it is human nature to make mistakes. Being able to accept their nature as imperfect and feeling comfortable about it establishes young children's realistic notions of their abilities and contributes to their feelings of self-acceptance. Furthermore, the self-acceptance gained during the preschool stage affects future learning experiences and supports the development of a healthy self-esteem (Bigner, 1998).

What This Means for Parents and Professionals Working With Parents.   Although it is important for parents to encourage their preschoolers' freedom to explore, thereby promoting their curiosity and sense of initiative, it is essential that parents closely monitor their youngsters' activities and establish reasonable parameters and rules of behavior. By establishing boundaries and regulations for young children, and at times redirecting their behavior, parents help them to understand which behaviors are safe and/or acceptable. The ways in which parents respond to their young children's mistakes are important as well. Because accidents and mishaps are a natural side effect of preschoolers' adventurous behavior, parents should expect (and be patient with) such things as spilled milk, accidental toppling of objects, and other blunders that are a natural part of an active preschooler's day.

Thinking Critically

In the preceding discussion, we have considered the ways in which the young child's sense of self is shaped by the parent's responses to the child. Drawing on Family Systems Theory (see chapter 1), in what ways do you think the parent's sense of self is shaped by the enthusiasm, affection, and curiosity of the preschooler?

THE ROLE OF PARENTS IN PROMOTING PRESCHOOLERS' PHYSICAL DEVELOPMENT

During the years that preschoolers are taking the initiative in accomplishing a variety of goals, developing their sense of self, and learning about personal boundaries, they are experiencing significant physical changes as well. The most obvious physical changes during those early years are in children's size and shape as chubby toddlers are transformed into slimmer and taller preschoolers. Less obvious, but more crucial, developmental changes occur in the preschool child's brain and central nervous system. Together, the growth and development of the body and the brain provide young children with the ability to explore and master their worlds primarily through play that is undertaken with joy and exuberance. Parents are better prepared to promote their preschoolers' physical development if they are aware of (a) the nutritional needs of their young children, (b) the brain development that occurs during those early years, and (c) the preschool child's development of gross and fine motor skills.

Meeting the Nutritional Needs of Preschoolers

Providing adequate nutrition to preschool children plays a central role in promoting their physical development. Although physical growth slows during the preschool years resulting in young children requiring fewer calories than toddlers, it is important that they have a nutritious diet. When family food is limited (primarily due to poverty), young children often suffer from malnutrition. In industrialized societies, the most common diet deficiency during the preschool years is **iron-deficiency anemia** and one of its main symptoms is chronic fatigue. Anemia, which stems from an

Providing balanced nutritional meals and limiting sweets promotes young children's healthy physical development.

insufficiency of quality meats, whole grains, eggs, and dark green vegetables, is three times more common in low-income families than in other families. Adding to the problem of providing adequate nutrition for their young children, parents of every social class tend to give their children candy, sugary drinks, sweetened cereals, and other sweets. Children who eat those foods are more likely to have a vitamin deficiency due to less consumption of nutritional foods and are vulnerable to early tooth decay, one of the most common health problems of early childhood in the United States (Lewit & Kerrebrock, 1998).

For all children, annual height and weight gains are much lower between ages 2 and 6 than they were during the first 2 years of life. As a result, preschool children need fewer calories per pound of body weight than they did as infants (Eveleth & Tanner, 1991). In addition to requiring fewer calories than they did as toddlers, young children are beginning to demonstrate their food preferences that show up in their refusal to eat certain foods. It is easy to understand that preschoolers are slowing in their growth and, therefore, requiring fewer calories than toddlers. Parents, however, are sometimes puzzled or aggravated by their preschoolers' refusal to eat certain foods that parents have chosen for the nutritional value. Besides their refusal to eat certain foods, preschoolers are quite compulsive about daily routines, including the placement of food on their plates. They are likely to insist that certain foods not touch other foods and might become very fussy if their expectations are not met (Evans et al., 1997).

What This Means for Parents and Professionals Working With Parents. Preschoolers' development of food preferences, as demonstrated by their refusal to eat certain foods, challenges parents to find creative approaches for assuring that their preschoolers receive adequate nutrition. The best way to resolve that issue is to search for solutions that balance the parent's goal of providing nutritional food with the preschooler's inability to tolerate certain tastes. When parents become annoyed with their preschool children because of their youngsters' refusal of certain dishes or when they attempt to force them to eat foods that they dislike, the dilemma is not resolved in a democratic fashion. A creative and understanding approach to meeting young children's nutritional needs is to offer a variety of nutritional foods and to allow them to select the foods they prefer. Parents should keep in mind that certain acidic foods, such as broccoli, might taste better to a young child if those foods are topped with cheese sauce (which tones down the acidic taste and provides a source of calcium and protein). Of course, parents might want to consider their children's reactions to the placement of food on their plates to determine if preschooler perfectionism is affecting their children's reaction to the food that is offered.

Even when parents are receptive to their preschoolers' tastes, preferences, and preferred placement of food, they might notice that their youngsters often dawdle over their food, eating very slowly and sometimes even forgetting to chew. It is helpful to give young children who dawdle over their food very small portions because nagging slow eaters only serves to compound the problem. Besides serving smaller amounts of food to preschoolers who tend to eat slowly, parents might keep in mind that young children sometimes take a longer time to eat when they know that they will be required to take a nap right after eating. As noted by Verville (1985), that problem can be avoided by changing the daily routine. Finally, as parents are attempting to resolve the dilemma of providing adequate nutrition while understanding preschoolers' taste preferences and tendency to dawdle over food, they should limit sugary snacks between meals. Thus, children's hunger needs will not be met at the expense of their nutritional requirements.

Thinking Critically

Based on Family Systems Theory, how would you explain the ways in which the picky eating behaviors of young children affect the behaviors of their parents?

THE BRAIN DEVELOPMENT OF YOUNG CHILDREN

During infancy and preschool, the brain develops faster than any other part of the body. By age 2, the brain has already reached 75% of its eventual adult weight and by age 5 it has reached 90% of its adult weight. Part of the reason for the increase in brain weight during the preschool years is due to the continued proliferation of communication pathways among the brain's various specialized areas. Another aspect of brain growth and development is due to ongoing **myelination**, which is the insulating process that speeds up the transmission of neural processes. Finally, several areas of the brain undergo considerable expansion, especially those areas dedicated to control and coordination of the body, the emotions, and the thinking processes. As a result of the brain growth and development that occurs during the preschool years, young children react more quickly to stimuli and become better at controlling their emotions. For example, compared to a toddler, a 5-year-old child more quickly notices that another child is playing with a favorite toy but is less likely to object by throwing a tantrum. Instead, the preschooler is able to come up with a number of tactics for retrieving the desired toy, such as explaining ownership, offering another toy, or even offering a trade, which 2-year-olds almost never do (Berger, 2001).

What This Means for Parents and Professionals Working With Parents.   The brain development that occurs during the preschool stage of development makes it easier for young children to control their emotions and to come up with a variety of tactics for getting their needs met in a socially acceptable way. Whether or not preschoolers develop those abilities, however, depends on the guidance they receive from parents and other caregivers. Unlike toddlers, preschoolers are amenable to parental suggestions regarding ways in which to handle conflicts. Young children who have parents who gently explain to them the options available for resolving conflict, such as

The active, spontaneous play of these young children provides the optimum type of movement for the development of their gross motor skills.

sharing, trading, or taking turns, incorporate those skills more readily into their behavioral repertoire than do preschoolers who are not provided that kind of guidance (Rogoff, 1990; Rogoff, Mistry, Goncu, & Mosier, 1993).

PROMOTION OF PRESCHOOLERS' FINE AND GROSS MOTOR SKILLS

During preschool, children of all cultures demonstrate a variety of skills that reveal increasing control and coordination of their gross and fine motor skills. **Gross motor skill** development requires the use of large muscles in the legs or arms as well as general strength and stamina. Running, jumping, skipping, hopping, throwing, catching, climbing up, jumping down, tumbling, and balancing are examples of gross motor skill abilities that develop during the early years. **Fine motor skill** development involves the ability to coordinate smaller muscles in the arms, hands, and fingers. Those abilities contribute to preschoolers' beginning attempts at writing, drawing, and other creative activities such as using scissors to cut out different shapes and using clay to represent objects in the environment. Another outcome of advancements in fine motor skill development in young children is that greater dexterity in the use of fine motor skills allows them to perform a variety of self-help skills (Trawick-Smith, 2000).

The Development of Gross Motor Skills

As preschoolers make notable progress in the development of their gross motor skills, they develop the ability to adapt those movements to meet varying environmental challenges, such as catching balls of different sizes and running up and down hills. Preschool children's proficiency in adapting their gross motor skills to the diverse challenges provided by the environment is critical for play as well as for participation in everyday activities in all cultures. For example, children in urban American settings learn not only to run but also to run up and down ramps, over tires, and along balance beams on the playground. In contrast, children in settings such as rural Guatemala learn to run, change directions, and stop quickly when herding farm animals (Keogh, 1977).

In the social realm, young children learn to coordinate the movements of their own bodies with the movements of other people. Being able to change directions while running in anticipation of another child's movement in a game of *tag* reflects the young child's development of **social coordination of movement**. Reaction time is another important component of developing gross motor skills. For developing reaction time, children must have experience in which they see or hear a stimulus and then quickly judge how to react. Traditional American games such as *musical chairs* or *red light, green light* require those kinds of quick motor reactions. In the game of *musical chairs*, for example, children learn to sit quickly after they notice that the music has stopped. They must make a quick decision regarding where they will sit (Connolly, 1970). Finally, play that incorporates the motor dimensions of coordination and speed of movement is associated with the development of cognitive abilities of preschoolers (Planinsec, 2002).

What This Means for Parents and Professionals Working With Parents.   There are a variety of ways in which parents might promote the development of their preschoolers' gross motor skills. First, parents should be alert to cues from their young children regarding their motivation to run, jump, skip, throw, kick, roll, tumble, and so forth. Second, parents need to be certain that preschoolers are provided sufficient space and appropriate structures on which to practice those skills. Third, it is essential for parents to take the necessary precautions for keeping their children safe from harm without holding them back in motor skill development. Because young children are not logical thinkers, it is imperative for parents to provide close supervision of their activities. And because preschoolers are highly motivated to climb up on things, parents need to check the stability of the structures their preschoolers attempt to climb, redirecting them when necessary. Finally, providing their preschool children with opportunities to play with other children supports the development of gross motor skills, social coordination of movement, and reaction time.

The Development of Fine Motor Skills

In all cultures, young children are engaged in activities that contribute to the development of their fine motor skills. In nonindustrialized societies where writing and drawing are not common, however, children are unlikely to learn a pencil grip or other fine motor skills common to children in industrialized societies. In societies and cultures in which writing or drawing are not emphasized, young children participate in other activities that promote the development of their fine motor skills. Among the Yup'ik Eskimo children in Southwestern Alaska, for example, children draw symbols in mud as they tell traditional stories and even preschoolers (called *tag-alongs* by older Yup'ik children) learn to knife their stories along the riverbank (DeMarrias, Nelson, & Baker, 1994).

Not only does the development of young children's fine motor skills not always include a pencil grip, but some cultures do not value or emphasize drawing or writing at all. Cultural differences in the development of young children's fine motor skills are exemplified in a study conducted in the 1970s of British and Zambian children. In that study, both British and Zambian children were asked to copy two-dimensional figures. The British children in the study were more competent in reproducing the figures with pencil and paper. The Zambian children, on the other hand, were advanced in their ability to accurately form the shapes with strips of wire. The findings of that study highlight the effect of experience on the development of fine motor skills. The British children had more experience with pencil and paper, and the Zambian children had more experience with sculpting with wire, which is more prevalent in the Zambian culture than are Western forms of drawing (Serpell, 1979).

What This Means for Parents and Professionals Working With Parents.   The foregoing discussion highlights the importance of providing young children with a variety of objects designed to help them gain fine motor dexterity. Although children need to be given the opportunity to manipulate a diverse number of objects, certain objects have greater significance depending on the culture in which the child is reared. In most cultures, proficiency in using writing and drawing tools is highly desirable. When choosing pencils and crayons for preschoolers, though, parents should keep in mind that fat pencils and fat crayons are best suited for the short, fat fingers of very young children. Moreover, parents should be aware that preschoolers are capable of developing dexterity in the use of a variety of tools. Parents, therefore, might consider the goals they have for their children in choosing the tools they provide for them. For example, parents who wish to see artistic ability in

Thinking Critically

Drawing on Bronfenbrenner's Ecological Model (see figure 1.3, chapter 1), how would you explain the role of cultural context in the development of young children's fine and gross motor skills? For example, how might differences in the child, the family, the community, the culture, and time, impact the development of those skills?

their preschoolers must provide items such as crayons, pencils, paper, finger paints, and modeling clay.

The Development of Personal and Family Life Skills

In addition to facilitating play and social interactions, advances in motor skills allow preschoolers to be more involved in self-care and to take on simple household responsibilities. As early as age 3, with some help from parents, young children can perform self-help tasks such as dressing themselves, picking up their toys, bathing, brushing their teeth, and eating with utensils. Even though assistance is needed in tying shoes, buttoning small buttons, or coordinating a fork and table knife at age 3, most children master those skills by age 5. Besides being able to take on increasing self-care responsibilities, preschoolers gain motor skill development through participation in household responsibilities (Berger, 2001).

What This Means for Parents and Professionals Working With Parents.   Even though it is helpful for young children to become responsible for self-care tasks and to be given household responsibilities, parents should take care that those responsibilities match the developmental capabilities of their preschool children. Parents need to be mindful as well of the requirement to guide, instruct, and support their youngsters' development of personal and family life skills. Showing youngsters how to brush their teeth, wash behind their ears, comb their hair, tie their shoes, and button their shirts are just a few of the ways that parents are consistently involved in promoting their children's self-care activities. Ongoing parental guidance as youngsters are learning family life skills include giving them responsibilities such as helping to straighten their rooms, putting dishes on the table at mealtimes, and helping with meal preparation. Examples of ways in which young children might assist with meal preparation include activities such as spreading mayonnaise on a slice of bread and placing slices of meat and/or cheese between slices of bread, and helping stir up cookie dough for making cookies. Children benefit too from being able to assist in feeding family pets, perhaps pouring water in the pet's water dish and putting pet food in the feeding dish.

The Household Responsibilities of Children in Traditional Cultures

In nonindustrialized societies, young children participate more extensively in household work than do young children in industrialized societies. For example, young children in India, Okinawa, the Philippines, Mexico, and Kenya carry out a range of jobs that most Canadian, European, and American children would not be expected to perform. Those household responsibilities include collecting firewood, fetching water, herding and tending livestock, grinding grain, and harvesting vegetables. Children in nonindustrialized societies perform universal household tasks as well, such as dressing or preparing food at an earlier age than would be expected in families in industrialized societies. Finally, in almost all cultures, young girls are more often assigned child care duties than are young boys (Weisner, 1982). The following vignette exemplifies the type of child care responsibilities that might be given to a young female living in a traditional culture:

> A 5-year-old girl in a small village in Kenya is up early. She has been assigned as the child nurse to her infant brother. Her mother and father have already gone to work in the garden, and she is left in full charge of her young sibling. When he awakes and cries, she picks him up and holds him close. As he calms down, she holds him on one arm and reaches with the other for a bottle to feed him. She must grip him tightly as she does this; he is 8-months-old and very big for his age. After feeding him, she places him into a sling. Her brother wiggles and kicks—he does not seem eager to be confined. She then straps the sling to her back. She stands up, maintaining her balance, then walks off to play with friends in another part of the village. (Trawick-Smith, 2000, pp. 217–218)

THE ROLE OF PARENTS IN PROMOTING YOUNG CHILDREN'S COGNITIVE DEVELOPMENT

Although the years between 2 and 6 are referred to as the preschool years in the United States, Leach (1997) points out that the term *preschool* is a mundane name for a magical time. Leach argues that the term implies that those early years represent a "waiting time"—before school or even before preparation for school. The reality of that early developmental stage is that young children have a developmental agenda of their own. Furthermore, recent research has led to an appreciation of the impressive cognitive abilities that manifest themselves during those early years, including mathematics, language, and social understanding. For parents, the cognitive development of their young children often fascinates and sometimes confuses them. On the one hand, parents everywhere are captivated and delighted by the magical thinking of young children who wonder where the sun sleeps or who chatter away with invisible playmates. On the other hand, parents are frequently surprised by their young children's failure to comprehend metaphors and other ways in which adults and older children express themselves. We will now examine the role of parents in promoting the cognitive development of their young children. A discussion of the role of parents in the promotion of young children's language development is included in this section as well.

Insights from Piaget

According to Piaget, a striking difference between infant and preschooler cognition is the ability to use **symbolic thinking**, which involves the use of words, gestures, pictures, or actions to represent ideas, things, or behaviors. Similar to motor skill development, the ability to symbolize occurs in gradual steps and is dependent on interactions with other persons and objects in the environment. As monumental as symbolic thought might be, Piaget referred to the cognitive development between ages 2 and 6 as **preoperational thought**. Due to the constraints of preoperational thought, preschoolers' first symbolic concepts are not as complete or as logical as are those of older children and adults; thus they are referred to as **preconcepts** (Piaget & Inhelder, 1969).

An illustration of a preconcept used by preschoolers is **overgeneralization**. Young children know, for example, that whoever walks on two legs, is tall (according to the standards of young children), and speaks in a deep voice belongs to a particular class of persons (Piaget & Inhelder, 1969). The English word they learn for that class of persons is usually *Daddy*; the Hindu term is *Bapu*, and the Xhosa (South African) word is *Tata*. So when young children use the terms *Daddy, Papa, Bapu, Tata,* or other linguistic variations to refer to all men, they are demonstrating the ability to use preconcepts. The same classification ability is demonstrated when English-speaking preschoolers call dogs, cows, and horses, *doggies*. Besides calling all men by the term their culture uses for *father* and using one term to distinguish all large, four-legged animals, young children have difficulty in distinguishing specific members of a species from each other. That inability is evident in a young child who has seen a kitten down the street thinking another kitten seen in another place is the same one (Elkind, 1976).

Preschoolers' Egocentrism. A primary limitation of preschoolers' thinking is that their thought processes are **egocentric**, which simply means that young children have an excessive reliance on their own point of view, coupled with a corresponding inability to be objective. Consequently, young children tend to focus on one feature or perspective at a time. Preschooler egocentrism shows up in young children's inability to share their toys, a fact that parents often fail to understand. Because parents frequently do not comprehend the limitations of young children's logic, they tend to scold them when they refuse to share their toys. The lack of ability to consider two perspectives at once, however, means that very young children are unable to comprehend the concept of sharing. The inability to consider two perspectives simultaneously can be seen too in young children's inability to **conserve** matter and volume. The failure to understand that the quantity of matter (such as clay) does not change when the shape changes, or that the volume of water remains the same if it is poured from a short squat glass to a tall narrow glass, is reflected in preschoolers' judgment (Piaget & Inhelder, 1969).

What This Means for Parents and Professionals Working With Parents. Rather than expressing impatience with preschoolers when they do not share, parents might take their young children's perspective in the matter. Parents can be certain that each child has an identical toy or when noticing that two children are insisting on having the same toy might distract one of the children by offering that child an equally attractive toy. Because preschoolers lack the ability to conserve matter and liquid, parents need to be patient with them when they complain that they have less lemonade than the other children whose glasses are taller (even though they are narrower). Instead of providing a logical explanation to the prelogical preschooler regarding how the width of one glass compensates for the height of the other glass, it is better to take care that glasses chosen for their liquid refreshments are all the same height and width.

Insights from Vygotsky

Vygotsky agreed with Piaget that preschoolers are active learners (Brandstadter, 1998), but Vygotsky emphasized another point: Children do not strive alone; their efforts to understand a world that fascinates and sometimes confuses them are imbedded in a social context. Preschoolers notice things that happen and ask "*Why?*" with the assumption that others know why—and they expect answers. Meanwhile, parents, older siblings, grandparents, preschool teachers, and many others do more than answer: They guide a young child's cognitive development by (a) presenting challenges for new learning, (b) offering assistance with difficult tasks, (c) providing instruction, and (d) encouraging the preschooler's interest and motivation. Accordingly, children learn much of what they need to know through **guided participation** in social experiences and in explorations of their world (Rogoff, 1990; Rogoff et al., 1993).

Thinking Critically

Drawing on your comprehension of the role of parents in promoting young children's cognitive development, from the perspective of Vygotsky, how would you recommend that parents help their children to learn to pick up their toys and put them in their toy boxes?

The parents in this picture understand that children are able to master tasks more quickly (and with less frustration) when assisted by adults.

The Role of Parents in Promoting Language Development

From infancy to early childhood, one undeniable change takes place—children learn to talk. During the preschool years, there is a language explosion, with words and sentences bursting forth. By age 6, the average child has a vocabulary of over 10,000 words because during the early preschool period children learn words at the rapid rate of 10 to 20 new words per day through a process called **fast mapping** (Jones, Smith, & Landau, 1991). Furthermore, even though different languages have different subject, verb, and object placement, young children's word placement matches the grammatical structure of their native language from the time they first string two words together (Allen & Crago, 1996). Moreover, young children demonstrate an understanding of verb tense in their language (Gleason, 1967).

An example of preschoolers' knowledge of verb tense is demonstrated in the following example. The young child who says "I played with Sally today" comprehends that *ed* is added to a verb to represent past tense. When that same child says "Sally and I goed to the park," the child is still demonstrating a basic understanding of past tense. In the second example, the child uses **overregularization**, whereby a standard rule of past tense is applied to the English language, which has many exceptions to the standard rules. The remarkable advances in language development during the preschool years are further exemplified in young children's social speech. Preschool children are extraordinarily adept at producing socially adaptive behavior in their verbal communication. For example, 4-year-old children speak differently to 2-year-olds when they see themselves in a teaching role than when they are attempting to engage a younger child in informal play. Additionally, young children's speech reflects the social skills of turn taking and topic maintenance (Woodward & Markman, 1998).

What This Means for Parents and Professionals Working With Parents. There is no question that the preschool stage of development is an impressive time of language development. The extraordinary growth of vocabulary that occurs during the preschool years is matched by an impressive understanding of basic grammar and socially adaptive language. There are, nevertheless, variations in language development and those variations can be traced to parent–child interactions. First of all, preschoolers need to hear new words in order to learn them. It is, hence, beneficial for young children when their parents continually engage them in verbal dialogues and respond to their questions and other verbal comments. Young children's language development (especially vocabulary expansion) is further promoted when adults label new things for them. For instance, a parent might point to some animals the child sees at a distance and say, "See the deer are running across the field." In less than a minute, the words *deer* and *field* enter the child's vocabulary.

Finally, whereas the language development that occurs during the preschool stage is impressive, young children's pronunciation takes a little longer to perfect. It is important that parents do not attempt to correct their young children's pronunciation because that approach actually hampers their preschoolers' language development. Instead of calling attention to their youngsters' mispronunciation, parents should respond to their preschoolers' speech as if they had pronounced the words correctly. In their responses to their young children's mispronunciations, however, it is important for parents to repeat back the words correctly, thereby modeling the correct pronunciation. For example, the child might say, "Mommy, Daddy said we are going on a twip!" In response, Mommy could say "Oh yes! We are going to go on a trip!"

How Young Children Understand Speech

Even though young children's speech reflects their social understanding of turn taking, topic maintenance, and social adaptation, they are somewhat limited in comprehending the speech of others. First, the preoperational thought of young children prevents them from understanding the concept of reversibility, which shows up in their failure to accurately comprehend **reverse-order sentences** (Woodward & Markman, 1998). An example of that misunderstanding can be detected in the statement whereby the parent says to the child, "You can have a cookie after you wash your hands." Because young children understand the sequence of action in the order that it is presented, the child believes the parent is actually saying, "You can have a cookie, then you should wash your hands." Not only does the child think that cookie eating precedes hand washing in that instance, the child is less likely to have paid attention to the second half of the sentence. The failure to attend to the second stated action in the sentence is due to preschoolers' egocentric tendency to focus on one thing at a time.

Still another limitation of children's linguistic understanding stems from their inability to comprehend metaphors—that one word or phrase can mean different things when used in different contexts (Woodward & Markman, 1998). Their inability to grasp metaphors means that young children are quite literal in their understanding and use of speech. As a case in point, if a father tells a preschool child on the phone that he will be home in a little while but that he is "tied up right now," the child believes the father is literally tied up. The concerned child might turn to the mother and ask, "How is Daddy going to get untied." The child's lack of understanding that words might mean different things in different contexts means their language understanding is very context bound. An illustration of that language limitation is apparent in the situation where a parent has taken the child into the deep end of the swimming pool and the child learns from that experience that *deep* means over one's head. When that same parent says to the young child the following week that it is okay to step in puddles after a rain while wearing rain boots, but not to step into deep puddles, the child will feel free to step into any puddle that is not over the child's head. Still another restriction of young children is their lack of ability to understand complex, multiaction sentences (Woodward & Markman, 1998). For instance, a young child would have trouble making sense of the following request: "Tommy, pick up your toys, go wash your hands, and put on your jacket." The parent who uses a sentence such as that expects the child to attend to several different requests, which is very difficult for the egocentric young child.

When parents speak face to face with their young children, those children are able to see how words are formed.

What This Means for Parents and Professionals Working With Parents.   First, parents should be certain that they speak clearly, and face-to-face, with their young children so that their children have the opportunity to watch the formation of their words and clearly hear how sentences are formed and words are pronounced. Second, it is better to use short, concrete sentences, state one request or idea at a time, and give the child an opportunity to think about and process each request separately. Third, it is important for parents not to use metaphors when talking to their preschool children, who rely on literal comprehension. Fourth, parents need to understand that even though a child has learned the meaning of a word, the child might not understand the usage of that word in a different context. Therefore, parents should be very patient with their young children and not assume that they are misbehaving when they have not followed through with instructions. It is possible

Thinking Critically

Drawing on the previous discussion that focused on how young children understand adult speech, describe how you might instruct preschoolers to come to dinner after they have put away their toys and washed their hands.

that the child has not clearly understood the meaning of words used in a context that does not match the one in which the words were learned. Finally, some parents need to be reminded of the importance of slowing down their pace when speaking to their young children, thus providing sufficient pauses to encourage parent–preschooler dialogue.

CHALLENGES AND CONCERNS OF PARENTS OF YOUNG CHILDREN

There are a number of areas in which young children sometimes experience problems and parents typically require additional information in order to help their children with those difficulties. Those problems not specifically related to the preschool children's developmental stage are presented in chapters 9 and 10. The two most common areas of concern for parents of preschool children are sleeping problems (including bed-wetting) and sibling conflict.

Sleeping Problems

Childhood sleep disturbance negatively impacts children as well as their parents. For parents, their young children's sleep problems are associated with parental fatigue, stress, depressed mood, marital tension, and negative parent–child interactions. Four sleep-related problems (bed-wetting, difficulty going to bed, waking up at night, and sleeping with parents) are at the top of parents' list of preschool children's behavior problems. Fortunately, most sleep problems are amenable to treatment, and much of the negative impact on family functioning is alleviated with successful intervention (Kuhn, Mayfield, & Kuhn, 1999). The importance of successful intervention for sleeping problems that arise during the preschool years is that early sleep problems might forecast later behavior and/or emotional problems. For instance, Gregory and O'Connor (2002) found that sleep problems at age 4 predicted behavioral–emotional problems in midadolescence.

The first step in alleviating childhood sleep disturbances is to determine if there are coexisting child behavior problems. Young children who are noncompliant, defiant, or aggressive, might respond paradoxically to sleepiness by exhibiting overactive behavior, irritability, or decreased attention span. In those situations, the combination of the child's sleep problem and a frustrated parent might lead to a family crisis. In some cases, treating the child's behavior problem might result in a resolution of the sleep problem. In other situations, treatment of the youngster's sleep disturbance alleviates the child's behavior problem. In situations where the child's sleep disturbance contributes to or reflects behavior problems, a comprehensive assessment of pediatric sleep disturbances within an outpatient clinic might be necessary before a plan of intervention can be developed. In the majority of families, however, parents and their children benefit greatly when parents learn ways to assist their children with their sleep problems (Kuhn et al., 1999).

Sleep Disturbance Related to Bed-Wetting

Among preschoolers, a common problem associated with sleeping is **enuresis**, defined as any instance of involuntary urination by a child over 3 years of age (Verville, 1985). Although, bed-wetting is sometimes related to psychological reasons, there are two biological reasons that are primarily associated with enuresis. First of all, the maturation of the nervous system (which helps children achieve bladder control) occurs at different rates among young children. Because the maturation of the nervous system occurs somewhat later for boys as compared to girls, bed-wetting is more common for boys than for girls. Finally, some children sleep more soundly than do others, and the combination of a very sound sleep pattern combined with less mature bladder control frequently contributes to bed-wetting. Although medical intervention is available for treatment of enuresis, more children benefit from psychological than pharmacological treatments. Moreover, psychological treatments involving a urine clock are more likely to yield benefits that are maintained once treatment has ended (Houts, Berman, & Abramson, 1994).

What This Means for Parents and Professionals Working With Parents. Because bed-wetting is not under young children's control, it is important that parents not overreact to wet sheets or hold children responsible for incidents of bed-wetting. It is recommended instead that parents adopt a detached attitude toward bed-wetting, providing encouragement to their children in their attempts to control their bed-wetting yet remaining unconcerned about the outcome. Although there are a number of techniques recommended for dealing with bed-wetting, ranging from medication to pad-buzzer systems, parents need to keep in mind that patience and bed pads will go a long way in getting both preschoolers and their parents past the bed-wetting problem. The most important recommendation in dealing with bed-wetting is that children not be made to feel ashamed or guilty for behavior that is not under their control.

Sleep Problems Not Associated with Other Childhood Problems

Most of the problems related to the sleep patterns of young children are night waking and failing to settle at night, calling persistently for parental attention. About 25% of preschoolers have sleep difficulties of those kinds (Houts et al., 1994). Another common sleep problem is that children sometimes develop fears related to going to bed, including a fear of monsters that might be lurking under their beds or in their closets.

When Children Have Trouble Going to Sleep. Many parents respond to young children's problems with going to sleep by forcing them to go to bed at a time the parents designate and failing to respond to their cries or pleas to get back up. Although that has become a popular method for dealing with young children's sleep problems, it is not a democratic approach to parenting children. Furthermore, based on the strong evidence that parental responsiveness is the best predictor of children's attachment, ignoring a child's pleas and cries is not a beneficial method for dealing with their problems associated with sleep. It is important to point out that sleep disturbances of young children might be culturally determined. Many Asian families, for instance, expect their young children to sleep in their siblings' or parents' bed and do not report any sleep disturbances (Brophy, 2000). To assist parents in alleviating problems related to getting their children to go to bed, Ansbaugh and Peck (1998) developed a procedure called *Faded Bedtime with Response Cost Intervention*, which they adapted from a similar procedure first introduced by Piazza and Fisher (1991). The procedure developed by Ansbaugh and Peck (described in Figure 4.2) helps parents to align their young children's bedtime with the children's normal onset of sleep.

Those Troublesome Monsters in Children's Bedrooms.   In addition to coordinating their children's bedtime with their normal onset of sleep, it is also beneficial when parents respond sensitively to children's nighttime fears. Those nighttime fears are related to young children's anxiety about being separated from parents and other family members when going to bed as well as children's active imaginations that cause them to interpret shadows and noises as monsters lurking in the dark. In response to their young children's worries about monsters, parents often attempt to alleviate children's feelings of anxiety by providing them with logical explanations of how there are no monsters and that they should not be afraid. One problem with such a response is that young children are not very logical in their thinking (Piaget & Inhelder, 1969); therefore, reasonable explanations from their parents do little to alleviate the fear of

---

- During the baseline period, no scheduled bedtime is implemented. During that period, parents note the times the child falls asleep at night.

- Before intervention, an initial bedtime is established by computing the average time the child falls asleep each night (e.g., 9:00) and adding 30 minutes (9:30).

- The fading procedure consists of adjusting the child's bedtime according to the actual onset of sleep for the previous night. Example: If the child falls asleep within 15 minutes of the scheduled bedtime, then the child's bedtime the next night is 30 minutes earlier. If the child does not fall asleep within 15 minutes of the scheduled bedtime, the bedtime for the next night is 30 minutes later.

- After setting the bedtime for 30 minutes later, the parents keep the child from falling asleep before the scheduled bedtime by playing with the child.

- This procedure is implemented with the goal of establishing a specific bedtime. If the child is not asleep within 15 minutes of being put to bed, the child is removed from the bed and played with for 30 minutes. The procedure is repeated until the child falls asleep within 15 minutes of being put to bed.

FIGURE 4.2   Faded Bedtime with Response Cost Intervention
Source: Adapted from "Treatment of Sleep Problems in a Toddler: A Replication of the Faded Bedtime with Response Cost Protocol," by R. Ansbaugh and S. Peck, 1998, *Journal of Applied Behavior Analysis, 31*, pp. 127–129.

monsters. Another problem with that rejoinder is that telling children that they should not be afraid minimizes children's feelings and does not provide them with the comfort they seek. As a reminder, parents of securely attached preschoolers are significantly more warm and accepting as well as less controlling of their young children in comparison to parents of insecurely attached preschoolers (Barnett et al., 1998).

What This Means for Parents and Professionals Working With Parents.   It is recommended that parents show their young children that they care about their concerns. Children need to have their parents reassure them that they can and will protect them and keep them safe. Accordingly, calm and loving reassurance from parents is the best approach for dealing with those troublesome monsters. A nightlight in the child's bedroom is another way to alleviate nighttime fears as children can notice familiar surroundings before dozing off. Finally, attachment objects such as stuffed animals tend to ease children's feelings of separation and make bedtime more calming.

Thinking Critically

Research findings have consistently demonstrated that sensitive, responsive caregiving predicts preschooler attachment, which contributes to a number of positive outcomes for young children. Do you think those findings mean that parents should respond sensitively to their young children throughout the day then ignore their pleas at bedtime? If not, what can American parents learn from Asian parents about handling bedtime?

Sibling Conflict

Ranking alongside sleep problems of young children is sibling conflict. Although problems with siblings certainly exist, the impact of siblings on the social development of children is more positive than negative. Children learn many social skills from brothers and sisters, and sibling influence is especially valuable in many cultures throughout the world in which older siblings act as caregivers of younger siblings (Schlegel & Barry, 1991; Whiting & Edwards, 1988). Furthermore, children learn valuable lessons when they adjust to the arrival of a new sibling (Dunn, 1992). Where there are siblings in a family, however, there are inevitable spats and conflicts. Although parents may fail to appreciate it at the time, those interactions usually have a positive influence on children's developing ability to resolve conflict. Furthermore, unilateral oppositions of young children are likely to be imbedded in the midst of positive interchanges and after their mild spats young children are likely to remain near one another and to continue their positive interaction (Laursen & Hartup, 1989; Vandell & Bailey, 1995).

How parents respond to young children's conflicts with their siblings makes a difference in how children resolve those conflicts, how they feel about themselves in relation to their siblings, and whether or not they will benefit from sibling rivalry and conflict. Vandell and Bailey (1995) summarized the following parental influences on siblings' ability to resolve conflict. First, punitive parenting approaches are associated with high levels of sibling conflict. Second, conflicts are minimized when children's emotional needs are met by their parents and there is no favored child in the family. Third, when parents act as mediators of siblings' conflicts by referring to moral principles as well as to children's feelings, young children engage in relatively mature forms of conflict, using justification for their actions and moral reasoning themselves. Fourth, parents need to be sensitive in their interventions, keeping in mind that parental interruption of constructive sibling conflicts might deprive young children of the opportunity to develop necessary social problem-solving skills.

What This Means for Parents and Professionals Working With Parents.   Even though siblings should be encouraged to work out their differences without parents taking sides or taking over, it is beneficial for parents to provide guidelines for conflict resolution that maximize the chances that cooperation will occur. For example, two young children might be arguing over which one of them should be able to play with a particular toy. Instead of telling the children how to resolve the spat, parents might express a belief in the children's ability to resolve the problem on their own. After showing confidence in their children's capability to settle the matter themselves, the parents might provide a couple simple guidelines regarding how to negotiate their differences. They might tell their children, for instance, that they should make a decision only after talking over the problem with each other. They might also tell their children that they should try to reach a compromise that makes both of them happy. When children work out their problems and come up with equitable solutions,

Children are better able to resolve conflict with each other when they receive guidance from an adult.

it is important that parents show approval of their children's problem-solving efforts. When parents congratulate their young children for resolving their conflicts, they encourage them to engage in problem solving in the future. Furthermore, as parents continually express a belief in their young children's capacity to resolve conflict, children become increasing more capable of conflict negotiation.

❧ SUMMARY

During the years between ages 3 and 6, young children in cultures throughout the world make tremendous advancements in the social–emotional, physical, and cognitive domains of development. They toddle into the preschool stage with the fundamental skills of reaching, grabbing, and discovering the properties of things through direct contact with those objects, and they leave by running, skipping, tumbling, jumping, and romping. Furthermore, by the end of the preschool years, young children have gained the ability and the skills necessary to begin to use the tools of their culture. As they gain a greater understanding of their environment and become skilled in the use of a variety of tools, young children start to form impressions about their competence and self-image.

Behind all of the remarkable achievements of children during those early years are parents who play a key role in supporting their children's goals to realize their developmental potential. The materials and objects that parents make available to their youngsters, and the freedom they grant them to move about within a safe environment, promote their preschoolers' development. Parents further support their young children's development by the ways in which they speak to and listen to them. Finally, when parents are confronted with problems related to getting their children to go to bed, bed-wetting, and sibling conflict, they need to be understanding and supportive of their children's feelings and to seek out information and guidance to match their care to their children's specific needs.

❧ KEY TERMS

- conserve
- egocentric
- enuresis
- fast mapping
- fine motor skill
- gross motor skill
- guided participation
- iron-deficiency anemia
- myelination
- overgeneralization
- overregularization
- personal boundaries
- preconcept
- preoperational thought
- reverse-order sentences
- self-esteem
- self-reliance
- sense of guilt
- sense of initiative
- social coordination of movement
- symbolic thinking

5

Interactions Between Parents and Their School-Age Children

If parents were asked to pick the easiest years of childrearing, they would probably choose the years from 7 to 11 when children (a) master dozens of new skills, (b) are able to learn quickly and think logically, and (c) live in a social world wherein most children think their parents are helpful, their teachers are fair, and their friends are loyal. As you will see in the forthcoming discussions, the interactions school-age children have with their parents are impacted by the cultures in which they live, the socioeconomic level of families, and parents' childrearing beliefs. Nevertheless, in all families, all cultures, and all socioeconomic levels, parents are important influences on every aspect of school-age children's social–emotional, physical, and cognitive development.

THE ROLE OF PARENTS IN PROMOTING SCHOOL-AGE CHILDREN'S SOCIAL–EMOTIONAL DEVELOPMENT

Around the age of 7, children move from the closely supervised and limited world of the younger child and begin to explore the wider world of neighborhood and school. In those broadening ventures, school-age children experience greater vulnerability, increasing competence, ongoing friendships, troubling rivalries, and deeper social understanding. Although not as closely supervised by parents and other adults as they were during the preschool years, school-age children's social and emotional lives continue to be shaped by family interaction patterns. Children's social–emotional development during that stage is influenced as well by the degree to which their parents provide organized activities for them and monitor their informal leisure activities. We will now examine the interplay between school-age children's expanding freedom and parents' guiding forces and the impact of those interactions on children's social and emotional development.

According to Erikson, parents and other significant adults in school-age children's lives play an important role in helping them develop a sense of industry.

The Ways in Which Parents Influence School-Age Children's Sense of Industry

According to Erikson (1982), during the school-age years, as children attempt to master the skills valued in their particular cultures, they experience a psychosocial crisis of **industry versus inferiority**. Based on their level of success in mastering the skills valued by their parents and other significant adults, school-age children judge themselves as competent or incompetent, productive or failing. The ways in which parents assist their children in resolving the industry versus inferiority crisis in a positive manner is by (a) providing experiences that promote the development of their children's skills and competencies, and (b) supporting their children in the process of acquiring those skills and competencies. If parents do not provide the experiences and guidance needed to support their children's sense of industriousness, their children are likely to develop feelings of inferiority. The development of a sense of industry during middle childhood is related to the development of **coregulation** as well as to the development of **competence**. The role of parents in supporting their children's development of coregulation and competence is explained in the upcoming discussion.

The Parental Role in School-Age Children's Development of Coregulation

Children learn self-control during early childhood and are prepared for a greater sharing of social power during middle childhood due to advances in cognitive development. The sharing of social power between parents and their school-age children (coregulation) thereby becomes a predominant aspect of appropriate child socialization during that developmental stage (Masten & Coatsworth, 1998). An example of coregulation is demonstrated in the following exchange: Charlie: "Mom, can I invite Tommy and Mike over for dinner? Mom: "Sure, that will be great. We're having spaghetti; I remember that those two seem to like my spaghetti. If Tommy and Mike come for dinner, will you please be sure that they pick up their dishes, rinse them off, and put them in the dishwasher after we have finished eating? Charlie: Okay, Mom.

What This Means for Parents and Professionals Working With Parents. It is important that parents make adjustments in their child socialization patterns to accommodate their children's need to move from self-regulation during the preschool years to coregulation during the school-age years. Whereas it is important that parents support parent–child coregulation in many daily activities, the entire parent–child relationship is not coregulated. It is essential that parents of school-age children continue to structure their school-age children's daily activities, monitor their whereabouts, require certain levels of responsible behavior, and step in as needed to exercise more control when they misbehave. It is possible, though, for parents to provide guidelines for their children's behavior and appropriate consequences when necessary without taking away their children's developing ability to work with parents in the coregulation of their behavior.

The Role of Parents in Promoting School-Age Children's Competence

If school-age children have several crucial strengths, they can sustain reasonably positive social–emotional development even when confronted with serious problems (Masten & Coatsworth, 1998). Especially important are social, academic, and creative skills that can help children to ward off or avoid many of the problems they might encounter at home or in the community (Conrad & Hammen, 1993). One of the main ways in which the development of competencies contributes to the resilience of school-age children is through the role of competence in enhancing self-esteem. Children who feel confident in at least one area of their lives are likely to have a higher self-esteem in comparison to those children who lack confidence in their abilities across several areas of their lives. Furthermore, high self-esteem helps children to view the rest of their lives from a more positive perspective. They are able to believe, for example, that even when their efforts are not successful in certain academic, athletic, or social situations, they are still worthwhile individuals (Harter, 1990).

What This Means for Parents and Professionals Working With Parents. It is important for parents to be supportive of their children's efforts to become self-sufficient and to develop various skills. Children are assisted in their quest for competence when their parents (a) encourage them to try out new things, (b) provide the materials and instruction needed to learn new skills, (c) pay attention to the progress their children are making in developing competence in a particular area, and (d) provide direct help when needed.

❦ ❦

Thinking Critically

Go back in your mind to middle childhood and consider some activity (such as sports, dance, or art) that you began to feel you were good at. What were the feelings of pride about being competent at that particular thing? What do you remember about the ways in which your parents or other caring adults supported your development of competence in that area?

❦ ❦

THE ROLE OF PARENTS IN THE DEVELOPMENT OF SCHOOL-AGE CHILDREN'S SOCIAL RELATIONSHIPS

During middle childhood, peer relationships become important, conformity to peers gradually increases, and acceptance into the peer group is of paramount interest. It has been found that children who are liked and accepted by their peers have positive social traits, better social problem-solving skills, more constructive social behavior, and better friendship relations in comparison to less popular children. On the other hand, rejected children are more aggressive, more withdrawn, and less socially skilled than are those children who are liked and accepted by their peers (Ginsburg, LaGreca, & Silverman, 1998; Marano, 1997). As will be demonstrated in the upcoming discussion, parents influence their children's development of the social skills necessary for making and sustaining friendships. Unfortunately, some parents influence their children's development of behaviors that contribute to their rejection by other children. By and large, the social relationships of school-age children are directly impacted by their parents' childrearing patterns and indirectly influenced by the neighborhoods in which parents are rearing their children.

The Ways in Which Childrearing Patterns Influence Children's Social Relationships

Findings from Baumrind's (1991b) research show that children of authoritative parents have more positive relationships with their peers than do children whose parents are authoritarian, permissive, indulgent, or uninvolved. The encouragement of children's participation in decision making by authoritative parents appears to provide children the experience needed to engage in thoughtful and responsible behaviors when interacting with their peers (Steinberg et al., 1991). That children's thoughtful and responsible behavior is associated with parental authoritativeness is demonstrated by findings that the authoritative parenting style is linked to childhood behaviors that reflect empathy and altruism (Aunola et al., 2000; Baumrind, 1989; Hetherington & Clingempeel, 1992). As noted by Marano (1997) children learn responsiveness, sensitivity, and a positive attitude toward others from the numerous everyday acts of positive parenting. Furthermore, parental coaching and discussion of peer problems help children to develop specific social strategies.

In comparison to children whose parents are authoritative, children of authoritarian, permissive, uninvolved, or indulgent parents have poorer peer relationships. Children whose parents are authoritarian tend to be less socially adept (Aunola et al., 2000) and more at risk for behavior problems (Baumrind, 1991b). Children of permissive parents are typically immature, often lack impulse control, and show less social responsibility in comparison to children whose parents are not permissive (Baumrind, 1971, 1973, 1991b). Children of uninvolved parents also tend to suffer socially (Patterson, Debaryshe, & Ramsey, 1989; Steinberg, 1996). Uninvolved parents demonstrate low levels of affection toward their children, and some uninvolved parents also display high levels of criticism and hostility toward their children. When parents show little affection for their children while being critical and hostile toward them, they contribute to the likelihood that their children will develop aggressive behaviors and have social problems. As early as preschool, such a pattern can manifest itself in the form of noncompliance that evolves into a behavior pattern characterized by peer rejection during the school-age years (Jacob, 1997).

Thinking Critically

What do you think the lives are like of children who do not experience sufficient affection from parents and whose parents are also critical and hostile toward them? Why do you think those children are at greater risk for being rejected by their peers?

The Influence of the Neighborhood on the Social Relationships of School-Age Children

Parents directly influence their school-age children's peer relationships by the parenting styles they adopt, and they indirectly influence those relationships by the neighborhoods in which they and their children live. In their study of the impact of neighborhoods on school-age children's aggression and peer relations, Kupersmidt, Griesler, DeRosier, Patterson, and Davis (1995) found support for the idea that the neighborhood is associated with childhood aggression and peer relations over and above family characteristics. According to those researchers, children's social development is particularly at risk in low socioeconomic status (SES) neighborhoods due to two primary reasons. In those communities, parental supervision often is lacking and children are likely to be exposed to peers who are involved in deviant behavior.

Unsupervised wandering, a typical outcome of low supervision, was associated with delinquent behavior in the Kupersmidt et al. (1995) study. A further finding of the study was that boys living in low-SES neighborhoods were more vulnerable to recruitment into antisocial gangs than were children living in mid-SES neighborhoods. Even when parental supervision and monitoring of children's activities are present in those communities, children have fewer opportunities to make friends due to more restrictive parental behavior based on efforts to ensure their children's safety. Consequently, the dilemma for children who are growing up in unsafe neighborhoods is that either (a) they do not receive the level of parental monitoring required to help them resist the negative influences of deviant peer groups, or (b) their parents' highly restrictive efforts to ensure their safety results in fewer opportunities to make and sustain friendships (Kupersmidt et al., 1995).

Thinking Critically

Many parents choose the neighborhoods in which they will live with their children based on whether or not those neighborhoods are safe places for children, whether there are neighborhood parks, what the schools are like, etc. Yet many parents are bringing up their children in unsafe neighborhoods. What societal factors, do you suppose, are associated with parents rearing their children in unsafe neighborhoods?

Providing Opportunities for Children's Peer Group Interactions

One of the ways that parents of school-age children provide opportunities for their children to make and sustain positive peer relationships is when they support their children's involvement in organized, adult-supervised, out-of-home activities. Those activities reflect parental involvement and monitoring, both of which are linked to more positive peer relations and fewer behavior problems among children (Jacob, 1997). For children in the United States, organized activities typically fall into the following categories: sports (soccer, football, baseball, etc.), music, band, dance lessons, drama, and crafts, Scouts, church activities, and recreational camps. Those activities assist children in achieving peer group status while broadening their scope of learning. Furthermore, being involved in positive peer group organizations extends children's peer group interactions beyond the classroom, exposes them to a variety of cultural backgrounds, and provides them with opportunities to interact with other children who share their interests (Elkind, 2003). Of the many possible activities that parents might choose for their children, youth sports has become a significant venue for parental socialization of school-age children. Through their involvement in sports, children experience parental satisfaction with and encouragement of their performance. Furthermore, parental involvement with their children is expressed in parents' commitment to and enduring involvement in the sports programs in which children are players (Green & Chalip, 1997).

The Overbooked Child.   Over the past 20 years, American children have been spending more time in supervised and structured settings. The findings of a 1998 longitudinal study demonstrated that children in the United States are leading far more organized and tightly sequenced lives. Although being involved in organized activities has many benefits for children, parents should be careful not to overbook their children's time. With their time carefully allocated to such activities as sports, school-age children have less time for unstructured play or for family activities (Fishman, 1999). In a recent article, Elkind (2003) expressed concern regarding the overscheduling of children's lives and emphasized the need for children to have a balanced childhood in which they go to school, do a little homework, and play fort or other childhood games after school. To illustrate the difficulties faced by children whose lives are highly organized, Elkind tells the story of 9-year-old Kevin who was anxious, having trouble sleeping, and complaining that he was tired all the time. When the mother was asked about her son's schedule, it was discovered that she had enrolled the child in "a dizzying number of extracurricular activities." In addition to school, Kevin had piano lessons twice a week and was involved in three team sports, church activities, and Scouts. In separate discussions with Kevin and his mother, Elkind discovered that Kevin, who was on the brink of depression, was not having a happy childhood as suggested by comments that he missed playing with his friends in the neighborhood. Kevin said that he missed the following activities that he used to do with friends: riding bikes, having water balloon fights, and building forts out of cardboard boxes.

According to Elkind, Kevin is not unusual; millions of school-age children across the United States feel overwhelmed and pressured. Elkind's concerns are echoed by Rosenfield and Wise (2000), who suggest that parents of school-age children avoid the "hyperparenting trap" of overscheduling their children. Rosenfield and Wise suggest that overscheduling of children's time is not only a widespread phenomenon but is how Americans parent today. Parents who overschedule their children's lives seem to feel remiss that they are not being good parents if their children are not in all kinds of activities, and children whose lives are overscheduled are under pressure to demonstrate success in many areas. Elkind stresses that children who are pressured to achieve to the extent that they are involved in too many activities miss out on important childhood experiences. Childhood experiences that overscheduled children miss out on are (a) time to play in a natural and creative way, (b) time to participate in family relationships, and (c) time to pursue self-awareness.

According to Rosenfield and Wise, time for unstructured play allows children to follow their interests, express their personalities, and learn ways in which to structure their own time. Furthermore, play is a natural mode of learning for children. When there is little or no time for play due to parental organization of children's activities, there is little time left for just being children. Besides time for natural, creative play, children benefit from downtime with parents and other family members, to relax, talk, read, play games, and just hang out. Unfortunately, families who are running from one activity to the next have little time for those family experiences.

Finally, to gain self-awareness, children need time to read, write, build, create, fantasize, and pursue special interests.

What This Means for Parents and Professionals Working With Parents.   First, it is important to remember that extracurricular activities per se are not the problem. Children who participate in such activities reap important rewards. Involvement in sports, for example, has been shown to be related to elevated self-confidence, higher levels of academic performance, more involvement with school, fewer behavior problems, less likelihood of taking drugs, and decreased probability of engaging in risky behavior (Elkind, 2003). Even though the provision of out-of-home organized activities is potentially advantageous to their children, parents need to avoid the "more is better" trap or the "my child is busier than your child" syndrome. Some parents overenroll their children in classes, leaving their children with less time for unstructured play with their friends, less time for meaningful family interactions, and less time to simply relax and do little or nothing.

Hamner and Turner (2001) provide several excellent guidelines for assisting parents in choosing out-of-home activities for their school-age children. They suggest that parents select activities for their children judiciously, being careful to not overcommit children's time. They also recommend that parents help children select activities in which they can be successful by (a) examining alternatives carefully, (b) considering the time commitment and competitive aspects of those activities as well as the characteristics of participating adults and children, and (c) assessing the child's interest in the activity and the fit between the activity and the child's developmental level. In addition to parental involvement in selection of activities for their children, Hamner and Turner recommend that parents provide encouragement and guidance as children select their own activities.

Besides supporting their children's involvement in organized out-of-home group activities, it is important that parents encourage leisurely group activities that promote their children's friendships such as skating parties and hiking trips. When promoting leisure activities for their children and their children's friends, parents need to carefully monitor and supervise those activities because higher rates of problem behaviors such as delinquency and the use of drugs and alcohol are associated with the lack of parental monitoring of their children's leisure activities (Cairns, Leung, Buchanan, & Cairns, 1995).

Thinking Critically

Consider the friendships of your school-age siblings or other school-age children that you know. Based on the previous discussion, see if you can identify the various ways in which their parents or guardians are involved in promoting those friendships.

Victims and Bullies.   We will now address a serious problem seen in school-age children's peer relations—the presence of bullies and victims in the neighborhood and in the school. **Bullying** was once considered to be a normal part of school-age children's play, an unpleasant experience, certainly, but of little long-range consequence. After having looked at the situation more closely, however, researchers now realize that bullying is a considerable problem for school-age children, harming both the bullies and the victims. Bullying is defined as repeated, systematic efforts to inflict harm through physical, verbal, or social attack. Bullying through physical attack includes behaviors such as hitting, punching, pinching, or kicking. Verbal bullying consists of threatening, teasing, taunting, or name-calling, and bullying in the form of social attack includes deliberate social exclusion or public mocking (Garrity & Baris, 1996).

There are gender differences in the type of bullying behavior engaged in by children as well as gender differences in the characteristics of the children who are likely to be the targets of bullies. Boys who bully other children tend to use force or the threat of force. Girls who bully other children often mock or ridicule their victims, making fun of their clothes, behavior, or appearance, or revealing their most embarrassing secrets. In comparison to other children, the victims of bullies tend to be less assertive and physically weaker (especially boys) and are more likely to be timid (especially girls) (Lagerspetz & Bjoerkqvist, 1994). Even though the behaviors of bullies take place in peer groups outside the family, important differences have been found between children who are bullies and children who are not bullies (Stevens, Bourdeaudhuij, & Oost, 2002). By and large, bullies are more likely to have behavior problems (Wolke, Woods, & Bloomfield, 2000), and children with behavior problems are more likely to have parents who are authoritarian, permissive, or indifferent (Baumrind, 1991b). In contrast, children from authoritative families are less likely to have behavior problems, including being bullies (Stevens et al., 2002).

FACTORS RELATED TO CHILDREN'S ABILITY TO COPE WITH SOCIAL PROBLEMS

In addition to difficulties they might encounter in making friends, coping with bullies, and dealing with overscheduled lives, school-age children encounter a number of other challenging circumstances that make their lives somewhat stressful. They have a number of household responsibilities that range from doing homework and daily chores to taking care of younger siblings and helping out with farmwork. They worry about such things as making and keeping friends, earning good grades, and getting on the team. The stresses and hassles of middle childhood are so common that all school-age children experience some level of anxiety, although many children appear to be "stress resistant" or even "resilient." The resilience of children to the stresses and hassles of middle childhood are associated with (a) children's problem-solving abilities (Compas, Banez, Malcarne, & Worsham, 1991), (b) their parents' childrearing practices (Wyman et al., 1999), and (c) the level of other social support they receive (Borland, Laybourn, Hill, & Brown, 1998; Garmezy, 1993).

Children's Problem-Solving Abilities

The advance of cognitive abilities that render school-age children logical thinkers provides the foundation for them to develop the necessary coping strategies to be able to deal with the stresses associated with middle childhood. Good coping skills help children to disguise their hurt feelings at times that they determine to be inappropriate for the expression of those feelings, to keep a bully at bay, to repair a broken friendship, and (when necessary) to make new friends to replace old ones (Compas et al., 1991).

Parental Contributions to Children's Problem-Solving Abilities.   There is an important link between children's adaptive functioning and their family transactional processes. Children with lower levels of social competence and more behavioral problems are likely to have parents who show negative affect during family problem solving. On the other hand, when parents are warm and supportive of their children during family problem solving, children develop more effective problem-solving skills (Hamilton, Asarnov, & Tompson, 1997).

PROMOTION OF SCHOOL-AGE CHILDREN'S PHYSICAL DEVELOPMENT

Now that we have considered the influence of parents on school-age children's social–emotional development, we will turn our attention to the ways in which parents contribute to the physical growth and development of their school-age children. As will become apparent in the upcoming discussion, during middle childhood, children are undergoing various physical changes, improving their bodily control, and refining their gross and fine motor skills. During that developmental stage, parents play a crucial role in keeping their children healthy and safe while promoting their children's involvement in activities necessary for optimal physical development. As we shall see, parents promote their school children's physical development when they (a) provide adequate nutrition for their children, (b) promote their children's motor skills through involvement of their children in physical activities, and (c) meet their children's safety needs. As will be revealed, children's physical growth and development are affected by the availability of food, their families' food habits, the degree to which children are engaged in daily physical activity, and the amount of television children watch.

The Importance of Meeting School-Age Children's Nutritional Needs

The level of nutrition received by school-age children affects their ongoing growth, height, weight, motor skill development, and social and emotional functioning. In more affluent countries, such as the United States, Canada, and Australia, heredity is the primary source of variation in children's height because most children in those countries get sufficient nutritious food to grow as tall as their genes permit (Troiano, Briefel, Carroll, & Bialostosky, 2000). In many countries of the world, however, most variation in children's height and weight is due to differences in the availability of nutritious food. In places such as Nairobi, Rio de Janeiro, or New Delhi, for example, school-age children from wealthier families are generally several inches taller than their classmates from impoverished families (Eveleth & Tanner, 1991). For school-age children who receive adequate nutrition, their growth and physical development give them the strength and agility to participate in games, sports, and a number of other physical activities (Parizkova, 1989, 1998).

The importance of children's involvement in games and sports that allow them to run, jump, throw, catch, climb, swim, tumble, and so on, is that those playful adventures promote the development of many motor skills. Although children who receive adequate nutrition are often less active than is desired due to environmental circumstances, numerous studies have demonstrated that malnourished children engage less in physical activity due to lack of available energy (e.g., Parizkova, 1989, 1998). In addition to the toll that malnutrition takes on school-age children's growth and motor skill development, considerable research indicates that the level of nutrition that children receive affects their social and emotional development. For example, Barrett and Frank (1987) found that, among Guatemalan children, those who received more nutrition were more self-confident, more alert, more socially involved with peers, showed less anxiety, and exhibited more positive emotional affect in comparison to children who received less adequate nutrition.

The Growing Problem of Childhood Obesity in the United States

Although children in poorer nations often suffer from malnutrition, children in the United States are likely to experience obesity. Between 20 and 30% of American children are obese, a rate that has doubled in the past 3 decades. It is now recognized that obesity is as much a risk factor as malnutrition and can lead to cognitive, physical, and social difficulties (Brown & Pollitt, 1996; McDonald, Sigman,

Unfortunately, many school-age children in the United States watch countless hours of television rather than being involved in physical activities.

Espinosa, & Neumann, 1994). Furthermore, children who are obese are especially vulnerable to orthopedic and respiratory problems. Although particular inherited genes might predispose certain children to be overweight, changes in population genetics occur slowly over generations (Dietz, 1999). Because childhood obesity is not common in other countries but has risen sharply in the past several decades in the United States, it is clear that social rather than genetic factors are associated with the rise in numbers of children affected by obesity in the United States.

The Link Between Childhood Obesity and Insufficient Physical Exercise.   A main contributor to childhood obesity is simply insufficient exercise. It is normal and natural for school-age children to expend large quantities of energy each day running about; however, many children today do not have that opportunity. In contrast to the past, countless schools today do not have recess and gymnastics classes during the school-age years (Armstrong & Welsman, 1997). Furthermore, many children who are not physically active during the school day have limited opportunities for physical activities after school as well. To be active after school, children need to have safe places to play and parents or other responsible adults to monitor their activities. Due to safety concerns of working parents, children who live in unsafe neighborhoods are frequently instructed by their parents to remain indoors after school (Garbarino, Kostelny, & Barry, 1997).

In demonstrating the link between childhood obesity and low levels of physical activity, Steinbeck (2001) emphasizes that excess fat is the result of an imbalance of energy intake (food) and energy output (physical activity). Steinbeck points to evidence that physical activity for the entire population of the United States is declining, and that declining physical activity is a major factor in the increasing prevalence of obesity among American children. One of the factors Steinbeck associated with declining physical activities among children is that many childhood leisure activities, including television viewing, contribute to children's lives becoming less active and more sedentary. Furthermore, the time that children might spend being engaged in physical activities is sometimes limited by safety concerns, lack of suitable environments, and a shortage of time spent with family. As noted by Steinbeck, even though providing healthy food for children remains important, parental goals of preventing the obesity of their children must focus as well on their children's need for physical exercise.

For school-age children who are already obese, Steinbeck recommends that parents increase their children's physical exercise to allow them to grow into their weight. Steinbeck emphasized that the parental goal of promoting children's involvement in physical activities must include considerations of space, access, and appropriate types of play for school-age children. Another emphasis of Steinbeck is the need for parents to understand that children model their behaviors on parental behaviors. Accordingly, the family activity model is an important one just as are the family's food beliefs and eating patterns. Thus, any proposed changes in physical activity for school-age children must take into account those three components.

Childhood Obesity and Television Viewing.   Closely associated with school-age children's declining participation in physical activity is the increase in the time they spend watching television. As noted by Steinbeck (2001), the increase of time children spend in leisure activities is a prime contributor to the increase in childhood obesity. There are three ways in which researchers have linked television watching and childhood obesity. First, the more children participate in sedentary leisure activities, such as watching television, the less they are engaged in physical activities (Steinbeck, 2001). Second, watching television lowers children's rates of metabolism. Klesges (1993) found that television watching lowers an individual's metabolism below its normal at-rest state, an average of 12% lower in children of normal weight and 16% lower in obese children. Third, researchers have consistently found that children eat more while watching television (Gortmaker et al., 1996).

Do Children Who Are Obese Eat Too Much?   A common belief regarding overweight adults and children is that those individuals eat too much. Based on that belief, reducing food intake by dieting is a popular approach to losing weight for adults. Even for adults, reducing calories without increasing exercise is likely to be a temporary solution to weight control. For children, that approach to preventing obesity or to helping obese children reach an appropriate height–weight ratio is not recommended due to the growing child's need for adequate nutrition. Although it appears that obese children are eating more than children who are not obese, the evidence from studies of children's eating habits does not support that belief. Using longitudinal data from the national health and nutritional surveys in the United States, Troiano et al. (2000) examined the trends in energy and fat intakes of youths between the ages of 2 and 19 from the years between 1988 and 1994. The findings from that study showed that despite an increase in the prevalence of overweight among children, there was a lack of evidence to support a general increase in food intake.

Although there were no significant differences in overall food intake between children who were obese and those who were not, there was a difference found between those two groups in the consumption of nonnutritive sources of energy. For overweight children, higher consumption of nonnutritious sources of energy in the form of soft drinks means that a higher percentage of their energy source is derived from nonnutritious sources. Based on that evidence, although the intake of food was comparable for obese and nonobese children, obese children's diets were less nutritious due to their greater reliance on soft drinks as a source of energy. The conclusion reached by Troiano and colleagues (2000) was that increasing physical exercise and limiting the consumption of soft drinks are effective approaches that parents might take to counter the rise in overweight prevalence of their children.

What This Means for Parents and Professionals Working With Parents.   To prevent obesity in their children and to respond to the needs of their children who are already overweight, there are several things that parents might do. First, parents need to understand that too much time spent watching television puts their school-age children at risk for the development of obesity. To offset that risk, parents should monitor the amount of time spent watching television and should be certain that their children are engaged in physical activities. In addition to providing opportunities for their children to be engaged in enjoyable physical exercise and limiting their children's television viewing, parents should be certain that the food their children consume is nutritious and that children are not deriving much of their energy from the consumption of nonnutritive beverages.

Thinking Critically

How do you feel about the finding that more American children are becoming obese while children in many other countries lack sufficient nutrition to reach their maximum growth? In what ways are malnourishment of some children and obesity of others related to those children's involvement in physical exercise?

PROMOTING THE MOTOR SKILLS OF SCHOOL-AGE CHILDREN

Children enter middle childhood having learned how to take care of their own self-care needs, and as their physical strength and coordination continues to develop they become competent in a variety of physical skills promoted by their particular cultures.

Fine Motor Skill Development

School-age children show continuous advancements in fine motor skills based on the materials and instruction provided by their cultures. Most children in the world become proficient in writing and drawing during middle childhood. Children in many cultures become skilled as well at other fine motor skills, such as weaving and pottery making. Children's fine motor skills reach adult levels by the end of middle childhood due to the ongoing process of myelination that allows children to have increasing neurological control over their motor functions and sensory abilities (Rice, 1997).

Gross Motor Skill Development

Although fine motor skill development reaches adult levels by the end of middle childhood, gross motor skill development does not reach adult levels until the end of adolescence because adult-level motor skills are dependent on strength, endurance, and reaction time that continue to develop across adolescence. Nevertheless, school-age children are able to master practically any gross motor skill so long as it does not require too much strength and/or fast judgments of speed and distance (Berger, 2001). School-age children in many countries of the world learn to ride bikes, in-line skate, ice skate, skate board, dive, swim, water ski, snow ski, snow sled, climb trees, jump rope, perform in gymnastics, and participate in a variety of other sports (e.g., soccer, baseball, football, hockey) and numerous other activities.

Many school-age children within and outside the United States develop gross motor skills as they learn to ride horses, herd cattle, and participate in a number of physical activities associated with rural life.

Children in rural farm settings learn to feed and herd livestock and many school-age children learn to hunt and fish. The kinds of skills taught to children during middle childhood vary cross-culturally. For example, most parents in the majority cultures of the United States and Canada do not expect their children to master the ability to ride horses, although some parents provide their children with that opportunity. In contrast, being able to ride horses is a skill that is expected to be cultivated during middle childhood for many Navajo American children (Armstrong & Welsman, 1997).

Influences of Gender and Genetics on Gross and Fine Motor Skill Development. In addition to the influence of culture on the development of motor skills during the school years, there are influences that are related to gender and genetics. Girls are ahead of boys in fine motor skill development (the skills required for writing and drawing), and boys are ahead of girls in gross motor skill development (the skills needed for running, catching, and throwing). It is important, however, not to exaggerate the motor skill differences between school-age boys and girls. Boys and girls are roughly equal in their physical abilities during that stage of development but boys tend to have better upper arm strength and girls are more likely to have greater overall flexibility. Consequently, boys have a slight edge in sports such as baseball, and girls have a small advantage in sports such as gymnastics. Nevertheless, for most physical activities during middle childhood, gender differences in motor skill abilities are minimal. Boys can do cartwheels; girls can hit home runs; and both girls and boys make tremendous strides in the development of writing and drawing (Armstrong & Welsman, 1997).

Influences of Motivation, Guidance, and Practice on Motor Skill Development. Expertise in many areas of motor skill development depends not so much on gender as on the following three factors: motivation, guidance, and many hours of practice. Those three factors are seldom equal, though, for both genders in any particular area. For instance, boys are more likely than are girls to be provided more opportunities and greater social support for playing sports, and girls are more likely than are boys to be encouraged to take dance lessons. National policy also affects the development of motor skills. An illustration of the effect of national policy on the development of children's motor skills is the way in which Japan values and supports physical activity for children. Japan requires physical activity for all school-age children; most Japanese schools are well equipped with gyms and fields; and 75% of those schools have swimming pools. In contrast, children in the United States get only about 1.5 hours a week of physical activity; and children in England or Ireland get only 1 hour a week of physical activity (Armstrong & Welsman, 1997).

Not only are opportunities for physical activity in schools limited for many children but many sports that North American adults value demand exactly those skills that are the most difficult for school-age children to attain. Softball and baseball, for example, are hard for school-age children to master because throwing, catching, and batting all require better distance judgment, more hand–eye coordination, and shorter reaction time than many school-age children have. The maxim, "Practice makes perfect," does not always hold true. For some skills, practice does lead to mastery; others require a certain body size, brain maturation, and/or inherited ability. Common experiences for younger school-age children who are attempting to play baseball include: (a) dropping the ball (even if it lands in their mitts) because they are slow to grasp the ball once it lands, and striking out because school-age children typically swing too late to hit a pitched ball. Furthermore, no matter how much they try, some children (due to hereditary differences) are unable to throw or pitch a baseball, or kick a football, with as much strength and accuracy as other children (Berger, 2001).

What This Means for Parents and Professionals Working With Parents. It is important for parents, teachers, and other adults to be certain that all children, of both genders, with all levels of ability, are included in play activities—whether those activities are part of a school curriculum or part of a group of neighborhood children playing together (Armstrong & Welsman, 1997). Parents should remember, however, that the skills necessary for playing organized sports (such as baseball, football, or soccer) are difficult for school-age children to master. On the other hand, parents might keep in mind that many games requiring movement (such as *tag, hopscotch*, and *hide-and-go-seek)* match the skills that school-age children have, assist in the further development of those skills, and allow children to have a lot of fun in the process. In

While it is important for parents to promote their school-age children's involvement in physical activities, safety precautions should be taken to prevent serious accidents.

addition to promoting children's participation in organized sports in the school and informal play in the neighborhood, parents might involve their older children in programs offered in the community that provide further development of gross motor skills, such as dance lessons or gymnastics. Finally, school-age children benefit from interactive play within the family. Many of the games that children play with their friends are fun to play with family members as well. Furthermore, parents have the opportunity to plan family activities that maximize the possibility of movement, such as touch football, hiking, swimming, and treasure hunts.

KEEPING SCHOOL-AGE CHILDREN SAFE

School-age children both enjoy and need to participate in many physical activities that require speed, a great deal of movement, and many other factors that potentially place the child at risk for incurring injury. Although children need to be involved in a variety of physical activities, it is important to ensure children's safety as they engage in those activities. Children will undoubtedly suffer minor injuries that are virtually impossible to prevent and still remain actively involved in play. On the other hand, many children are seriously injured or die as a result of injuries that could have been avoided. Worldwide, despite several decades of concerted efforts, unintentional injuries remain a significant health problem for children. Among school-age children, traffic accidents as well as accidents at playgrounds and at sports facilities cause the most serious injuries. With the goals of preventing serious injury to children and demonstrating that child safety is an attainable goal, Timpka and Lindqvist (2001) set up the Safe Community Model, designed by the World Health Organization (WHO), in a target community.

The purpose of the implementation of the Safe Community Model was to determine if the residents of a community could work together to decrease the incidents of serious injury to children. A follow-up assessment of the effectiveness of the program showed that total child injuries in the intervention community decreased significantly more than did total child injuries in a control community using the national level injury prevention program. The effectiveness of the WHO intervention model was credited to a shift from focusing on individual responsibility to ensuring that the entire community was involved in safety promotion. The results of the study by Timpka and Lindquist (2001) demonstrate that coordinated efforts by parents, children, and a concerned community can reduce serious injury and possible deaths of children.

The Steps Involved in the WHO Safe Community Model

The first step in the WHO Safe Community Model was to be certain that all parents received information about risk factors for child injuries. Thereafter, both structural and educational measures were put into place with the goal of improving child safety. A program called "A safe way to school" was implemented at every primary school. That program included a "Cut your garden hedge" initiative to increase driveway visibility for child pedestrians and child bikers. Additionally, voluntary organizations and the police provided traffic safety education programs in the schools. A 1-hour traffic lesson was scheduled each week for all fourth graders. A safe cycling program also was initiated to subsidize the price of bike helmets and to promote helmet usage. As a part of the safe cycling program, children were offered courses to "shape up their bikes" to reduce risks of equipment failure.

What This Means for Parents and Professionals Working With Parents.   The foregoing discussion is vitally important for parents of active school-age children. Parents everywhere want their children to be able to enjoy playful activities but want them to remain safe while doing so. The effectiveness of the WHO Model of Prevention points out the value of open discussion of safety with children and their parents. At the family level, parents might emphasize the guidelines outlined in that model for their own children. For example, parents might walk the route with their children to their schools to determine if there are obstacles to seeing driveways, such as overgrown bushes. If parents should discover such visual obstructions, they might voice their concerns to the owners. If parents are unable to get obstacles such as bushes removed, they might map out a safer route for their children to walk or bike. Finally, the outcomes of the WHO program suggest that parents, teachers, coaches, police persons, and other adults should let children know they are concerned about their safety and outline for them ways in which they can engage in various activities, such as playing, skating, cycling, and climbing, without encountering injury.

There are numerous ways in which parents can promote their children's cognitive development, including providing them opportunities to become adept at computer usage.

Thinking Critically

You might not have considered that safety awareness and advocacy for child safety within the community are a part of the responsibilities of parents. Why do you suppose that parents might be the ideal persons to become involved in community action to make children's play spaces safer?

PROMOTING THE COGNITIVE DEVELOPMENT OF SCHOOL-AGE CHILDREN

Now that we have examined the ways in which parents impact the social–emotional and physical development of their school-age children, we will turn our attention to the role of parents in promoting the cognitive development of their school-age children. Although parents, teachers, and researchers have tended to underestimate the cognitive capability of infants, toddlers, and young children, that is not the case with school-age children whose cognitive skills are constantly on display. Parents and other adults are consistently impressed with school-age children's ability to learn rapidly at home and at school. Their computer skills tend to progress more rapidly than do those of adults. They recognize out-of-towners simply by the clothes they are wearing. They know the brand names and desirable features of popular items such as skateboards; and they repeat the rapid-fire lyrics of a rap song—accomplishment beyond many people twice their age (Berger, 2001). In the upcoming discussion, we will examine the cognitive changes underlying the school-age child's impressive cognitive abilities and consider ways in which parents might maximize their school-age children's cognitive potential.

Development of School-Age Children's Ability to Use Logical Reasoning: A Piagetian Perspective

In comparison to preschoolers, who make judgments based on intuitive thinking and are easily fooled by appearances, school-age children are logical thinkers. The **logical thinking** of school-age children emerges as egocentrism decreases, allowing children to decenter their attention. As children develop the ability to decenter their attention, they are able to take into account multiple aspects of a situation, which greatly enhances their problem-solving ability. One advantage of school-age children's ability to decenter their attention is that they are able to focus on present, past, and future events. They are, therefore, capable of planning ahead and considering how current efforts relate to future accomplishments (Piaget & Inhelder, 1969).

A main advance in school-age children's thinking involves the **ability to conserve** volume and mass that comes about as they develop the concepts of **compensation** and **reversibility**. For example, whereas preschoolers think a tall, narrow glass contains more juice than does a short, squat glass, school-age children understand that both glasses contain the same amount of juice because the wideness of the short glass compensates for the tallness of the other glass. Furthermore, unlike preschoolers who do not understand the concept of reversibility, school-age children realize that one could pour the juice from the short glass to the taller glass (reversal of the operation) and it would still be the same amount of juice. Another aspect of school-age children's reasoning ability is the emergence of the ability to classify. Being able to classify allows children to apply order to their world by correctly recognizing and assigning categories to objects in their environment. School-age children's development of the ability to classify is demonstrated in their heightened interest in having collections of objects from baseball cards to seashells (Gelman & Baillargeon, 1983).

What This Means for Parents and Professionals Working With Parents.   The logical thinking abilities of school-age children means that parents no longer have to be concerned that their children will feel short-changed if their juice or lemonade is in a shorter, but wider, glass than that of other children. Another advantage is that parents are able to feel freer to use more complex speech with them because school-age children are able to understand metaphors, realize that some words have multiple meanings, and comprehend reverse-order sentences. Capitalizing on their children's developing ability to decenter their concentration, parents can point out to their children the ways in which their behaviors affect others, thereby promoting their development of empathy. For example, parents could say to their first-graders that when they share with other children those other children are pleased and are more likely to share with them. Parents might assist their school-age children in the development of their ability to classify by supporting their interests in collections of various objects and by making recommendations for categorization, ordering, and collecting that their children might not have considered. Parents can promote their children's ability to consider past, present, and future events by providing them with calendars and watches. By encouraging school-age children to use their watches to monitor events in their daily lives and assisting them in the use of their calendars to keep up with and plan for future events, parents offer their children the experiences they require for continued development of their ability to decenter their attention.

Thinking Critically

Try to recall the ways that you as a school-age child expressed your ability to classify by collecting certain objects. What were the ways in which your parents, or other significant adults in your life, supported your interest in having a collection?

The Views of Vygotsky Regarding the Parental Influence of School-Age Children's Cognitive Development

As explained in chapter 3, Vygotsky recognized the role of parents and other members of children's culture in shaping children's cognitive development. In that chapter, we contemplated the ways in which children's learning is extended by parents and other more capable individuals through the process of guided participation. As a reminder, Vygotsky pointed out that, with the assistance of parents, teachers, and older more capable individuals, children often demonstrate higher level, problem-solving abilities. Drawing on Vygotsky's perspective, Wood, Bruner, and Ross (1976) introduced the concept of **scaffolding** to describe the supportive strategies parents use to guide their children in solving cognitive tasks. According to Kermani and Brenner (2000), through the process of scaffolding, parents, caregivers, or teachers lead children toward greater understanding of the task at hand while assisting children in the development of their own conceptions of the task. Successful scaffolding, therefore, requires the establishment of **intersubjectivity** or a shared understanding of the task.

What This Means for Parents and Professionals Working With Parents.   We will now consider two examples of ways in which parents might scaffold the cognitive development of their school-age children.

> *Example 1:* Suppose a child attempts to solve a jigsaw puzzle, gets discouraged and stops trying. Although it appears at first glance as if the task is beyond the child's ability to accomplish, that is not necessarily the case. The challenge might actually be within that child's zone of proximal development, meaning that the child might be successful in putting the puzzle together if the parent provides guided participation to facilitate the child's learning experience. Guided participation might include: (a) remarks designed to motivate the child to solve the problem, "Oh, I think you can do it; let me help you;" (b) assisting the child in focusing attention on the important steps, "First, we have to study the picture,

then try to match the puzzle pieces to the picture;" (c) providing instruction, "Sometimes, we need to rotate the pieces to get them to fit into a certain space;" and (d) encouraging the child's interest and motivation, "See, you're making progress. I thought you could do it."

Example 2: A classic example of the use of guided participation can be observed in the assistance parents typically provide to a child who is attempting to learn to ride a bicycle. Children who are physically mature enough to learn to ride a bicycle will learn through independent attempts if they continue trying, but will learn more quickly with parental scaffolding. In the first step of that process, the parent determines (based on the child's age, interest, and level of physical ability) that the task is within the child's zone of proximal development. Next, the parent explains that the child will need to go slowly at first, because it takes practice to learn to balance oneself on a bike and ride at the same time. Then, the parent holds the bike up as the child makes the initial attempts to balance the bicycle and pedal forward. Throughout the entire process, the parent talks the child through initial feelings of trepidation and expresses confidence in the child's ability to become a bicyclist. Emphasizing process rather than outcome, encouraging the child's ability and effort, and focusing on the child's feelings are all aspects of guided participation.

Cognitive Limitations of School-Age Children

Respecting the limitations of school-age children's ability to reason is as important as understanding their cognitive potential. The primary limitation of children's thoughts during middle childhood is that they remain tied to a concrete, physical reality, which means that school-age children are unable to think hypothetically or abstractly. The focus on a concrete, physical reality prevents school-age children from being able to consider abstract notions or possibilities that are not tied to their experienced reality (Elkind, 1976). Their inability to think abstractly might be observed in school-age children's insistence on sticking to the rules in various aspects of their lives. Thus, school-age children are not trendsetters; instead, they tend to wear a similar style of dress and have the same kinds of haircuts. Their insistence on following the rules is most evident in the way they play an organized game, whether it is baseball or monopoly. Anyone who does not follow the rules of the game or suggests that the rules might be altered will be told firmly by the school-age child that, "That is not the rule!"

Thinking Critically

If you know a school-age child, try to think of the various situations in which someone has suggested another way of playing a game or doing a particular activity that has resulted in the school-age child insisting on "playing by the rules."

What This Means for Parents and Professionals Working With Parents.   The best way for parents to respond to their school-age children's inability to understand abstract notions (such as changing the rules of the game) is to be patient with them and to realize that children at that age are busily learning to order their worlds, to plan ahead, and to understand the rules and norms that govern certain activities. They will venture out into a consideration of other possible ways of dressing, problem solving, and questioning of the status quo when they develop abstract reasoning ability during adolescence.

The Ways in Which Parents Promote the Language Development of Their School-Age Children

The language of school-age children is highly expressive; they enjoy words and often play at language. Their enjoyment of language is illustrated in their writing of poems and in their creation of secret codes (Anglin, 1993). Taking pleasure in the use of language is also exemplified in school-age children's ability to understand and tell jokes, which verifies their emergence from the strictly literal perspective of preschool. Joke telling actually demands several skills not apparent in younger children: (a) the ability to listen carefully, (b) the ability to know what someone else will think is funny, (c) and, hardest of all, the ability to remember the right way to tell a joke. Vocabulary also is a key ingredient in the ability to understand and tell jokes, and puns are a mainstay of school-age humor. Furthermore, the telling and understanding of jokes reflects several aspects of their ongoing cognitive development, including the ability to understand and use metaphors as well as the realization that certain words have multiple meanings (Berger, 2001).

An example of a classic school-age child's joke, as told to a parent, is illustrated in the following parent–child exchange: Child: "Knock, knock," Parent: "Who's there?" Child: "Knock, knock," Parent: "Who's there?" Child: "Knock, knock," Parent: "Who's there?" Child: "Orange," Parent: "Orange Who?" Child (delightedly): "Orange you glad I didn't say 'knock, knock'?" The child in that example realizes that the words *orange you* sound like the words *aren't you.* Another typical joke of school-age children is as follows: Child: "Why did the elephant stand on the marshmallow?" Parent: "I don't know, why?" Child: "So he wouldn't fall into the hot chocolate." Even though the elephant joke does not contain a metaphor or a word with multiple meanings, it demonstrates the ability of the school-age child to move beyond a literal interpretation of things.

What This Means for Parents and Professionals Working With Parents.   The vocabulary increase of middle childhood does not represent the "language explosion" seen during preschool. Instead, school-age children become more analytical and logical in their comprehension of vocabulary. They, therefore, are able to benefit from explicit instruction from parents and other adults (Anglin, 1993). Besides providing instruction for their children, parents have many opportunities to become the audience for their children who have taken on the role of comedian. The recommendation for parents, regarding their children's telling of the many "knock, knock" jokes and elephant jokes, is to be patient with their emerging comedians (even when the jokes are silly and parents have, undoubtedly, heard them countless times). First of all, one should never underestimate the benefits of play in parent–child interactions (whether it comes in the form of joke telling or other playful encounters). Next, parents should be aware that the telling of jokes is an example of children's playing with language because they have now obtained the ability to understand the aspects of language exemplified in joke telling. Finally, as children are learning to tell jokes, they might pick up some inappropriate jokes, such as sexist, racist, or crude jokes. In those cases, the parent should not laugh at those jokes but should take the opportunity to explain to their children that jokes are funny and appropriate only when they do not make fun of or hurt other people.

School-Age Children's Development of the Ability to Use Code-Switching

Another important development in language ability seen in the speech of school-age children is the use of **code-switching,** which parallels their achievement of the ability to decenter their attention. The ability to code-switch is reflected in school-age children's capability of switching from one form of speech to another depending on the context and the audience. An example of school-age children's usage of code-switching is demonstrated by their informal speech with friends, formal speech with teachers, and more intimate speech with family members. By and large, the development of language norms governing school, peer groups, and family inform school-age children as to which type of speech is appropriate in particular settings (Berger, 2001).

What This Means for Parents and Professionals Working With Parents. In the home, parents model language usage and instruct their children as to what constitutes appropriate language to use with other family members. For example, parents whose own language is friendly and respectful toward other family members have children who incorporate that example of language into their more intimate speech. Parents also guide their children in the formal speech they use with teachers and other adults by instructing children on how to address adults, how to request the assistance they require from adults, and so on. Children are further guided by their parents regarding the informal speech they use with their peers. As parents monitor the speech they hear their children use with their peers, they both support and reprimand their children's usage of informal speech, depending on the situation. An example of parental support of children's informal speech with peers is when a parent overhears a child engage in successful problem solving with a peer and shows approval for the way the child handled that verbal exchange. An example of the way in which a parent might reprimand the informal speech of a child is when a child repeats a curse word learned by a peer. In that case, a parent is likely to inform the child that the use of that word is inappropriate and unacceptable.

PROMOTING CHILDREN'S SCHOOL ACHIEVEMENT

Now that we have examined the development of school-age children's logical reasoning and language development, we turn our attention to the role of parents in helping their children to demonstrate their cognitive ability through various measures of school achievement. In attempting to distinguish the factors that promote children's school achievement, researchers have repeatedly demonstrated positive correlations between authoritative parenting and children's school achievement (e.g., Dornbusch et al., 1987; Paulson et al., 1998). As discussed in chapter 2, authoritative parents exhibit demandingness (having high expectations of their children) as well as responsiveness (to their children's feelings and needs).

There are a number of ways in which authoritative parenting enhances children's achievement behavior. For example, positive parental beliefs and attributions emphasizing children's abilities support children's positive self-perceptions. Moreover, a tendency of authoritative parents to provide optimal challenges for their children fosters their children's self-regulation and control beliefs, thereby encouraging independent and active problem solving (Aunola et al., 2000; Ginsburg & Bronstein, 1993). In comparison to children of authoritative parents, children of authoritarian parents (high on demandingness but low on responsiveness) have been found to have lower achievement motivation. Lower achievement motivation has been linked to maladaptive achievement strategies, particularly passive behavior, and a lack of use of self-enhancing attributions (Aunola et al., 2000).

Children's academic success is associated not only with the authoritative parenting style but also with parental values that attribute academic success to ability and lack of academic success to lack of effort. The link between parental attributions of their children's academic success and their children's academic performance was demonstrated by Bempechat, Graham, and Jimenez (1999). Those researchers studied parents' socialization practices reflecting attributions of success and failure and compared those practices to their school-age children's mathematics achievement scores. In their study of African American, Latino American, Indo-Chinese American, and European American fifth and sixth graders from families with low socioeconomic levels, they found that (across all groups) higher levels of attributing success to ability were associated with higher mathematics scores. In contrast, regardless of ethnic group membership, children's lower mathematics scores were associated with stronger beliefs that failure is due to lack of ability.

What This Means for Parents and Professionals Working With Parents.   The foregoing discussion emphasizes how important it is for children to have parents who have effective childrearing approaches and who have confidence in their children's ability to succeed. When parents have ineffective childrearing patterns and/or do not show a belief in their children's abilities, those children do not develop a positive assessment of their abilities and the lack of belief in their abilities shows up in lower academic achievement. On the other hand, those children who have authoritative parents who demonstrate a belief in their children's capacity to achieve come to realize that they are capable of accomplishment, which is reflected in their higher academic success.

❧ SUMMARY

In this chapter, we have examined the lives of school-age children as they are engaged in the ongoing process of developing proficiency in manipulating the tools of their particular culture, becoming more physically capable of playing organized games and sports, and becoming progressively more competent at social interactions with others. We have learned that during middle childhood, children master dozens of new skills that vary according to cultural context. We also discovered that during that stage of development children are able to learn quickly and think logically and that those emerging cognitive abilities are expressed in their language, their greater understanding of other people, their increasing competence, and their school achievement. As was demonstrated, parents play a primary role in determining the positive outcomes of children during that developmental stage. We also considered challenges faced by parents of school-age children, such as the need to ensure their children's safety and to prevent childhood obesity. Difficulties that many school-age children encounter such as malnutrition, childhood obesity, living in unsafe neighborhoods, difficulties in achieving peer acceptance, and dealing with bullies were addressed as well. For each of those problems, suggestions were provided regarding the ways in which parents might meet the needs of their school-age children.

❧ KEY TERMS

- ability to conserve
- bullying
- code-switching
- compensation
- competence
- coregulation

- industry versus inferiority
- intersubjectivity
- logical thinking
- reversibility
- scaffolding

6

Parent–Adolescent Interactions

"My parents and I got along okay during my adolescence. When I was about 12-years-old, my dad sat down with me and told me that I would be going through a lot of changes over the next few years and there would be times that we might not see things eye to eye. He told me not to worry about it, that we would talk things over but mostly we were going to have a good time with it."

—Unpublished quotation from a 20-year-old male

Adolescence is a stage of major developmental changes, which calls for a number of alterations in the parent–adolescent relationship. In this chapter, we will explore the ways in which the developmental changes of adolescents affect their relationships with their parents and the ways in which their relationships with their parents impact adolescents' development. First, we will consider the various parenting styles, presented in chapter 2, as they relate to adolescent development. We then will focus attention on two important aspects of adolescent development: (a) adolescents' attachments to their parents and (b) the role of parents in supporting adolescents' self-esteem and quest for identity. Next, drawing from Family Systems Theory, we will examine the disequilibrium that occurs in the family system as parents and other family members adapt to the developmental changes of adolescents. In the second half of the chapter, we will turn our attention to challenges encountered in parent–adolescent relationships. We will examine parent–adolescent conflict, followed by a presentation of the role of parents in the prevention of adolescent depression. Next, the link between parent–adolescent relationships and adolescent risk behaviors will be discussed.

PARENTAL STYLES AND ADOLESCENT DEVELOPMENT

As earlier noted, the study of parenting styles has been exclusively an American scholarly focus, probably due to the parental role being more isolated from other adult roles in the American culture. As a reminder, the parenting styles identified by Baumrind (1971, 1987) include permissive, authoritative, authoritarian, indifferent, indulgent, and more recently, traditional. Please refer to chapter 2 for a complete description of each of those styles. To distinguish the socialization styles of parents of American adolescents, Lamborn et al. (1991) studied over 4,000 adolescents,

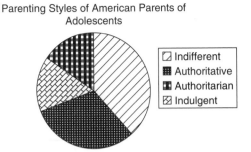

Parenting Styles of American Parents of
Adolescents

Legend:
☐ Indifferent
▦ Authoritative
▉ Authoritarian
☒ Indulgent

FIGURE 6.1

Source: "Patterns of Competence and Adjustment Among Adolescents from Authoritative, Authoritarian, Indulgent, and Neglectful Families," by S. D. Lamborn, N. S. Mounts, L. Steinberg, & S. M. Dornbusch, 1991, *Child Development, 62,* pp. 1049–1065.

aged 14 to 18, from diverse socioeconomic and ethnic backgrounds that included both urban and rural communities. Figure 6.1 shows the results of that study.

As demonstrated in Figure 6.1, the most common pattern of parenting among the parents in the Lamborn et al. study was indifferent (37%), followed closely by the authoritative parenting style (32%). Less commonly seen were the indulgent parenting style (15%), and the authoritarian parenting style (15%). As suggested by Arnett (2001), the high proportion of indifferent parents in the study is striking and might perhaps be understood in light of parent midlife development. In considering that 85% of the parents in the Lamborn et al. (1991) study had authoritative, indulgent, or indifferent parenting styles, we see a clear preference by American parents to socialize their adolescents toward a goal of independence.

THE WAYS IN WHICH PARENTING PATTERNS IMPACT ADOLESCENTS' LIVES

As with other developmental stages, the most favorable outcomes for adolescents (by American standards) have been associated with the authoritative parenting style. Parenting styles other than authoritative have been associated with various negative outcomes for adolescents, depending on the specific parenting style.

Adolescent Children of Authoritative, Permissive, Authoritarian, or Indulgent Parents

Adolescents whose parents have adopted an authoritative approach to parenting tend to be independent, self-assured, creative, and socially skilled, to achieve in school, and to have positive relationships with peers and adults (Baumrind, 1991a, 1991b; Fuligni & Eccles, 1993; Lamborn et al., 1991; Steinberg, 2000). Adolescents whose parents are authoritarian have a tendency to be dependent, passive, conforming, less self-assured, less creative, and less socially skilled than other adolescents. Adolescents who have indulgent parents are more likely than other adolescents to be immature and irresponsible and they tend to conform to their peers. In comparison to adolescents whose parents are authoritative, adolescent children of permissive parents are more immature, less self-reliant, less socially responsible, less independent, and inclined to have lower academic achievement (Baumrind, 1991a, 1991b; Dornbusch, Ritter, Mont-Reynaud, & Chien, 1990; Durbin, Darling, Steinberg, & Brown, 1993; Lamborn et al., 1991; Paulson et al., 1998; Steinberg, 1996, 2000; Steinberg, Fletcher, & Darling, 1994).

When Parents Are Indifferent

Adolescents whose parents are indifferent tend to be impulsive. Because of their greater tendency to act impulsively and their parents' lack of involvement with them, adolescents of indifferent parents have higher rates of behavioral problems than do other adolescents. Delinquency, early sexual involvement, and the use of drugs and alcohol are greater among that group of adolescents (Maccoby & Martin, 1983; Steinberg, 1996). When we examine the associations between parental styles and adolescent development in light of Lamborn et al.'s finding that indifferent parenting is the pattern most commonly used by American parents of adolescents, it raises concerns for the well-being of many American youth.

The Traditional Parenting Style

In the Lamborn et al. study, the authoritative parenting style was found more often in European American than in ethnic minority American families. As discussed in chapter 2, parents in non-Western cultures as well as many parents in ethnic minority cultures within the United States have a style of parenting that has been designated by Baumrind

High levels of parental responsiveness in traditional cultures contributes to close parent-adolescent relationships.

(1987) as traditional. As a reminder, the traditional parenting pattern is high in responsiveness accompanied by a type of demandingness that does not encourage discussion or debate. Similar to the authoritative parenting pattern, the traditional parenting pattern is associated with fewer negative outcomes for children and adolescents than are authoritarian, permissive, indulgent, or involved parenting patterns (Arnett, 2000).

The parenting patterns of Asian American and Latino American parents exemplify the traditional parenting pattern, although the parenting pattern observed in those families has been consistently labeled as authoritarian. Chao (1994) presents a persuasive argument that researchers have misunderstood Asian American parents when they have labeled them as authoritarian. That researcher points out that Asian American adolescents do not exhibit the negative effects typically found to be associated with authoritarian parenting. On the contrary, Asian American adolescents have higher achievement and fewer behavioral and psychological problems than do European American adolescents. That Latino American families have also been inappropriately labeled as authoritarian is evident in the emphasis on **familism**, which is the pillar of Latino culture. Familism, which emphasizes the love, closeness, and mutual obligation of family members, certainly does not fit into the low-responsiveness aspect of authoritarian parenting. Furthermore, the positive effects of familism on Latino American adolescents have been documented (Fuligni et al., 1999; Suarez-Orozco & Suarez-Orozco, 1996).

What This Means for Parents and Professionals Working With Parents.   In light of the overwhelming evidence that authoritative and traditional parenting patterns are associated with positive outcomes for adolescents, it is important for parents to consider what those two parenting patterns have in common. Whereas the goal of the authoritative parenting style is the promotion of *in*dependence and the goal of the traditional parenting style is the promotion of *inter*dependence, both of those parenting patterns combine high parental expectations with high parental support. In the case of the traditional parenting style, the support provided by the parent is further augmented by support from extended family members. Whether parents value independence or interdependence for their adolescent children, the message is clear—adolescents fare better in homes where their parents and/or other caregivers are involved in their daily lives, provide clear guidelines for their behavior, and support them in their attempts to live up to parental and societal expectations.

The Issue of Parental Inconsistency

In examining the effects of parenting styles on adolescents, most researchers have either studied one parent or combined ratings of the two parents into one. That approach does not address the issue, however, of parental inconsistency, which has been related to negative outcomes for adolescents. Adolescents who perceive inconsistency between their parents have been found to be lower on self-esteem (Johnson, Shulman, & Collins, 1991), school performance (Johnson et al., 1991; Juang & Silbereisen, 1999), self-control, and academic motivation (Wentzel & Feldman, 1993). Inconsistent parenting also has been found to be related to adolescents' deviant peer affiliations (Brody et al., 2001), externalizing behaviors (Lindahl & Malik, 1999), delinquency, and depression (Juang & Silbereisen, 1999).

What This Means for Parents and Professionals Working With Parents. The finding that parental inconsistency between parents detrimentally impacts their adolescent children's development does not mean that parents must always agree with the other's views regarding ways to socialize their adolescents. When parents disagree about the socialization of their adolescent children, it is important for them to discuss their points of disagreement. By talking over their dissimilar points of view, they are better prepared to negotiate their differences, rather than presenting their adolescents with conflicting expectations. When adolescents are confronted with differing expectations from their parents, they are placed in a difficult position. They must make the tough decision of either going against the wishes of one of their parents or rejecting the requests of both parents.

Bidirectional Effects of Parents and Children

Adolescents are, undoubtedly, affected by parents but they in turn influence their parents. As discussed in chapter 1, there are reciprocal or bidirectional effects between parents and children (Mussen, Conger, Kagan, & Huston, 1990). Adolescents have personalities of their own that they bring to the parent–adolescent relationship (Scarr, 1992). Accordingly, adolescents with different personality types might induce varying behaviors from their parents. An especially active child might evoke authoritarian parenting and a very shy child might encourage indulgent parenting. Research supports the possibility that parents' socialization approaches are influenced by the characteristics of their children. For example, adolescent siblings within the same family often report that their parents respond differently to them (Daniels, Dunn, Furstenberg, & Plomin, 1985; Hoffman, 1991; Plomin & Daniels, 1987). In the Daniels et al. (1985) study, there were significant differences found in adolescents' perceptions of their parents' love for them, their parents' use of discipline with them, and the degree to which they were involved in family decision making.

Thinking Critically

Perhaps you had not considered that during adolescence you influenced your parents' behavior at the same time that your parents influenced your behavior. In what ways do you think your gender, personality type, or special needs influenced the ways in which your parents interacted with you during your adolescence?

Informal discussions between adolescents and their parents help to prevent many problems and contribute to better resolution of differences that occur.

DEVELOPMENTAL CHANGES AND THE PARENT–ADOLESCENT RELATIONSHIP

Now that we have called attention to the impact of different parenting styles on adolescent development, we will address the ways in which the developmental changes of adolescents alter the parent–child relationship. The parental influence on two important aspects of adolescent development will be addressed in this section: (a) the adolescent's attachment to parents and (b) the adolescent's conception of self which includes self-esteem and the quest for identity.

Adolescents' Attachment to Their Parents

That adolescents are attached to their parents is evident. Adolescents consistently report that their parents are the most important people in their lives and most of them maintain emotional closeness to their parents throughout adolescence. As the adolescent is transforming from child to adult, parents remain a source of love, support, protection, and comfort (Allen & Land, 1999; Steinberg, 1990). Parents are the persons that adolescents say they admire most (Offer & Schonert-Reichl, 1992), the persons that serve as the primary identification models for them (Facio & Batistuta, 1998), and among the people to whom they are most closely attached (Allen & Land, 1999). Furthermore, the core moral values of adolescents are typically attributed to parental influence (Facio & Batistuta, 1998; Offer & Schonert-Reichl, 1992).

Research that has focused on adolescent attachment to parents has provided evidence that secure attachment to parents during adolescence is related to a variety of favorable outcomes, including higher self-esteem, better physical health, and positive social relations (Allen & Kuppermine, 1995; Allen & Land, 1999; Juang & Nguyen, 1997). For instance, adolescents with closer relationships to their parents have been found to have closer relationships to friends and romantic partners (Allen & Bell, 1995; Allen, Hauser, Bell, & O'Connor, 1994). One of the advantages of adolescent attachment to parents is that closeness to parents and confidence in their parents' love predicts a healthy sense of autonomy from parents (Allen & Bell, 1995). The way that works is that secure attachment to parents provides adolescents with the confidence to venture forth into the world using the refuge of parental attachment as a secure base from which to explore. Support for the link between secure attachment and adolescent autonomy has been demonstrated by findings showing that adolescents who are autonomous and self-reliant report close, supportive relationships with their parents (Allen et al., 1994; Chirkov & Ryan, 2001).

What This Means for Parents and Professionals Working With Parents. The research that has related positive adolescent outcomes to parent–adolescent attachment highlights the importance of a close relationship between the adolescent and the parent. It particularly emphasizes that parents need to be responsive to their adolescents' feelings because responsiveness is the single best predictor of the development or maintenance of attachment. Unfortunately, as noted earlier, many parents of adolescents adopt an indifferent parenting pattern that reflects a lack of sufficient parental involvement. One of the problems associated with a parenting style that does not include involvement of the parents is that the parents are not maintaining an attachment to the adolescent. You might recall that parent–child attachment is associated with ongoing parental responsiveness to the child. Thus, parents preserve parent–adolescent attachment when they attend to their adolescent children's basic needs, support their goals of becoming increasingly more autonomous, and respond to their need to feel that their parents love and understand them.

Thinking Critically

Consider an example of an interaction between you and your parents or guardians when you were an adolescent that demonstrates the concept of parent–adolescent attachment. See if you can identify the elements of parental responsiveness in your example.

The Link Between Parent–Adolescent Relationships and Adolescents' Conceptions of Self

Advances in cognitive abilities during adolescence result in the tendency of adolescents to engage in self-reflection. The newly acquired ability to use abstract thinking leads to adolescents asking questions about themselves such as "Who am I?" "What am I good at?" "How do others see me?" "What is my future life likely to be like?" Those questions represent adolescents' **quest for identity** and the answers to those questions impact adolescents' self-esteem as well as their identity achievement.

Adolescent Self-Esteem.   Several longitudinal studies following children from preadolescence to adolescence have shown that self-esteem declines in early adolescence, especially for females (Block & Robins, 1993; Savin-Williams & Demo, 1983). Although a substantial number of adolescents experience a decline in self-esteem, many others do not, and only a small percentage of adolescents follow a pattern of steep decline (Hirsch & DuBois, 1991). In attempts to understand environmental factors that might account for variations in adolescent self-esteem, researchers have identified the following influences: physical appearance (Dubois, Felner, Brand, Phillip, & Lease, 1996), academic success (Dubois & Tevendale, 1999), peer relationships, and parent–child relationships (Harter, 1999). Of those, parent–child relationships have been found to be particularly important. Harter (1999) found that adolescent self-esteem is enhanced if parents provide love and encouragement. The importance of the nurturing aspect of parenting for promoting adolescent self-esteem is further supported by numerous findings that higher self-esteem levels of adolescents are related to the authoritative parenting pattern (Baumrind, 1991a, 1991b; Fuligni & Eccles, 1993; Lamborn et al., 1991; Steinberg, 2000) and consistent parenting practices (Johnson et al., 1991).

What This Means for Parents and Professionals Working With Parents.   Probably the most important goal of parenting is to promote a child's self-esteem. We know that an adolescent's self-esteem and positive development is impacted by the love and encouragement they receive from their parents. Based on those findings, the direction is clear—parents should find ways to send a clear message to their adolescents that they love them and that they believe in them. Noticing the things that adolescents care about, spending quality time with them, asking them how they feel about things, and including them in important family decisions can go a long way toward building adolescents' self-esteem.

The Adolescent Quest for Identity

Adolescents' greater cognitive capacity for self-reflective thought influences their self-esteem while contributing to their quest for identity. As more fully described in chapter 2, each stage of life has a central psychosocial issue to be resolved. According to Erikson (1968, 1982), the issue to be resolved during adolescence is **identity achievement** versus **identity diffusion**. Identity achievement consists of being able to establish a clear and definite sense of who one is and where one fits into one's particular culture. It should be noted that the achievement of identity is based on Western values emphasizing the goal of independence that forms the basis of the identity formation theories (Marcia, Waterman, Matteson, Archer, & Orlofsky, 1993). Identity is achieved in Western cultures by trying out various possibilities and ultimately making commitments in the key areas of love (personal relationships), work (occupation), and ideology (beliefs and values). Erikson theorized that a failure to establish commitments in those areas by the end of adolescence results in identity diffusion.

What This Means for Parents and Professionals Working With Parents.   Research findings show that adolescents are better able to explore identity issues in families where disagreements with parents are permitted. Furthermore, differentiation from parents, an essential aspect of identity formation, is encouraged when parents allow their adolescents to develop their own opinions (Holmbeck, Paikoff, & Brooks-Gunn, 1995).

The Identity Quest of Adolescents in Ethnic Minority Cultures.   Adolescents who are members of ethnic minority groups within a society, such as the United States, experience more than one culture when growing up and face the challenge of incorporating those diverse influences into their identity (Phinney, Romero, & Nava, 2001; Tse, 1999). For a large and growing proportion of adolescents in American society, their identity quest includes coming to terms with what it means to be a member of an ethnic minority within a society dominated by the European American culture. Due to adolescents' greater cognitive capacity to consider what others think of them, ethnic minority adolescents become acutely aware of stereotypes and prejudices that others might hold about their ethnic group. Because ethnic minority adolescents must confront such issues, their identity development is likely to be more complicated than is identity formation for adolescents in the American majority culture. Furthermore, because norms and values of the minority culture often differ from those of the majority culture, the identity quest might be confusing and challenging for ethnic minority adolescents (Phinney, 1990).

Due to the confusion and challenge associated with the identity quest for ethnic minority youths, it is important that their parents help them to have pride in their ethnic minority membership. As emphasized in chapter 2, an important component of child socialization in ethnic minority families is racial socialization, which acts as a buffer against negative racial messages in the environment (Peters, 1985; Stevenson, 1994, 1995). You might recall that racial socialization includes providing a home that is rich in racial culture and socializing children to be proud of their racial heritage (O'Brien et al., 2002). Because parenting styles in minority ethnic groups do not promote independence, African American, Native American, Latino American, and Asian American adolescents are more in danger of choosing foreclosed identity in comparison to European American adolescents (Rotheram-Borus & Wyche, 1994).

To prevent **identity foreclosure** whereby their adolescent children identify either with their ethnic group or with the majority culture without sufficient exploration of the values of the other culture, parents in ethnic minority families make a valuable contribution to their adolescent children's identity quest when they assist them in seeking a bicultural identity. To promote their children's bicultural identity, parents should (a) preserve ethnic traditions so that their children have pride in their ethnic heritage and (b) simultaneously provide support for their children's membership in the mainstream culture. To determine the value of assisting ethnic minority adolescents in their quest to achieve a bicultural identity, Tse (1999) analyzed published autobiographical accounts of Asian American adolescents. The analysis of those reports revealed that after a period of searching and finding out that they were not fully comfortable with either the mainstream culture or the ethnic culture, adolescents of Asian descent were able to achieve an Asian American identity as positive and self-validating.

In the process of choosing an identity that incorporates positive aspects of both cultures, ethnic minority youths tend to experience a cultural conflict in values. An example of cultural conflict that might impact an adolescent's quest for identity is seen in the area of love, which includes dating and sex. An aspect of identity development in the American majority culture includes experimenting with various possibilities in love by dating different people. By participating in dating, adolescents develop intimate relationships with others and gain sexual experience with them. The practice of dating, however, conflicts sharply with the values of certain American minority groups. For Asian American adolescents, for example, dating is frowned upon and premarital sexual experimentation is considered disreputable—especially for females (Miller, 1995; Wong, 1997).

What This Means for Parents and Professionals Working With Parents.   It is important for parents in varied cultures within the United States to be sensitive to, and supportive of, the unique identity challenges faced by their adolescent children. Conflicts between the values of ethnic minority groups and those of the majority culture, however, make that parental responsibility especially problematic. The challenge for parents in ethnic minority cultures in the United States is to be certain that their adolescent children respect the values of their ethnic group as well as those of the majority culture of which they also are members. By providing their children with information designed to promote their ethnic identity while emphasizing the opportunities that are available in American society, parents in ethnic minority groups help their children to develop a bicultural identity. According to Phinney et al. (2001), a primary way for immigrant parents to integrate the values of their ethnic minority group into their adolescent children's ethnic identity is by preserving their ethnic language proficiency. In their survey of immigrant families in the United States of Armenian, Vietnamese, and Mexican descent, those researchers found that across all groups, ethnic language proficiency and in-group peer interaction predicted ethnic identity and that parental cultural maintenance predicted adolescent language proficiency.

The Identity Quest of Gay and Lesbian Adolescents in the United States.   The identity quest of gay and lesbian adolescents is a complex process and parents are important influences of that process. A number of studies have addressed the relations among parental influences, the coming out process, and gay and lesbian adolescents' self-concept, self-esteem, and identity formation (Cramer & Roach, 1988; Flowers & Buston, 2001; Newman & Muzzonigro, 1993; Parish & McCluskey, 1992; Savin-Williams, 1989). It has been found that gay and lesbian adolescents feel most comfortable with their sexual orientation when their parents accept their homosexuality. Although parental acceptance of their adolescents' sexual orientation is beneficial to gay and lesbian youth, the reactions of parents to the disclosure of homosexuality are often unpredictable, making the decision to come out difficult (Flowers & Buston, 2001; Savin-Williams, 1989).

The Concerns and Fears Associated with Coming Out During Adolescence. Many gay or lesbian adolescents fear that their parents might reject them should they reveal their sexual orientation. In their study that examined gay men's retrospective accounts of their gay identity formation during adolescence, Flowers and Buston (2001) identified a number of concerns of gay adolescents. The comments of those men in recalling their adolescent years reflected fears related to being perceived as being different: "I was terrified of being different." Comments also showed that those men felt their identity quest was "defined by differences" during a stage of development in which acceptance by others contributes to positive social–emotional development. Their concerns regarding lack of acceptance by parents and peers were demonstrated in comments that reflected feelings of "alienation and isolation." The need to achieve an identity that incorporated their sexual orientation was evident in comments related to wanting to be open about their sexuality but being plagued by "fears of telling others." Finally, their comments included a need to achieve an identity that included acknowledgment of their sexual identity to achieve "wholeness and integrity."

The Importance of Parents in Supporting the Coming Out Process. A study of gay male adolescents by Cramer and Roach (1988) found that, although sexual revelation causes stress in the parent–child relationship, the affiliation between gay adolescents and their parents tends to improve over time and in many cases becomes better than before the disclosure of sexual orientation. It has been conjectured that adolescents from highly supportive families tend to come out at a younger age because of higher self-esteem and greater feelings of security in terms of their relationships with their family members. Conversely, family environments that are low in support hamper the gay or lesbian adolescent in the coming out process. In a study of parents and their gay and lesbian adolescent children, Floyd, Stein, and Harter (1999) found that when youths perceived their parents had relatively accepting attitudes regarding sexual orientation, they had greater consolidation of sexual orientation identity.

The Ways in Which Parents Influence Sexual Orientation Identity Formation. Similar to other adolescents, gay and lesbian adolescents face normative developmental challenges associated with renegotiating relationships with their parents. Like most youths, gay and lesbian adolescents undergo the process of separation–individuation from their parents in order to establish an autonomous adult identity. Concurrently, they face unique challenges associated with sexual orientation identity development. According to Floyd et al. (1999), sexual orientation identity formation for gay and lesbian youths involves personal acknowledgment of sexual orientation as well as public presentation and public recognition. In the consolidation of their sexual orientation, gay and lesbian adolescents become more comfortable and open about their sexual orientation. Rather than being supportive of the progress their gay and lesbian adolescents have achieved in becoming comfortable with their sexual orientation, however, many parents are not accepting of their youths' sexual orientation.

The result of parental lack of acceptance of their adolescent children's sexual orientation sometimes contributes to some adolescents feeling that they must hide their sexual orientation from their parents to maintain parent–child harmony. In other families with a gay or lesbian adolescent member, lack of acceptance of the youth's sexual orientation leads to significant stress in the parent–child relationship. Whether parental disapproval contributes to gay or lesbian adolescents concealing their sexual orientation to get along with their parents or whether parental disapproval contributes to strained parent–child relationships, the lack of parental support interrupts the separation–individuation process of identity formation. Acceptance by parents, on the other hand, helps to bolster and reinforce gay and lesbian adolescents' progress in this aspect of their identity development.

What This Means for Parents and Professionals Working With Parents.   Parental acceptance is one of the most important components of effective child socialization patterns. Parental acceptance and support predicts parent–adolescent attachment and is a critical component of both authoritative and traditional parenting styles. Furthermore, having parents that are warm and supportive predicts positive outcomes for all adolescents, not just those adolescents who have the same sexual orientation as their parents. Parental warmth and acceptance are especially critical to the adjustment of gay and lesbian youth who must confront negative attitudes regarding their sexual orientation from peers and the general public. As they work through the challenges related to being gay or lesbian in a primarily heterosexual society, having parents who demonstrate that they love and respect them (regardless of their sexual orientation) is especially beneficial. An example of the importance of parental support of their gay and lesbian adolescents is shown in the findings of Newman and Muzzonigro (1993) that gay adolescent males in traditional families are less likely to come out to their parents than are those whose parents have less traditional family values. Thus, strong parental support is important

Parent–adolescent conflict is a normal part of parent–adolescent relationships and usually occurs within the context of a close parent–adolescent relationship.

in reducing the personal and social conflicts that plague many homosexual adolescents during the important period of identity formation (Heights & Beaty, 1999).

PARENT–ADOLESCENT CONFLICT

Adolescence is a challenging time for adolescents as well as for their parents. The degree of parent–adolescent conflict that has been attributed to that stage, however, has been largely exaggerated. Early Western theorists such as G. Stanley Hall (1904) and Anna Freud (1946) made it seem as if parent–adolescent conflict is universal and inevitable and that all adolescents and their parents experience intense conflict over many years due to adolescent rebellion. The earlier conceptions of adolescence as a time of storm and stress, due to high levels of conflict between adolescents and their parents, have generally been denounced as numerous studies in the past several decades have indicated otherwise. Two studies during the 1960s were instrumental in dispelling the stereotype of "adolescence as a time of storm and stress." Both of those studies showed that although parents and adolescents often disagree, their arguments are mostly over minor issues, such as curfew and cannot be characterized as highly conflicted. Furthermore, those researchers discovered that the majority of adolescents like, trust, and admire their parents (Douvan & Adelson, 1966; Offer, 1969). Current empirical evidence indicates that adolescents and their parents are likely to agree on the most important aspects of their lives (Offer & Schonert-Reichl, 1992; Smetana, Abernathy, & Harris, 2000). They tend to see eye to eye on issues such as the value of education, the importance of hard work, and the desirability of being honest and trustworthy (Gecas & Seff, 1990). Actually, high levels of conflict characterize only 5 to 10% of parent–adolescent relationships (Larson, Richards, & Moneta, 1996; Steinberg, 1990).

Before we get carried away by a rosy picture of family harmony during adolescence, it is important to acknowledge that conflicts between parents and adolescents are higher during adolescence than during childhood. The picture of parent–adolescent conflict looks like this: Studies show an increase in parent–child conflict during early adolescence (Paikoff & Brooks-Gunn, 1991), which is especially intense between mothers and daughters (Montmeyer, 1982; Steinberg, 1990). By middle adolescence, conflict with parents becomes less frequent but more forceful, followed by a substantial diminishing of conflict by late adolescence (Laursen, Coy, & Collins, 1998).

Sources of Parent–Adolescent Conflict

So far, we have not addressed the following questions: (a) Why does conflict with parents rise when children become adolescents? (b) Why is conflict with parents during early adolescence especially high? (c) How do we account for gender differences in parent–adolescent conflict? Biological, cognitive, and psychological changes of adolescents can be pointed to as part of the explanation for parent–adolescent conflict and further understanding is possible if we consider the role of cultural norms. Biologically, the increased size and strength of adolescents make it more difficult for parents to impose their authority on them than it was when they were younger. Another source of parent–adolescent conflict is adolescent sexual maturity where parental concerns regarding their adolescents' sexual behaviors might provoke conflict (Arnett, 1999, 2001; Steinberg, 1990).

Cognitively, adolescents' increased capacity for abstract thinking makes them more capable of presenting an argument in the face of parental directives. Parents, therefore, face more difficulty in quickly prevailing when engaged in verbal conflicts with their adolescents in comparison with verbal conflicts when their children are younger. Still another source of parent–adolescent conflict is when there is a mismatch between parent and adolescent expectations of autonomy for the adolescent (Smetana, 1988; Smetana et al., 2000). Research shows that, particularly in early adolescence, parents and adolescents have disagreements focused on the adolescent's increasing quest for the expression of personal choice in dress, hairstyle, choice of friends, and the order or disorder of the adolescent's bedroom (Smetana, 1989; Smetana & Asquith, 1994). Finally, although both parents and adolescents in Western societies generally agree on the ultimate goal of adolescent independence, there are often conflicts associated with the pace of that independence. In the West, young persons' independence is not fully recognized until they, as emerging adults, no longer live in their parents' home and no longer depend on their parents financially (Arnett, 1998).

Conflict and Closeness in Parent–Child Relations

The findings that parent–adolescent conflict increases during adolescence do not contradict research findings that point to parent–adolescent closeness and mutual respect. Conflict and closeness in relationships are not mutually exclusive. As noted by Collins and Laursen (1992), conflicts (defined as oppositional interactions) are natural interpersonal exchanges that accompany shifts in role expectations associated with maturational changes. In their longitudinal research, Walker and Taylor (1991) revealed that a parental style that involves supportive but challenging discussions of issues helps promote the adolescent's advanced reasoning skills. Moreover, qualities of family conflict resolution have been linked to aspects of psychosocial development, including identity formation and the development of social cognitive skills (Grotevant & Cooper, 1985; Smetana et al., 2000). Furthermore, effectively managed parent–adolescent conflict fosters the interpersonal adaptations necessitated by the physical, social, and cognitive changes of adolescents (Paikoff & Brooks-Gunn, 1991; Smetana et al., 2000; Steinberg, 1990).

Conflict Arising from Indirect Communication

As clarified earlier, most parent–adolescent conflict is over relatively minor issues. Arnett (2001) suggests that some of those arguments might stem from parental expressions of disapproval that are substitutes for unexpressed parental concerns regarding their adolescents. For example, parents tend to have limited communication with their adolescents about sexual matters. Given the risks associated with sexual activity during adolescence such as sexually transmitted diseases and pregnancy, it is unlikely that the typical parent is unconcerned with those issues. Statements such as "You can't go out of the house wearing that dress" might mean "You look too sexually provocative in that dress, and I'm worried about what others will think of you." Arnett speculated that sexual matters are not the only issues that tend to be argued over in that indirect manner. A comment by a parent, such as "I don't want you hanging out with those two boys," might reflect the following parental concern: "I've seen those boys smoking and have overheard them using some tough language. I'm afraid that they might be using drugs and will influence you to do the same." Although American parents might have legitimate concerns for the safety and welfare of their adolescent children, they must balance those concerns with the cultural emphasis on promoting the independence of their adolescents. That mismatch of parental concern and cultural beliefs regarding the parental role in relation to adolescents undoubtedly promotes the indirect style of communication described here.

What This Means for Parents and Professionals Working With Parents.   Although concern about their adolescent children's sexual behavior and affiliation with peers who are exhibiting risky behaviors is natural, indirect communication about such concerns is not the best approach for parents to take. Not only does indirect communication frequently insult the adolescent, it is typically confusing and often leads to parent–adolescent conflict. When the parent says *"The movie is over by 9:00, and I want you home by 10:00,"* the adolescent does not realize what is going on in the mind of the parent and the directive sounds arbitrary and authoritarian. If parents are concerned about their children making responsible choices, it is better that they sit down with their adolescents and let them know that they care about them and want to be sure that they will be careful in making decisions in those areas.

The Role of Culture in Parent–Adolescent Conflict

Although the same biological and cognitive changes occur in adolescents throughout the world, parent–adolescent conflict is not universal (Arnett, 1999). Actually, it is rare for parents and adolescents in traditional cultures to engage in the kind of frequent bickering typical of parent–adolescent relationships in the American majority culture (Rothbaum, Pott, & Azuma, 2000; Schlegel & Barry, 1991; Whiting & Edwards, 1988). The reason for low conflict between adolescents and their parents in traditional cultures is partly due to the economic interdependence of parents and children in those cultures wherein family members rely on each other economically. As pointed out in chapter 2, independence is not a highly valued outcome of child and adolescent development outside the West (Schlegel & Barry, 1991). In non-Western cultures, interdependence (financially, socially, and psychologically) is more highly valued than is independence.

An example of parent–adolescent interdependence in traditional cultures is seen in the common practice of adolescents sharing child care responsibilities with their parents. In traditional cultures, the sibling–caregiver relationship is the most common type of sibling relationship with over 80% of adolescent boys and girls having frequent responsibility for younger siblings (Schlegel & Barry, 1991). In traditional cultures, age is considered a powerful determinant of status, with an understanding that older siblings have authority over younger siblings (Whiting & Edwards, 1988). More than economic considerations, shared child care responsibilities account for the low level of parent–adolescent conflict in non-Western families. As pointed out by Zhou (1997), parent–adolescent conflict is low not only in traditional cultures but also in highly industrialized societies such as Japan and Taiwan that have maintained their traditional beliefs. Other scholars have reported low parent–adolescent conflict in Asian American and Latino American families (Chao, 1994; Suarez-Orozco & Suarez-Orozco, 1996). Those findings suggest that cultural beliefs regarding parental authority and adolescent autonomy override economic considerations as explanations of cross-cultural differences in parent–adolescent conflict.

CHANGES IN THE FAMILY SYSTEM WHEN CHILDREN REACH ADOLESCENCE

When children become adolescents, they undergo physical, cognitive, and social–emotional changes. Those developmental changes contribute to changes in their behavior and their behavioral changes impact other family members' behaviors. As their children reach adolescence, their parents are typically experiencing a mid-life transition and that parental transition also influences parent–adolescent relationships. The result is a certain amount of imbalance or disequilibrium in the family system as family members adjust to those changes (Minuchin, 1974).

The Changes in the Family System to Accommodate Changes in the Adolescent

The time of greatest disequilibrium in the family system occurs during early adolescence (ages 10 to 14) when puberty and sexual maturity occur, the cognitive capability of **abstract thought** is achieved, and the psychological quest for a unique identity begins. The hallmark of the ability to engage in abstract thinking is that adolescent thought is no longer tied to a concrete reality. Adolescents begin to consider life's problems and challenges in terms of possibilities (Piaget & Inhelder, 1958). The ability to consider many possible alternatives to the established order of things, coupled with their quest to discover who they are and what future goals they will choose for themselves, is a normal and natural aspect of adolescent development.

The social–emotional and cognitive changes that occur during adolescence are manifested in American adolescents' questioning of parents' authority and challenging previously established rules and boundaries. It is, therefore, important for parents to make adjustments in their guidance style that allow for the exploration of possible exceptions to the usual while encouraging their adolescent children's quest to understand who they are. As previously noted, although parent–adolescent relationships are more conflicted during early adolescence as parents are adjusting to their young adolescent children's developmental transition (e.g., Paikoff & Brooks-Gunn, 1991; Smetana et al., 2000), they are less conflicted during late adolescence when a balance toward greater equilibrium in the family system has been achieved (Laursen et al., 1998; Smetana et al., 2000).

After a period of relative family stability, disequilibrium once more occurs as older adolescents leave home. As noted by O'Connor, Allen, Bell, and Hauser (1996), adolescents leaving home affects parent–adolescent relationships in either a positive or a negative direction depending on the timing of and reason for the move and how parents and adolescents handle that important transition. There is a tremendous difference between the young adolescent who runs away from an abusive or neglectful home and an older adolescent who goes off to college with the full involvement and support of parents.

Thinking Critically

Consider an example of disequilibrium that occurred in your family during your adolescent years. How did you, your parents, and other family members adapt to that imbalance?

This mother and daughter are in the process of altering their roles to suit the mother's transition into middle-age and the daughter's into adolescence.

The Dual Transitions of Adolescent Children and Midlife Parents

It is important to point out that while adolescents are experiencing many changes related to development, their parents are undergoing development change as well. Some of the disequilibrium experienced in the family system with an adolescent member might, therefore, be related to parents reaching midlife (Steinberg & Steinberg, 1994). For the majority of parents, changes occurring in their adolescents coincide with their own midlife development. As noted in chapter 1, the median age for marriage, and for the birth of a first child, is typically in the mid- to late 20s in industrialized societies. Because adolescence begins at around 10, most parents in industrialized countries are around 40 when their first child begins adolescence. Even with those who have children relatively early or late, their children's adolescence is likely to overlap at least in part with their own midlife development (Arnett, 2001).

The Launching of Young Adults

As children enter adolescence, there is greater disequilibrium; and throughout adolescence, a state of stability is gradually regained as both parents and adolescents adjust to each other's developmental changes. Then, as adolescents make the next major transition, from adolescence to emerging adulthood, disequilibrium again manifests itself in the parent–child relationship. The challenge at that point is a test of both the parent's and the adolescent's ability to adapt to greater independence from each other. Although the implication in the popular literature is that the empty nest is a syndrome reflecting especially difficult psychological development for parents, the reality is that most parents handle that transition relatively well. In fact, the majority of parents report that transition as a positive, rather than a negative, adjustment (Harris, Ellicott, & Holmes, 1986; Raymond, 2000). The finding that the launching of young adults is a rewarding experience, for the most part, suggests that the disequilibrium associated with that major development change is growth producing for both parents and children.

What This Means for Parents and Professionals Working With Parents.   Families are dynamic systems characterized by stability and change. Although family stability contributes to a sense of shared history and a certain degree of predictability, the changes in the family system challenge members to adapt to those changes and to redefine their roles in relation to family members. It is important for parents to consider the growth-producing aspects of the disequilibrium that occurs in the family system when their children reach adolescence. The physical, cognitive, and social–emotional advances that accompany the transition from childhood to adolescence call for adaptations in adolescents' roles in relation to their parents and other family members. When parents enfranchise their adolescent children into increasingly more responsible roles, parents and adolescents both benefit as the family system integrates the development of those new family roles into a family system marked by vitality and growth.

Thinking Critically

Why do you think that parents generally respond favorably to their young adult children leaving home? What are some examples of disequilibrium that required adjustment by you and your parents when you left home?

PROBLEMS THAT ADOLESCENTS SOMETIMES FACE

Although the typical adolescent does not experience internalizing problems such as depression or eating disorders or become involved with risky behaviors such as drug usage, crime, or delinquency, there is a sizable number of adolescents for whom those problems occur. By understanding the role that parents play in the development of those problems, it is possible to provide recommendations regarding the ways in which parents might prevent such problems from occurring.

Adolescent Depression

According to Larson and Richards (1994), the newly developed capacities for abstract reasoning allow adolescents to see beneath the surface of things and envision

Although adolescents report more negative moods than do preadolescents or adults, those adolescents who have close relationships with parents are less likely to experience depression.

hidden threats to their welfare. Even in response to the same events, adolescents re-port more negative moods than do preadolescents or adults. The self-reflective ca-pacity for picking up on real or imagined intimidation comes at a time when there are a number of other changes in their lives that potentially increase the stress level for adolescents. As previously discussed, early adolescence is a stage of transition from childhood into the increasingly complex time of adolescence wherein signifi-cant developmental changes are occurring (Petersen, Leffert, Graham, Alwin, & Ding, 1997). Social interactions with peers and family members are altered during that period (Petersen, 1988) and developmental changes are compounded by the early adolescent's transition from elementary to middle level school (Petersen, 1987). Those changes are challenging and commonly stressful, which might explain why early adolescence has been identified as a time when adolescents are especially vulnerable for the development of depressed mood (Clarizio, 1994).

Although studies have documented increases in depressed affect during adoles-cence, recent findings of Heath and Camarena (2002) demonstrate that (a) most ado-lescents do not show increases in depressed mood during early adolescence and that (b) depressed mood is typically followed by a decrease in depression symptoms. Un-fortunately, though not typical, a smaller proportion of adolescents experience chronic symptoms of depression and those adolescents are more at risk for problem-atic behaviors. Researchers studying adolescent depressed affect have shown that the experience of depressed mood is related to other serious consequences for adoles-cents such as emotional and disruptive behavior, truancy, drug abuse, pregnancy (Dryfoos, 1991; Eccles, Wigfield, & Harold, 1993), and suicide attempts (DiFilippo & Overholser, 2000; Heath & Camarena, 2002).

The Role of Parents in Adolescent Depression.   Research findings that have shown that adolescent depressed affect is not a typical experience, and that it is most often short lived, suggest that the adolescent's social environment plays a role in the occur-rence or nonoccurrence of depression symptoms. Because parents are important influ-ences in their adolescents' lives, it seems reasonable to conclude that the parent–child relationship plays a role in the development or prevention of adolescent depression. Abundant research findings support that conclusion. Although other factors such as poor peer relations, academic concerns, and moving from one school to another, are associated with adolescent depressed mood (Petersen et al., 1993), a variety of family factors have been found to be particularly relevant. Conditions in the family that con-tribute to adolescent depressed affect include emotional unavailability of parents, high family conflict, economic difficulties, parental divorce (Asarmov & Horton, 1990; Lee & Gotlib, 1990), and parental depression (Sarigiani, Heath, & Camarena, 2003).

The relation between family factors and adolescent depression is expressed in the following case level analysis of a young adolescent identified as having chronic depressed mood:

> He mentioned that . . . he was getting into fights at school, and that he had been sus-pended from school for fighting. He also described arguments with his brothers and his parents. His reports further indicated that he was having academic difficulties including 'getting a terrible grade on a test' and being concerned about 'flunking seventh grade.' He

also reported that he had attempted suicide by hanging himself and that his mother had 'found him hanging there and called the police.' His mother reported that he had a bad attitude. . . . (Heath & Camarena, 2002, p. 276)

The Link Between Adolescent Depression and Adolescent Suicide. Although depressed mood is typically a transient experience and does not affect all adolescents (Heath & Camarena, 2002), parents need to take adolescent depression seriously. If parents are concerned about adolescent depression, they might be able to prevent depression symptoms from becoming chronic; and timely intervention could prevent some of the problems associated with adolescent depression. A compelling reason for considering adolescent depression as worthy of response is that it is a risk factor for suicide. Parents need to understand that adolescent suicide attempts are usually preceded by symptoms of depression (Pfeffer, 1986; Shagle & Barber, 1994). Based on the relation that has been found between suicide and symptoms of depression, a recommended response to the treatment of adolescents exhibiting suicidal behavior is parenting strategies that focus on reducing feelings of depression.

Assessing Adolescent Suicide Risk. Although depression is a symptom associated with suicide behavior among adolescents, parents need to look further than the adolescent's mood in assessing the risk of suicide. Although most suicide attempters are depressed (Andrews & Lewinsohn, 1992), not all depressed individuals are suicidal (Rao, Weissman, Martin, & Hammond, 1993). The findings of Dori and Overholser (1999) suggest that adolescents who experience higher levels of hopelessness during a depressed episode are at increased risk for suicidal behavior. Those researchers found that both severity of depression and level of hopelessness differentiated between adolescents who had recently, or repeatedly, attempted suicide in comparison to adolescents who had never attempted suicide.

What This Means for Parents and Professionals Working With Parents. The implications of the foregoing discussion are that parents should be mindful that adolescents experiencing depression need to be assisted in seeing that there is hope in their lives. Although there are many experiences outside the home that might discourage an adolescent (such as romantic breakups), parents are in a unique position to help adolescents regain hope by sensitive responsiveness to their feelings. To provide the necessary support for adolescents experiencing depressed affect, parents need to be aware of the changes in their adolescent children's behavior that might forewarn others of the risk of actual or attempted suicide (see Figure 6.2).

Adolescent Eating Disorders

Eating disorders that occur during adolescence primarily affect adolescent girls living in Western societies, particularly those living in the United States. American adolescent girls are presented with a cultural ideal that portrays the ideal female body as slim at a time when their bodies are biologically tending to become less slim and more rounded. In response to that dilemma, many adolescent females become distressed at the biological changes taking place in their bodies and attempt to resist

1. **A preoccupation with the themes of death and dying. This is a primary warning sign, and it is a myth that those persons who talk about suicide do not carry it out.** Many young people write stories, essays, poems, and songs about suicide shortly before their own self-inflicted death. Some adolescents provide verbal clues, sometimes actually and directly threatening suicide ("I think I'll just kill myself") but the clues are often more subtle ("You'd all be better off if I were dead"). Others make jokes about suicide. Although suicide is no laughing matter, the adolescent sometimes clothes suicidal thoughts in humor to assess other people's reactions.

2. **One or more signs of serious depression,** including sadness, extreme mood fluctuations, feelings of helplessness, pessimism about the future, sleep disturbances, increased or decreased appetite, the inability to play and have fun, and/or disturbing physical symptoms such as a persistent headache.

3. **A sudden change in habits, attitudes, or personality.** A confident, outgoing adolescent might become passive and withdrawn or an adolescent who is usually reserved might become very talkative.

4. **A sudden or pronounced decline in school.** A student who was previously doing average or above average school work might begin to have a hard time keeping up with required studies.

5. **Neglect of appearance and hygiene.** After usually being well-groomed, an adolescent who is contemplating suicide might suddenly become disheveled, dirty, or poorly groomed.

6. **Signs that the adolescent is "putting affairs in order."** Adolescents who begin to give away prized possessions are at extremely high risk for suicide.

7. **Losing interest in friends and activities that were once important.** The adolescent might refuse to socialize with friends or look for excuses to avoid other people, especially in organized activities.

8. **Sudden difficulty in communicating with other people.** Suicidal adolescents might especially have a difficult time establishing eye contact with others. Speech might be slow, faltering, or stumbling.

FIGURE 6.2   Warning Signs of Adolescent Suicide
Source: Adapted from *Youth Suicide: Depression and Loneliness*, by B. Hafen and K. Frandsen, 1986, Evergreen, CO: Cordillera Press; and *A Time to Listen*, by P. Hermes, 1987, San Diego, CA: Harcourt.

those changes. Various studies show that up to three fourths of American adolescent females believe they weigh too much; although fewer than 20% are actually overweight (Davies & Furnham, 1986; French, Story, Downes, Resnick, & Blum, 1995; Paxton et al., 1991). Concerns with the American ideal of slimness for women contribute to female adolescents being unsatisfied with their bodies (Phelps et al., 1993), and that dissatisfaction increases throughout adolescence. Many of those adolescent females develop extreme weight-loss behaviors such as fasting, "crash dieting" and skipping meals (Rosenblum & Lewis, 1999).

Although many adolescents in cultures emphasizing female thinness strive to be slender themselves, only a small percentage of them reach the extremes of actually developing eating disorders (Garner & Garfinkel, 1997). Evidence shows that girls with eating disorders tend to have parents who are warm but also highly controlling (Caspar, 1992; Kenny & Hart, 1992). Outwardly those girls appear to be well behaved and even perfectionists in efforts to please their parents. Some clinicians, however, have suggested that the eating disorder is a way to assert control over their lives in the face of overly controlling parents (Caspar, 1992). Other researchers have shown a link between parental eating patterns and adolescent eating disorders. For instance, many adolescent girls with excessive weight-loss behaviors have mothers who model weight-loss behaviors (Benedikt, Wertheim, & Love, 1998).

What This Means for Parents and Professionals Working With Parents.   First and foremost, it is imperative that parents not send the message to their adolescents that their acceptance of them is related to their performance or achievement, but that they accept their adolescents as they are. Second, parents need to understand that being overly controlling is not beneficial for children and is particularly detrimental to adolescents who need to become increasingly more self-reliant. Third, parents should be aware of the cultural ideals that adolescent girls in the United States must confront and be certain that their adolescent daughters are able to put those idealized images of female slimness into perspective. Finally, because adolescent eating problems primarily affect adolescent girls, mothers should be mindful of their own concerns with slimness and the dieting behaviors they are modeling for their adolescent daughters.

Adolescent Substance Abuse

Children whose family environments reflect high levels of conflict between parents or between parents and children, combined with low levels of parental support, tend to develop alienation and low self-control that are sometimes expressed during

The maintenance of a nutritious diet is important for promoting adolescent growth and development.

When parental monitoring is low, adolescents are at greater risk for involvement in crime and delinquency.

adolescence through drug use and affiliation with drug-using peers. In contrast, experiencing close and supportive relationships with parents during childhood and adolescence serves as a protective factor against substance use, even in communities where drug use is common (Brook, Brook, Gordon, & Whiteman, 1990). The way in which close parent–adolescent relations serve as protective factors against substance abuse is that a close parent–adolescent relationship is linked to lower orientation to peers, which is in turn related to lower substance use (Bogenschneider, Wu, Raffaelli, & Tsay, 1998; Myers, Wagner, & Brown, 1997). Moreover, adolescents are more likely to use substances when one or more members of the family use substances or when parents have a lenient attitude toward substance abuse (Bogenschneider et al., 1998; Peterson, Hawkins, Abbott, & Catalano, 1994).

Adolescent Crime and Delinquency

Parental inconsistency, leniency, and lack of monitoring have been specifically associated with adolescent delinquency. Several decades ago, McCord and McCord (1959) found that delinquents were twice as likely to have parents who practiced inconsistent or lenient discipline, and that finding has been replicated many times over the years since then. Parental monitoring, an aspect of parental control, has been found to be an especially important factor in adolescent delinquency. Adolescents are considerably more likely to engage in delinquent acts when parental monitoring is lacking (Jacobson & Crockett, 2000; Patterson & Yoerger, 1997).

Adolescents Who Run Away from Home

For some adolescents, the situation in their homes is so intolerable that for one reason or another they run away. In the United States, as many as one million adolescents run away from home (Flanagan & Maguire, 1992; Tomb, 1991) and one quarter of those young people are not runaways but rather throwaways. Their parents have forced them to leave (Tomb, 1991). Not surprisingly, adolescents who run away from home have frequently experienced high levels of conflict with parents; and many of those adolescents have experienced physical or sexual abuse by parents. Other factors associated with running away from home include low family income, conflict between parents, parental alcohol usage, and parental neglect of the adolescent (McCarthy, 1994; Rotheram-Borus, Koopman, & Ehrhardt, 1991). Although the majority of runaways stay within 50 miles of their homes with friends or relatives and return within a week, those who stay away for weeks, months, or longer, are at high risk for a variety of problems. Adolescent runaways tend to be highly vulnerable to exploitation. Many are robbed, beaten, and malnourished, and in their desperation to survive they might seek money through prostitution or pornography (Rotheram-Borus et al., 1991). Adolescents who run away also are likely to steal food, to be involved in other thefts, and to use drugs. Furthermore, suicidal behavior is common among runaways (Rotheram-Borus, 1993; Yoder, Hoyt, & Whitbeck, 1998).

The Influence of Parents and Peers on Adolescent Risk Behavior

A great deal of research has focused on the ways that family circumstances are related to adolescent risk behavior. That research consistently supports a relation between parenting styles and risk behavior. Specifically, adolescents with authoritative parents (who combine demandingness and responsiveness) are less involved in risk behaviors than are other adolescents (Baumrind, 1991b). Similarly, less risk behavior has been found among adolescents whose parents have a traditional parenting style that also represents a combination of demandingness and responsiveness (Chao, 1994; Fuligni et al., 1999; Suarez-Orozco & Suarez-Orozco, 1996). In comparison, adolescents whose parents are authoritarian, indulgent, or indifferent tend to have higher levels of participation in problem behaviors. Other factors associated with adolescent risk behaviors are high levels of family conflict and family disorganization (Martin & Pritchard, 1991; Protinsky & Shilts, 1990).

What This Means for Parents and Professionals Working With Parents. Research findings have demonstrated the importance of parental warmth and acceptance for helping adolescents to go in a positive direction with their lives and for preventing them from engaging in risky behaviors. Whether parents are considering ways to keep their adolescent children on a positive path or preventing them from engaging in risk behaviors, the message is clear—adolescents need parents who are involved with them and who use child socialization styles marked by warmth and acceptance. Furthermore, parents who are distant, uninvolved, neglectful, or abusive, place their adolescents at the greatest risk for engaging in risk behaviors.

❧ SUMMARY

In this chapter, the key role that parents play in the lives of their adolescent children has been examined. A consistent theme of this chapter has been the significance of parental styles that emphasize authority coupled with responsiveness. As has been shown, the parenting patterns that integrate parental authority with parental responsiveness are found not only in the authoritative pattern practiced by many parents in the United States but also in the traditional pattern found in many American ethnic minority families as well as in traditional cultures throughout the world. Attention has been drawn to research findings that demonstrate that those patterns of parenting are instrumental in promoting adolescents' higher self-esteem, higher achievement, and more positive relationships with others. The role that parent–adolescent conflict plays in adolescent development has been discussed as well. Finally, being mindful of the detrimental outcomes of adolescents who experience depression and/or engage in risk behaviors, research evidence has been presented showing the ways in which adolescent depression and adolescent risk behavior are related to parent–adolescent relationships. Based on the examination of adolescents and their parents in different cultures and in various circumstances, one factor stands out—close, supportive interactions with parents are crucial to the positive development of adolescents.

❧ KEY TERMS

- abstract thought
- familism
- identity achievement

- identity diffusion
- identity foreclosure
- quest for identity

7

The Relationships of Young Adults, Their Parents, and Their Children

The roles and responsibilities that define adulthood, such as marriage, parenthood and employment, vary considerably throughout the world. Some individuals take on adult responsibilities while still in their teenage years or early 20s; others delay those responsibilities until they are in their late 20s or 30s. At the same time that young adults are assuming adult responsibilities, they are altering the relationships they have with their parents. Then, as many young adults become parents themselves, they align their parenthood roles with those of their own parents who become grandparents to their children. The arenas in which those parent–child relationships are played out differ according to a number of factors such as socioeconomic status and cultural context. Across all contexts, however, the intergenerational relationships in which young adults participate affect their emotional, social, and cognitive development. The interactions between parents and children contribute as well to the development of the social roles of young adults and their parents and to the ongoing development of the family systems in which those interactions occur.

VARIATIONS IN THE ECONOMIC INTERDEPENDENCE OF YOUNG ADULTS AND THEIR PARENTS

In much of the world, such as in China, India, and Mexico, working to help support the family is expected of young adults. In China, for example, when children become young adults they have the **filial duty** to financially support their parents (Lee & Sung, 1998). Furthermore, it is in the context of poverty and dependence on family members for survival that we see the greatest emphasis on the older generation's economic dependence on the younger generation. In many industrialized societies (such as the United States and Canada), on the other hand, most young adults are not expected to contribute to the financial support of their parents. In societies in which it is not anticipated that young adults will contribute to the economic maintenance of their parents, financial aid is typically from the parent to the child. For example, those young adults who go to college typically receive considerable monetary help from their parents. Even those who do not go to college usually accept some form of financial assistance from their parents (Zarit & Eggebeen, 1995).

VARIATIONS IN THE LIVING ARRANGEMENTS OF YOUNG ADULTS AND THEIR PARENTS

In addition to considerable variation in economic interdependence between young adults and their parents, there is diversity in the living arrangements of the two generations. Young adults in traditional cultures typically continue to live with their parents but the roles of parents and children are somewhat shifted such that adult children are expected to begin contributing to the financial welfare of their parents (Lee & Sung, 1998). Those living arrangements are quite different from those seen in Western societies, where most young adults move out of their parents' home sometime during young adulthood. For young people in the United States and Canada, that move typically occurs around the ages of 18 to 19, which is several years earlier than in most other Western countries (Goldscheider & Goldscheider, 1999). In contrast to the early exodus of young adults in the United States and Canada, young adults in European countries are more likely to continue to live at home even while attending college. For example, in Germany, the typical ages for leaving home are 23 for males and 21 for females; and those ages of departure from their parents' home are similar in most other European countries (Silbereisen, Meschke, & Schwarz, 1996).

Adult Children Living with Their Parents in Industrialized Societies

In the past, most young adults in industrialized societies left home to go to college, to marry, and/or to set up separate households. Hence, the term **"empty nest"** came to describe the home from which those young adults were launched into independent living. Although that pattern of transition into adulthood continues to define most living arrangements of young adults in industrialized societies today, there have been recent changes in the patterns of intergenerational living in some countries. In the United States, increasing numbers of young adults are now living with their parents well into their 20s. For example, more than 20% of 25-year-old Americans continue to reside with their parents (Mogelonsky, 1996). In Greece, Spain, and Italy, more than half of 30-year-olds still have not achieved the full autonomy associated with a job and a home of their own (Fernandez & Antonio, 1997), and in Japan there are at least 10 million single young adults living at home with their parents (Masahiro, 2001). The increase in the numbers of young adults who live at home with their parents has led to the empty nest being redefined as the **"full nest."**

Factors Influencing Young Adults' Coresidence with Parents.   In the United States, the timing of departure from the family home is related to ethnicity (Mogelonsky, 1996), whether the young adults' biological parents are still married to each other, parental expectations of when their adult children should leave home, parental resources, and other economic dimensions such as housing costs, job opportunities, whether or not adult children have remained single, and, for women in particular, the extent of government-provided cash assistance to low-income parents and their children (Goldscheider, 1997). The clearest change in parent–child relationships that affects young adults' living arrangements in the United States is the increase in parental divorce and remarriage. The most consistent finding in the literature focusing on whether young adults live with or apart from their parents is whether the parents of those young persons continue to be married to each other. Young adults leave home sooner from nontraditional families than from two-biological-parent households. Furthermore, the differences are particularly large when leaving home to attend college because that is one route that young adults in never-divorced families are significantly more likely to take in comparison to young adults in other families (Goldscheider, 1997). Ethnic differences also have been identified in patterns of coresidence of young adults and their parents. Those differences show that the full-nest syndrome is more pronounced among European Americans than among Americans of other ethnicities (Mogelonsky, 1996).

Thinking Critically

Why do you suppose adult children of two-biological-parent households are more likely to live with their parents than adult children from other households?

Living Arrangements in Full-Nest Families.   Contemporary living arrangements between parents and their young adult children in industrialized societies are in sharp contrast to the economic interdependence between the generations that is seen in many traditional cultures. Whereas adult children in traditional cultures are expected to contribute to the economic well-being of their parents (Hinton, 1986; Lee & Sung, 1998), most young adults living with parents in industrialized societies do not contribute to the financial resources of the parental household. In contrast, many adult children living with their parents are permitted to spend their wages on luxuries without paying rent or contributing to expenses related to running the household (Mogelonsky, 1996). An example of that pattern of coresidence among Japanese single adults and their parents was described by Masahiro (2001) who pointed out that the majority of young Japanese single adults who live with their parents have jobs and are able to enjoy affluent lifestyles while their fundamental needs are met by their parents. Furthermore, most of those young Japanese single men and women do very little housework. Instead, their mothers do the housework for their sons and daughters after they become adults.

Thinking Critically

Given the large numbers of adult children living at home with their parents, you probably know a family that includes at least one adult child member. Based on your observations, in what ways does that family fit the characteristics previously described?

PARENTHOOD AND THE SOCIAL–EMOTIONAL DEVELOPMENT OF YOUNG ADULTS

Whether living together or apart, individuals become less dependent on their parents during young adulthood in comparison to earlier years. Nevertheless, the parent–child relationships in which they continue to be involved are important influences of young adults' social and emotional development. Participation in parent–child relationships as adult children contributes to individuals' ongoing attachment to their parents (Leonardari & Kiosseoglou, 2000; Wels, Linssen, & Abna, 2000) and the achievement of **intimacy** with others (Goldhaber, 2000; Robinson, 2000; Stollberg & Van Schaick, 2001; Wels et al., 2000). For those young adults who become parents, participation in simultaneous relationships with their parents and with their children is related to their development of a sense of generativity (Erikson, 1968; Goldhaber, 2000).

The Attachment of Young Adults to Their Parents

The central theme of attachment theory, which was explained in chapter 2, relates to the implications of optimal and nonoptimal social attachments for psychological well-being (Ainsworth et al., 1978; Bretherton, 1985). A related perspective empha-sizes a balance between **individuation** and **connectiveness** (Baumrind, 1991a;

The parent-child attachment which begins during infancy and continues throughout adulthood is obvious in the scene depicted here.

Kenny, 1987). According to that view, attachment and individuation should be considered as dual and equally important pathways to development (Josselson, 1988). Thus, a differentiated sense of self (individuation) can be achieved without severing emotional ties (connectiveness) with parents; and young persons benefit from relationships with their parents in which both their separateness and their individuality are supported (Kaplan & Klein, 1985). Following those theoretical suggestions, researchers have demonstrated that relationships with parents that are marked by supportive forms of connectiveness and satisfying forms of separateness contribute to young adults' adaptive functioning (Leonardari & Kiosseoglou, 2000).

An example of the benefit of young adults' attachment to their parents was demonstrated by Leonardari and Kiosseoglou (2000), who explored the links among attachment patterns, psychological separation from parents, and young adults' adaptive functioning. In their study of university students in Greece, they found a positive association between security of attachment and freedom from guilt, anxiety, and resentment toward parents. Additionally, those students with secure attachment to their parents scored higher on self-esteem and lower on measures of anxiety and loneliness. Further evidence of the importance of young adults' attachment to their parents comes from the findings of Mayseless, Daniel, and Sharabang (1996) who found that young adults' patterns of attachment were related to the ways in which they coped with separation from significant others. Those who were securely attached to their parents coped well with separations from significant others. They tended to live outside their parental homes and attribute high significance to their romantic partners while sustaining close communication with their mothers. Those with ambivalent attachments to their parents also tended to live away from the parental home but were less committed to their relationships with romantic partners. When separated from romantic partners, however, young adults who had ambivalent attachments to their parents reacted with strong anxiety, rejection, and self-blame. Furthermore, even mild separations from romantic partners elicited strong reactions from young adults with ambivalent attachment to parents.

Thinking Critically

How would you explain the association between young adults' patterns of attachment to their parents and their reaction to separation from significant others?

The Role of Parents in Promoting Young Adults' Achievement of Intimacy

It is easy to confuse the concepts of attachment and intimacy especially because both are related to parent–child closeness. The distinction is that attachment to parents is related to the individual's psychological well-being, such as to levels of self-esteem and to feelings of security versus feelings of loneliness or anxiety (Leonardari & Kiosseoglou, 2000). In contrast, successful resolution of the issue of intimacy enables the young adult to maintain committed, enduring intimate relationships (Erikson, 1968; Orlofsky, 1993). The role of parents in promoting young adults' achievement of a sense of intimacy is that many of the patterns that young adults bring into their intimate relationships with significant others are developed in the relationships they have with their parents. As noted by Van Schaick and Stollberg (2001), the impact of parental involvement is a significant influence on all relationship dimensions in the lives of young adults. Although the parental influence on young adults' achievement of intimacy is similar for young men and young women, research suggests that there are gender differences in that influence. For example, Robinson (2000) demonstrated that a positive relationship with one's mother during adolescence was related to more positive intimate relationships in young adulthood.

Thinking Critically

Why do you suppose that a positive relationship with one's mother during adolescence was found to be related to more positive intimate relationships in young adulthood?

Parent–Child Relationships and the Achievement of a Sense of Generativity

We will now turn our attention to the ways in which the achievement of a sense of generativity derives from the parent–child relationships in which young adults participate with their children and with their parents. Included also in this discussion are the contributions that young adults make to their parent's ongoing generativity needs.

Parenthood and the Development of a Sense of Generativity.   As noted by Goldhaber (2000), each of Erikson's stages builds upon those that precede it and each moves the individuals more fully into the role of a mature, active participant in one's culture. Therefore, the achievement of a sense of intimacy, whereby individuals have been able to join their lives with others, better prepares them for the next step in which they consider the significance of their efforts for the next generation. According to Erikson (1968, 1982), after the achievement of intimacy, young adults seek to attain a sense of **generativity**. As Erikson points out, even though generativity might take a variety of forms, its chief expression is found in "establishing and guiding the next generation." In any culture, when one stranger asks another "What do you do?" the answer is not likely to be "Raise children." Although raising children is not the way that young men and young women typically describe what they do, the reality is that they are as likely to be parents as to be employed. Furthermore, many of those young people consider the successful rearing of their children to be their most important accomplishment. In their establishment of a sense of generativity, young adults develop the ability to care for others, which is a basic strength that reflects young adult maturity.

Generativity and Gender. In cultures throughout the world, maintaining a household and caring for children has been a primary source of generativity for women. Conversely, providing food and other goods for the family has been the main way in which men have been able to achieve a sense of generativity (Furstenberg, Hoffman, & Shrestha, 1995). Although in many cultures the socialization into distinct gender roles (emphasizing men's roles as family providers and women's roles as wives and mothers) continues to occur, that picture has shifted considerably during the past 50 years in most industrialized societies. The most current U.S. census data show that the majority of married women in the United States were working in paid employment outside the home, including those whose youngest child was in school (U.S. Bureau of the Census, 2000). The husbands of almost all of those women also were employed, and the majority of those husbands shared household responsibilities with their wives—sometimes providing a major portion of child care responsibilities. In spite of the fact that in the United States, both parents are likely to be working, not all couples work out an amicable dual-worker, dual-parent relationship. Nevertheless, it has been found that the happiest couples do not work either very long or very few hours. That balance allows both parents to contribute to the household finances as well as to the unpaid labor needed to maintain a household (Moen & Yu, 1999).

Thinking Critically

Why do you suppose that young people do not typically mention that they are engaged in rearing children when they are asked the question "What do you do?" Consider your answer in terms of gender and cultural norms.

Generativity and Culture. The drive to be generative is a powerful theme of adulthood and occurs in two major ways—through parenthood and through employment. The expression of that desire is variable, however, and is dependent on the diverse roles of individuals in various cultures. At the cultural level, there are differences in generativity goals related to individualism and collectivism. For a parent in an individualist culture, such as the majority culture of the United States, generativity needs might take any of the following forms: (a) being the best parents they can be, (b) achieving individual success in their occupational roles, or (c) seeking to be the best parents possible while being highly competitive in their occupational roles. In contrast to the drive for individual success in their work and family roles, young adults in collectivist cultures, such as ethnic minority cultures in the United States, are more likely to link generativity with communal living. Those parents are able to attain a sense of generativity through being involved in cooperative efforts that maximize the likelihood of group success in the family as well as in the workplace (Bean, Curtis, & Marcum, 1977; Goduka & Kunnie, 2003; Ramirez & Acre, 1981; Suarez-Orozco & Suarez-Orozco, 1996).

The emphasis on success in collectivist cultures is derived from being a good parent and/or a good worker and simultaneously earning the respect of their children, their grandchildren, their parents, their coworkers, and individuals in their community. An example of cultural collectivism is found in Latino family life wherein *la familia*, or **familism**, is a core family value. Familism is the constellation of beliefs that define the roles and expectations of family members in relation to the needs of the collective, as opposed to needs of the individual. *La familia* refers to the cultural belief that families should live near their extended kin and have strong kinship ties, particularly in times of need (Fuligni et al., 1999; Ramirez & Acre, 1981; Suarez-Orozco & Suarez-Orozco, 1996). Whether one lives in an individualistic culture or in a collectivist culture, at the individual level, the roles of parent and worker contribute to a sense that one's contributions to the family and/or to the workplace are valuable. The evaluation of one's success in those roles contributes to a sense of generativity, which becomes integrated into the individual's sense of self (Erikson, 1982; Goldhaber, 2000).

What This Means for Young Adult Parents and Professionals.   For young adult parents in collectivist cultures, it is important to align their quest for generativity with the values of their extended families and their communities. By recognizing the important roles of family and community members, young parents in those communities are able to access

One of the ways that families maintain their cohesiveness is through their participation in family rituals that mark significant transitions in family members' lives.

valuable support of their efforts to achieve a sense of generativity. For professionals working with parents in collectivist cultures, it is helpful when they recognize that the young adult's role as parent is likely to be integrated with extended family and community roles. Therefore, the establishment of a relationship with those young parents must be based on a respect for the traditions of shared caregiving and other family and community supports that are an integral part of collectivist cultures. For example, in referring to a young adult's family, a teacher or other professional might keep in mind that a person who is living in a collectivist culture might consider parents, siblings, aunts, uncles, and cousins as family members in addition to children and a spouse or partner.

Generativity Is a Two-Way Street.   The achievement of a sense of generativity is linked not only to childrearing but also to the quality of adults' relationships with their parents. Young adults' development of a sense of generativity, therefore, is related to caring for their children as well as being responsive to the needs of their parents. As noted by Erikson (1982), the young adult still relies on the support and guidance of parents, and the mature adult, in turn, "needs to be needed." Thus, the interdependence of parents and children is a lifelong process. Examples of that interdependence can be observed in the ways in which young adults involve their parents in the planning of and participation in their weddings, the births or adoptions of their children, family birthday parties, and graduation celebrations. Additionally, families develop many rituals for celebrating religious and other holidays in which young adults, their children, and their parents are all included. Furthermore, young adults and their parents regularly visit, have family meals together, share caregiving responsibilities, and participate in a number of other activities designed to maintain family cohesiveness across generations (Imber-Black & Roberts, 1993; Richlin-Klonsky & Bengston, 1996). Finally, young adults and their parents support each other at times of family crises such as illness or death (Murphy et al., 1998). All those activities provide ways in which young adults and their parents contribute to each other's development of a sense of generativity.

Thinking Critically

What examples of interdependence have you observed between young adults and their parents in the planning and carrying out of family celebrations and/or the mutual support demonstrated during family crises?

A Challenge to the Development of Generativity: Unintentional Parenthood.   Most adults choose to become parents, and the universal reason for choosing parenthood is the expectation of achieving a sense of generativity (Erikson, 1982; Goldhaber, 2000). Many parents, however, have children without weighing the costs or advantages of childrearing. For numerous young persons, the pregnancy is unintentional due to not having used birth control or as a result of the failure of birth control methods. For some would-be parents, the unplanned pregnancy is not considered undesirable and might even be welcomed; for others, who had not wanted to have children or who were not ready to have children, the pregnancy might be viewed as problematic (Clinton & Kelber, 1993).

Those individuals who are most likely to have unwanted pregnancies are typically the most vulnerable because younger, poorer, and less educated adolescents and young adults are more likely to experience unplanned pregnancies (Monahan, 2001). Moreover, young adults who began their childbearing during adolescence are the most vulnerable in terms of their ability to care for and provide the basic necessities for their children. A further complication of unplanned early parenthood is that the experience of childbirth for those young parents is likely to be associated with the trauma of having a low-birth-weight baby and/or a premature birth (Cornell, 2001).

What This Means for Young Adults, Their Parents, and Professionals.   Based on the preceding discussion, young parents who have unplanned pregnancies are the least prepared for parenthood and have the fewest resources to help them to be successful in their roles as parents. In those situations, their parents are typically willing to provide financial support for them while also supporting and providing care for their grandchildren. In addition to requiring assistance from their parents, young adults who give birth to children who were not planned for generally benefit from the support of professionals who can help them to adapt to their roles of early parenthood and to ensure that their children receive the care and attention needed for positive development.

The professional services needed by young parents in those situations include programs designed to help them remain in school so that they have more occupational opportunities. In addition to the advantages of education focused on career preparation, parent education courses help unprepared young parents adjust to their role of parent, help them to understand their children's normal development, and assist them in the development of skills designed to enhance parent–child interaction. Because their children are often designated as being at risk for developmental problems associated with low socioeconomic status, there are subsidized day care programs that are available for those children. Community organizations that ensure that their children will receive medical care and adequate nutrition are also beneficial for parents whose pregnancies were not planned.

THE INFLUENCE OF PARENT–CHILD RELATIONSHIPS ON YOUNG ADULTS' COGNITIVE DEVELOPMENT

Now that we have examined the ways in which young adults' parent–child relationships contribute to their social–emotional development, we will consider the impact of those relationships on young adults' cognitive development. The following discussion examines the ways in which the challenges of working out their relationships with their parents influence the ability of young adults to reason at higher cognitive levels. Also included in the upcoming discussion are the various ways that taking on the responsibilities of parenthood during young adulthood provoke advanced problem-solving abilities.

Parenthood and Postformal Thinking

Followers of Piaget believe that during adulthood the complex, often ambiguous, and frequently conflicting demands of daily life produce a higher level of reasoning capability. According to those theorists, higher reasoning capabilities of adults emerge during the Stage of Postformal Operations. That stage of cognitive development has been described by Arlin (1975) as a problem-finding stage and by Riegel (1976) as a dialectical stage. As emphasized in the discussion of Piaget's Theory of Cognitive Development in chapter 1, the development of higher levels of reasoning is gradual and dependent on particular experiences and education rather than being chronologically determined. As young adults thoughtfully consider the real-life dilemmas that are a necessary part of their relationships with their parents and with their children, they increasingly align their thinking processes with their contextual awareness. For many problems in young adults' parent–child relationships, there are no single solutions, no predetermined right answers, and no absolute rules. The ups and downs in the lives of their parents and children often lead young adults to consider the world in novel, more complex, and less rigid ways. By and large, **postformal thought**, which is reflected in problem finding and **dialectical thinking**, allows individuals to deal more effectively with the complex social worlds of which they are a part.

Examples of Young Parents' Problem-Finding Ability.   The problem-finding capability, seen in adulthood, emphasizes that the ability to provide solutions to problems can only be applied once those problems have been identified. For instance, to remedy a child's earache or stomach upset, the parent must first determine that a problem exists as well as what that problem is likely to be. Similarly, buying a child a new pair of shoes must be preceded by a realization that the shoes the child is currently wearing are getting too small or are becoming too worn. Moreover, providing emotional support to a child who is feeling disappointed or depressed must be preceded by the ability of a parent to recognize that something seems to be bothering the child.

The Dialectical Thinking of Young Parents.   After problem finding, young parents typically engage in dialectical reasoning whereby they are compelled to make logical decisions for which there are a number of possible solutions. Those decisions involve the recognition of ambiguities and contradictions in many life dilemmas for which adults become increasingly tolerant. An example of dialectical thinking is seen in the situation in which young parents, in considering day care for their children, are confronted with the dilemma of whether to choose the child care program that is less expensive and closer to their home or the one that costs more and is farther away from their home. The easier solution to the problem is to choose the less expensive and more conveniently located child care setting. If the less costly and more opportunely situated day care facility has child care providers who use a form of discipline that is not consistent with the values of the parents, however, those parents might engage in dialectical reasoning to resolve the child care dilemma. An example of dialectical reasoning in that situation would take into account the expense and expediency as well as values regarding what those young parents consider to be the best environment for their children. Like the child care quandary, there are numerous other childrearing challenges in which the ability to use dialectical reasoning helps young parents to arrive at more satisfactory solutions.

Thinking Critically

What examples come to mind of issues that young parents face that demonstrate the concept of dialectical thinking?

Experiences That Promote Young Parents' Postformal Thinking.   A variety of complex life circumstances associated with adulthood provide opportunities for young parents to develop the problem finding and dialectical thinking found in postformal thought. While in the process of pursuing an advanced degree, for example, individuals are challenged to engage in the critical thinking process which is based on problem finding and dialectical thinking. Moreover, it has been demonstrated that the critical thinking process engaged in within college classrooms impacts the parenting decisions of young adults. Researchers have found, for instance, that college-educated persons are more likely than are those who are not college educated to have an authoritative child socialization pattern (Hoff-Ginsberg & Tardif, 1995). One of the primary features of the authoritative pattern of parenting is the willingness of parents to provide reasons for their actions and to engage their children in problem-solving activities (Baumrind, 1971, 1991a; Steinberg & Levine, 1997).

Real-life experiences that promote higher level reasoning processes occur both inside and outside formal educational settings. For those young adults who do not go to college, they typically take responsibility for their own financial well-being while considering their future direction in life, such as gaining and keeping employment. While struggling with those real-life decisions, many of those young people enter into committed partnerships and/or become parents and begin to make multifaceted decisions—including ways in which to provide suitable housing for their families and how to feed and care for their infants and children. Because their real-life circumstances do not provide easy answers, those responsibilities are likely to promote young adults' ability to engage in problem finding and dialectical thinking.

Parenthood and Vygotsky's Concept of Scaffolding

Another theoretical approach to understanding the ways in which parent–child relationships contribute to young adults' cognitive development is provided by Lev Vygotsky. Vygotsky (1978) postulated that individuals are better able to demonstrate proficiency in various activities when supported by persons with specialized expertise. As noted in chapter 1, Vygotsky emphasized that with the help of their parents or other more accomplished persons, individuals can often reason at a higher level than they can by themselves. Through activities, such as modeling, instruction, and direct support, more competent persons provide **scaffolding** for the skill development of less experienced individuals. Although discussions of the concept of scaffolding typically focus on the role that parents and teachers play in sustaining the learning experiences of young children, there are many occasions whereby the problem solving of young adults is scaffolded by interactions with their own parents and/or their spouses or partners.

Parental Scaffolding of Young Adults' Academic Success.   Findings from a number of surveys have demonstrated that routine help to adult children characterizes the majority of parent–adult child ties (e.g., Rossi & Rossi, 1990; Spitze & Logan, 1992; Zarit & Eggebeen, 1995). As noted earlier, college students typically receive financial assistance from their parents that enables them to pursue studies in preparation for careers. In addition to financial backing, young adults often benefit from consultation with their parents regarding important decisions they are making, such as the selection of a major and/or the choice of a career. Furthermore, findings cited earlier showing a link between parental support and academic success suggest that young adults' academic success is scaffolded by the relationships they have had and continue to have with their parents (e.g., Fuligni et al., 1999; Paulson et al., 1998).

Behind the academic success of most young adults are parents who are emotionally and financially involved in helping their children achieve their dreams.

❦ ❦

Thinking Critically

What are the various ways that your parents or other parental figures in your life are currently involved in the scaffolding of your academic success and/or career preparation?

❦ ❦

Parental Scaffolding of Young Parents' Childrearing Efforts.   The role that parents play in scaffolding the ongoing development of their young adult children is not limited to assistance provided to those who are pursuing academic degrees and making choices regarding future careers. Most young adults benefit as well from parental support when they become parents. Even when young adults have been financially independent for a period of time, their parents are likely to provide financial, practical, and emotional assistance to them after they become parents. Examples of intergenerational financial support range from the gifts or loans parents provide their young adult children for buying their first house to the clothing and toys they buy for their grandchildren. Even though financial and practical support are excellent examples of ways in which the older generation of parents scaffolds the efforts of the younger generation of parents, perhaps the most important scaffolding role of older parents is that of emotional supporter. When young adults experience real-life problems, such as difficulties with the rearing of their children, illnesses, or life crises, they typically turn to the same individuals who were there for them at earlier developmental stages when they had skinned knees or wounded hearts (Zarit & Eggebeen, 1995).

Finally, the most common practical help that parents make available to their young adult children is related to assistance with child care (Cherlin & Furstenberg, 1986; Cornell, 2001; Kivett, 1991). Even in the majority cultures of the United States and Canada, where grandparents, aunts, and uncles do not typically assume coparenting roles, they frequently provide some level of child care if they live in close proximity to their children and grandchildren. Furthermore, circumstances such as parental death, illness, or teenage parenthood often influence those relatives to step in and scaffold young parents' childrearing efforts. The majority of unmarried adolescent parents live with their parents who provide financial, practical, and emotional support, thereby extending the childrearing efforts of those young parents. The scaffolding provided by older parents to unmarried young parents is particularly important for those young parents who are the most vulnerable in terms of their ability to care for and provide the basic necessities for their children (Cornell, 2001).

What This Means for Young Adults, Their Parents, and Professionals.   The foregoing discussion emphasizes the important role of parents in providing continuing support for their children in a variety of areas. Being able to scaffold the success of their adult children provides parents with an important role in relation to their children and also helps them to feel as if they are able to contribute to their children's ongoing development. The benefit for adult children is the realization that parents are there to support and assist them when needed. Parental scaffolding also sends the important message to children that parents are interested in their well-being and want to help them toward the achievement of their goals.

Thinking Critically

Do you know of a situation involving unmarried young parents where their parents have stepped in to scaffold the parenting efforts of those young parents? If so, in what ways do you think those young parents benefit from the scaffolding efforts of their parents?

The Scaffolding of Childrearing Efforts by Parental Partners. Finally, the important role that parental partners play in supporting young parents' childrearing efforts has been well documented. An important aspect of scaffolding seen in two-parent families is emotional support of each other's parenting efforts. In addition to emotional support, there are numerous practical opportunities for sustaining each other's childrearing efforts in the typical family. Examples of practical help that support childrearing efforts include taking turns getting up with a crying baby, participating in the bathing of the children, preparing meals for the family, taking the children to school, entertaining the children by playing with them, and helping the children with their homework. When parents work together to provide for

In this scene, the father and mother are working together to sustain each other's child-rearing efforts.

the needs of their children, the effectiveness of each parent's childrearing efforts is promoted (Ambert, 1992).

Thinking Critically

Have you observed a young couple at home with their young child or young children? If so, what examples of scaffolding of each other's childrearing efforts were you able to discern between those two parents?

THE ASSUMPTION OF ADULT SOCIAL ROLES

We will now consider the effect of parental socialization patterns on the social roles that individuals assume during early adulthood. We will consider as well the ways in which young adults and their parents influence the development of each other's social roles through a process known as parallel development.

The Selection of Adult Gender Roles

At some point after leaving home, the majority of young adults enter into domestic partnerships wherein they must make joint decisions with their spouses or partners regarding the division of household labor. In those choices, we see the influence of gender socialization processes as they occur in the family context. To provide an understanding of parental influences on young adults' adoption of gender roles, Cunningham (2001) conducted a study that compared the relative influence of parental characteristics assessed at different points in young adults' upbringing. The findings from that study provided evidence of the importance of parental modeling of household task division and parental attitudes about gender in the formation of young adults' gender role beliefs.

Among the most significant of the findings in that study was the strong impact of the mothers' gender role attitudes during the early years on the young adults' views regarding the ideal division of household labor. Cunningham's (2001) findings also demonstrated that the parental division of labor during their midadolescence had a significant effect on young adults' interpretation of the way that household tasks should be divided between women and men. Specifically, the higher levels of participation in housework by their fathers were associated with young adults' greater support for men's participation in stereotypically female housework. Based on those findings, Cunningham concluded that fathers' participation in household tasks during the adolescent years, when children are likely to be responsible for a greater proportion of the domestic labor, plays an important behavioral role in leading their children to support household task sharing.

Thinking Critically

It might not have occurred to you that the degree to which fathers are involved in sharing household tasks during their adolescent years is related to the values that young adults have regarding the gender division of household tasks. Consider the sharing of household tasks that you observed during your own adolescence, in your own or in another household. Are you able to see a link between your own gender role attitudes and those earlier observations?

The Parallel Development of the Social Roles of Young Adults and Their Parents

Although parents influence the development of the social roles that their children assume during young adulthood, the roles of young adults and their parents continue to be redefined in relation to each other's. Parents and their young adult children exert a strong influence on each other's role development through a process that contributes to their **parallel development**. To achieve parallel development with their parents, young adults must develop **filial maturity**. Blenkner (1965) introduced the concept of filial maturity to describe an adult's capability of responding to the needs of the parent, which represents a move away from egocentrism and a step toward the development of a more mature adult role. Forcefully rejecting the notion of role reversal, Blenkner emphasized that mature sons or daughters do not take on a parental role in relation to their parents but rather they assume a filial role, which involves the ability to be depended on by their parents.

Dimensions of Filial Maturity.   Two dimensions are essential to the development of filial maturity: **distancing** and **comprehending**. Distancing is necessary in the parent and adult child relationship to allow each party a certain level of independence from one another, and comprehending serves to keep the parent and adult child close to each other. Development in each of these dimensions requires the ability to balance the two forces (Nydegger & Mitteness, 1991). In the following discussion, we will examine the concepts of distancing and comprehending from the perspective of the role of the adult child.

Parental Distancing.   A critical task for personal development during young adulthood is to distance oneself from one's parents and to establish one's separate identity as an adult. As one begins the process of separating from one's parents, however, it is important to simultaneously take the first step toward development in the filial role (being responsive to the needs of one's parents). The challenge, therefore, is to achieve emotional emancipation while remaining engaged as a son or daughter. Establishing a psychological distance from their parents is a necessary step for young adults to take in order to be able to see both themselves and their parents more objectively. Acquiring a level of objectivity in relation to their parents allows young adults to perceive their parents as persons, apart from the parental role (Nydegger & Mitteness, 1991).

Although parental distancing is a normal and beneficial process, the course of emotional weaning is likely to be slow and painful for parents as well as for their adult children (Colarusso & Nemiroff, 1981; Erikson, 1963). The initial phase of parental distancing is triggered by the physical separation from parents typical of early adulthood in industrialized countries (which occurs earlier in the majority culture of the United States than in most other cultures). That period of adjustment is likely to be characterized by elevated criticism and reduced contact (Nydegger & Mitteness, 1991), and it is important to examine the processes underlying those interactions. Transitions such as physical separations from parents can be stressful because they challenge attachment bonds between family members. Therefore, open communication and the processing of emotions are crucial when family members change. The expression of emotions fosters the renegotiation of bonds and the clarification of family members' needs and concerns (Dankoski, 2001).

Renewed Acquaintance.   The separation phase wherein young adults temporarily withdraw from their parents is generally followed by a stage of **renewed acquaintance**. The emancipation that occurs during the withdrawal phase tempers young adults' egocentrism, thereby helping them to see their parents more realistically during the phase of renewed acquaintance. The more realistic perception of the parent, which occurs in the reconnecting phase of the parent–child relationship, is typically accompanied by a greater appreciation of the parent as an individual. A second outcome of young adults' distancing and renegotiated relationships with their parents is their improving ability to perceive themselves in the adult child role, from the viewpoint of what their parents need from them (Nydegger & Mitteness, 1991).

A concern of young adults that emerges during the emancipation stage and continues during the stage of renegotiated relationships with parents is the issue of privacy. It is, therefore, important to devise a family etiquette to handle the delicate balance between the parents' interest in knowing what is going on in their adult

Thinking Critically

What is an example of family etiquette that you and your parents have worked out (or are currently in the process of working out) to handle the delicate balance between your parents' interest in knowing what is going on in your life and your right to privacy?

children's lives and their adult children's right to privacy (Nydegger & Mitteness, 1988). Just as there are hindrances to parental distancing, there are factors that serve to promote the level of distancing necessary for the development of mature relationships between adult children and their parents. Interviews of young adults and their parents have suggested that demonstrating maturity in other adult roles promotes young adults' self-confidence, which in turn encourages parental distancing. Another factor that has been suggested as important in the promotion of parental distancing is the maturity of the parents themselves (Nydegger & Mitteness, 1991).

Parental Comprehending. There is much emphasis on the need of parents to understand their children and that is an appropriate focus of parent–child relationships when children are developing toward adulthood. When children become young adults, however, they develop filial maturity, which includes the capability of comprehending their parents. As might be expected, the ability to comprehend one's own parents requires considerable objectivity. The development of the ability to comprehend their parents brings adult children to the place whereby they realize that their parents had their own existence prior to assuming the role of parent and continue to exist as individuals outside their parental role (Blenkner, 1965; Nydegger & Mitteness, 1991).

The development of the ability to comprehend one's own parents not only lags behind parental distancing but also is a slower process. Most adults can remember a time when they began to really understand their parents (typically in their early 20s). They usually realize that their understanding of their parents was a gradual process that occurred as they themselves began to take on the adult roles held by their parents—those of spouse, parent, and worker. A positive outcome of young adults' development of the capability of comprehending their parents is the reduction of conflict with parents (Suitor & Pillemer, 1988). Finally, the comprehension of mothers happens earlier than does the comprehension of fathers. The level of comprehension of fathers is not expected to be achieved during early adulthood but instead is anticipated to occur during the 40s. Although, for many adults, comprehension of their fathers does not occur until their fathers are very old and may not take place until after their fathers' deaths (Nydegger & Mitteness, 1991; Nydegger, Mitteness, & O'Neil, 1983).

Thinking Critically

Can you identify the ways in which you distanced yourself from your parents as you became young adults? Are you currently in the process of comprehending your parents? If so, what have you discovered about your parents that helps you to appreciate them as individuals apart from their parental role?

YOUNG ADULTHOOD AND PARENT–CHILD RELATIONSHIPS: A FAMILY SYSTEMS PERSPECTIVE

So far we have discussed the various ways in which the parent–child relationships of young adults impact the emotional, social, and cognitive development of young adults. We considered as well the influence of parents on the development of young adults' social roles and the parallel development of the roles of parents and children in relation to each other. We will now examine the ways in the relationships of young adults and their parents alter the family system in which they occur by viewing that family from the perspective of Family Systems Theory. As a reminder, according to Family Systems Theory, which was discussed in chapter 1, each family member's behavior affects the behavior of all other family members. Furthermore, all individuals in a family work together to maintain the stability of the family system in the face of change. The changes that require adjustment of expectations, roles, and behaviors of family members include the arrival or departure of any family member, the experience of a family crisis, and the ongoing developmental changes of family members (Beevar & Beevar, 1988; Steinberg & Steinberg, 1994).

When Young Adults Establish Separate Residences

According to Family Systems Theory, whenever young adults leave home, a disruption occurs in the family system. That disruption requires all family members, including the departing member, to adapt to a change in the family system (Steinberg & Steinberg, 1994). A common disruption of the family occurs when young adults leave home to go to college. As young adults move out of the homes they lived in with their parents, a number of changes occur in their parent–child relationships that necessitate that both generations readjust their expectations of each other and modify their roles in relation to each other. Furthermore, there are different degrees of leaving home. For college students in the United States, even though they *live* in college residences they typically still *go home* for holidays, for many weekends, and for the summer. When college students go home, they often are surprised and/or disappointed to discover that their rooms have been taken over by younger siblings or that younger siblings have achieved a status in the family hierarchy that they (the college student) held prior to leaving home. Similarly, parents of young adult college students are frequently taken aback by their children's new independence. For example, parents might expect their college-age children to observe an earlier curfew when home for weekends and for holidays than those young adults adhere to while away at college. The following example is a reaction of a college student to a suggested change in the parental household after that student had been living away from home for 2 years while attending a state university.

> My Mom wanted to turn my room into a sewing room and I said "no way—that is my room." I know she will have sewing things all over the place and I won't feel like it's my room anymore. I told her that I am not ready to give up my room. (Unpublished interview of a 20-year-old college student)

Thinking Critically

In what ways have you observed that roles, rules, and other alterations in the household changed after you went away to college?

The Changes That Occur in Parent–Child Relationships When Members Are Added to the Family System

Not only do family roles and expectations change when young adults leave their parents' home, the rules and roles are further modified when young adults enter into committed relationships of marriage or other partnerships and/or when they have children. The integration of each of these new family members into the existing family system triggers a further shift in family roles (Steinberg & Steinberg, 1994).

Parents-in-Law and Children-in-Law. Parents of newlywed young adults take on the roles of mothers-in-law and fathers-in-law; and their children's spouses assume the roles of daughters-in-law and sons-in-law. The challenge for parents, when children-in-law enter into the family system, is that the previous relationships they had with their adult children require alterations to support their children's allegiance to their spouses or partners. Helping the partners or spouses of adult children feel welcome in the family requires an understanding that those individuals have come from family systems with roles, expectations, and boundaries that differ from those of their new family (Steinberg & Steinberg, 1994).

From the perspectives of both parents-in-law and children-in-law, there will be times when family members feel that "This is not the way we did things in our family." Those discoveries will sometimes be pleasant surprises and at times will be disappointing. The degree to which family members are sufficiently open minded and flexible to incorporate the needs of old and new family members makes a difference in the level of satisfaction experienced by all members of the expanded family system. Successful assimilation of new family members into an existing family system requires that all members receive encouragement to openly discuss their feelings and expectations. A positive integration of new family members into the existing family system is more likely to occur in families that respect the feelings of all family members. Furthermore, a willingness of family members to alter expectations to ensure that all members' needs are met is a positive step toward family cohesiveness (Steinberg & Steinberg, 1994).

When Young Adult Children Enter Gay or Lesbian Unions. Whereas the unions of most young adults are supported by their parents, young adults who are gay and lesbian do not typically have the support of their parents for their partnerships. In their study of the intergenerational relationships of gay men and lesbian women, LaSala (2002) found that the majority of those young adults experience parental disapproval, which might interfere with their union if both of the partners fail to prioritize the needs of the partner relationship over the parent relationship. The disappointment expressed in the following comment of a gay man discussing his partner's parents demonstrates the effect of parental disapproval on the lives of that couple: "Anytime he wants to go to see them, which is frequent . . . we have this whole conversation about whether I should go or shouldn't go. . . . If they were accepting, there would be no friction" (p. 331).

Although failure to prioritize the needs of the partner relationship often occurs, most gay men and lesbian women defend the partnership boundaries against intergenerational pressures (LaSala, 2002). An example of the way in which young adults in gay or lesbian unions defend their partnerships in the face of parental disapproval is illustrated in the comment of another gay man: "I respect her right to feel that way about my homosexuality. I recognize that her experiences are different from mine. I can validate her feelings and not buy into them. Just because my mother does not want to see me in a gay relationship does not mean I'm going to leave the one I'm in" (p. 332). Another way that gay men and lesbian women maintain intergenerational boundaries is by distancing themselves from their disapproving parents, as seen in the next comment: "My parents' religious objections don't affect the relationship. I don't see them very much" (p. 332).

Whereas both gay men and lesbian women who are in committed relationships typically experience moderate to strong parental disapproval of their homosexual unions, there are gender differences in the relationships those young adults have with their parents. Lesbian women experience less parental disapproval of their homosexual lifestyle than do gay men, and compared with gay men they are able to identify parental support for themselves even when parents are not supportive of their lifestyles (LaSala, 2002). The following statement reflects the value a lesbian woman places on the relationship she has with a parent who does not support her homosexual lifestyle: "It's positive, my parental relationship, because she comes over and we have dinner together and talk. . . . If I couldn't talk with my mother, I would feel closed off, and that would affect me and my relationship" (p. 332).

Even though gay men and lesbian women are frequently able to identify support for themselves, when parents disapprove of their partnerships the lack of parental support makes those relationships more challenging. One of the ways that young adults in those situations tend to cope with those challenges is by avoidance strategies designed to keep the peace. Either they do not discuss their sexuality with their parents or they hide negative comments from their partners. The next statement is an example of such a strategy, which is more likely to be used by lesbian women than by gay men: "When my father says something homophobic or ignorant, I jump in quick to correct it. I don't tell my partner because I don't want her to be hurt. She really needs my parents so much in light of her own parents' rejection" (p. 332).

Whereas most parents of gay men and lesbian women do not fully support their children's homosexual lifestyle, there are parents who demonstrate support of their young adult children's unions with their partners (LaSala, 2002). The benefit of that support in the lives of those individuals is demonstrated in the following statement of a young lesbian woman. "My parents being fully invested in my relationship has a positive effect. It lets me be fully present because my family is very close and important to me. I wouldn't be successful in a relationship without their support" (p. 332).

The Ways in Which the Arrival of Children Alters the Family System.   The arrival of children changes the family system of young adults and their parents. The primary impact of the birth or adoption of children, though, is on the members of the family system wherein those children reside. For new parents, they are suddenly placed in the largely expanded roles of *mother* and *father*. Those novel role positions contribute to alterations of their roles as members of a couple. For many couples, the strains accompanying the arrival of children result in the lowest level of marital satisfaction of any point in their relationship. That is particularly true for women, who (as discussed in chapter 3) tend to be less satisfied with their partners in the months after birth or adoption (Belsky & Kelly, 1994; Kluwer et al., 2002; Kurdek, 1993).

As explained in chapter 3, the most likely reason for young mothers' greater dissatisfaction with their partners or spouses following the advent of parenthood is that new mothers usually take on more child care and related household responsibilities than do new fathers. Even when both parents are employed outside the home and work similar hours, young mothers typically spend more time taking care of the children and doing housework than do young fathers (Belsky & Kelly, 1994; Glenn & Weaver, 1990; Kluwer et al., 2002). On the other hand, not all new parents experience a decline in satisfaction with their relationship or with each other. Indeed, some individuals experience greater satisfaction with their relationship during the years that they are most involved in childrearing. That is particularly true for those couples with realistic expectations regarding the extent of work involved in childrearing when there are infants and young children in the home (Kurdek, 1993). Additionally, young parents who are able to have an egalitarian relationship while rearing their young children tend to achieve greater satisfaction in their couple relationship (Hackel & Ruble, 1992; Kurdek, 1993; Patterson, 1995).

Those working mothers and fathers who share household responsibilities and child care experience greater satisfaction with their relationship.

COMBINING WORK AND PARENTAL ROLES

During the same time that young adults are adapting to their roles as parents and redefining their couple relationship to include parental responsibilities, most young adults are engaged as well in aligning family and work responsibilities. The fundamental problem for parents when both of them work outside the home is being able to coordinate family and work obligations. **Role overload** occurs when the demands of work and family roles result in a person feeling strained and overwhelmed. A number of researchers have documented the negative effects of role overload on family relationships (e.g., Erdwins, Buffardi, & Casper, 2001; Goldscheider & Waite, 1991; Kooreman & Kapteyn, 1987). The findings of those studies have contributed to the belief that dual-income families typically have mothers who suffer from role overload and children who are neglected.

Moving beyond the problems associated with role overload, recent evidence has provided a more positive scenario of families in which both fathers and mothers are working. First, studies of working parents have not provided evidence that children in dual-income families are more likely to suffer from neglect than are children in families with only one employed parent (Bryant & Zick, 1996). Second, women who are simultaneously carrying out the roles of wife, mother, and employee do not necessarily suffer role overload. Third, role overload is less common in dual-worker families than is **role buffering**. In many dual-income families, both parents act in many ways to buffer the impact of stress associated with performing the dual roles of parent and paid worker. Moreover, those young adults who are able to balance parental and vocational roles are healthier, happier, and more successful in their combined roles than are parents who function well in only one of those roles (Hochschild, 1997).

❧ SUMMARY

In this chapter, we have explored the relationships of young adults and their parents as well as young adults and their children in diverse circumstances and in varied cultures within the United States and throughout the world. We examined the parent–child relationship from the perspective of the impact of that relationship on the emotional, social, and cognitive development of young adults. Also discussed in this chapter were the ways in which the alterations in the lives of young adults impact the family system. The main emphases were (a) that parent–child relationships undergo considerable modification after children reach adulthood, (b) that those relationships remain important to young adults as well as to their parents, and (c) that participation in parent–child relationships (as parents and as adult children) impacts the social, emotional, and cognitive development of young adults.

❧ KEY TERMS

- comprehending
- connectiveness
- dialectical thinking
- distancing
- empty nest
- familism
- filial duty
- filial maturity
- full nest

- generativity
- individuation
- intimacy
- parallel development
- postformal thought
- renewed acquaintance
- role buffering
- role overload
- scaffolding

8

Middle Age and Older Parenthood and Grandparenthood

The psychological and social development of middle-aged and older adults is affected by the relationships in which they participate with their parents, with their children, and with their grandchildren. Furthermore, those relationships influence the continuing growth and development of the family systems in which they take place. In the upcoming discussion, we will take a look at middle age and elderly parenthood and grandparenthood in diverse cultures within the United States as well as in cultures throughout the world. We also will consider the influence of varied life circumstances (such as divorce, remarriage, retirement, and widowhood) on those relationships.

THE INFLUENCE OF PARENTHOOD ON THE SOCIAL–EMOTIONAL DEVELOPMENT OF MIDDLE-AGED ADULTS

The development of a sense of generativity has its beginnings during early adulthood when young adults become parents. During middle age, most people become grandparents, and the relationships grandparents develop with their grandchildren contribute to further development of a sense of generativity (Ryff, Lee, Essex, & Schmitte, 1994). A second type of continuing generativity development occurs among many middle-aged and elderly parents who are continuing in the roles of caregivers to their adult children with special needs and/or become the custodial caregivers of their grandchildren (Gibson, 2002; Karp, 1996). Still another kind of generativity development is found in a growing number of middle-aged fathers who have children by a second spouse or partner after they have reared other children (Cleaver, 1999). As we will see in the upcoming discussions, whether middle-aged adults develop a sense of generativity versus a sense of despair is influenced by a number of transitions that happen in their lives and in the lives of their adult children.

The Impact of Adult Children's Social Status Transitions

Beginning when their children are in early adulthood, the relationships of middle-aged adults and their children are altered along a series of social status transitions. **Social status transitions** refer to those changes in an individual's life that modify that person's social role. Normative status transitions occur as young adults graduate from college, enter a career, get married, or have children. Nonnormative social status transitions result from experiences such as getting divorced or losing one's job. Numerous studies have demonstrated a pattern of increased intergenerational closeness and contact when adult children experience normative transitions (e.g., Larson & Richards, 1994; Nydegger & Mitteness, 1991). Nonnormative transitions, on the other hand, tend to negatively affect parent and adult–child relationships (LaSala, 2002).

The Impact of Normative Social Status Transitions.   Middle-aged parents and their adult children typically become closer when children establish separate households (Aquilino & Supple, 1991; Larson & Richards, 1994), marry, and become parents (Larson & Richards, 1994; Nydegger & Mitteness, 1991). The positive change that occurs in intergenerational relations when adult children experience normative transitions has been attributed to two factors. First, such transitions verify that the adult child is conforming to social norms in terms of maturational development. Second, the transitions themselves increase the number of adult social roles that adult children share with their parents (Suitor, Pillemer, Keeton, & Robison, 1994).

Thinking Critically

What are the normative status transitions that you have experienced that met with approval from your parents? What are the positive effects of those transitions on your parent–child relationship?

The Consequences of Nonnormative Status Transitions.   Whereas normative status transitions generally enhance affectionate ties between middle-aged parents and their adult children, nonnormative status transitions frequently have a detrimental affect on those relations. Parents tend to have strong developmental expectations for their children. They hope that their children will mature into functioning adults and become important parental supports. Furthermore, parents often feel they cannot carry on with their own lives until their children have made those important transitions. Children who have not established their own households or who have not become independent of their parents serve as a reminder that parents have not achieved their goal of socializing their children to become independent, capable adults (Aquilino & Supple, 1991).

In addition to violating parental expectations, many nonnormative transitions of adult children increase adult children's demands on their parents, and those unanticipated burdens tend to have a negative effect on parent–child relations. Studies that document the impact of adult children's job loss support that argument. Parent–child relationships often become strained when sons lose their jobs (Newman, 1988), and adult children's unemployment has been found to be one of the main factors in parental conflict when generations share a home (Aquilino & Supple, 1991; Clarke, Preston, & Raskin, 1999).

The Impact of Middle-Aged Parents' Social Status Transitions

As their young adult children are making the normative transitions into their adult roles and sometimes undergoing nonnormative transitions, middle-aged parents are experiencing transitions in their own lives. The transitions in the lives of both generations affect their relationships with each other.

The Normative Transition into Grandparenthood.   A universal social status transition of middle age occurs when parents become grandparents. Even though the birth or adoption of the first grandchild marks the move into the role of grandparent, most individuals have more than one grandchild and the arrival of each grandchild further alters the grandparent role. Becoming a grandparent is a welcome role shift for most individuals and provides the opportunity for the acquisition of new roles. Many grandparents (particularly grandmothers) perceive the role of grandparent as easier, and more gratifying, than the role of parent, affording them pleasure and gratification without requiring them to take on the major responsibility for the care and socialization of the children (Emick & Hayslip, 1996). In addition to the satisfaction derived from becoming grandparents, parents of adult children gain satisfaction from knowing their children have assumed the status of parenthood, which becomes a social role shared by adult children and their parents (Suitor et al., 1994).

Middle-Aged Parents' Nonnormative Transitions.   Serious illness, death, divorce, remarriage, and second-generation fatherhood, represent social status transitions in the lives of middle-aged adults that might negatively impact their relationships with their adult children.

Serious Illness or Death.   The impact of serious illness or death of an adult child or parent on the well-being of middle-aged adults represents a nonnormative transition that calls for considerable social support. Because those transitions are highly important in the lives of middle-aged adults and their families, in the interest of providing a more comprehensive coverage of the topic, the discussion related to those losses is reserved for chapter 10, *Grief and Loss in Parent–Child Relationships.*

Parental Divorce and Remarriage.   Divorce of middle-aged adults is a nonnormative transition that impacts the relationships those older adults have with their adult children. The most consistent finding is that divorce in later life adversely affects parent–child relationships (Kaufman & Uhlenberg, 1998). Both divorced and re-married middle-aged parents provide less emotional support to their adult children and have lower levels of parent–child solidarity in comparison to parents who have not divorced (White, 1992). A number of studies have found a decrease in contact between older parents and their adult children following parental divorce (e.g., Aquilino, 1994; Umberson, 1992). Studies also have shown that the later life divorce of parents is associated with reduced relationship quality (Aquilino, 1994) and greater strain in the parent–adult child relationship (Umberson, 1992). Further-more, gender differences have been noted in the effects that older parents' divorce has on their relationships with their adult children. The effect of divorce on inter-generational relationships is particularly detrimental to the relationships between fathers and their children (Amato & Booth, 1996), and father–daughter relationships are more detrimentally affected by the divorce of an older parent than are father–son relationships (Aquilino, 1994).

Second-Generation Fathers.   Not only are relationships between middle-aged fathers and their adult children likely to be strained following the older parents' divorce and/or remarriage, those relationships are further altered in cases when older fathers have more children. Although the population of middle-aged, **second-generation fathers** is growing, only a few researchers have studied the relationships between those fathers and their adult children. According to that research, most men who become "refathers" are not doing so because they have discovered a need to father late in life. Instead, most of those fathers love their wives or partners who want to have children, like the idea of having more children, and have more time to spend with children than they had when their adult children were younger. Because there is often a generation difference between second-generation fathers and their wives or partners, those fathers are usually learning how to parent all over again.

This second-generation fa-ther faces the challenge of expanding his paternal role to include parenting a young child while also being the par-ent of adult children.

When rearing their first set of children, older fathers often have been part of the old male model of the father as the disciplinarian and financial provider and are typically grateful to have a second chance to parent (Cleaver, 1999).

Although second-generation fathers are given the opportunity to adapt their fatherhood role according to the contemporary model of involved father, observation of their father's new role might contribute to resentment by their older children. Possibilities of tension between second-generation fathers and their adult children center around three issues: (a) seeing their fathers spend more leisure time with their younger siblings than they had experienced as children, (b) concern about division of family financial resources, and (c) not being as free to rely on their fathers' assistance with their own children. The adult children of second-generation fathers might interpret their father's greater involvement with their younger siblings as evidence that their fathers have a greater affection for their younger siblings. What older siblings are witnessing, however, is an example of an alteration in the fatherhood role across the two generations. "Refatherhood" is an example of the way in which the parenthood role changes from one generation to the next and is influenced by social and societal changes (Cleaver, 1999).

THE RELATIONSHIPS OF OLDER PARENTS AND THEIR MIDDLE-AGED CHILDREN

We will now change the focus from middle-aged adults and their children to middle-aged adults and their older parents. In distinguishing middle-aged parents from older parents, it is important to keep in mind that some of those older parents might be considered elderly; whereas some might be viewed as merely older. In the past, it was easier to distinguish between older persons and middle-aged individuals. People who had reached their 60s were thought to be old. Today, due to better health, an increase in longevity, and variation in lifestyles among older persons, those distinctions are less clear. Keeping those considerations in mind, the following discussions focus on the lives of individuals who are 60 and older and their relationships with their middle-aged children. The majority of older persons in the United States (approximately 80%) have living children, and many of those older individuals (the oldest old—about 10%) have children who are 65 or older. As will become clear in the upcoming discussions, older persons and their children have relationships that vary in terms of residential proximity, frequency of interaction, mutual aid, feelings of affection, and beliefs regarding filial duty and obligation.

PARENT–CHILD RELATIONSHIPS AND THE SOCIAL–EMOTIONAL DEVELOPMENT OF OLDER PERSONS

The quality of the relationships that elderly individuals have with their children and grandchildren contributes to the development of the older person's sense of integrity versus despair (Erikson, Erikson, & Kivnick, 1986). According to Erikson (1968), during old age, individuals reexamine their lives and make a judgment regarding whether they have accomplished the things they had hoped for in their work as well as in their personal relationships. If their interpretation of their lives is a positive one, they incorporate a **sense of integrity**. If they look back with regrets, they develop a **sense of despair**.

Because parent–child relations play such an integral role in the life of an individual, the development of a sense of integrity or a sense of despair is linked to whether or not their children have turned out as parents had hoped they would. The attainment of a sense of integrity is related as well to whether parents have been able to maintain satisfactory relations with those children over the years. Both older men and older women evaluate their life histories in terms of the social networks of which they have been a part but there is a gender difference in those life reviews. In their remembered past, feeling as if they have had social influence on others is more highly valued for men, whereas for women **social anchorage** (maintaining connections to others) is seen as more important (McCamish-Svenson, Samuelsson, & Hagberg, 1999).

The Transitions of Elderly Parents and Their Middle-Aged Children

We will now explore the ways in which the transitions experienced by older persons and their middle-aged children affect their relationships with each other. We also will examine the impact on older persons' lives when their middle-aged children do not make the expected transition into independent living.

The Influence of Elderly Parents' Transitions.   There are a number of status transitions that older parents must make in their lives such as the adjustment to retirement and/or the death of a spouse or partner. Furthermore, older parents make accommodations in their lives to respond to the needs of their children as well as to the needs of their grandchildren. Those life course alterations affect the nature and quality of those intergenerational relationships.

The Normative Transitions of Older Parents.   The two primary normative transitions of older adults that affect their relationships with their middle-aged children are retirement and widowhood. In the case of retirement, the support required by older parents from their children in coping with retirement is minimal. Moreover, the adjustment made by the family following the older parent's retirement is likely to be increased family participation by the retiree. Although the retirement of older parents is associated with increased family participation, there are a number of factors that influence the degree to which retired parents interact with their adult children. Those include the geographic distance between parents and children, the gender of the retired person, and the presence or absence of grandchildren. For those children living within 10 miles, their mothers' retirement is associated with fewer visits and their fathers' retirement is associated with more visits. In contrast, for children living more than 10 miles away, mothers increase and fathers decrease their visits. Interestingly, retired mothers are more likely to visit their children who have children living in the household, whereas retired fathers are more likely to visit their childless children (Szinovacz & Davey, 2002).

In contrast to the minimal adjustment of family members following a parent's retirement, the widowhood of a parent signifies a radical change in the life of the surviving parent. Adult children are a particularly important source of emotional support and assistance to the surviving parent (Roan & Raley, 1996; Silverstein & Bengston, 1994), and there is a general pattern of stability and continuity in parent–child relations following widowhood (Dean, Matt, & Wood, 1992). See chapter 10, *Grief and Loss in Parent–Child Relationships* for a more in-depth discussion of the impact of the death of an older parent on the psychological development of middle-aged adults and their families.

Older Parents' Adjustment to Their Children's Transitions. In addition to the effects of transitions associated with aging such as retirement and the death of a spouse or partner, older adults also are affected by the transitions in their children's lives, such as their children's career changes and geographic locations. The normative transitions in the lives of middle-aged children generally do not strain the relations between older parents and their children. The nonnormative transitions of middle-aged adults, on the other hand, tend to burden older parents. When older parents are troubled by the nonnormative transitions of their middle-aged children, there are likely to be difficulties in the parent–child relationship.

The Impact of Middle-Aged Children's Stressful Life Circumstances. Stressful life circumstances and prolonged dependency are two primary problems that middle-aged adults encounter that tend to negatively affect their older parents' psychological adjustment and have a harmful effect on the relationships they have with their aging parents. For example, Pillemer and Suitor (1991) found that parents of adult children who have mental or physical impairments, substance abuse, or stress-related problems experience more depression than do parents whose children do not have those problems. Another factor that detrimentally impacts the psychological adjustment of older parents is when their adult children fail to become emotionally and economically independent. The morale of older parents suffers if their middle-aged children's problems necessitate older parents continuing to provide them with high levels of care and support. Thus, to the extent that the problems of middle-aged adults lead to their continued or increased dependency on their older parents, the quality of those intergenerational relationships tends to decline and the psychological well-being of older parents might be compromised (Clarke et al., 1999; Gibson, 2002).

Thinking Critically

Consider the relationships your grandparents have with their children, including your own parents, and see if you can identify the normative and nonnormative transitions that have altered or currently impact those relationships.

GRANDPARENTHOOD, PERSONHOOD, AND THE LIFE COURSE

Earlier in the chapter we discussed the ways in which becoming a grandparent represents a social status transition that typically occurs during middle adulthood and alters the relationship between middle-aged parents and their adult children. We now will explore the ways in which participation in the role of grandparent affects the lives of middle-aged and older individuals, their children, and their grandchildren.

The Greater Number and Various Roles of Grandparents Today

Today, an unprecedented number of people in American society are grandparents, and with the increase of grandparents has been a parallel boost in the variety of ways in which the grandparent role has come to be defined. Thinking of grandparents in terms of the stereotype of persons with a common lifestyle who have few roles outside their role as grandparent is very difficult to maintain. Although, we still see grandparents at home baking cookies for their grandchildren, we also encounter them on the jogging track and the hiking trail, watch them perform as rock stars, and are likely to be working for them in the corporations that they head. Not only do we have difficulty identifying grandparents by the roles they play in society, we also are unable to pin them down in terms of a life stage since they range in age from 30 to 110!

In addition to variations in age and alterations in the lifestyle of grandparents, the route to grandparenthood has shifted as well. Due to changed configurations of families through divorce, remarriage, and older child adoptions, the new grandchild might be an infant, an older adopted child, a young or middle-aged adult, or even a retiree. Increased longevity also means that the grandparent role has been extended. It is becoming increasingly common for women to be grandmothers for more than 4 decades. Additionally, the grandparent role has been expanded; it has become gradually more integrated into other family and societal roles. Many individuals who are grandparents are still involved in rearing their own children and are very active in their careers, counteracting the image of grandparents who spend their days taking care of household tasks and talking to neighbors across the back fence (Pruchno & Johnson, 1996).

The Cultural Role of Grandparent

In addition to variations in age and lifestyles of grandparents, there are cultural differences in the roles grandparents play in relation to their grandchildren. Those cultural roles differ according to the degree to which there is a cultural norm of independence (found in individualistic cultures) or a cultural norm of interdependence (seen in collectivistic cultures).

The Grandparent Role in Traditional Cultures.   Because traditional cultures value family interdependence, the lives of grandparents in those cultures are more integrated into the daily lives of grandchildren, and grandparents are expected to play a central role in the upbringing of grandchildren. In cultures characterized by large extended families and a reverence for elders, grandparents are likely to live with their adult children and grandchildren and to be part of the social support system of the family. An example of the integration of the grandparent into the daily lives of grandchildren in traditional cultures can be observed in the Japanese culture. Japanese tradition emphasizes that grandparents be respected and honored and that grandmothers be provided with a ritualized status, through a rite of passage that allows them to wear the color red as a symbol of that status (Kornhaber, 1996).

The Grandparent Role in Western Societies. Within the majority cultures of the United States, Canada, and Western Europe, grandparents are not expected to play a primary role in the socialization of grandchildren. Moreover, the role of grandparent in Western societies is less clear than the grandparent role in traditional cultures. Despite the lack of clarity of the grandparent role in Western societies, a couple of general rules govern that role. The first of those rules is the norm of noninterference, which specifies that under normal circumstances grandparents should not interfere with the way their adult children are rearing their grandchildren. The second general rule of grandparenthood is the norm of independence, which prescribes that parents and their children live independently and autonomously from the older generation (Lockery, 1991).

The Grandparent Role in the United States. The role of grandparent in the United States varies according to ethnic diversity. According to Lockery (1991), grandparents of Asian American, African American, and Latino American backgrounds are more likely, in comparison to grandparents of other ethnicities, to play an active role in the lives of their grandchildren. Furthermore, grandparents in ethnic minority cultures are more integrated into the social support system of the family than are grandparents in the European American majority. An illustration of the integration of grandparents into

The role of grandparent in ethnic minority families in the United States is typically integrated into the social support system of the family.

the social support system of ethnic minority families in the United States is found in the central role that elders play in the Latino American culture. In that culture, older adults are twice as likely to influence childrearing, family decision making, and advising, in comparison to their African American or European American peers (Burnett, 1999). In contrast to the role of the grandparent in ethnic minority cultures, European American grandparents are more likely to take on roles in relation to their grandchildren whereby they maintain close relationships with their grandchildren while living independently from the parent–child household.

The Functions of Grandparents.   Despite cultural and social differences in the expectations associated with the grandparent role, grandparents everywhere make valuable contributions to the lives of their grandchildren. One of the most important types of support provided by grandparents is that they help their families by just being there (Bengston, 1985). Their presence in the lives of their children and grandchildren provides symbols of longevity and continuity and having grandparents who are available increases feelings of security in younger generations. Another important role served by grandparents is that of family historian. The evolution of the family is passed down from generation to generation by the stories told by grandparents and great-grandparents. Grandparents also sometimes serve as mentors and role models to their grandchildren. Additionally, grandparents fulfill the role of crisis managers in the family. As noted earlier, when crises such as divorce, death, or prolonged unemployment occur, older parents often provide substantial assistance to their children and grandchildren (Gibson, 2002). For example, Cherlin and Furstenberg (1986) reported that when divorce occurs, the norm of noninterference (common in individualistic cultures) is temporarily set aside. Finally, many grandparents assume the role of custodial parents when neither of their grandchildren's parents is able to fulfill that responsibility. In the United States, a large number of children are permanently in the care of their grandparents (Gibson, 2002). The rapid growth of grandparent-maintained households is due in large part to the growth of recent health problems among younger parents, including substance abuse and HIV/AIDS. Other factors that are associated with an increase in the number of children being raised by grandparents include high rates of teen pregnancy, child abuse and neglect, and the increased incarceration of women of childbearing ages (Fuller-Thomson & Minkler, 2001).

Thinking Critically

If you have (or had) grandparents, or older adults in your life that fulfilled the role of grandparent, see if you can identify the various roles that those individuals have played or are currently playing in your life.

The Impact of Grandparenthood on Older Adults' Psychological Development.
According to Erikson et al. (1986), grandparenthood offers many individuals a "second chance" at generativity because it provides the possibility of caring for the newest generation more vigorously and less ambivalently than they did with their own children. With grandchildren, elders might participate in any number of ways of guiding and maintaining those children. By taking children for the weekend, for example, grandparents are caring for their grandchildren as well as for their children. Furthermore, the distance of the next generation frequently allows those grandparents who had difficulty with parenthood to experience feelings of pride in their grandchildren that they might not have experienced with their children. Finally, participation in the role of grandparent contributes to the psychological development of older adults based on the inclusion of that experience in the older adult's life review. Kivnick (1982) identified five distinct dimensions of meaning that grandparenthood brings to the life review process: (a) role centrality, (b) valued eldership, (c) immortality through clan, (d) reinvolvement with personal past, and (e) indulgence.

OLDER ADULT CAREGIVERS OF GRANDCHILDREN AND/OR ELDERLY PARENTS

We will now turn our attention to the ways in which intergenerational relations are altered in situations when older parents become the caregivers of their grandchildren and/or their parents.

The grandmother and grandchild in this scene represent a growing trend in the United States, where a substantial number of grandparents are assuming responsibility for rearing their grandchildren.

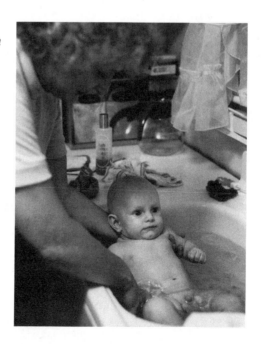

Custodial Grandparents

As previously noted, there has been a substantial increase in the number of grandparents who are assuming the role of primary caregivers of their grandchildren in the United States. Although there has been an increase in grandparent-headed households in the United States, there are ethnic differences in the prevalence of those households. African Americans are three times as likely and Latino Americans twice as likely as other grandparents to be providing custodial care for their grandchildren. The skipped-generation caregiving by grandparents in those ethnic groups does not reflect less parental responsibility among African American and Latino American parents in comparison to parents in other ethnic groups but rather an integration of cultural norms with social forces. There has been a recent increase in the United States of children who are cared for by nonbiological parents and many of those children are growing up in foster care or adoptive families (Fuller-Thomson, Minkler, & Driver, 1997; Roche, 2000). Rather than watch their grandchildren being placed in foster care or adoption, when their adult children are unable or unwilling to provide the care they need, African American and Latino American grandparents are likely to step into the vacated parental role. The role of grandparents as primary caregivers of their grandchildren is a culturally congruent social role in those communities for a couple of reasons. First, it fits with the African American and Latino American commitment of assisting family members by providing a safety net for children. Second, kinship care in African American and Latino American families is an acceptable response to family member loss and separation.

Challenges Faced by Custodial Grandparents.   Although the role of primary care grandparent is on the rise in the United States, caring for one's grandchildren is not as simple as transferring residences. To better understand the challenges faced by second-generation grandparents, Gibson (2002) interviewed a number of those grandparents to determine their concerns about their grandchildren and their adult children. One of the findings from the study was that after assuming their role of primary care grandparent, those older adults became aware of previously unknown problems faced by their grandchildren. Those problems included a lack of age-appropriate skills, low self-esteem, developmental delays, sexualized behaviors, and hyperactive behavior. As they became aware of their grandchildren's troubles, those grandparents began to realize that their grandchildren behaved differently than did their parents at similar ages.

The following quote exemplifies a custodial grandmother's reaction to her residential grandchildren's behaviors: "M. was so hyper and he was so angry . . . and he broke everything. I mean he fought constantly. He would just . . . he had a foul mouth that was hard for me to get used to" (p. 6). The next quote demonstrates a grandmother's worries regarding her grandchildren's low self-esteem: ". . . I'm trying to work on the children's self-esteem. . . . They are missing a lot of things, and I want them to be proud of who they are and what they can do" (p. 6). The comments of the grandparents in Gibson's study demonstrated that as their awareness increased, they were often surprised at their grandchildren's idiosyncrasies. For instance, one grandmother remarked: "M. will not wear a shirt with buttons on it . . . . So I don't press the issue. If I buy, I buy a shirt that goes over his head . . . . Friends give me a lot of things . . . so I either give those shirts to someone else or save them 'til the next child grows into them (Gibson, 2002, p. 7).

Besides the adjustments related to the direct care of their grandchildren, skipped-generation parents are often burdened with worries about their children who are parents of the children in their care. For example, Gibson found expressions of disappointment related to their children's present and past behaviors and attitudes. Those disappointments centered around three primary themes: parenting skills, parenting attitudes, and irresponsible behavior. "She's always complaining either she's ill or she just doesn't feel good when she has the children. But she can always go out on Thursdays and Fridays. She's just . . . I don't know . . . she always said, 'Well, I just shouldn't have had those kids.' Well, since you have, you're supposed to love them and give them all you can. You're supposed to be devoted to them" (p. 6). Another grandparent's remark expresses her lack of understanding of the attitude of the parent: "I couldn't understand how she could not want to be a part of her baby's life. I couldn't understand it because she wasn't raised that way" (p. 6).

Gibson found that chief among the concerns of those custodial grandparents was ensuring the safety of their grandchildren by keeping them out of foster care and monitoring interactions between them and their parents. For some of the custodial grandparents, there were no concerns regarding grandchildren safety when interacting with their parents. When there were concerns, the grandparents reacted by supervising the interactions between the parents and the grandchildren and by placing limits on those interactions. Examples of ways in which primary care grandparents put themselves between their grandchildren and the parents in those situations are exemplified in the following statements. In referring to her daughter, one mother said "She couldn't stay here and disrupt the kids. If she wanted to stay, long as she was attempting to help herself, or like, get a job, but she could not bother the kids" (p. 8). In the next comment, it is evident that the grandmother's role in protecting her grandchild has taken its toll on her relationship with her son who is the child's father: "I feel like we're [grandmother and parent] not as close as we used to be because like I said, now that he's out [prison] and out of trouble, he wants to come in [exert authority] and I have my own set of rules" (p. 8, brackets added by author).

Many middle-aged daughters or daughters-in-law take on the role of caregiver for elderly parents when those parents become ill or frail.

The Challenges Associated with Providing Care for Elderly Parents

In addition to an increase in the number of grandparents who have assumed the role of caregiver to their grandchildren, many older adults provide care for their aging parents. Furthermore, those older adults who are in the role of custodial grandparents might be simultaneously providing care for their aging parents. In the following discussion, we will focus on the lives of adults who serve as caregivers of their parents.

Who Are the Caregivers of Elderly Parents?   First, it is important to emphasize that not all older persons require assistance with the tasks of daily living. Second, older persons are more likely to be in a role whereby they are coming to the aid of their adult children rather than receiving assistance from them (Bengston, Rosenthal, & Burton, 1990; Kelly & Kropf, 1995). Third, when elderly parents become frail or suffer from disabilities, their children do not necessarily take on the caregiver role. In the United States, the first choice related to the care provision of their parents by the majority of adults is to provide no care. The second choice of adults faced with their parents' need for care is to designate one child as the caregiver. The third choice for parental care is for siblings to share the responsibilities related to the care of an elderly parent. Whether a child takes on the caregiver role or shares parental care with siblings is affected by a number of child and parent characteristics (Checkovich & Stern, 2002).

Child Characteristics That Influence Decisions Regarding Parental Care.   Characteristics of the child that influence whether or not that person will become a caregiver of an aging parent include geographic location, employment, age, and gender. The further children live from their parents the less likely they are to provide care, although modern technologies as simple as the telephone and cheaper and faster forms of travel have made it increasingly possible for children to provide some form of long-term care from a considerable distance. Another influence of whether or not children provide direct care for their parents is related to their work responsibilities. Less care is devoted to parental care by children who work. The age of children is another factor that impacts the decision of whether or not they will assume the caregiver role, with older children less likely to be in that role than younger children. The link between older children's decreased likelihood of becoming caregivers might reflect situations in which frailty or disability is more common among the oldest of the elderly population whose oldest children are more likely to be elderly themselves. Finally, all things being equal, women provide considerably more care of aging parents than do men. Both daughters and daughters-in-law are more likely to assume the role of caregiver of older parents than are sons or sons-in-law (Checkovich & Stern, 2002).

Child Versus Spousal Care.   In the United States, women are more likely than men to take on the responsibilities of caring for their aging parents but spouses are more likely to become caregivers than are adult children. Because women typically outlive their husbands, older fathers who become ill, frail, or disabled, typically have wives who provide the care they require. Older women who become ill, frail, or disabled, however, are more likely to be widows. Therefore, older fathers who require assistance with the tasks of daily living are likely to be cared for by their wives, and older mothers in that same situation are more likely to be cared for by their daughters or daughters-in-law (Checkovich & Stern, 2002).

Parental Characteristics That Influence Decisions Regarding Parental Care.   The characteristics of parents that influence whether or not they will be cared for by their children include marital status, level of education, as well as the number of children they have and the presence or absence of a disability. Married parents are less likely to receive direct care from their children than are parents who are not married, which reflects the tendency of spouses to take on the role of caregiver for their spouses who are ill or disabled. More educated parents also are less likely to have children in the role of caregivers because each year of parental education decreases the amount of long-term care provided by children. The relation between parental education and decreased care by children might reflect the link between education and income. Those parents with more education typically have higher incomes and are, therefore, better able to provide for their own care by funding in-home care, opting to pay for institutionalized services, or living in a retirement community that offers appropriate services. Finally, the level of parental need as well as the presence of children to meet those needs affect the decisions that children make related to parental care. That children consider parental need in making caregiving decisions is reflected in findings that parents with disabilities receive more assistance from children than do parents without disabilities. When there are several children in the family that can divide the caregiver responsibilities among themselves, those children are more likely to provide direct care for their parents. In that situation, more total care is received by the parents in comparison to families where there are fewer children, but less care is provided by each individual child (Checkovich & Stern, 2002).

Reactions of Caregivers to the Demands of Caring for Elderly Parents.   The literature confirms that the care of elderly parents has negative effects on the caregivers, who show more financial, physical, and emotional strains than do noncaregivers (Braus, 1998; Clyburn, Stones, & Hadjistavropoulos, 2000). Moreover, caring for one's elderly parents is not a homogeneous experience but varies according to gender and residential status. Because women provide more intensive personal care than do men, they tend to experience more problems and strains related to caregiving than do men (Barusch & Spaid, 1989; Braus, 1998; Clyburn et al., 2000); and coresident caregivers tolerate more than do those who live apart from the care recipient (Hoyert & Seltzer, 1992).

The Stresses of Caregivers.   One example of the effects of stress on caregivers of their parents was shown by Braus (1998), who documented that family caregivers often must juggle work responsibilities and stretch their finances while dealing with the additional stress of caring for an elderly parent. Braus found that those caregivers benefit from informal supports provided by family and friends and that they are most in need of the kind of support that allows them to catch up on needed rest. Another example of the stresses associated with providing care for a parent was provided by Clyburn et al. (2000) who studied the stresses incurred by family caregivers of persons with Alzheimers' disease. Those researchers found that a higher frequency of disturbing behaviors exhibited by the family member in their care, combined with low informal help from family and friends, was related to a higher burden for the caregiver. Furthermore, caregivers of family members exhibiting more disturbing behaviors and functional limitations received less informal help from family and friends.

Adaptation to the Role of Caregiver.   Whereas the stresses related to assumption of the role of caregiver of one's parents has received much research attention, it is important to emphasize that there is variation in the coping behaviors of those caregivers. One approach to understanding the ways in which caregivers cope with caring for their elderly parents is to examine the ways in which individuals change when they first take on the caregiver responsibility and how they are affected during the course of caregiving. The small body of longitudinal research on caregiving indicates that, as time goes by, a process of adaptation to the caregiver role occurs. For example, Townsend, Noelker, Deimling, and Bass (1989) studied nonresidential caregivers of their parents over a 14-month period and found the following: (a) the majority of those caregivers improved in their ability to cope with the problem behaviors manifested by their parents and (b) most of the caregivers showed no increase in levels of depression. Similar findings were reported by Zarit, Todd, and Zarit (1986), who found that caregivers of their elderly family members improved over time in their ability to cope with the problem behaviors manifested by their care recipients in spite of the fact that those behaviors became increasingly more extreme throughout the course of caregiving. Chirobogo, Yee, and Weiler (1992) also reported that caregivers showed improvement over time in the ability to cope with the stresses of caregiving. Those researchers studied the stress responses of adult children of parents with Alzheimer's disease and found that the longer the time since the parent's diagnosis, the less the burden on the caregiver.

The preceding findings indicate that the highest level of stress associated with the care of one's parents occurs as the caregiver assumes that new role but that, with the passage of time, enactment of the caregiving role might contribute to the development of coping strategies. Finally, informed by the coping and adaptation literature, Noonan, Tennstedt, and Rebelsky (1996) interviewed caregivers of elderly family members in an attempt to discern the meaning of the experience on a personal level. The results of those interviews revealed several common ways in which caregivers were able to find meaning in their caregiver roles, including: (a) gratification and satisfaction with the caregiver role, (b) a sense of family responsibility/reciprocity, (c) the friendship and company that caregiving offered, and (d) a commitment to doing what needs to be done. Less common themes that emerged from that investigation were having the ability to express a caring personality, experiencing personal growth, and having an improved relationship with the elderly parent.

Thinking Critically

Were you surprised to learn that the experience of caring for one's parents might, despite the stresses involved, contribute to the development of a caregiver's coping strategies? In what ways do you think that the development of coping strategies associated with caring for one's parents might influence the ongoing development of the adult child?

Interventions That Support and Provide Relief for Caregivers. As noted in the foregoing discussion, being in the caregiver role potentially impacts the caregiver's development of positive coping skills. Nevertheless, the responsibilities associated with that role sometimes detrimentally impact the psychological well-being of the caregiver and the relationships of older parents and their children. Whether assuming the role of caregiver of one's parents has a positive or negative impact on individual development and intergenerational relationships depends on whether or not caregivers receive the necessary support to effectively carry out their caregiver responsibilities. A number of interventions have been designed to provide support and relief for persons who are the primary care providers for their parents.

In a study of respite service for caregivers of parents with Alzheimer's disease, Lawton, Brody, and Saperstein (1989) pointed out the need for a number of services that could be made available by informal sources (family and friends) as well as formal sources (government, social, or health agencies, or independent paid workers). Those researchers emphasized that respite services could take place in the home or out of the home (e.g., in a day care setting or in a facility such as a nursing home) and might be planned in advance for special purposes, used regularly for periodic relief, or utilized in response to emergencies. Furthermore, as noted by Lawton and colleagues, transportation to bring the patient to the site of service delivery is a primary component of respite service that is delivered outside the home. In their evaluation of the impact of respite care on the lives of caregivers and their families, Lawton et al. found that families with respite care maintained their relatives, who had impairments, significantly longer in the community and had higher levels of satisfaction when respite care was used.

THE ABLE ELDERLY IN THE FAMILY CONTEXT

So far we have considered the relationships of older adults and their children in terms of transitions, life stresses, and altered roles. We also examined the lives of older adults who take on the roles of caregivers of their grandchildren and/or elderly parents. We will now take a look at the able elderly in the family context, including the importance and quality of those intergenerational relationships.

Measures of Relationship Quality

The quality of the relationships of older parents and their children are reflected in (a) how close they live to one another, (b) the frequency of their interactions with each other, (c) the degree to which they provide mutual aid to one another, and (d) the closeness or strength of feelings between them.

Residential Proximity.   One indicator of the importance of the relationships of middle-aged children and their older parents is the effect of those relationships on where people live. In regard to residential proximity, it is clear that older persons prefer to live near their children. The majority of older adults have children who live less than an hour away (Fingerman, 2001). Furthermore, the geographic distance is lessened between older parents and their children as older parents get older. For example, many elderly individuals, 75 or older, mention proximity to children as a primary reason for geographic relocation (Atchley, 1991). Even for elderly parents and grown children who do not live in close proximity to each other, their relationships with each other are typically close. Surprisingly, geographic distance does not seem to detrimentally affect those close ties. Technological advances over the years such as cheaper telephone rates, the availability of electronic mail, and increased air travel, allow frequent contact between parents and children who reside at a distance (Fingerman, 2001).

Frequency of Interaction.   Not only are older persons inclined to live near their children, but also interaction frequency between older persons and their children tends to be high. There are several status factors that influence the frequency of those interactions. First, the gender of each party plays an important role in the interaction patterns of older adults and their children. Women's intergenerational ties tend to be characterized by greater intimacy than men's intergenerational ties. Therefore, mothers and daughters are likely to experience greater intimacy in comparison to fathers and sons. The marital status of older parents is another factor that influences intergenerational relationships. Married older women interact less with their children than do those who are widowed or divorced (Fingerman, 2001). The nature of the frequent interactions between older children and their parents is primarily to serve as a means of checking that all is well through brief encounters. Moreover, that type of monitoring typically increases with the age of the parent, such that adult children are likely to learn quickly if their parents have a problem or need something (Atchley, 1991).

Mutual Aid.   The crucial dimension of the relationship between adult children and their older parents is mutual aid. Mutual aid flows in both directions and is multidimensional, consisting of services such as child care and/or housework, information and advice, as well as money and gifts. Although the stereotypical view of dependency is that older parents are dependent on their children, research findings have demonstrated that older parents are primarily donors who provide substantial aid to their middle-aged adult children (Bengston et al., 1990; Kelly & Kropf, 1995). What is more, the level of assistance that older parents make available to their children is directly proportional to parents' perceptions of their children's level of need. For example, elderly parents provide much of the care of adult children who are developmentally disabled or mentally impaired and not living in institutions (Kelly & Kropf, 1995).

For children who are living independently, when events occur in their lives, creating a period of greater need, elderly parents typically step in to assist them. An example of elderly parents providing greater assistance to their children in times of need is shown in the case of midlife widowhood. Bankoff (1983) found that older parents were by far the most important source of emotional support to women who became widowed in middle age. Bankoff concluded that of all the possible sources of comfort, including children and friends, parents were best able to fulfill the middle-aged widow's need for nurturance. The relief older parents frequently provide for their adult children benefits older parents as well as their children. For instance, there is evidence that being able to offer help to their adult children increases the psychological well-being of older women (Spitze, Logan, & Joseph, 1994).

Degree of Closeness.   Whereas proximity, interaction frequency, and mutual aid are significant indicators of the quality of relationships between middle-aged adults and their older parents, qualitative aspects of the relationship, such as the degree of closeness or strength of feelings might be even more revealing. Intimacy between aging parents and their offspring are marked by two features: (a) recognition of the other person as an individual with strengths and weaknesses and (b) a deep concern for the other party's well-being. The acceptance of each other's weaknesses and foibles allows adult children and their aging parents to achieve a closeness that was not available to them in their earlier relationship. Unlike other intimate relationships, such as those between romantic partners, the increased closeness of aging parents and their offspring does not typically include a greater sharing of problems. As offspring pass through early and middle adulthood, each party realizes the other has different needs and limitations requiring a new kind of distance. The type of mutual respect that marks the relationships of older parents and their adult children influences parents to cease trying to direct their children's lives and influences children to seek to protect their parents from worry (Fingerman, 2001).

Thinking Critically

Consider your parents, in terms of their relationships with their own parents (your grandparents). How would you assess the importance of those relationships for both generations?

Factors Influencing Relationship Quality

There are three social structural positions that play an important role in determining the quality of parent–child relationships during later life: age, gender, and ethnicity.

Age and Relationship Quality.   Age generally has a positive influence on intergenerational relationships. As adults grow older, they experience less conflict and greater closeness in the relationships they have with their children as well as with their parents (Aldous, Klaus, & Klein, 1985; Fingerman, 2001). An example of the positive effect of age on intergenerational relationships is the finding that both elderly mothers and elderly fathers are more likely to choose their older rather than their younger children as confidants (Aldous et al., 1985). The tendency toward more positive parent–child relationships as a function of age has been explained in various ways. Bengston (1979) suggested that as children become more mature, their orientations become more similar to those of their parents. Blenkner (1965) proposed that adult children's identification with their parents increases as part of the process of developing filial maturity. Hagestad (1987) posited that differences between parents and children become subdued as years go by and that both parents and children tend to develop a greater tolerance for the differences that remain.

Gender and Relationship Quality.   In addition to age, the gender both of older parents and of their middle-aged children impacts their intergenerational relations. There are more affectionate ties between mother and daughter than any other combination and less affectionate ties between son and father than any other combination. Both sons and daughters report greater closeness to their mothers than to their fathers, and both mothers and fathers report greater closeness to their daughters than to their sons (Rossi & Rossi, 1990). Mothers have a greater likelihood to rely on their daughters in comparison to their sons as confidants and comforters and are less likely to be angry or disappointed with their daughters than with their sons (Aldous et al., 1985). An important gender role that contributes to relationship quality across the generations is that of **kinkeeper**. The kinkeepers of an extended family are typically middle-aged older women who tend to provide the key connections between families. Kinkeepers gather the family together for celebrations and keep family members in touch with each other (Greene & Boxer, 1986). Kinkeeping appears to be a mechanism for the achievement of social anchorage that has been linked to the realization of a sense of generativity for women (McCamish-Svenson et al., 1999).

Ethnicity and Relationship Quality.   The relationship quality of older parents and their adult children is clearly influenced by the culture in which those relationships are played out. For example, cultural beliefs influence whether or not middle-aged and older parents will live in the same household. In individualist cultures, such as the majority cultures of the United States, Britain, and Canada, middle-aged persons and their elderly parents are not expected to live together. In collectivist cultures such as India, South America, and much of Asia and Africa, it is anticipated that older persons will live with their middle-aged children. For instance, normative expectations

Thinking Critically

In considering the extended family relationships (including older parents and/or grandparents) of your family (or someone' else's family), can you identify the kinkeepers of the family? What are some of the behaviors of the kinkeepers that promote family closeness?

that adult children will care for their elderly parents in Thailand result in the common arrangement that at least one adult child lives in the same household or close by, thereby providing a minimum level of social support (Gardiner, Mutter, & Kosmitzki, 1998). Within the United States, African American, Latino American, and Asian American middle-aged parents are more likely to have their parents living with them in comparison to European American middle-aged parents (Emick & Hayslip, 1996; Phua, Kaufman, & Park, 2001).

Time Usage and the Quality of Intergenerational Relationships

We will now explore the ways in which older parents, their children, and their grandchildren spend their time together, by participating in leisure activities, carrying out everyday routine activities, and simply relaxing.

The Role of Leisure and Recreation on Continued Family Development.   Despite the failure to assign a high level of priority to the leisure experiences of family members, there is considerable evidence that those activities provide unique opportunities for family members to experience feelings of security and connectedness with one another. A specific role that leisure and recreation serve in family members' interactions is in promoting feelings of attachment. As a reminder, *attachment* is an intense association between individuals that brings both to the level of human experience whereby the feelings of connectedness and belongingness are experienced. The importance that family members attach to leisurely activities and the benefits they are able to gain from them contribute to continued attachment between older parents and their children as well as to family maintenance and continued family development (Orthner & Mancini, 1990).

Leisure Activities and the Meanings They Provide.   There are various ways in which leisure activities provide meaning for intergenerational relationships involving grandparents, parents, and children. Leisure can be a platform on which aspects of a family's history are replayed (such as rituals associated with family holidays or family vacations). Leisure activities in the form of rituals also support alterations in family composition or roles (such as celebrations of birth, adoption, marriage, or graduation). As celebrations of those family events, leisure activities have the potential for promoting family harmony and cohesion. Of course, whether the meanings associated with

The intergenerational dynamics of families are played out in many activities shared by older persons, their adult children, and their grandchildren.

leisure activities are exhilarating and hopeful or tedious and discouraging depend on the family dynamics that accompany spending time together (Orthner & Mancini, 1990). In planning intergenerational leisure activities, it is important to consider the activities themselves as well as the context in which those interactions will occur. For example, Kelly, Steinkamp, and Kelly (1987) found that for adults aged 75 years and older, home-based family activities are related more to their well-being than are activities engaged in outside the home.

Leisure Activities as Reflections of Intergenerational Dynamics.   In addition to promoting family harmony and cohesion, leisure activities of older parents, their children, and their grandchildren provide some illumination of the family dynamics across generations. For example, whether family members are engaged in putting together a family celebration, traveling together, or simply deciding which restaurant to go to for dinner, action, interaction, and transaction are all occurring. In the course of sharing ideas, opinions, and feelings, a shared reality develops; and within that shared reality, negotiation and decision making are required. Negotiation might be as simple as when to leave an event or as complex as the planning of a trip (where to go, when to begin the trip, how long to stay, which mode of travel to use, and so forth). The decisions that revolve around the planning and carrying out of those activities reflect the ways in which parents, children, and grandchildren interact and through which they sustain their relationships. Furthermore, the degree to which all family members are actively engaged in the planning and carrying out of various leisurely activities influences the satisfaction of individual family members as well as the overall success of those leisurely pursuits (Orthner & Mancini, 1990).

Thinking Critically

What are the leisurely activities in your family that involve your parents and your grandparents? What benefits do you think those activities provide for family members of various ages?

The Importance of Everyday Routine Activities.   Although there is a tendency to assume that only leisure activities or employment can give meaning to life, that belief overlooks the importance that older parents and grandparents attach to ordinary activities such as personal care, housekeeping, cooking, shopping, puttering, and tinkering. As noted by Atchley (1991), in later life those activities reflect the continued ability to be independent. Being able to comprehend older parents' need to engage in the everyday activities that reflect their ability to remain independent, rather than insisting that they allow other people to do those things for them, shows support for the feelings of older parents.

Time for Restoration.   Just as there is a common misperception of the importance of everyday activities in the lives of older parents or grandparents, there is also a misconception that inactivity is undoubtedly harmful. That view of how older persons ought to be spending their time often contributes to attempts to fill the day with activities that require the participation of all family members. Whether older parents are living with their middle-aged children or visiting with them (at either's home or on vacation) it is beneficial to recognize the value of passive activity. In massive

Passive activity, such as the one demonstrated here, serves as a respite for older adults. Such activities are restorative in that they allow for the pursuit of individual interests in a restful environment.

doses, certainly, inactivity is detrimental; but as noted by Atchley (1991), what appears to be inactivity often overlooks the inner activity in which the person is involved. Sitting on the beach and watching the seagulls fly overhead while smelling the scent of the salty ocean might represent a time of restoration for an individual. Likewise, to others, a person who is sitting quietly reading a book appears to be engaged in a passive activity. The inner thoughts of the reader, however, might reflect an involvement in a moving experience. Especially for older persons who do not have people in their homes on a daily basis, or who live alone, being able to go for a solitary walk or briefly retreat to their room to read or rest might provide a welcome respite before reengaging with family members.

❦ SUMMARY

In this chapter, we contemplated the ways in which the psychological and social development of middle-aged and older adults is influenced by their relationships with their parents, with their children, and with their grandchildren. We considered as well the ways in which those relationships impact the family systems in which they occur. To gain a broad understanding of those relationships, we explored those multigenerational relationships in diverse cultures within the United States as well as in cultures throughout the world. In looking at the influence of varied life circumstances on those relationships, we found that there exists considerable variability in the level of interdependence, the living arrangements, and the roles of older adults in relation to their adult children and their grandchildren. In spite of the diversity in intergenerational relationships, we have seen evidence that parent–child–grandchild relations are important in the lives of middle-aged and older adults in all walks of life. The intergenerational relationships examined in this chapter suggest that older adults experience continued parental imperatives that are rooted in the adult child's continued need for security and the older parent's enduring desire to protect the welfare of continuing generations of family.

❦ KEY TERMS

- kinkeeper
- refathers
- second-generation fathers
- sense of despair
- sense of integrity
- social anchorage
- social status transitions

9

Children at Risk: Special Challenges in Parent–Child Relationships

In this chapter, we will examine a number of challenges that confront parents and place children at risk for not developing their full potential. First, we will consider the difficulties encountered by parents of children with varied **exceptionalities** or chronic illnesses and provide recommendations for optimizing the developmental potential of those children. Next, we will focus on the problems associated with child abuse and neglect including the link between maltreatment and the development of social and psychological problems. We then will turn our attention to the ways in which the dynamics in families, with at least one alcoholic parent, impact the development of the children in those families.

PARENTING CHILDREN WHO HAVE EXCEPTIONALITIES

Whenever the development of a child deviates from the expected norm, that child is considered to be **exceptional**. Exceptionalities are classified either as **impairments** or as **giftedness** depending on the nature of the exceptionality. Children with impairments have physical, psychological, mental, intellectual, or medical conditions that make it difficult for them to learn and/or behave according to normal expectations. Children identified as **gifted** deviate from the norm in that their talents and/or academic capabilities exceed normal expectations. Children whose developmental progress places them outside the realm of normal expectations, whether impaired or gifted, require special attention from parents, educators, and other professionals to realize their developmental capability (Chan, 2002; Gill & Maynard, 1995; Lynch, Thuli, & Groombridge, 1994).

The purpose of the following discussion is not to address all the exceptionalities of children that parents contend with but rather to provide an overview of some of the common experiences of parents and their children with exceptionalities. The exceptionalities discussed in this chapter include mental and physical impairments, autism, attention deficit/hyperactivity disorder (ADHD), learning disability (LD), chronic illness, and giftedness. Although the parent–child relations associated with each of those exceptionalities will be presented separately, some children have a combination of exceptionalities such as mental and physical impairments, and parents of those children face multiple challenges. Furthermore, even though the needs of children with different exceptionalities vary, most children with exceptionalities require higher levels of understanding and patience from their parents and many require specialized care. Thus, children with various exceptionalities challenge parents to gain an understanding of their special needs and to develop specific skills for caring for them.

The Importance of Child-First Language

The first thing that parents should be aware of, in addressing the specialized needs of their children who have exceptionalities, is the importance of seeing the child first and the exceptionality second. Rehabilitation professionals have been strongly encouraged to adopt person-first language that focuses on the person rather than on the exceptionality. That perspective helps parents of children who have impairments to understand the whole child and also assists parents in focusing on the things a child *can do* or is able to learn rather than on the things a child has difficulty in achieving or cannot do. For parents of children who are gifted, seeing the child first helps them to appreciate that, although their child has special gifts and talents, that child also has needs and abilities that fall within the normal range. Perceiving the child before the exceptionality is reflected in the terminology that a parent uses (and teach others to use) in referring to their child. Terminology that places the child before the exceptionality consists of language like *the child who is blind* rather than *the blind child* and the *child who has a mental impairment* rather than *a mentally impaired child* (Lynch et al., 1994).

PARENTING THE CHILD WITH A PHYSICAL OR MENTAL IMPAIRMENT

Physical or mental impairments of children take many forms and are designated according to various criteria. Parents of those children experience difficult feelings whether they are aware of their children's impairments from the beginning or whether they slowly become aware that their children are not developing as expected. On learning of their child's impairment, parental adjustment is required to accept the reality of the exceptional child rather than the wished-for child. Some feelings that are common during that adjustment stage include grief over the loss of the child parents expected to have, feeling guilty about their disappointment, and being resentful of the time and energy that caring for their child will require (Cook, Kieffer, & Charak, 1993).

Although the reactions to having a child with a disability are initially negative, and there are many difficulties associated with caring for children with special needs, parents typically face up to the challenges connected with that role. In their acceptance of their role as parents of exceptional children, parents undergo tremendous development as they gain knowledge of the skills necessary to meet their children's special needs. As they undertake the growth required to become skilled parents of exceptional children, parents typically report that the role brings joy and satisfaction in addition to the obvious adjustments. The road from disappointment and self-blame to joy and acceptance, however, is not an easy one for parents. Larson (1998) found that parents of children with disabilities express contradictory emotions of grief and joy as well as hope and fear that influence their well-being. In a study of mothers of children with various exceptionalities, Larson found that parents of children with exceptionalities learn to embrace a paradox of emotions.

The paradox of emotions experienced by parents of children with exceptionalities include (a) learning to manage internal opposing forces between loving the child as he or she is and wanting to erase the disability, (b) dealing with the child's incurability while pursuing solutions, and (c) maintaining hopefulness for their child's future while being given negative messages and battling their own fears. Due to the paradox of conflicting emotions that are typical experiences for parents of children who have disabilities or impairments, much effort is required in their development of their parental roles. That work promotes an extension of parental skills as they develop hopeful life trajectories for themselves and their children. In their embrace of the paradox, parents of exceptional children create a positive bias that helps them to regain a sense of control that fuels the optimism they need to do the required parental work (Larson, 1998).

Parenting Children with Mental Impairments

A child with **mental impairment** is a slow learner in all, or almost all, intellectual pursuits (Shaffer, Fisher, & Dulcan, 1996). In young children, mental impairment is frequently labeled as **pervasive developmental delay** to allow for the possibility that the child will catch up to normal, age-appropriate development. Pervasive developmental delay is characterized by patterns of impediment in the development of communicative, social, and cognitive skills that arise in the first year of life (Volkmar, Cook, & Pomeroy, 1999). An important first step in matching parental care to the special needs of a child who is mentally impaired comes with the recognition, and acceptance, of the child's impairment. When parents initially fail to recognize that their child has a mental impairment, they might regard that child as fussy, disinterested, or unresponsive and react by being punitive or less spontaneous toward the child. In contrast, when parents are aware of their child's mental impairment from the beginning, they have an advantage in that they might be more prepared to respond to their child in appropriate ways (Volkmar et al., 1999).

Although parents of children with mental impairments encounter different challenges, a primary concern for those parents is the education of their children. Changes in sibling relationships when there are younger siblings in the family that developmentally overtake the child with a mental impairment represent another common challenge for those parents. For example, a 3-year-old child with a mental impairment, who still wets the bed, is likely to object to wearing diapers at night "like the baby." Parents of children with mental impairments report also that they experience stress and difficulties in coping with many of the everyday situations related to caring for their children (Bower & Hayes, 1998).

Parenting the Autistic Child

Living with a child who is autistic is not easy. The combination and severity of their children's behavior and communication deficits presents parents of children who have autism with unique challenges (Dunn, Burbine, & Bowers, 2001; Volkmar et al., 1999). Although there are variations, characteristics of children with **autism** include some combination of those listed in Figure 9.1.

Due to their cognitive deficits, children with autism experience a prolonged infant–toddler stage that creates practical problems related to teaching self-help behaviors and managing difficult behavior. As a result, social activities for the family might be severely curtailed and financial burdens are often great. Furthermore, because children with autism typically appear normal, strangers might not realize that a child with autism has a disability and might blame the child's parents when the child publicly displays aggressive or bizarre behavior. Additionally, parents and other family members frequently become aware that the child shows precocity in memory, artistic tendencies, or mathematical skills, which might contribute to unrealistic expectations for the child. Those idealistic hopes contribute to feelings of disappointment or blame as parents are consistently confronted by their child's lack of progress. A further challenge for parents is that children with autism typically show little affection, instead appearing aloof. Their parents,

---

1. The inability to relate to other people in an ordinary manner, including an absence of social smiling, a preference for interaction with objects rather than people, and the absence of distress when a parent leaves the room;

2. Language deficits, including mutism, echolalia, noncommunicative speech, pronoun reversals, and immature grammar;

3. Sensory impairment characterized by over- or underresponding to noise, touch, and visual stimuli;

4. Abnormal affect, including extreme or no fear reactions, tantrums, and uncontrolled giggling and crying;

5. Self-stimulation, including spinning self and objects, repetitive hand movements, rocking, humming, etc.;

6. Inappropriate play, including self-stimulation;

7. Extreme resistance to environmental changes, food, everyday schedule, familiar routes, etc.

FIGURE 9.1 Characteristics of Autistic Children
Source: Adapted from "Behavioral assessment and curriculum development," in R. Koegel, A. Rincover, and A. Egel (Eds.), *Educating and Understanding Autistic Children* (pp. 1–32), by J. Johnson and R. Koegel, 1982, San Diego, CA: College-Hill Press.

therefore, receive little reinforcement from those children for the care they provide them (Fine, 1991).

For all those reasons, parents whose children are autistic endure more stress than do parents whose children do not have disabilities and parents of children with other disabilities (Dunn et al., 2001). The strain experienced by parents of children with autism comes from dealing with the difficult behaviors of their children as well as from the reactions of others to them and their children. In response to those difficulties, parents of children with autism often become socially isolated, and the more stress that is experienced the more socially isolated those parents become. In their social isolation, parents of children with autism are cut off from needed social support that has been found to be an important moderator of parental stress. Practitioners would, for that reason, be well advised to facilitate social support for those parents (Dunn et al., 2001).

Community Services for Children with Autism. In addition to needing social support, securing appropriate direct services for their child with autism is a high-priority need for parents and is a goal that will typically override all other family considerations. Finding suitable educational, residential, and treatment programs is of such urgency that parents have observed that, until they had identified an appropriate school or program for their child with autism, they were unable to adequately address their own needs and the needs of their other family members. The direct services parents are able to obtain for their autistic child impact the lives of that child as well as the lives of other family members (Fine, 1991). Although children with autism will inevitably have a significant effect on their families, the nature and extent of that effect can be guided by awareness and sensitivity to family issues on the part of friends and professionals who come into contact with the autistic child and the family of that child (Dunn et al., 2001).

Parenting Children with Learning Disabilities

A child with a **learning disability** (LD) has at least a normal intelligence level but has problems with achievement in a particular subject area. A learning disability is part of a larger diagnosis of underachievement, which might represent a number of different areas, including difficulty in perceiving, processing, storing, and understanding information. The problems that children with LD experience are compounded by the difficulties they encounter in their social relations (Sprouse, Hall, Webster, & Bolen, 1998; White, Saudargas, & Zanolli, 1991). One social problem they sometimes face is the negative perception of their behavior by teachers in regular classrooms. Paradoxically, the special assistance that is provided to children with LD has been found to be associated with negative evaluations of their behaviors by teachers when they return to regular classrooms. White et al. (1991) found that teachers in regular classrooms, who did not disapprove of those children's behaviors prior to their placement in special education classrooms, evaluated their behaviors as disruptive upon their return to the regular classroom. In attempting to determine the reasons for regular classroom teachers' negative assessments of their students with LD, White and colleagues found that after experiencing greater student–teacher contact in the special resource room (where the teacher–student ratio is very low), children with LD were much more likely to initiate questions with their teachers in regular classrooms than were the other students.

In addition to being viewed as disruptive by many of their teachers in regular classrooms, children with LD often have problems relating to other children. They tend to be less popular than their peers and are likely to be rejected or neglected by their peers (Sprouse et al., 1998; Wiener, Harris, & Shirer, 1990). One of the reasons for the troubles children with LD have in social relations appears to be related to their problems in accurately perceiving social cues. Sprouse et al. (1998) demonstrated that children with LD have more difficulty in the accurate perception of social cues than do children without LD. Those researchers recommended that parents and other adults who interact with children classified as having LD should consider the possibility that there might be a social perceptual component to the disorder.

The Family Relations of Children with Learning Disabilities.   Even though professionals recommend that parents of children with LD provide a supportive environment for their special needs children, the reality is that the home environments of children with LD tend to be less rather than more supportive. Parents of children with LD tend to establish a more rigid home environment wherein they demand more achievement from their special needs child while expecting less personal growth. Moreover, the interpersonal relationships in those families have been found to be more conflicted than relationships in other families (Margalit & Almougy, 1991).

Children who have learning disabilities need encouragement from parents and other adults to prevent the development of low self-esteem.

What This Means for Parents and Professionals.   Parents and professionals should be aware that children with LD are at risk for developing low self-esteem. Because other individuals tend to be annoyed by their behavior and respond to it disapprovingly, that sets up a negative cycle with playmates, teachers, and parents (Bryan, 1988; Jerome, Fujiki, Brinton, & James, 2002; Sprouse et al., 1998). One of the outcomes of having experienced a preponderance of negative reactions from others is that those experiences contribute to the likelihood that a child will develop low self-esteem. The link between LD and low self-esteem is that children with LD frequently encounter demanding contexts in school whereby they must expend considerable energy attending to and accomplishing schoolwork that is much easier for their peers. The distractibility and impulsivity exhibited by those children might stem from fatigue or might reflect their disappointment with themselves in trying to master tasks that are difficult for them to perform. In either case, children with LD need encouragement to persevere in difficult situations. Through encouragement, children develop higher self-esteem; and a positive self-esteem could be an important factor in motivating children with LD to persevere when confronted with challenging tasks (Jerome et al., 2002).

Parenting Children with Attention Deficit/Hyperactivity Disorder

Children with **attention deficit/hyperactivity disorder** (ADHD) have difficulty in focusing their attention, are easily distracted, display impulsive behavior, have trouble waiting their turn when playing games with other children, and tend to begin but not finish numerous activities (American Psychiatric Association, 1987). They also are unable to remain seated or calm for periods of time that are perceived as normal for other children their age. Those children tend to have problems with school because to be successful in the school setting they must be able to pay attention and follow rules. Due to their difficulty in sitting still, paying attention, and following instructions, children with ADHD are typically placed in special education classrooms; although some researchers have questioned the overuse of the hyperactive diagnosis for children who display boredom in learning and impatience with repetitive activities. Besides placement in special education classrooms, children with ADHD are frequently prescribed stimulant medication that is often effective for helping them manage their behavior (Thiruchelvam, Charach, & Schachar, 2001).

The Social Problems Faced by Children with ADHD.   Children with ADHD are at risk for problems in relationships with parents, teachers, siblings, and peers. The primary social problem experienced by highly active children is that others perceive them in negative ways (Cunningham & Boyle, 2002; Podolski, 2001). Whether the negative behaviors associated with highly active children are qualities directly attributable to their high activity levels is questionable. Researchers have suggested that the undesirable traits credited to highly active children might be related to the unconstructive responses of those parents and teachers who lack an understanding of the special needs of very active children. Both mothers and fathers of highly active children tend to be directive, intrusive, and authoritarian. They get into power struggles and competition with their children and appear to be hostile and unresponsive to their children's needs and interests (Cunningham & Boyle, 2002; Harrison & Sofronoff, 2002; Podolski, 2001).

One of the reasons that parents are likely to react negatively toward their children with ADHD is that those parents have higher levels of stress and depression than do other parents (Harrison & Sofronoff, 2002). Another explanation is that parents of children with exceptionalities are more likely to hold their children responsible for their problem behaviors when the exceptionality is characterized as a behavioral excess (Chavira, Lopez, & Blacher, 2000). When parents have higher levels of stress and depression and also hold their children responsible for problem behaviors, they tend to respond to unwanted behaviors with controlling negative suggestions and with decreased positive or preventive suggestions. Furthermore, parents respond more negatively to their sons who have ADHD in comparison to their daughters with ADHD. For example, it has been shown that mothers of girls with ADHD give more rewards for positive behavior than do mothers of boys with ADHD (Cunningham & Boyle, 2002).

What This Means for Parents and Professionals. Although parents of children with ADHD might be expected to be challenged by their children's higher than usual activity levels, it is important that they not develop a pattern of disapproving responses. Consistent pessimistic responses to children contribute to a negative cycle of parent–child interactions and to less positive developmental progress for children. It is important that parents of children with ADHD consciously work on ways to prevent the development of negative parent–child interactions. One approach for helping parents to interact more positively with their children with ADHD is suggested by findings of Podolski (2001). In a study of parents of children with ADHD, Podolski found that parental coping through the use of reframing—thinking about problems as challenges that could be overcome—was related to higher satisfaction in the parental role for both mothers and fathers of children with ADHD.

Recognizing that parents who have developed a harmful interaction pattern with their highly active children might need assistance in establishing harmonious relationships with them, Barkley (1990) developed specific guidelines designed to interrupt the negative cycle of parent–child interactions. Those guidelines, outlined in Figure 9.2, reflect the need for highly active children to (a) have positive interactions

---

1. Spend at least 15 minutes per day doing what the child would like to do such as playing a game or reading a story.

2. Do not express disapproval of the child's behavior unless some extreme behavior occurs.

3. Establish daily routines that place highly active children in an active role and allow their high energy levels to be put to constructive use.

4. Assist highly active children to create order in their lives by providing structure, including:

   a. Places for books, toys, and clothes that the child can easily access (such as child-level hooks for coats and hats), and

   b. Regular times for meals, snacks, playtime, bathtime, and bedtime.

FIGURE 9.2 Developing Positive Interactions with Highly Active Children
Source: Adapted from *Attention Deficit Hyperactivity Disorder: A Handbook for Diagnosis and Treatment*, by R. A. Barkley, 1990, New York, Guilford Press.

with their parents, (b) be engaged in carrying out constructive activities, and (c) have structure in their daily routines to increase the predictability in their lives.

❧ ❧

Thinking Critically

If you were speaking to a group of parents who had children with either LD or ADHD, what would you say to those parents about the common needs of their children with either of those exceptionalities? How would you address the necessity of promoting the self-esteem of children with LD or ADHD?

❧ ❧

Parenting the Physically Impaired Child

Children who are **physically impaired** have diseases such as cerebral palsy or muscular dystrophy or have been involved in accidents that have caused them to have impaired motor control, which often affects their ability to be ambulatory. Melissa Crisp (2001), an active teenager who has cerebral palsy, provides several guidelines for parents to remember when interacting with and guiding their children with physical impairments. First, she advises parents to "let go a little," emphasizing that, in addition to a need to experience their parents' love, all children need to experience as normal a childhood as possible. According to Melissa, having a normal childhood means being involved in after-school activities, doing household chores, going to slumber parties, attending camp, participating in adapted sports, and, yes, even dating.

Being the parent of a child with a physical impairment requires providing the child with needed assistance while simultaneously recognizing and promoting the child's capabilities.

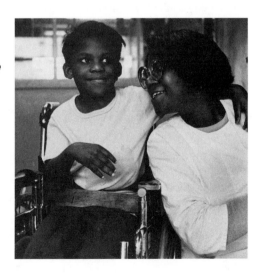

Another guideline that Melissa has for parents of children with physical disabilities is to "remember the importance of mobility" for a child with an ambulatory limitation. To ensure the greatest level of mobility, Melissa emphasizes how critical it is for parents to select the appropriate mobility device (wheelchair, scooter, crutches, etc.). The next piece of advice Melissa offers parents of children, with physical impairments, is to "teach their children and themselves about the disability." She points out that people with disabilities are typically willing to discuss the challenges they face. Through talking with other individuals with impairments as well as with parents of children with disabilities, parents are better prepared to teach their children about what it means to have exceptionalities.

Still another recommendation that Melissa has for parents is to work to "increase public awareness" of what it means to have an impairment. She calls attention to the fact that many people do not understand how to react to individuals with disabilities and frequently feel uncomfortable or embarrassed by their own curiosity. She suggests that by speaking openly about their child's physical challenges, welcoming questions, and if possible using humor, parents can put others more at ease. According to Melissa, speaking openly about a child's special needs not only helps others gain a better understanding of the child's exceptionality but also shows children with obvious disabilities how to deal with strangers' questions. Finally, Melissa suggests that parents of children with physical disabilities "take it easy" by practicing patience. She points out that absolutely nothing is more frustrating to the child with a disability than when parents become agitated because that child cannot perform a task with the speed and accuracy of a child who does not have a disability.

Thinking Critically

What do you think qualifies Melissa as an expert in how to parent a child with a physical impairment? What insights do you think she can offer parents that others cannot?

PARENTING CHILDREN WITH CHRONIC ILLNESS

There are a number of chronic illnesses that are generally associated with children: spina bifida, cystic fibrosis, and sickle-cell anemia. Children are sometimes born with, or develop shortly thereafter, a number of other diseases, such as leukemia, cancer, diabetes, kidney disease, and heart disease. In recent years, there has been an increase in children who are born with fetal alcohol syndrome (FAS), are addicted to drugs, and/or are HIV-positive. Those chronic illnesses that result from prenatal exposure to alcohol, drugs, or the HIV virus present novel and challenging problems for their parents or caregivers—many of whom are adoptive or foster parents.

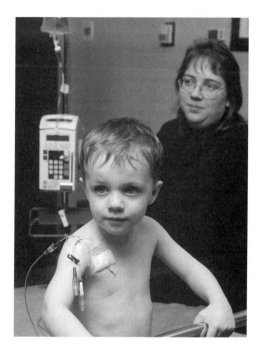

Children who experience the stresses of chronic illness need extra support from their parents or guardians.

Helping Children Who Are Chronically Ill Cope with Hospitalization

Children who are chronically ill require more care within the household as well as more medical assistance outside the household in comparison to healthy children. Because frequent hospitalization is often necessary to keep those children alive, the medical treatment and periods of recuperation (in the hospital as well as at home) are stressful on the child as well as on the parent. Children's reactions to the stresses of chronic illness, however, depend a great deal on the ways in which their parents, foster parents, or guardians respond to their special needs. One of the difficulties associated with periods of hospitalization is a great deal of waiting and subsequent boredom, which is experienced by both children and parents or other caregivers. Furthermore, it is not only the physical or emotional pain that must be endured by children who are ill but also the lack of activity. Healthy, active children are able to gain attention from adults and entertain themselves in ways that are difficult or impossible for sick children. In recognition of their children's emotional needs, parents might use times of waiting to read or sing to their children, to play games with them, to tell stories, or jokes, or to inform them about what is happening in the family and in the neighborhood. Parents might also provide play materials or books that match their children's interests, energy level, and ability to concentrate. As trying and as difficult as recuperation times can be for children as well as for their parents, those are also times that parents and children often become closer because they have the time together that they might not have otherwise taken (Fine, 1991).

The Effects of a Child's Chronic Illness on Family Relationships

For parents, caring for a chronically ill child evokes an intense emotional interdependence with the sick child and involves a range of tasks including brokering information for the child and gaining the child's cooperation with treatment. When faced with a severe or life-threatening illness, everyday concerns about the child's diet or management of the child's behavior take on a new significance and are likely to contribute to heightened parental stress. A primary stressor for a parent who is caring for a sick child is that the caregiver role tends to compromise the parent's ability to function in other roles, including the role of parent to the other children in the family. Thus, the stress of a child's chronic illness alters the relationships parents have with the child that is ill as well as the relationships they have with each other and with their other children (Young, Dixon-Woods, Findlay, & Henry, 2002).

Family relationships are impacted by the length of time of the illness, the degree of medical involvement, and the interruption of normal family activities. As a result of having a member with a chronic illness, other family members might develop special needs and require specialized care and/or family therapy. One alteration in the family that occurs when a child is chronically ill is that parents (especially mothers) tend to modify the family environment to better accommodate the child who is ill. Because the family environment is typically altered to meet the needs of the sick child, keeping the lines of communication open becomes especially important for the marital bond (in families in which there are two parents) as well as for relationships between parents and the other children. It is important that parents openly discuss the needs of the child with the chronic illness as well as the requirements of the other children in the family. With honest communication and cooperation, parents have a greater chance of dealing successfully with the challenges of their child who is chronically ill as well as with the needs of their other children (Hurley, 1987).

PARENTING CHILDREN WHO HAVE SENSORY IMPAIRMENTS

In the upcoming discussion, the focus will be on children who have profound sensory impairments and the parents of those children. The descriptors of *blind* and *deaf* and of *visual impairment* and *auditory impairment* will be used interchangeably in recognition of the lack of agreement regarding the use of those terms.

Parents' Concerns for Their Children Who Are Visually Impaired

A review of the research literature focused on families with children who are visually impaired shows that the experience of caring for a child who is blind is frequently stressful and can be challenging as well as threatening to family members. In a study of parents of children with visual impairments, Leyser and Heinze (2001) asked parents about the particular concerns they had which were related to their child's impairment. The primary concern voiced by those parents was anxiety regarding their child's future (96.8%). The apprehension regarding the future of their child with a visual impairment focused on uneasiness regarding the child's independence and ability to achieve, concerns related to their child's self-esteem, and worries about their child's future job opportunities. Another primary concern, expressed by parents of a child with a visual impairment, was questions regarding their ability to provide for the needs of their child. Other concerns of those parents, in order of importance, were finances, adequate services, and the effects of their child's disability on their other children.

Enhancing the Development of Children Who Are Visually Impaired. Whereas parents of children with visual impairments have many concerns about their children's future, and their ability to provide appropriate care for their children, there are a number of ways those parents might enhance the development of their children. Mary Zabelski (2001), President of the National Association for Parents of Children with Visual Impairments (NAPVI) and a parent of a grown child who is blind, offers a number of recommendations regarding ways in which to encourage self-esteem in children who are visually impaired. Her first recommendation is that children with visual impairments be given opportunities to help others. Zabelski points out that most people want to help individuals who are blind and that children who are blind also need to have opportunities to help others. Zabelski shared a story about when her daughter brought her guide dog to a grade school where several other children who were blind could meet her and her dog. In that visit, her daughter demonstrated how she used her dog to assist her in daily tasks, explaining that first she had to be a good cane user. By her demonstration, Zabelski's daughter was

The independence enjoyed by this child, who has a visual impairment, is crucial to the child's well-being.

able to provide other children with hope for their future and a belief in their ability to be independent.

Besides providing their children with opportunities to help other people, Zabelski emphasizes the importance of parents giving children domestic responsibilities (such as putting toys away, walking the dog with parents, and setting the table) at a very early age. She stresses that a child's ability to perform small domestic chores might represent a critical step toward independence in later years. Zabelski calls attention to the fact that children who have visual impairments benefit greatly when parents express confidence in them. She, therefore, cautions parents not to feel sorry for their children and not to always do everything for them because that attitude lowers the child's feelings of self-worth.

Based on her belief that all children need structure and discipline, Zabelski advises parents to let their children with visual impairments know that they are expected to behave according to the rules of the family just like their brothers and sisters. She points out that when the expectations parents have of their child who is visually impaired are similar to those of their siblings, they show confidence in all their children. Finally, Zabelski suggests that when children with visual impairments are provided opportunities to demonstrate their capabilities in various areas, those incremental successes build on each other, leading to self-assurance and self-esteem.

Adjustment to the Role of Parent of a Child with a Visual Impairment.   It is not only important that parents foster the independence and self-worth of their child who is visually impaired but also that they be able to adapt positively to their role as parents of a child who is visually impaired. Successful adaptation to that role is closely tied to the resources available to those parents as well as to the degree to which they take advantage of those resources. It has been found that parents who utilize support systems, both inside and outside the family, are more likely to experience positive adjustment to the challenges of parenting a child who has a visual impairment than are parents who do not utilize support systems (Moore, Van Hasselt, Ammerman, & Hersen, 1994).

Parenting Children Who Have Auditory Impairments

Of all the areas of childhood disability, deafness is probably the most confusing and controversial because the ability to speak is so closely connected in our minds with thought, communication, and intelligence. For children whose lack of hearing begins at a very early age, their most serious problem is not their hearing loss but rather their challenge to develop an adequate communication system. For 200 years, the major controversy in the field of deafness has been what method of communication (oral or manual) should be used with the child who is deaf. Furthermore, the means of communication chosen can profoundly affect almost every area of the child's life, including the hopes and expectations for the child, selection of educational and recreational programs, and how best to include the child in family communication.

Whether verbal or manual, effective parent–child communication contributes to more satisfactory parent–child relationships.

The Challenges for Parents of Children Who Have Hearing Impairments.   Parents who have lived their entire lives using and depending on their hearing and speech are handicapped in their attempts to understand their child who is deaf. On the other hand, parents who are deaf themselves are better able to understand their child who is deaf and to teach that child valuable communication skills. In families where the parents are deaf, over 90% communicate with each other and with their children primarily in sign language; although speech is used in conjunction with sign language by many of those with adequate skills. In contrast to parents who are deaf, fewer hearing parents use sign language with their child who is deaf and very few of those do so from the time of diagnosis. Because the majority of parents of children who are deaf are members of the hearing world, the decision regarding whether or not to learn to use and to teach sign language to their child must be addressed very early (Berger, 2001).

There are differing beliefs regarding whether the child who is deaf should be taught sign language or should be expected to learn to lip read and speak, but the reality is that not all individuals who are deaf can readily learn to lip read. On the other hand, studies have shown that children who are deaf readily learn sign language as easily as hearing children learn spoken language (Berger, 2001). Furthermore, sign language is more easily mastered during the first years of the child's life, which represents the critical period of language development. Although babies who are deaf begin to make babbling sounds later than do hearing babies (Oller & Eilers, 1988; Petitto, Holowka, Sergio, & Ostry, 2001), they begin babbling manually at about the same time that hearing babies begin babbling orally (about 6 or 7 months of age).

Whereas **oral babbling** consists of the repetition of certain syllables (such as *ba-ba-ba*), manual babbling consists of repetitive gestures of communication. Moreover, **manual babbling** is innate for all infants, who communicate with various gestures such as lifting their hands to be picked up and pointing to the things they want. For obvious reasons, babies who are deaf reduce their oral babbling and increase their manual babbling just when babies who can hear do the opposite (Petitto & Marentette, 1991). Therefore, for children with hearing impairments who are provided instruction in sign language, beginning during infancy or early childhood, their deafness might not be viewed as a handicap. An example of a nonhandicapped person, who was born deaf to parents who were also deaf, is illustrated in the following quote by Leo Jacobs, who earned a master's degree and became a teacher of mathematics.

> I never noticed my own handicap nor came up against discrimination or unfair treatment until I began my own personal contacts with hearing people when I entered school. . . . I felt more handicapped from the treatment I received at the hands of hearing people than from my deafness. . . . The real ills of deaf people lie more with minority group dynamics than with their deafness. (Jacobs, 1974, p. 99)

Thinking Critically

The exceptionality of the child does not necessarily represent a handicap. A child might feel handicapped, however, if others respond negatively toward the child based on the child's exceptionality. What are some parental attitudes and behaviors that prevent a child's exceptionality from becoming handicapping?

PARENTS AND THEIR GIFTED CHILDREN

Unlike other exceptionalities that reflect some aspect of disability, giftedness is not generally considered to be a disability but rather a welcome exceptionality. Children are identified as gifted when they have demonstrated exceptional abilities and shown themselves to be capable of high academic performance. In comparison to the past, when high scores on intelligence tests were the measure of giftedness, today children identified as gifted are viewed as representing a number of abilities. Their higher than average performance is demonstrated in such areas as general intellectual ability, specific academic aptitude, creative thinking, leadership ability, and ability in visual and performing arts. Even though more positive self-concepts might derive from being labeled as gifted, the labeling process often communicates high expectations to which children sometimes feel they cannot measure up. Furthermore, although gifted children might perceive their giftedness as positive, they often believe that others view their giftedness as negative (Chan, 2002).

Gifted Families

Not only is giftedness generally welcomed, there is evidence that parents might play an important role in the promotion of giftedness in their children. Children's giftedness appears to be present at birth and needs only the opportunity to develop. In numerous studies, the families of children who have been identified as gifted have been found to have certain characteristics in common. By and large, the profile of "**gifted families**" epitomizes the self-actualizing family system. In families wherein at least one child participates in a gifted education program, the following family interactions have been documented: (a) mutually supportive relationships, (b) appropriate degrees of closeness, (c) flexibility, and (d) open expression of thoughts and feelings (Cornell, 1983; Moon & Hall, 1998). Parental perceptions of their child as gifted (whether or not the child has been formally identified) also has been found to be associated with positive labeling of the child, taking pride in the child's accomplishments, better parent–child communication patterns, and more intimacy in the parent–child relationship (Cornell & Grossberg, 1988; Moon & Hall, 1998).

The Challenges of Parenting the Child Who Is Gifted

Having a child who is gifted is typically a source of pride for parents but the presence of a gifted child sometimes has a negative impact on family relations. First, making the child who is gifted the focus of parental attention can lead to inappropriate comparisons between that child and the other children in the family. Second, because highly intelligent children often demonstrate advanced reasoning abilities, parents might find themselves treating their children who are gifted as more mature than those children actually are, thereby blurring role distinctions between children and adults. When parents treat children who are gifted as more mature than they are, an imbalance of power tends to occur in the family such that parents relinquish control of family interactions in the direction of the child's ideas and decisions. Finally, discovering that their child is gifted sometimes contributes to parents experiencing an exaggerated sense of responsibility to "do right by" their child (Hackney, 1981; Moon & Hall, 1998).

The exaggerated sense of responsibility, on the part of some parents of children who are gifted, includes fears regarding their adequacy to raise the child or feelings of guilt that they are neglecting their child's development. To the degree that parents experience feelings of inadequacy in meeting the developmental needs of their children who are gifted, family interactions might be adversely affected. To compensate for their feelings of inadequacy, parents sometimes place excessive performance demands on themselves as well as on their children. That approach to parenting a child who is gifted not only negatively affects the child but also contributes to psychological problems for the entire family (Fine, 1991; Moon & Hall, 1998). It is recommended, instead, that parents of a child who is gifted (a) see the child before the exceptionality, (b) make efforts to treat their child who is gifted like the other children in the family thereby normalizing the daily experiences of the child, and (c) provide the educational enrichment that their child requires.

FAMILY ENVIRONMENTS THAT PLACE CHILDREN AT DEVELOPMENT RISK

When children have exceptionalities, they present unique challenges to their parents, and the degree to which their parents are able to meet their children's exceptional needs impacts their children's developmental outcomes. When children, with or without exceptionalities, grow up in a **dysfunctional family** environment, characterized by **child maltreatment** (physical abuse, sexual abuse, and/or neglect), family violence, or parental substance abuse, the adults in the family present challenges to children that place those children at risk for developmental problems. Consequently, as a result of the home life experienced by children in dysfunctional families, many of those children develop social, psychological, and behavioral problems as well as difficulties related to school achievement.

CHILD MALTREATMENT

When parents (or other persons who are responsible for children's welfare) inflict nonaccidental physical injury on children under the age of 18, that act is legally defined as **physical abuse** and is prohibited by law in all states within the United States. When parents, or other persons responsible for the child's well-being, engage in sexual activity with children under the age of 18, that act is legally defined as **sexual abuse** and is prohibited also by state law. When parents (or other designated caregivers) fail to provide children with basic care and protection, those persons can be held legally accountable for **child neglect**. Children's development is compromised not only by various forms of abuse and neglect but also by exposure to acts of violence between parents or other family members. By definition, family violence includes abusive and violent acts of a family member against another family member, and the most common form of family violence is spousal abuse. Today's household, though, often consists of persons who might not be related to each other (such as a parent's romantic partner) and the witnessing of violence between those members of the household is traumatizing for children as well (Kashani & Allan, 1998).

The History of Child Maltreatment in the United States

Child maltreatment has been a common occurrence for many centuries but the public objection to child maltreatment in the United States is a relatively new phenomenon. In the past, it was believed that "child discipline" needed to be maintained even if "harsh corporal punishment had to be used" (Radbill, 1974). The first scientific documentation in the literature of the harmful effects of child abuse did not occur in the United States until 1962, with the publication of a revolutionary article by Kempe, Silverman, Steele, Droegenmueller, and Silver who coined the phrase, the **"battered-child syndrome."** According to Kempe and colleagues, the **battered child** is a child who has sustained serious physical injury from an adult caregiver. It was noted by the authors of the article that child battering is frequently undiagnosed and mishandled by professionals, due to a hesitancy to report such violence to the authorities. The public reaction to the article was extraordinary and child abuse soon became a topic that was openly discussed in the research literature as well as in the media (Newberger, 1991).

Several years after the publication of the article by Kempe and colleagues (1962), the first documented use of the phrase "**family violence**," referring to violent acts of family members against each other, and the effects of those actions on children, was in an article entitled "Youth, Violence, and the Nature of Family Life" by Havens (1972). Havens suggested that, due to the increasing awareness of child abuse within the family, medical and health professionals should stop idealizing family life and accept the fact that some parents intentionally injure and sometimes kill their children. The work of Kempe and colleagues in the 1960s and Havens in the 1970s led to laws in the United States that were designed to protect children from violence, as well as mandatory reporting laws for mental health and other professionals who work with children (such as teachers and counselors). Subsequently, the identification of other types of family violence including spouse and elder abuse, which might be witnessed by children, has received considerable attention (Kashani, Daniel, Dandoy, & Holcomb, 1992).

Children at Greatest Risk for Being Abused.   Bottom and Lancaster (1981) found that children whose births resulted from unwanted pregnancies, children with special needs (including those born prematurely), and children with a chronic illness are all at higher risk for being abused than are other children. Child temperament and stages of development that are frequently experienced as being more challenging (such as toddlerhood and adolescence) are other characteristics that are associated with child maltreatment.

The Conditions of Family Violence.   There are a number of factors that have been found to be linked with family violence, including the intergenerational transmission of abuse, systemic beliefs of parents who abuse, family stress factors, individual parental characteristics, and parental alcohol abuse.

The Intergenerational Transmission of Family Violence.   The intergenerational transmission of family violence, which has received a great deal of research attention, involves the relation between having experienced or witnessed abuse during childhood and subsequent violence toward children during adulthood. Specifically, adults are predicted to replicate the aggressive behaviors of their parents. Whereas results of a number of studies have supported the intergenerational transmission model of child abuse, some of those studies have been sharply criticized due to methodological problems (Widom, 1989). Kaufman and Zigler (1987) summarized the relevant research focused on abuse across generations and concluded that, although being maltreated as a child puts an individual more at risk for becoming abusive toward one's own children, the path between the two points is neither direct nor inevitable. Furthermore, most children who are abused do not later become violent. As noted by

Gelles and Maynard (1987), a number of factors tend to moderate or mediate that relationship, including childhood resilience and social support outside the family.

Family Stress Factors Associated with Child Abuse.   Child maltreatment has been related to family stress and socioeconomic factors. By and large, stress in the family has been suggested as the mechanism through which low socioeconomic status sometimes contributes to child abuse. Parental unemployment (particularly unemployment of fathers) is a major stressor in a family and a possible contributor to violence among family members (Gillham, Tanner, & Cheyne, 1998). For example, women who are battered are more likely to have spouses who are unemployed than are women who are not battered (McClosky, Treviso, & Scionti, 2002). Barton and Baglio (1993) identified a number of other stressors in the family, in addition to financial strains, that contribute to a risk of child abuse. Those include legal violations, stresses related to work, family loss, illness of a family member, major changes in a family situation, and difficulties associated with the management of young children.

Parental Characteristics Associated with Child Abuse.   A number of individual characteristics have been found to be common in parents who abuse their children: Those include (a) a tendency toward role reversal (whereby the parent depends on the child to gratify certain needs), (b) parental impulse control problems (learned from being exposed to family violence during childhood), (c) low self-esteem, (d) defensiveness (that aims to defend one's low self-esteem), (e) the propensity to blame others for their problems (which is seen when a parent scapegoats a child), and (f) parenting attitudes that devalue children (Jackson, Thompson, & Christiansen, 1999). The age of a parent is another factor that has been found to be associated with child abuse and neglect. More adolescent mothers abuse their children than do older mothers, probably due to the effects of poverty and limited education. Furthermore, young mothers are more likely to leave their children with a potentially abusive person, such as a young friend (Klerman, 1993).

Family Constellation and Child Abuse.   Child abuse and neglect occurs in all family configurations but single parenthood has been linked to an increased risk for child maltreatment. The link between single parenthood and child mistreatment appears to be related to the strain of economic hardship, which is more common in single-parent households than in married households. Furthermore, father-custody single parenthood combined with economic hardship places the child at especially high risk for familial violence (Gelles, 1989; Jackson et al., 1999).

Child Abuse and Dysfunctional Problem-Solving Patterns.   Within violent families, family members hold certain beliefs, such as the acceptability of violence, that hinder the family members' ability to solve problems in an effective and nonviolent manner (Robinson, Wright, & Watson, 1994). There is also evidence that members of abusive families have not developed the skills to discuss stressful circumstances, examine options or actions, and come up with effective ways for solving family problems. For example, Cantos, Neale, and O'Leary (1997) found that mothers who physically abuse their children have a general lack of coping skills.

The Impact of Maltreatment on Children's Lives

Experiencing child abuse and/or neglect has been associated with a full range of problems for children, including difficulties in adjusting to the school environment, poor academic performance, troubles with regulating emotions, and disturbances in the attachment process.

School Adjustment and Performance.   Even at a very young age, children who have been maltreated have trouble adapting to their child care and preschool environments. Children who have suffered from any form of maltreatment demonstrate more cognitive deficits as they get older and are considered to be more at risk for school failure and drop out than are their nonmaltreated peers. Child neglect is particularly detrimental to children's ability to achieve in school. In comparison to other groups of maltreated children, those who have experienced neglect have been found to have the poorest academic achievement (Eckenrode, Laird, & Doris, 1993; Kinard, 2001).

Disturbances in the Attachment Process.   Parents of securely attached children nurture, comfort, and protect them, thereby promoting their sense of security, trust, and self-esteem. Moreover, secure attachments assist children in the establishment of self-identity and self-worth. Those children who have been neglected and abused, rather than nurtured, comforted, and protected, typically do not develop the sense of security, trust, and self-esteem associated with secure attachment (Weinfield, Sroufe, & Egeland, 2000).

Interventions to Prevent or Interrupt the Cycle of Child Maltreatment

Because children who are maltreated are at risk for the development of psychological, social, and cognitive impairments (Gibson, 2002; Shaw, Lewis, Loeb, Rosado, & Rodriquez, 2001), it is important to understand the steps that can be taken to prevent or interrupt the cycle of child maltreatment. A number of interventions have been suggested by Lowenthal (1999) as ways to promote the resiliency of children who have experienced abuse and/or neglect, including the availability of alternative caregivers and social support intervention programs for child victims.

Availability of Alternative Caregivers.   When children are removed from their homes due to maltreatment, they are placed with other relatives or foster families; and in cases in which parental rights are severed, they become available for adoption. Those alternative caregivers frequently encounter immense challenges as they attempt to gain the trust of children who have been traumatized. Not only do maltreated children have lower levels of trust, they frequently exhibit challenging behaviors and/or a lack of basic skills that reflect the maltreatment they have received (Gibson, 2002). Relatives, the wider community, foster care parents, and adoptive parents can play a vital role in providing maltreated children with the safety, dedication, and nurturance they need to recover from their traumas. Having at least one adult in their lives, who nurtures them and provides for their basic needs, helps maltreated children to develop resiliency in the face of risk. Crucial to the resiliency of maltreated children is their response to supportive influences in the extended family and the wider community as well as children's determination to be different from abusive parents (Herrenkohl, Herrenkohl, & Egolf, 1994).

Social Support Intervention.   Parents who abuse or neglect their children often have suffered from maltreatment when they were children (Pears & Capaldi, 2001). Furthermore, poverty and unemployment increase parental stress, sometimes leading to child maltreatment (Gillham et al., 1998). Based on their previous experiences and present life circumstances, parents who are at risk for abusing their children are in need of informal and formal intervention. The first step toward intervention for potentially abusive or neglectful parents typically comes from informal support systems. Informal support from family members, friends, and community members, in the form of child care, respite care, transportation, or financial assistance, might relieve the stress of parents and in so doing reduce the possibility of child maltreatment. Second, formal community supports, such as family therapy, food, and clothing, can go a long way toward mediating the stresses experienced by parents. Third, programs that teach basic parenting skills are particularly helpful in reducing family stress and pathology. DePanfelis and Zuravin (2002) found that after abuse had occurred, families who attended the services outlined in their service plan were much less likely to abuse their children. Based on those findings, they concluded that actively engaging families in a helping alliance and encouraging them to accept and receive services might help reduce the likelihood of further maltreatment.

Intervention Programs for Child and Adolescent Victims.   The use of therapeutic techniques by child care professionals and therapists has been linked to improvements in the adaptive, cognitive, and social–emotional skills of children who have been maltreated. Intervention services, such as child care and preschool classes that specialize in the treatment of young children who have been maltreated, are becoming increasingly available. Because children who have been abused and/or neglected frequently have a combination of language, cognitive, and social–emotional delays, they benefit from placement in child care settings in which child care providers are trained to use therapeutic techniques. Parent education and family counseling are other valuable intervention approaches for families in which abuse and/or neglect has occurred (Fine, 1991).

CHILDREN OF PARENTS WHO ARE ALCOHOLICS

The most frequent form of substance abuse found among parents is alcohol abuse. A person whose use of alcohol is excessive and whose drinking creates problems in their social relationships, and/or careers, is considered to be an **alcoholic**. The following discussion focuses on the family relations, family roles, and developmental outcomes of children who grow up in homes where at least one parent was an alcoholic.

The Ways in Which Problem Drinking Affects Parenting Skills

Problem drinking by parents negatively impacts important parenting skills, including (a) inconsistency or unpredictability in parenting behaviors, (b) poorer monitoring of children's behaviors, (c) lower levels of parental nurturing and emotional availability, (d) a greater likelihood to use harsh punishment, and (e) a higher tolerance for adolescent drinking and other substance abuse (Windle, 1996).

Inconsistency or Unpredictability in Parenting Behaviors. While intoxicated, some parents become more (or less) accepting of their child's failure to perform household tasks, do their homework, and act responsibly in a number of other ways. It has been determined that such inconsistency in parenting might undermine a child's sense of order, control, and stability in the family relationship, thereby reducing feelings of self-esteem and perceptions of self-competence (Windle, 1996).

Poor Monitoring of Children's Behavior. **Parental monitoring** consists of establishing rules for appropriate and inappropriate behaviors for children, consistently providing penalties for violation of rules, and overseeing leisure activities including friendship choices and peer group activities. Parental monitoring helps establish an orderly structure in which children are better able to distinguish between healthy and unhealthy choices. By decreasing monitoring behaviors, parental problem drinking tends to undermine children's healthy adjustment and places them at greater risk for involvement in antisocial behavior (Windle, 1996). For example, the research literature has consistently shown that higher levels of parental monitoring are associated with lower levels of adolescent alcohol and other drug use as well as other delinquent behavior (e.g., Jacobson & Crockett, 2000; Patterson & Dishion, 1985; Steinberg et al., 1994).

Lower Levels of Parental Nurturing and Emotional Availability. Children rely on parents for emotional support to assist them with challenges such as handling conflicts with others and for guidance in making healthy choices for themselves. Higher levels of parental nurturance and warmth of expression have been linked with lower levels of problematic behavior during childhood and adolescence (Barrera & Stice, 1998). In comparison to other parents, parents who abuse alcohol are less emotionally available to their spouses and children as a result of drinking-related consequences, including hangovers, irritability, and negative mood states. Thus, decreased parental nurturing, as a result of alcoholism, tends to disrupt healthy emotional development in children (Barnes, 1990; Whipple, Fitzgerald, & Zucker, 1995).

Greater Likelihood to Use Harsh Punishment. Parents who are inebriated tend to exercise poorer judgment in disciplining their children and might become less inhibited and overly aggressive (Whipple et al., 1995). Harsh disciplinary practices contribute to a variety of detrimental outcomes for children including a greater emotional distance from parents; lower psychosocial maturity (Mantzipoulos & Oh-Hwang, 1998); lower achievement (Aunola et al., 2000); an increased risk for behavior problems such as substance abuse, crime, and delinquency (Baumrind, 1991a); poorer school performance; and early affiliation with deviant peer groups (Patterson, 1986).

Greater Tolerance of Adolescent Drinking and Other Substance Abuse.   Research has consistently demonstrated that parental tolerance of adolescent alcohol usage is associated with an earlier onset of drinking among children as well as with the escalation to higher levels of alcohol usage. Parents who are problem drinkers not only model alcohol abuse but are more likely than other parents to show a greater tolerance of adolescent drinking and substance use, thereby providing implicit approval for their children's alcohol use (Hill & Yuan, 1999; Windle, 1996). Children's increased alcohol use, in turn, is linked to adverse social consequences such as problems at school or with the legal system (Johnson & Pandina, 1991).

Parental Alcoholism and the Abuse and Neglect of Children

Alcoholism is not always associated with family violence but it is a common contributor to domestic abuse as well as to child abuse and neglect. Even though alcohol abuse has been found to increase the likelihood of domestic violence, the association seems to disappear once alcohol use becomes severe. It has been speculated that the weaker link between family violence and heavy alcohol usage is because large quantities of alcohol tend to have an anesthetizing effect on users. Furthermore, alcohol abuse is more highly related to spousal violence than to child abuse (Yegidis, 1992). Finally, it should be noted that, although alcohol might be prevalent in some abusive families, the relation between alcoholism and child and/or spousal abuse is complex. Other factors, such as the observation of marital violence in childhood, gender role ideology, self-esteem, marital stress, and attitudes reflecting approval of marital violence play a role in mediating the effects of alcohol abuse on family violence (Rosen & Stith, 1993).

Relationships and Roles in Families of Alcoholic Parents

In addition to affecting parenting skills and contributing to a greater likelihood of abuse and neglect, a parent's alcohol abuse frequently places a strain on family relations, which in turn impacts children's development of healthy family roles. In a family where a parent is an alcoholic, the primary focus of the parents is usually on the problems associated with alcoholism rather than on the children. The main focus of the alcoholic parent is on obtaining and using alcohol. As a **codependent**, the spouse of an alcoholic typically spends a great deal of energy trying to control the drinking of the alcoholic spouse while enabling that person to continue drinking by covering up or denying the problem. One of the difficulties for children growing up in alcoholic families is that the feelings of family members are not openly discussed. Additionally, all family members are typically engaged in a conspiracy of silence regarding the issue of alcoholism. Although family members are generally aware when a parent drinks too much, one of the main rules in the alcoholic family is to behave as if the problem does not exist. In those families, children are typically exposed to a high level of stress while receiving the consistent message that they are not to acknowledge the predicament the family is in or to talk about their feelings (Seixas & Youcha, 1985).

Children's Roles in Dysfunctional Families.   Whenever individuals in a family are expected to consistently suppress their feelings, interactions between family members are restricted and family members are likely to view each other in terms of their family role positions. Furthermore, the role positions of family members reflect the ways in which each person in the family adapts to living in a dysfunctional family system. As previously explained, the role of the alcoholic parent's spouse or partner is that of a codependent (Seixas & Youcha, 1985). The roles assumed by children in an alcoholic family have been carefully detailed by Wegscheider (1989) and include (a) the **family scapegoat**, (b) the **family hero**, (c) the **family mascot or clown**, and (d) the **lost child in the family** (see Figure 9.3). Those childhood roles are found not only in alcoholic families but in other dysfunctional families as well.

Although enactment of the roles described in Figure 9.3 helps children to adapt to the dysfunction in their families, the problems associated with taking on one of those roles is that the role limits children's development of other aspects of themselves. Furthermore, parents and other family members in alcoholic families tend to see children in terms of their role positions rather than in relation to their feelings or developmental potential. Finally, even though the roles are developed to help children cope with a dysfunctional family system, those roles tend to persist into adulthood.

Adult Children of Alcoholic Parents.   Because growing up in a dysfunctional family contributes to the development of roles that help children adapt to a dysfunctional way of life, adult children of alcoholics have not typically developed roles that cultivate their ability to achieve happiness and fulfillment in the adult world. On the other hand, adults whose behaviors reflect those of the family scapegoat, the family hero, the family clown, or the lost child in the family often benefit from caring relationships and professional help. Being able to recognize the adult behaviors and needs associated with each of the childhood roles helps family members, friends, and therapists to better understand the feelings and behaviors of adult children of alcoholics (see Figure 9.4).

Thinking Critically

Parents are presented with unique challenges when their children have impairments or are critically ill. Children face challenges when they are abused and/or neglected. Which of these situations has a more detrimental impact on parent-child relations? Why?

The family scapegoat

The scapegoat in a dysfunctional family is viewed as a troublemaker, whose visible traits include hostility, defiance, and sullenness. Those behaviors are designed to draw attention away from the real problem and direct negative attention toward the scapegoat. Instead of admitting that there is a problem in a dysfunctional family system, such as physical abuse, incest, or parental alcoholism, family members are encouraged to blame the scapegoat for the family's difficulties. The child who has the role of scapegoat might also learn to exhibit problem behaviors to disrupt the fighting between parents, who must then stop fighting to work out solutions to the child's problems.

The family hero

The family hero in a dysfunctional family is a super responsible overachiever, typically does what is right, and needs everyone's approval. Often the oldest child, or in very traditional families, the first boy, the family hero provides family members with a sense of self-worth. In their denial that there exists a problem in the family, parents point to the family hero as an example of their parenting effectiveness and as a symbol of family normalcy. Whereas the child in the role of family hero appears to have it all together, what others do not see is a child who has low self-esteem and feels okay only when accomplishing a goal. Furthermore, the family hero is overly needy of attention, because that child typically lacks the ability to provide self-reinforcement.

The family mascot or the family clown

The family mascot or family clown is considered to be especially cute and will usually do anything for a laugh or to gain attention. What the child in that role represents to the family, and why they play along, is comic relief, fun, and humor. From the perspective of others, the family clown is having a great time and sees life from a fun, laughable point of view. The hidden, unrevealed feelings of the family mascot, however, are low self-esteem, terror, and loneliness. Whereas the hero child's acceptance in the family is associated with personal achievements, the family clown's recognition in the family is tied to the ability to keep everyone laughing.

The lost child in the family

Another role that is common in dysfunctional families is that of the lost child, who is quiet and generally ignored. The lost child is a loner and a daydreamer who engages in solitary play and is withdrawn from other family members. The benefit the lost child provides for the dysfunctional family system is relief, because the lost child does not cause any problem or inconvenience. By and large, lost children have been given the message that parents do not want to have to worry about them. Although on the surface the lost child appears to be independent and content to spend time alone, the reality is that the child feels unimportant, hurt, and abandoned. The lost child also feels defeated in efforts to gain attention, and the behavior of the lost child reflects the feelings of having given up.

FIGURE 9.3   Roles Assumed by Children in an Alcoholic Family
Source: Adapted from *The Impact of Family Violence on Children and Adolescents*, by J. Kashani and W. Allan, 1998, Thousand Oaks, CA: Sage; and *Children of Alcoholism*, by J. Seixas and G. Youcha, 1985, New York: Crown.

The Family Scapegoat

Behaviors

Tends to keep people at a distance

Works hard to hide the hurt inside

Elicits anger from employers and family

Is likely to abuse chemicals

Might become involved with the law

Needs

Support of feelings

Acceptance from others

Challenge of inappropriate behavior

To be listened to

To accept responsibility for own behavior

To learn appropriate expression of anger

To get in touch with a range of inner feelings

The Family Hero

Behaviors

Ties self-worth to accomplishments

Tends toward "workaholism"

Is too serious and rigid to enjoy self and others

Continuously seeks approval

Has expectations of self and others that are unrealistic

Takes on leadership roles

Might be emotionally or chemically dependent

Needs

To become tolerant of mistakes of self and others

To learn to play

To learn to take risks and be vulnerable

To learn to accept self

To learn to express feelings

The Family Mascot

Behaviors

Appears cheerful and witty

Is entertaining

Experiences sense of impending doom

Continued

Might have an eating disorder

Has sense of obligation to others

Needs
Physical touch

To be asked for input

To be taken seriously

To learn to laugh on the inside as well

To develop alternative ways of interacting with others

The Lost Child

Behaviors
Concerns regarding being boring

Is afraid to take risks, of being hurt

Suffers from stress-related problems (e.g., anxiety attacks, asthma)

Is quiet, aloof, isolated, passive (feels helpless)

Experiences difficulty in making decisions and takes whatever comes

Might have eating disorder

Needs
Invitation to join in group discussion or activity

Encouragement and reward for efforts

To consider self needs

To learn to accept and receive from others

To let others be responsible for their lives and mistakes

FIGURE 9.4   Behaviors and Needs of Adult Children of Alcoholic Parents
Source: Adapted from *Another Chance: Hope and Health for the Alcoholic Family,* by S. Wegscheider, 1989, Palo Alto, CA: Science and Behavior Books.

❧ SUMMARY

In this chapter, we examined a variety of circumstances that place children at risk for not realizing their developmental potential. First, we considered the challenges faced by parents of children who have exceptionalities and included recommendations by professionals, parents, and children for maximizing the developmental potential of children with exceptionalities. Next, we discussed the problems of child maltreatment, and the difficulties confronted by children living in those families. That presentation focused on the ways in which maltreatment places children at risk for the development of social and psychological problems. Recommendations were provided for disrupting the cycle of child maltreatment and increasing resiliency in children who have experienced abuse or neglect. Following the presentation related to parental abuse and neglect of children, the problems encountered by children growing up in alcoholic families were addressed. That discussion focused on (a) the ways in which alcohol abuse affects parenting skills, (b) an examination of the roles that children take on in alcoholic families, and (c) the effects of parental alcoholism on adult children.

❧ KEY TERMS

- alcoholic
- attention deficit/hyperactivity disorder
- autism
- battered-child syndrome
- child maltreatment
- child neglect
- codependent
- dysfunctional family
- exceptionality
- family hero
- family mascot or clown
- family scapegoat
- family violence
- gifted
- gifted families
- impairment
- learning disability
- lost child in the family
- manual babbling
- mental impairment
- oral babbling
- parental monitoring
- pervasive developmental delay
- physical abuse
- physically impaired
- sexual abuse

10

Loss and Grief in Parent–Child Relationships

In previous chapters, the importance of the parent–child relationship, and the ways in which that relationship shapes individuals' lives, was emphasized. In this chapter, we will examine the grief associated with the losses that occur in relationships through death, divorce, foster care or adoption placement, and parental incarceration. We begin by exploring the ways in which children cope with feelings of loss and grief following (a) the death of a parent or sibling, (b) the separation or divorce of their parents, or (c) the placement in foster care or with adoptive parents following their removal from their biological parents. We will then consider the feelings of loss and grief of adults who lose a parent or child through death or who deal with loss and grief in their role as foster parents. Finally, we will examine the grief experienced by children and their parents when they are separated due to parental incarceration. For each of the various circumstances of parent–child separation, we will consider strategies for helping children and parents handle the grief that accompanies such a loss.

THE IMPACT OF A FAMILY MEMBER'S DEATH ON CHILDREN

The death of a family member impacts the lives of children as well as adults. Many parents are unable to adequately, discuss death with their children, however; and relatives and friends are typically more supportive of parents than of children following the death of a close relative. An impediment related to discussing death with children is that most grown-ups have a limited understanding of children's concept of death. Many people do not realize that children's comprehension of death is different from that of adults and that it is learned in a developmental progression. Because an adult realizes that death is irreversible, universal, and involves the cessation of sensory and bodily functions, they tend to believe that young children also apply those concepts to their understanding of death.

Children's Understanding of Death

For children 2-years-old or younger, the notion of death is incomplete or does not exist. For those children, death is equated with separation from or absence of the person. Preschool children (3 to 5 years of age) also view death as separation and do not understand that cessation of sensory and bodily functions occurs at death. Furthermore, because preschool children have not yet achieved the cognitive ability to classify (being able to distinguish between categories based on differences), they confuse attributes of the dead with attributes of the living and think that people who are dead can think, feel, move, eat, and drink. Those cognitive limitations, coupled with young children's tendency toward **magical thinking** (that they can make things happen by wishing for them), can be seen in their belief that their wishes, prayers, or other activities can bring the loved one back to life. Moreover, preschool children's egocentric thinking (the tendency to perceive and interpret events from a self-centered point of view) contributes to their belief that death does not occur for everyone, such as themselves, their family members, or their friends. Finally, preschoolers do not comprehend the finality of death. For them, *dead* means being in a reclining position with one's eyes closed, and most preschoolers can "play dead," then jump back up and resume their active play (Hanna, 1996).

As children enter middle childhood (ages 5 to about 11), their thinking becomes logical and they can readily distinguish between life and death. They also understand that death is universal, irreversible, and that the movement of the body, and the functioning of the body's organs, ceases at death. Despite their comprehension that death happens to every living thing, elementary children's understanding of death is still somewhat limited by their own experience and personal reality. They tend to view death as personally distant, occurring with old age (Hanna, 1996). Elementary school children's emphasis on the concrete reality of things reflects their having reached Piaget's stage of concrete operations, wherein they are able to interpret experiences objectively and rationally rather than subjectively and intuitively (Gelman & Baillargeon, 1983). The school-age child's approach to reality from an objective and rational point of view is often expressed in their responses to the death of a family member. Parents and other adults should recognize that, during middle childhood, children who are grieving the loss of a close relative might ask questions that reflect their tendency to view events from a concrete perspective of reality. For instance, a child at that age is likely to ask "What happens to the body when it dies?" or "Who will take me to school and pick me up, now?" Questions such as that should not be interpreted as a child's lack of grief, but rather as an example of the child's endeavor to understand death from the child's own level of comprehension.

It is not until adolescence, when the individual acquires the ability to engage in abstract thinking (a consideration of various possibilities), that life after death is contemplated. Due to their ability to apply abstract thinking to their experience of death, adolescents are more likely than are younger children to ponder the meaning of life and death (Hanna, 1996). An example of the adolescent's propensity to contemplate life after death was revealed in a study by Morin and Welsh (1996) who reported that, although adolescents' beliefs about death varied, "spiritual continuation after death" was the most frequently reported belief.

Thinking Critically

Perhaps you had not considered the fact that death is a complex concept for children to understand. Look back over your own childhood and remember your first awareness that a person you know had died. Then, see if you can link the concepts of death you had during that developmental stage with those outlined in the previous discussion.

Guidelines for Explaining Death to Children. In explaining death to a child, parents must keep in mind the cognitive limitations of children at varying levels of development so that their explanations do not go over the heads of their children. The first step in clarifying death for a child is to provide a nonjudgmental environment in which a discussion can occur regarding how the child views death. The conversation might begin with a statement about how the child is thinking or feeling so that the child feels comfortable about expressing personal thoughts. For example, the parent could say to the child, "You might be feeling confused or mixed up right now about your Mommy's death." Then, the child's understanding of death might be assessed with open-ended questions, such as "What happened when your mother died?" If a child is hesitant to talk about the death, the parent might ask the child to draw a picture of what death is. Before the child begins the drawing, it might be helpful to ask the child what color death is, how big it is, and how it feels. Once the parent has determined the child's point of view regarding death, the parent is better prepared to explain death to the child, based on the child's level of understanding (Hanna, 1996).

In their conversations with children about death, it is recommended that parents focus on the death of humans rather than that of plants and animals because death for humans is different. For preschool children, the parent should explain death in descriptive language and in terms of separation. For example, a preschool child might be told that a person who is dead is lying down, with eyes closed, and is no longer able to move the body. For the young child, answers to their questions about death should be kept simple and factual, and misconceptions and magical thinking should be gently corrected. It is important as well to avoid nonfactual statements when discussing death with young children, such as "the person is now a star in the sky," or "the person has gone to sleep." Furthermore, telling a young child that a person who has died has gone to sleep might reinforce the child's view of death as reversible or could contribute to the child's fear of going to sleep. For school-age children, a parent might explain that, when a person dies, that person is no longer able to move the body, the person's heart stops beating, the person's breathing stops, and the person can no longer think. Younger school-age children might be told that death is universal (that it happens to everyone at some time). For an adolescent, a parent might engage in discussions regarding the abstract notion of death, including the adolescent's spiritual perspective of death (Hanna, 1996).

The Grief of Children When a Family Member Dies

Even though children have different conceptions of death at different developmental stages, they nevertheless experience grief when a family member dies. Young children are not only saddened by the loss of a family member but are at a disadvantage when they attempt to understand why a parent, sibling, or other close relative has disappeared from their lives, as indicated by the 5-year-old child who asks, "When is my mommy coming home from heaven? I've been waiting and waiting" (Perry, 2001, p. 22).

The Death of a Parent During Childhood or Adolescence.   In the normal course of life, most individuals will deal with the deaths of their parents. When the death of a parent occurs earlier in life, however, it triggers more distress than when the parent dies at an advanced age (Cicirelli, 1991). The loss of a parent during childhood or adolescence represents a profound psychological insult that threatens a person's social and emotional development (Dietrich, 1984). According to Perry (2001), a child experiences the most distress following a death when the child is close to and dependent on the one from whom that child is separated. Listed in Figure 10.1 are the various reactions of children following parental death.

1. Denial

2. Emotional numbing

3. Fear, accompanied by pangs of anxiety

4. Confusion

5. Disturbances in sleep patterns

6. Physical symptoms, such as stomachaches or headaches

7. Changes in eating habits, either overeating or a lack of interest in eating

8. Visual or auditory misperceptions, such as thinking they see or hear the deceased parent

FIGURE 10.1   The Feelings and Behaviors of Parentally Bereaved Children
Source: Adapted from "Death and Loss: Helping Children Manage Their Grief," by B. Perry, 2001, *Scholastic Early Childhood Today, 15*, pp. 22–23.

As shown in Figure 10.1, it is usual for children and adolescents to experience a sense of unreality or numbness as they are faced with the pain of separation from the parent; then the grief sets in. As children move beyond the initial feelings of grief, disorganization is common since familiar routines, habits, and roles become disrupted. Mourning children must confront the reality of facing life without the presence and support of the deceased parent. Eventually, a period of reorganization or recovery occurs and even though the sadness is still felt, its intensity is somewhat diminished (Perry, 2001). With the passing of time, most children and adolescents who have experienced the death of a parent find that they carry that parent with them in numerous memories. Thus, the strength of the parent–child relationship endures even beyond the life of the parent.

Factors That Influence a Child's Adjustment to Parental Death.   A number of circumstances have been found to affect a child's adjustment to a parent's death. If the death is sudden and unexpected, there is no opportunity to prepare the child for the sudden loss of the parent and that is particularly disturbing for the child (Kranzler, Shaffer, & Wasserman, 1990). Even when a parent has been ill for a period of time (and children might have had some time to prepare for the parent's death), those children are in need of ongoing support. The stresses of a fatal illness and the changes accompanying the progression of the illness, such as alterations in lifestyle, the absence or withdrawal of the ill parent from family functions, and household economic changes, often adversely affect a child's well-being (Raveis et al., 1999).

Whether a parent's death is sudden or expected, the degree to which a child adjusts to the loss of a parent depends to a large extent on the surviving parent's own distress and adjustment to the death (Worden, 1996). The quality of care provided by the grieving parent, and the degree to which the child's basic physical and emotional needs are met during the period of time following the loss of a parent, can affect the bereaved child's adjustment (Strength, 1991; Worden, 1996). When family members share information and support open expression of feelings about the deceased, healthy adaptation to parental loss is more likely to occur (Black & Urbanowicz, 1987). On the other hand, when family members avoid talking about a parent's death or have inadequate communication regarding the death, pathological mourning or other unfavorable outcomes are likely to be increased (Rosenthal, 1980).

Changes in the Child's Family System Following Parental Death.   As pointed out in earlier discussions, when members enter or leave the family system, that system is altered as members of the family attempt to regain family stability. An important aspect of the changes that occur in the family following a parent's death involves **rescripting of family interactions**. During the rescripting process, wherein the roles in the families are redefined, some old relationship habits are given up and new connections are established. Because the child must learn to adapt to those various changes in the family system during a time of grief and confusion, it is particularly important that discussions occur regarding the changes that are taking place. It is reassuring for children to know that someone will be able to take over some of the activities that the departed parent had carried out. After a parent has died, children might be worried, for example, about who is going to take them to school or to the ball game or who will help them with their homework. When adults reassure children that they will be able to take over some of the functions previously carried out by the deceased, they provide a sense of security for children. That type of reassurance is important for children who worry about how they will be able to live in the present without the material or physical aid of the parent who has died (Raveis et al., 1999).

The Death of a Sibling

Siblings form strong attachments to one another and have a shared history together that they expect to continue into adulthood and old age. The childhood loss of a sibling through death is, therefore, a painful and traumatic loss. The death of a sibling during childhood is complicated by the fact that children and adolescents are at high risk for failing to grieve that loss. According to Bowlby (1982) and Kubler-Ross (1969), central to the despondent person's successful resolution of grief associated with the death of a loved one is the opportunity to express feelings related to that loss. Furthermore, grief is a healthy and essential means for coping with the death of a family member. Unfortunately, being able to mourn the death of a sibling and receiving the assistance necessary to cope with that loss is problematic for children.

There are a number of circumstances that make it difficult for a child to mourn the death of a sibling. First, because it is commonly understood that the death of a child is the most unbearable loss that an adult can experience, family members and social groups tend to focus exclusively on the needs of the bereaved parents. At the same time that family members and friends are rallying to support grieving parents, they are simultaneously sending messages (implicit and explicit) to surviving siblings not to mourn. At the family level, children and adolescents are prohibited from mourning by the explicit instructions they receive from adults, telling them not to cry "so that they will not upset their grieving parents." A way that grieving siblings receive implicit prohibitions from grieving is when parents or other adults fail to communicate with them about their sibling's death. The unsympathetic messages that adults communicate to children, coupled with children's tendency to deny the loss, might severely impede the mourning of surviving siblings (Rosen, 1984–1985). When children are not permitted to mourn, they are not assisted in the grief work that could help them to maintain their personal attachment to their deceased sibling.

The adult in this scene understands that grieving children need to be comforted.

Help for Grieving Children

It is helpful to children if parents and/or other caring adults acknowledge the grief children feel when a family member dies and support children's expressions of their grief (anger, crying, bewilderment, etc.). One of the primary reasons that people typically do not talk about death to children is that they sometimes consider the topic taboo and are afraid that discussing a loved one's death with children will increase children's feelings of sadness. It is helpful, though, when adults are willing to talk with children about the feelings those children are having. Neither children nor adults benefit from admonitions to "not think about it" or "put it out of their minds." In discussing the death of a family member with a child, it is important to attempt to get a sense of what children are thinking about the loss they have experienced and to try to find out how they view death in general (Perry, 2001).

Grieving children need to be given information about the circumstances of a family member's death (according to the child's ability to understand). When providing children with information about a loved one's death, adults should be prepared to repeat the same information time and again because children generally are not capable of processing complex or distressing information in the midst of a stressful experience. In addition to providing information to children about a family member's death, it is helpful for grieving children when adults share some of their own feelings and thoughts about the loss. Comments such as "I feel really sad about Daddy's death and I think you must be feeling sad too" can be very useful in helping children to talk about their grief. Children need to be able to discuss their feelings and might need an invitation from a parent or other caring adult before opening up. Finally, it is essential that adults avoid the tendency to do most of the talking when discussing death with children. After inviting a child to talk about feelings related to the loss, the adult should let the child take the lead as to when, how long, and how much is discussed (Perry, 2001).

Thinking Critically

There are two related problems associated with talking with children about the death of a family member. First, adults frequently do not talk with children about the experience of death. Second, those who talk with children about death tend to talk too much. Why do you suppose those two approaches are so common and how do you think they are related?

The Role of Narrative in Helping Children Cope with Death.   The narrative approach is commonly used by adults to deal with grief and loss and adults can assist children through their grief by that same method. Three ways that the narrative approach might be used for assisting children in their effort to cope with the death of a family member include (a) supporting children in telling the story of the death,

(b) helping children to develop a personal narrative that focuses on the life and death of their deceased family member, and (c) sustaining children in their efforts to construct a mental representation of the deceased in order to maintain their attachment to that person (Angell, Dennis, & Dumain, 1998).

The Story of a Death.   A first step in understanding and coping with a death is the telling of the story of the death. Stories and rituals have long been recognized by family therapists as playing an important role in the healing process following the death of a loved one. Every death creates a story, and the **story of a death** in the family is the family members' account of what happened when one of their members dies. "The story" includes (a) an explanation of how the person died, (b) details about the circumstances surrounding the death, (c) the sequence of events preceding and following the death, and (d) each family member's experience of the death, including when and how each person learned of the death. Every family member's story is an individual construction and is based on that person's relationship with the deceased, relationships with other family members, role in the event, and preexisting and current circumstances in the person's life (Sedney & Baker, 1994).

The Function of the Death Story.   Stories help individuals to recall emotional events and thus achieve mastery of those events. The telling of their stories of the grief associated with the death of a family member can provide emotional relief for the bereaved, help to make the experience meaningful, and bring people together to provide mutual support. The importance of the story for children is that children have very strong needs for emotional relief, understanding, and inclusion when they are attempting to understand and cope with the death of a family member. Unfortunately, adults often shut children out of conversations about the person who has died. The consequences of children not being told "the story" is that they tend to create false or inaccurate stories to explain what is happening in their family. One of the reasons adults have difficulty listening to children's stories of death is that hearing children's accounts of their grief is painful for adults (especially at a time when they are grieving the same loss). Another factor that makes it difficult for adults to listen to children's stories of death is that sometimes children misrepresent events as part of their effort to accomplish a sense of mastery. Because children tend to feel powerless when confronted with a major loss, they might imagine themselves as having been capable of preventing the death by attempting a rescue of the deceased (Sedney & Baker, 1994).

Helping Children Tell Their Stories.   There are a variety of ways that parents and/or other supportive adults can help children to tell their stories related to the death of a family member. First, asking questions is a fundamental step in the direction of breaking the taboo that says death is so terrible it cannot be talked about. Second, adults should expect children to display strong affect when talking about the death of a loved one because the expression of difficult feelings (sadness and/or anger) is fundamental to stories of death. If parents cannot bear their children's grief alone, another family member or a grief counselor might be asked to be present (along with the parents) when children tell their story of the death. Third, the child needs an atmosphere of psychological safety to be able to help put together the story, which is accomplished by their parents' or guardians' expressions of acceptance and empathy. Finally, it is important for adults to remember that "the story" is an ongoing process that (as it is retold) can be expanded to accommodate new information, to reflect developmental abilities, or to more fully understand what happened (Sedney & Baker, 1994).

Helping Children Develop a Personal Narrative.   After having conceptualized a story of the death, children must find ways of living with their feelings of loss while struggling to reestablish self-confidence, self-esteem, and identity in a biography colored by the death of a loved one. As they contemplate, fantasize, and dream about their dead parent or sibling in the hope of tempering their feelings of loss, bereaved children struggle to fill in gaps of knowledge through remembering something forgotten or discovering something new in an effort to make sense of the loss. Parents, guardians, and/or other caring adults can assist bereaved children toward recovery by helping them to incorporate the trauma of their loss into a narrative of personal resiliency. The development of a **personal narrative** about the parent or sibling who has died assists children in reshaping their biography, which includes the life and death of their deceased family member (Angell et al., 1998).

Helping Children to Build an Inner Representation of the Deceased.   In addition to helping children tell the story of the death and develop a personal narrative about the parent or sibling who has died, parents, guardians, or other caring adults might help children to find a way to maintain a connection to that person. Children who sustain a tie to a deceased family member are better able to cope with the loss of that person and the accompanying changes in their lives. The child's preoccupation with preserving a connection to the deceased family member has been described by Nickman, Silverman, and Normand (1998) as an activity they refer to as constructing an **inner representation of the deceased**. Those researchers found that children are able to describe a set of memories, feelings, and actions that they view as keeping them joined to the parent or sibling. Similar to the development of a personal narrative, constructions of inner representations of the deceased family member provide children with a sense of continuity—from the past, to the present, and into the future. Outlined in Figure 10.2 are a number of ways that surviving parents, or other caregivers, might assist their children in remembering a deceased family member.

Although there are a variety of approaches that parents might use for supporting children through the grieving process, the research findings point to three basic requirements: (a) acknowledge the child's loss and the sadness associated with the loss, (b) exercise caution in making decisions related to the deceased (e.g., about disposal of possessions of the deceased), and (c) proceed carefully in making further changes in the family during the days, weeks, and months following a family member's death (e.g., changing residences).

1. Talk with the child about the deceased.

2. Provide the child with opportunities to participate in memorializing activities.

3. Give the child mementos of the deceased (belongings, photographs, jewelry, articles of clothing).

4. Be alert to the child's feelings about the deceased, as those feelings are communicated verbally and nonverbally.

5. Help the child find the language to express feelings.

6. Show the child respect for the deceased and for the child's relationship to the deceased.

7. Use humor, when appropriate, to modulate the pain of loss when talking about the deceased.

FIGURE 10.2   Parental Contributions to Remembering
Source: Adapted from "Children's Construction of a Deceased Parent: The Surviving Parent's Contribution," by S. Nickman, P. Silverman, and C. Normand, 1998, *American Journal of Psychiatry, 68*, pp. 126–134.

THE DISENFRANCHISED LOSS AND GRIEF OF CHILDREN

Although it is generally recognized that members of a family endure loss and are expected to grieve following the death of a loved one, there are many situations whereby children experience **disenfranchised loss and grief**. Disenfranchised loss and grief is encountered when a person incurs a loss that is not openly acknowledged, publicly mourned, or socially supported (Zupanick, 1994). Children whose parents have divorced, children who have parents from whom they have been removed due to abuse and/or neglect, and children of incarcerated parents are likely to experience disenfranchised grief.

The Loss and Grief of Parental Divorce Versus Parental Death

Children of divorce and children of bereavement share in their awareness that a shadow has been cast over their lives; and both experiences contribute to feelings of loss and grief as well as to thoughts of anxiety regarding their future lives. Comprehending the differences between children's loss and grief associated with bereavement and their loss and grief related to divorce is important for understanding the nature of each of those losses from the child's perspective. According to Wallerstein (1989), the similarities and differences between children's experience of loss related to parental divorce or parental death include: (a) a recognition that death is final and a belief that divorce might not be, (b) an understanding that divorce is a voluntary decision, unlike most death, (c) feelings of anger and guilt associated with parental death or parental divorce, (d) the realization that death, but not divorce, is a universal experience, and (e) differences in family and community support for children whose parents have divorced or died.

The Finality of Death.   A primary difference between the child's experiences of death and divorce is that loss due to death is final and the loss of a loved one who has died is irretrievable. Although very young children do not fully comprehend the finality of death, they will realize the irrevocability of the loss of a parent or sibling as they develop greater cognitive comprehension. A consequence of being able to understand the finality of death is that the reality of death is easier to acknowledge than is the actuality of divorce. When children face the divorce of their parents, finality is not present in the same way as it is in death, so children often believe that the loss of divorce can be modified. Consequently, children whose parents have divorced frequently have a persistent, gnawing sense that the loss lacks conclusiveness and can be undone (Wallerstein, 1989).

Not only is there a difference between divorce and death in terms of finality, but divorce is typically only a partial loss because children frequently continue to be involved with the noncustodial parent. For children whose parents have joint custody, those children might spend approximately equal amounts of time with each parent. Even when one parent has sole custody and takes on the bulk of responsibility for the care of the children, those children are likely to have regular visits with their noncustodial parent, and to be in frequent contact with that parent via telephone, letters or cards, and/or E-mail. Even though children of divorce are likely to have regular visitations with their noncustodial parents, the reality is that they are just as likely not to be in contact with their custodial parents. In a study of disengaged noncustodial fathers, Kruk (1994) found that maternal custody with paternal visitation continues as the dominant structural arrangement, and that paternal disengagement is identical, in postdivorce families in the United States, Canada, and Great Britain. In all those countries, half of all noncustodial fathers gradually lose contact with their children.

Divorce as a Voluntary Decision.   Another distinction between children's experience of loss associated with parental divorce and the loss related to parental death is that divorce, unlike death, is always a voluntary decision for at least one of the partners, and children are keenly aware of that reality. The grief experienced by children as a result of parental divorce always includes the knowledge that the divorce might have been avoided and that at least one of their parents is culpable for the unhappiness the children are experiencing. That knowledge burdens children, who recognize that the persons responsible for their pain are the same persons they count on for protection and care. The realization that their parents are the agents of their distress poses a dilemma for children, who believe that their anguish or sense of vulnerability cannot be expressed without hurting or angering the parent or parents (Wallerstein, 1989).

Feelings of Anger.   A third difference in children's experience of loss related to parental death or parental divorce might be observed in their expressions of anger. Feelings of anger are normal grief reactions with any kind of major loss. Nevertheless, there are distinctive differences in the expression of those feelings, depending on the nature of the loss. Although anger is often present in bereavement (toward the bereaved due to feelings of being abandoned or toward the self for failure to prevent a parent's death), the anger of a child of divorce stems from the child holding one or both parents responsible for the disruption of the family (Wallerstein, 1989).

Feelings of Guilt.   In addition to anger, guilt is a common feeling associated with parental death or parental divorce. Bereaved children suffer from the guilt related to a belief that they should have been able to rescue the parent who has died. Similar to the guilt experienced by children whose parents have died, children whose parents have divorced often believe that something they did or did not do might have contributed to their parents' decision to divorce. Although children of all ages blame themselves for what they perceive as their part in causing the divorce of their parents, preschool children (who have an egocentric perspective of the world) are especially prone to feelings of guilt related to their parents' marital disruption: "I didn't bring in my bike like I was supposed to," or "My brother and I were noisy and argued a lot—that got on my Dad's nerves." Such beliefs are likely to survive a long time, especially in the minds of young children. Finally, the guilt feelings of children whose parents have divorced tend to be stronger and more persistent than those experienced by bereaved children because they are reinforced by the presence of both parents. The fantasy guilt of children of divorce often contributes to a wish to undo their perceived misdeed and by so doing to restore their parents' marriage (Wallerstein, 1989).

Death as a Universal Experience.   The primary contrast between the loss associated with parental death or divorce is that death, unlike divorce, is a universal experience and although young children might not fully comprehend that reality, older children and adolescents know it. The acceptance of death as a universal experience mutes the guilt of a survivor of parental death. Parental divorce, on the other hand, invites the core question: "Will I also experience a disruption in my future marriage?" That question remains a continuing concern for children of divorce and reemerges as they progress through each developmental stage, frequently occurring with the greatest intensity during adolescence as youths begin to look ahead to what their lives are likely to be like during adulthood (Wallerstein, 1989).

Differences in Family and Community Support.   Finally, the social milieu and the available community support are different for children whose parents have divorced and children whose parents have died. The road to recovery is lonelier for children and adolescents who have experienced parental divorce in comparison to children and adolescents who have suffered the loss of a parent through death. Unlike the family and

Thinking Critically

Why do you suppose that the circumstances surrounding parental death and parental divorce contribute to differing levels of family and community support? How do you think that differences in family and community support contribute to children's judgments regarding the legitimacy of their feelings of loss and grief?

community network that rallies for the ceremonies of death, and the support for the bereaved in the immediate aftermath of parental death, when divorce occurs such supports are generally unavailable. Rather than receiving support from a network of caring individuals during parental separation or divorce, children and adolescents notice that friends and family members often stay away and that their grandparents take sides in the conflict or frown on the decision of their parents to divorce (Wallerstein, 1989).

Helping Children Cope with Parental Divorce

Marital disruption is distressing for children and adolescents, and they need emotional support in reconciling themselves to their parents' divorce. There are a number of ways that parents might assist their children in that process, including (a) maintaining open communication with their children, (b) providing children with favorable information about the other parent, and (c) providing a stable environment for their children following their divorce.

Maintaining Open Communication with Children Regarding Parental Divorce.
Children should be informed regarding their parents' decision to divorce and the changes that will be occurring in their lives due to the marital disruption. When telling children about the impending divorce, it is essential that parents reassure them that the divorce is not their fault and that both their parents still love them. Although there are usually resentful feelings between parents who are divorcing, they should be careful not to burden their children with those negative feelings (Kelly, 2000). On the other hand, children should be allowed to express their anxious or angry feelings related to the divorce and be provided emotional support for those feelings (Frieman, Garon, & Garon, 2000).

Providing Adequate and Favorable Information About the Absent Parent.
Although it might be a challenging task for the custodial parent to undertake, it is very beneficial for children to be given favorable information about their absent parent. Like children whose parents have died, children whose parents are divorced must find a way to maintain their attachment to their noncustodial parent. Unfortunately, little attention has been given to the way in which a child's sense of loss following divorce is sometimes compounded by a lack of favorable information about the noncustodial parent. Children tend to carry parental images with them when they are apart from their parents for any period of time. Even when they have never seen their parents, children have an idealized picture of those absent parents' physical characteristics and social backgrounds. Irrespective of the reasons for parental absence, children who possess adequate and favorable information about the missing parent fare better on a variety of measures of well-being than do children who possess little, unfavorable, or no information about their absent parent. When the noncustodial parent is devalued or disconfirmed over time by the custodial parent, a child's sense of trust in the world is diminished (Owusu-Bempah, 1995).

The availability and support of their parents aid children's adjustment to parental divorce.

Providing a Stable Environment for Children Following Parental Divorce.   The quality of care provided by divorced parents, and the degree to which children's basic physical and emotional needs are met during the period of time following parental divorce, affects children's adjustment. Children fare better in the aftermath of divorce when (a) the noncustodial parent remains actively involved in the children's lives (Kruk, 1994), (b) their parents maintain a cooperative relationship (Heath & MacKinnon, 1988; Hoffman & Ledford, 1995; Toews & McHenry, 2001), and (c) custodial parents have an authoritative approach to childrearing (Heath & MacKinnon, 1988; Lamborn et al., 1991).

The Loss and Grief of Children in Foster Care and Adoptive Families

Each year, thousands of children in the United States are taken from their biological families and placed in the care of foster parents or become available for adoption (Roche, 2000). The rise in the numbers of children removed from the homes in which they have resided with their biological parents coincides with an increase of reported cases of child abuse and neglect (Carney, 1997). Although there are a number of psychological difficulties associated with having experienced abuse and neglect at the hand of their parents, children who have been removed from their parents suffer feelings of grief related to the loss of the only parents they have known (Edelstein & Burge, 2001).

The Loss of Familiar People and Places.   When children are placed in foster care, they encounter the loss of their biological parents or previous caregivers, the loss of a familiar environment, and the loss of a number of established and ongoing relationships with other family members, friends, and teachers. Despite the fact that the child's prior living arrangements might not have been healthy and family relationships were neglectful and/or abusive, the child, nevertheless, grieves the loss. Foster parents might have difficulty understanding the child's feelings of grief associated with their separation from abusive or neglectful parents, especially given that foster parents are providing a safer and more nurturing environment than the one from which the child was removed (Edelstein & Burge, 2001).

Foster Children's Behaviors Related to Loss and Grief.   For adults, it is easier to recognize grieving in children who display sadness or who withdraw from social relationships. They might have difficulty understanding that many foster children tend to express their feelings of loss and grief through acting out behaviors toward the most available adult target—the foster parent. It is helpful if foster parents are able to recognize the various problems associated with foster children's feelings of grief. For example, feelings of anxiety and wishes to search for their parents or previous caregivers might interfere with foster children's ability to settle into their new home. Furthermore, it is not unusual for children who are being placed in an unfamiliar environment to have problems in their sleeping, elimination, and eating patterns. Troubles in paying attention and remembering things they are told are other common problems for children during this adjustment phase (Edelstein & Burge, 2001).

The Honeymoon Period.   A further confusing aspect of the grief of children in foster placement is that initially foster parents and their foster children experience a "honeymoon period," during which the children are on their best behavior. Then, several weeks or months after a child has seemingly adjusted to the new environment, that child might suddenly begin to display behavior problems (a testing of the limits) or emotional withdrawal. That behavior is often distressing to their foster or adoptive parents who are prepared to give emotionally but who encounter an emotional void instead. The child's inability to respond emotionally to the foster or adoptive parents who are caring for them sometimes elicits unexpected anger from those parents (Edelstein & Burge, 2001).

Thinking Critically

Imagine yourself at any point in your childhood and try to picture a typical day from that period of your life. Think about the home in which you lived, the people with whom you shared your home, the neighborhood in which you played, and the school you attended. Then, imagine the feelings you might have had if strangers had come into your home and told you to pack up only what you could put in a paper bag. After being told you could no longer live with the only parents you had known, you began to try to put your life together again in a new home, with a new family, in an unfamiliar neighborhood, and at a strange school. In that situation, how do you think you might have felt and behaved? Now, consider how a child in foster care might feel in those circumstances.

THE GRIEF OF ADULTS WHO LOSE PARENTS OR CHILDREN

We will turn our attention now to the experiences of loss and grief of adults who lose parents or children through death or who deal with grief and loss associated with foster parenthood.

The Emotional Stages of Grief

The premise that individuals pass through sequential emotional phases as they are confronted with death comes from two primary sources: Bowlby (1982), who emphasized the phases of grief experienced by a person whose parent or child has died, and Kubler-Ross (1969), whose interviews of dying persons and their families provided an in-depth account of the feelings and thoughts of bereaved persons at five consecutive stages of grief.

Bowlby's Four Phases of Grief.   Bowlby (1982) enumerated four emotional states through which individuals pass as they are grieving the loss of a loved one: (a) a state of numbness lasting from a few hours to a week, periodically interrupted by outbursts of annoyance or grief; (b) a state of yearning and searching for the deceased, lasting from a few months to years; (c) a state of disorganization and depression; and (d) a state of reorganization.

Kubler-Ross' Five Stages of Grief.   Kubler-Ross (1969), whose record-breaking study of dying patients brought death out of the darkness, showed how the human spirit composes itself for death and how family members react to terminal illness or death. Based on her study, Kubler-Ross conceptualized five stages of grief: stage one—Denial, stage two—Anger, stage three—-Bargaining, stage four—Depression, and stage five—Acceptance (see Figure 10.3).

The Impact of a Family Member's Death on Adults

When adults experience the death of a family member, the grief associated with that loss impacts the well-being of those individuals and alters the relationships in their families. Although all persons mourn the death of a loved one and are expected to go through the stages of grief described by Kubler-Ross (1969) in Figure 10.3, there are no hard and fast rules related to the personal experience of grief. First, the length and intensity of grief following the death of a parent or the death of a child does not correlate with the length of a relationship. For example, an adult might sustain a more intense and longer period of grief related to the death of a baby in comparison to the death of an older parent. Also, the length of time required for a person to move through the grief process varies from one individual to another. Two years is not an inappropriate length of time to spend moving through the grief process. Finally, time itself cannot heal grief, but time in conjunction with care and support eases the pain connected with the loss of a parent or a child. Even when the grief has subsided, one never really "gets over" certain losses such as the loss of a child or the death of a family

Stage One—Denial

The first response to news that a loved one has died, or that death is imminent, for one's self or for a family member, is to deny it—by not hearing it, by not believing it, by refusing to talk about it, or by attempting to run away from it. Denial functions as a buffer after a person has received unexpected shocking news and allows individuals to collect themselves and, with time, to mobilize other less radical defenses. It is important for family members and friends to understand that denial is a temporary defense and will soon be replaced by partial acceptance.

Stage Two—Anger

During the second stage of grief, feelings of anger, rage, envy, and resentment replace feelings of denial. At that point, the grieving person confronts feelings of "Why me?" (in the case of learning of one's own terminal illness), or "Why him or her?" (when confronting the reality of the terminal illness or death of a loved one). In comparison to the stage of denial, the stage of anger is very difficult for family members to cope with because the grieving person's anger is displaced in all directions, almost at random. During this stage, it is helpful to remember that the person whose feelings are respected and understood, given attention and a little time, will become less angry.

Stage Three—Bargaining

During the bargaining stage of grief, individuals who are dealing with their own, or a loved one's, imminent death start to believe that they can be successful in entering into some sort of agreement that will postpone the inevitable occurrence. For persons going through the bargaining stage following a family member's death, the bargaining takes the form of guilt regarding *what they might have done*. Most bargains with death are associated with feelings of guilt and should not be brushed aside by family members or friends, who might be helpful in easing individuals past those complicated feelings.

Stage Four—Depression

When individuals become depressed because of impending or actual death, they have made considerable progress toward the acceptance of death. The initial reaction by others to a person's sadness is to try to cheer that person up, by encouraging the despondent person to look at the bright side of life. Such responses are not helpful to the grieving person, who is confronting the impending loss of all that person loves (in the case of one's own terminal illness), or the impending or actual loss of a loved one. If individuals are allowed to convey their feelings of sorrow, acceptance of death is easier, and people are generally grateful to those who will sit with them through their grief without telling them not to be sad.

Stage Five—Acceptance

When a person has had enough time, and has been given sufficient support in working through the stages of denial, anger, bargaining, and depression, that individual will reach a stage of acceptance, where there is an absence of anger or depression related to the contemplation or experience of death. For the dying individual, the final stage of the grieving process is peaceful, accompanied by a need for fewer visitors and more quiet time. The presence of a few loved ones who can reassure the person of their presence by the touch of a hand and brief reassuring words, however, is important. For a person who has lost a family member through death, the stage of acceptance marks a time when that individual begins to reestablish a daily routine, makes readjustments in plans for the future, and searches for meaning associated with their experience of loss.

FIGURE 10.3 Kubler-Ross' Five Stages of Grief
Source: Adapted from *On Death and Dying*, by E. Kubler-Ross, 1969, New York: Macmillan.

member through tragic circumstances. There will be many times in the months and years following the loss when an individual will be aware of a sense of sadness and/or anxiety, especially around certain holidays, birthdays, and (when one has suffered the loss of a child) the beginning of school (Chin-Yee, 1990).

THE DEATH OF AN OLDER PARENT

Most research on the effects of parental death has been concerned with the impact of a parent's death on the lives of minor children. Actually, the death of a parent is much more likely to occur when one is an adult than when one is a child. Even though adults are not as dependent on their parents as are children, the loss of a parent during adulthood is a significant loss due to the importance of the parent–child relationship at any age. Relationships with parents have unique symbolic importance for adult children because of special aspects of the parent–child bond that set it apart from other types of kinship relations. Parents socialize the person during childhood and help shape the person's definition of self. Furthermore, the parental influence continues to be important throughout adulthood because social interaction patterns learned during childhood remain central to adult children's lives. Parents and children typically remain in frequent contact with each other, share many values and attitudes, engage in mutual exchanges of support and services, and experience high levels of positive sentiment from one another (Umberson & Chen, 1994).

The Impact of Parental Death on an Adult's Well-Being.   Based on the symbolic importance of the relationship between adults and their parents, and the ongoing communal interaction between the generations, it would be expected that the loss of an older parent would have a negative impact on an individual. That supposition has been substantiated by Umberson and Chen's (1994) findings linking the death of a father or of a mother to a decline in adult children's self-reported physical health.

Changes in Adults' Family Interaction Patterns Following Parental Death.   An example of the impact of parental death on the family interactions of adults can be observed in the changes in communication patterns between adult siblings following the death of a parent. Generally, the death of a parent negatively impacts the relationships adults have with their siblings. One of the roles that older parents (particularly mothers) serve in their relationships with their adult children is that of kinkeeper. As noted in previous chapters, kinkeepers are responsible for getting families together for family social occasions, for promoting cooperation among family members, and for sharing news about siblings' well-being. Although siblings typically rally following the death of a parent who has served as kinkeeper, after the initial period of grieving there tends to be a decline in sibling closeness and in some families a reactivation of childhood power struggles. Persons who have experienced the death of at least one parent are more likely to report that they do not get along with at least one sibling in comparison to persons with two living parents (Fuller-Thomson, 1999–2000).

There is no greater loss than the death of one's child, and bereaved parents need the support of family members and friends.

Thinking Critically

In your experience or awareness of the death of an older person (such as a grandparent), what have you observed regarding the effect of that family member's death on the relationships of his or her adult children?

THE DEATH OF A CHILD

The death of one's parents is a common experience of middle-aged adults; but the death of a child is a nonnormative occurrence at any age. The death of a child is a devastating life experience and disbelief that one's offspring has died before oneself is a common response regardless of the age of the child or the cause of the death. A child's death causes parents intense personal suffering and affects family reorganization and reintegration into community life. Furthermore, despite the cause of death and irrespective of whether accountability and blame are established, parents typically feel responsible for their children's deaths because the role of the parent is to protect the child and to contribute to the child's continued growth and development (Murphy et al., 1998).

When their child dies, the grief that parents feel encompasses their lives in a variety of ways, including every aspect of day-to-day living. To be able to move through the necessary period of mourning, adults who have lost a child through death must make their way through a maze of grief. During the grief process, many parents feel trapped in the labyrinth of overwhelming sadness. The feeling of being unable to escape the pain associated with the death of their child contributes to various reactions. Some bereaved parents tend to panic and run in all directions in an attempt to return to a normal life, whereas others are inclined to sit and wait for the hurting to subside. Each bereaved parent must make a tremendous endeavor to get through the grief associated with the death of a child but that effort is more effective when it occurs within the framework of supportive people. The most helpful way for others to support grieving parents is by providing love, comfort, and encouragement (Murphy et al., 1998).

Parents Bereaved by the Violent Deaths of Their Children.   Even though all parents experience disbelief when their children's deaths precede their own and tend to assume responsibility for their children's deaths, there are, nevertheless, unique bereavement responses to the violent death of one's child. After the suicidal death of a child, parents perceive rejection and abandonment by their child, report thoughts of "why didn't I know?" and are painfully aware of the social stigma directed toward them. Bereavement responses of a parent whose child has died as a result of homicide might consist of rage, revenge toward the child's killer, and frustration with the criminal justice system (Murphy et al., 1998).

The violent death of one's child affects all domains of a parent's personal and social functioning and legal and economic problems are common as well. Furthermore, the troubles associated with coping with the violent death of one's child occur very early in bereavement and persist for many years. The struggle to deal with their child's violent death tends to alter parents' views of themselves and the world. Persons generally regard the world they live in as benevolent and meaningful and their selves as worthy; but the trauma that accompanies the violent death of one's child brings about an abrupt change in one's perception of oneself and the world. Following the violent death of their child, parents frequently report that they feel helpless and weak in a malevolent, meaningless world. Finally, parents whose children have experienced a violent death frequently believe, correctly or incorrectly, that others blame them for their child's death (Murphy et al., 1998).

Helping Parents Cope with the Death of a Child.   Even though family members and friends would like to help parents who are grieving the loss of a child, they often feel helpless and unsure about what to say or what to do in that situation. Several guidelines have been suggested by Chin-Yee (1990) for assisting parents in dealing with the death of a child, including (a) recognizing that there is variation in the ways in which individuals respond to grief, (b) educating parents' family members and friends regarding the circumstances of the death, (c) recognizing the child's identity, (d) encouraging bereaved parents to initiate contact with others, and (e) expecting to deal with bereaved parents' anger.

Understanding a Parent's Unique Response to Death.   The first step in assisting grieving parents is to understand that one person's way of coping with the death of a child cannot be compared to someone else's. People tend to deal with loss based on how their family of origin coped with loss. The most helpful approach others can take to assist grieving parents is to allow them the freedom to express their grief according to their individual way of coping. While accepting grieving parents' unique responses to loss, family members and friends can validate their feelings related to the death of a child by being willing to listen and by being supportive when they talk about their worries and anxieties.

Educate Family Members and Friends.   When a child dies, the whole community reacts with shock and disbelief and attempts to find an adequate explanation for the death, sometimes at the expense of the grieving parents who might be blamed. When supportive persons act on behalf of the bereaved parents by informing those parents' family members and friends of the circumstances of the child's death, they spare parents the agonizing task of answering a number of painful questions. Educating family members and friends about the conditions of the child's death might also reduce the burden of guilt that is sometimes placed on the family. That is especially true in the case of sudden infant death syndrome (SIDS) and violent death.

Reinforce the Child's Identity.   A third recommendation for helping bereaved parents to deal with the loss of a child is to reinforce that child's identity by encouraging parents to talk about the events surrounding their child's birth, life, and death. To grieve for a loved one, that person needs to have an identity, a history, and a place in the family. When a baby is stillborn or dies shortly after birth, having a photo, a lock of hair, and/or a footprint is helpful. It is beneficial as well for family members and friends to always refer to the baby or the child by name and to call the parents *mother* or *father* and the siblings *brother* and/or *sister*.

Encourage Bereaved Parents to Initiate Contact with Others.   Along with confusion over the death, many family members and friends experience a lack of confidence regarding initiating contact with bereaved persons. Therefore, parents who are grieving the loss of a child should be encouraged to take the first step in making contact with others. It is particularly beneficial for grieving parents to initiate communication with others at anniversaries of 1 week, 1 month, 6 months, and 1 year after their child's death as well as on special occasions such as holidays and the child's birthday.

Expect to Deal with a Bereaved Parent's Anger.   It is not unusual for parents who have lost a child through death to have feelings of anger; and family members and friends sometimes bear the brunt of that fury. Parents whose child has died are simply lashing out at the world and those people just happened to get in the way. Persons who are providing support to sorrowful parents should therefore expect to deal with a bereaved parent's anger. It is important for others not to take those outbursts personally but to realize that anger is a natural expression of anguish when one's child has died.

Provide Support for Their Other Children.   An important, but often overlooked step, in helping bereaved parents who have other children is to talk to those children about the death of their sibling, and in the case of the death of a newborn, to talk about the birth and death of the baby. When talking to those children, it is valuable to reassure them that, although their parents are very sad, they still love their children, will continue to take care of them, and will be available to talk with and play with them soon. Offering to take their children out for brief periods of time is typically beneficial to grieving parents as well.

Consider Mutual Support Groups.   All parents who have experienced the death of a child might benefit from the interventions described above but those parents who are trying to cope with the violent death of a child are typically in need of assistance beyond their own social network. Their persistent need to talk about the violent death of their child allows them to revise some circumstances in ways that make their loss more tolerable and imposes some order on their experience. Sadly, the lack of nonjudgmental listeners during bereavement is well documented. For that reason, mutual support groups have been found to be the predominant source of help for parents following the violent deaths of their children.

THE LOSS AND GRIEF EXPERIENCES OF FOSTER PARENTS

Foster parents continuously deal with loss and grief including (a) the grief of the children in their care, (b) the grief of the parents whose children are in their care, (c) their own grief upon losing children who are reunited with their parents, and (d) the grief of other family members when foster children leave. Although each of these circumstances of loss and grief are hard, perhaps the greatest challenge for foster parents is the ability to comprehend and respond to the grief of their foster children. To understand the demanding behaviors that foster children frequently display, foster parents must be able to empathize with the loss and grief those children experience. One of the obstacles to helping a grieving foster child is when a child's sorrow reawakens memories of past losses in the foster parent. In that situation, a particular child's heartache might have a stronger than expected impact on a foster parent. How well foster parents are able to handle a foster child's feelings of loss and grief is related to those parents' own style of coping and the kinds of losses they have encountered and mastered in the past. Having successfully coped with past losses better prepares a foster parent to support a foster child's feelings of loss and grief. In contrast, a foster parent who is in the process of grieving a recent loss or who has experienced multiple losses might feel overwhelmed by a foster child's painful emotions and difficult behavior (Edelstein & Burge, 2001).

Help for Grieving Foster Parents

There are three primary sources of social support that can alleviate some of the pain associated with foster parents' experiences of loss and grief: (a) educational programs, (b) emotional support from friends and families, and (c) mutual support groups. Educational programs can prepare foster parents for the feelings of loss and grief that they will likely experience when their foster children leave. By gaining an awareness of the stages of grief a person goes through following any major loss, foster parents are better able to understand and acknowledge their feelings of grief following a child's departure from their lives. Although educational programs are valuable for helping foster parents to discern the feelings they might encounter, it is helpful as well when they have a network of family members and friends who are willing to support their feelings of loss and grief. Sometimes, though, family members or friends have suffered the same loss and are in too much denial or pain to be helpful. In those situations, they might cut off the bereaved foster parent's attempts to communicate sad feelings in a misguided attempt to be helpful. Alternatively, foster parent support groups provide an environment wherein feelings of loss and grief can be openly discussed, listened to, and supported. Members of those groups are familiar with and empathic toward the feelings of anticipated grief, fears of loss, and actual loss that are so much a part of the lives of foster parents (Edelstein & Burge, 2001).

THE LOSS AND GRIEF OF PARENTS AND CHILDREN WHEN PARENTS ARE INCARCERATED

The parent–child relationship is abruptly changed when a parent goes to prison but there are gender differences in parental incarceration. The overwhelming majority of the children of incarcerated fathers are in the care of their biological mothers (87%). In contrast, the minority of the children of incarcerated mothers are in the care of their biological fathers (20%) (Reed & Reed, 1997). Because women are among the fastest growing group of prisoners (Bloom & Steinhart, 1993), and the majority of incarcerated mothers of minor children were the primary caregivers for their children, that leaves large numbers of children who experience the loss of their primary caregivers.

Just as children show grief related to the loss associated with parental death divorce, or foster care placement, children whose parents are incarcerated grieve the

When parents and children are separated due to parental incarceration, feelings of loss and grief are usually accompanied by feelings of shame and embarrassment.

loss of their absent parents. Children of incarcerated parents respond to the mandatory severance from the parent by sadness, withdrawal, low self-esteem, depression, lower school performance, truancy, discipline problems, alcohol and other drug usage, running away, and aggressive behavior (Myers, Smarsh, & Amlund-Hagen, 1999). Children typically feel vulnerable and frightened about losing their parent and that loss is further exacerbated for siblings who might be separated from each other following the imprisonment of their parent. Furthermore, many children of incarcerated parents blame themselves for the parents' absence. Sometimes children are not told where their parent really is, and most children of incarcerated parents get little or no emotional support to process their feelings of grief, loss, shame, anger, anxiety, and fear. Instead of receiving support to deal with those difficult feelings, children of incarcerated parents are often not allowed to talk about their feelings or to tell others about their parent's incarceration (Reed & Reed, 1997).

Responding to the Needs of Children of Incarcerated Parents

Interventions designed to alleviate the suffering of children whose parents are incarcerated need to address the recurrent traumatic events that affect children of parents involved in the criminal justice system. Those children usually live in poverty before, during, and after their parents' incarceration, reside in substandard housing, and typically lack the means to visit their incarcerated parents (Reed & Reed, 1997). Johnston and Gabel (1995) described several models that could lessen the problems faced by children as a consequence of their parents' incarceration. Those include crisis nurseries for very young children that are designed to alleviate the trauma experienced by young children who have witnessed their parents' arrest. Crisis intervention counseling for children after the arrest of a parent is another approach that is needed to reduce the immediate and long-term negative effects of that experience. Such a program could provide reliable information to children regarding the process in which the parent is involved and furnish referrals to sources of ongoing support for family members. Parent–child visitations programs held in child-centered settings in the correctional facility are needed as well to make visits with incarcerated parents a more positive experience for children.

Incarcerated Mothers

In many situations, the care provided to one's children prior to imprisonment is far from optimum but prison time gives incarcerated mothers an opportunity to work on their parenting shortcomings. "When a woman goes to prison, her relationship to her children is a central emotional focus: she is torn by guilt, anxiety and a sense of failure, yet, at the same time, her child continues to be a source of hope, a connection to a part of herself, a motivation for her to change. This crisis is potentially an opportunity for enormous growth if it is faced . . ." (p. 104). Even though their children are a central focus in the lives of incarcerated mothers, the lack of involvement in the daily lives of their children is one of the hardest things that imprisoned mothers have to bear. They have many concerns about their relationships with their children, including fears that their infants and young children will not know who they are. Mothers in prison experience high levels of stress that correspond to high levels of depression and a greater number of physical symptoms in comparison to incarcerated women who are not mothers. Besides depression and physical symptoms, guilt, decreased self-esteem, and a sense of tremendous loss are common experiences of incarcerated mothers (Young & Smith, 2000).

Interventions for Incarcerated Mothers.   In addition to the ongoing physical separation from their children, correctional policies related to visitation and telephone calls make it problematic for mothers to remain in touch with and informed about their children. There is a need for culturally responsive family support programs to assist incarcerated mothers in maintaining connections with their children. Community-based organizations and social service agencies might serve as host agencies for services considered necessary for maintaining relationships with children following incarceration. Needed services include emotional support, individual and family counseling, and transportation and housing to facilitate visitation. Finally, mentoring and big brother/big sister programs are likely to benefit those children who require additional attention and direction while their mothers are incarcerated.

❧ SUMMARY

In this chapter, we focused on loss and grief as it relates to the parent–child relationship. We first considered the ways in which children cope with their feelings of loss and grief following (a) the death of a parent or sibling, (b) the separation or divorce of their parents, or (c) their placement in foster care or with adoptive parents. We then considered the feelings of loss and grief of adults (a) who lose a parent or child through death, or (b) who deal with loss and grief in their role as foster parents. Finally, we addressed the feelings of loss and grief experienced by children and mothers that occur following parental incarceration. For each of the various circumstances of loss, we considered strategies for helping children and parents to cope with feelings of grief, including ways to rebuild their lives following such losses.

❧ KEY TERMS

- disenfranchised loss and grief
- inner representation of the deceased
- magical thinking
- personal narrative
- rescripting of family interactions
- story of a death

11

Child Socialization Strategies and Techniques

As we have seen in previous chapters, children construct their social world from their everyday experiences. It is, therefore, essential for parents to carefully consider the guidance strategies they will use in the rearing of their children. When parents have ineffective parenting skills or rely chiefly on how they were raised, the resulting childrearing approach might not be as well thought out or as effective as when parents are prepared for that important career. The child socialization strategies presented in this final chapter are based on a philosophy of democratic parent–child relationships (Dreikurs & Soltz, 1964), which is represented in the authoritative parenting style (Baumrind, 1967, 1971). The democratic approach to child socialization focuses on process rather than consensus, attends to long-range as well as short-range goals, and recognizes the impact of parental actions on the child.

The parenting skills described in the first part of the chapter reflect a prevention-of-problems approach, which includes a variety of strategies designed to assist children in meeting their goals and to motivate them toward cooperative behavior. Following the presentation of strategies intended to prevent problems from occurring is a discussion of the ways in which parents might reinforce their children's appropriate behaviors and serve as effective models for their children's behaviors. After that discussion is a presentation of a strategy designed to foster effective parent–child communication. Then, several childrearing methods are explained to help parents in (a) establishing boundaries, (b) setting limits, and (c) providing consequences that are developmentally appropriate and growth-producing for the child.

GUIDANCE AS PREVENTION OF PROBLEMS

There are a number of effective strategies parents might use to prevent their children's misbehavior, to motivate their children to behave in appropriate ways, to understand the feelings and concerns that underlie their children's misbehavior, and to promote open communication between their children and themselves. Those strategies include a method for establishing an atmosphere of psychological safety for children, the technique of encouragement, an approach called *four pluses and a wish*, a procedure that focuses on children's four goals of misbehavior, and a method for improving parent–child communication skills that includes problem ownership, active listening, and I-messages.

Establishing an Atmosphere of Psychological Safety

Dorothy Briggs (1975) developed a prevention-of-problems approach to guidance wherein parents are enjoined to create an **atmosphere of psychological safety** for their children. That model is based on Briggs' position that the chief goal of parenting is to build a strong sense of self-worth in children. According to Briggs, there are three levels of self-esteem, each of which reflects children's ongoing interactions with their parents. Children with high self-esteem have experienced unconditional love from their parents. Children with low self-esteem have had interactions with parents that have contributed to questions regarding their lovability. Children with middle-level self-esteem have had interactions with their parents that have contributed to the belief that their lovability derives from performance that pleases others.

The House of Self.   Briggs uses the analogy of "house of self" to explain how each level of self-esteem is built. According to that perspective, the house of self is constructed by developing children from the words, body language, and treatment by important others in their environment, particularly parents. Every day, children are asking, "Who am I?" The answer to that question consists of the collection of messages

When children experience their parent's unconditional love, they develop a positive sense of self.

reflected back to them. Accordingly, the self-image of children matches how they are treated regardless of their actual potential. In determining how parent–child interactions impact a child's self-esteem, the issue is not "Does the parent love the child?" but "Does the child feel and experience the parent's love?" Briggs' emphasis on the promotion of the child's self-esteem highlights the belief that technique and love must be interwoven. Briggs recommends that parents examine all guidance decisions in light of two questions, (a) "Does this approach encourage or discourage a child's sense of self-worth?" and (b) "Would I like to be my own child?"

Because a child's house of self is constructed during everyday interactions with parents and others, it is important that parents attend to their children's feelings as they are instructing them and as they are responding to their behavioral challenges. In those interactions, children need to receive messages that contribute to beliefs that they are competent and lovable. Briggs outlined several ways in which parents might foster their children's self-esteem. She emphasized first and foremost that, in all of their interactions with their children, parents should express unconditional love. Children are more likely to develop a high self-esteem when they feel cherished. For children to feel cherished, they need to be able to get parents' focused attention, to be really seen (not just looked at). According to Briggs, to truly see a child, the parent must connect to each child with fresh eyes, to attend to that child's *particularness.* She further stressed that children need to know they can trust the adults around them. According to Briggs, children are able to trust their parents when (a) their real needs are met, (b) parental promises are kept, and (c) parents are not afraid to apologize or to say "no" when a refusal is necessary. Finally, Briggs highlighted the value of having humor in the parent–child relationship. She noted that children are more likely to trust parents who are capable of having fun with them. Laughing, joking, and playing with children dissolve the barriers between parents and children and helps to foster a trusting relationship.

Research Findings That Demonstrate the Value of Promoting Children's Self-Esteem.   The importance of using socialization strategies that promote children's self-esteem cannot be overemphasized. The self-acceptance that children gain during the early years reflects the degree to which they feel that they are valued by their parents (Bigner, 1998). Furthermore, high self-esteem helps children to view the rest of their lives from a more positive perspective. They are able to believe, for example, that even when their efforts are not successful in certain academic, athletic, or social situations, they are still worthwhile individuals (Harter, 1990). Moreover, children with supportive families develop both higher self-esteem and more positive social relationships (Franco & Levitt, 1998). Higher self-esteem also mediates a variety of negative outcomes for children, including eating disorders, depression, and antisocial behavior (Harter, 1998).

Guidance as Encouragement of Children

Encouragement is one of the most beneficial skills that parents might use for assisting children in meeting their goals and for boosting their children's self-esteem. Parental encouragement helps children to believe in themselves and their abilities and motivates them to try new things. By and large, parental encouragement of children helps children to have the courage not to be perfect. The strategy of encouragement fits into the democratic model of parenting by shifting the parental focus from children's mistakes to what parents like and appreciate about their children. Parents encourage their children when they (a) avoid placing value judgments on them, (b) focus on their feelings, (c) concentrate on process rather than outcome, and (d) separate children's worth from their accomplishments or their mistakes (Dinkmeyer & McKay, 1989).

Avoiding Value Judgments of Children.   The most beneficial effect of encouragement is that it does not place value judgments on children. Too often, when parents make positive comments about their children, those comments are laden with negative values and opinions and as such do not assist their children in believing in themselves. For parents who learn to use the influential strategy of encouragement, value-laden words of praise are replaced by non-evaluative phrases of encouragement that assist children to continue trying when things are difficult and to feel proud of their hard work and positive outcomes.

Focusing on the Feelings of Children.   To help children feel encouraged, parents need to emphasize the importance of how children feel about what they do and who they are. Instead of sending messages of encouragement that focus on the importance of a child's feelings and beliefs, parents frequently convey messages of **praise** that emphasize the parents' feelings. If, for example, a child has achieved a particular goal, parents often praise the child by saying: "I'm proud of you." To convert that statement of praise into a statement of encouragement, the focus must change from a focus on the feelings of the parent to a focus on the feelings of the child. Examples of statements of encouragement are, "You must feel proud of yourself," or "Well, I guess you feel pretty good about that," or "How do you feel about that?"

This mother is encouraging her child's self-reliance.

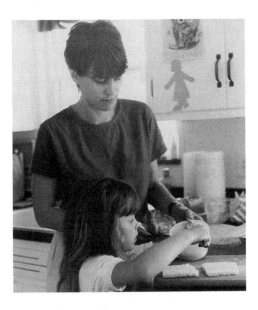

Focusing on Process Rather Than Outcome.   When parents wait until their children have achieved a desired outcome before providing a positive appraisal of them, they miss out on the opportunity to provide motivation for their children as they are work- ing toward their goal. To attain distinction in a specific area requires ability and effort; and excellence develops along many steps. Encouragement is, thus, more valuable along the way than it is after the child has already reached a goal. A state- ment such as "Look at the progress you've made in putting together that model" focuses on the process rather than the outcome and encourages children to perse- vere in the face of a challenge. Even when children have reached a desired goal, it is more encouraging for children when parents focus on the process that led to the achievement of that goal rather than placing the emphasis on the outcome. After a child has completed a project, an encouraging statement (which focuses on process), such as "You really worked hard on that science project, and your hard work paid off," is better than words of praise (that focus on outcome) such as "Good job." Finally, as recommended by Popkin (1987), parents should provide encouragement for children's efforts regardless of whether or not those efforts result in success. An example of a statement of encouragement that concentrates on improvement, rather than perfection, is something like this: "James, you are really improving in your read- ing. I can tell a big difference in the last few weeks."

Separating Children's Worth from Their Accomplishments.   Although it is impor- tant to admire children's accomplishments and to encourage the steps along the way to success, it is essential that parents make it clear that they love and appreciate their children independent of what they do. As emphasized by Popkin (1987), children's worth depends on who they are, not on what they do. Suggested ways for parents to separate their children's worth from their accomplishments include: (a) taking the time to sit and talk with their children, (b) listening to their children's funny stories as well as their tales of woe, and (c) telling their children that they are loved and fun to be with.

Separating Children's Worth from Their Mistakes.   Just as children's worth is some- thing different from their accomplishments, their worth is different also from their mistakes or failures. Mistakes, such as misbehavior, do not reflect a lack of worth but are actually an aspect of growth and development. An error or a slipup by a child can show that child what not to do in the future, which is a valuable lesson (Popkin, 1987). An example of a way to respond to children's mistakes includes the following phrase. "Don't worry about having made a mistake. Making mistakes is how we learn. Instead of blaming yourself, let's see how we can correct it."

Attitudes and Behaviors That Discourage Children.   To assist parents in becoming more encouraging to their children, Dinkmeyer and McKay (1989) described sev- eral attitudes and behaviors that parents need to eliminate because those behaviors discourage children: (a) negative expectations of their children, (b) unreasonably high demands of their children, (c) competition between or among their children, (d) being overly ambitious, and (e) the double standard (see Figure 11.1).

Negative Expectations
One of the most powerful forces in human relationships is expectations, and parents sometimes express negative expectations of their children in their day-to-day relationships with them (by word and by gesture). When parents do not believe a child will succeed at something, they subtly (and sometimes not so subtly) communicate that belief to the child. The typical result of negative parental expectations is that the child behaves in the manner expected (a self-fulfilling prophecy).

Unusually High Standards
Parents sometimes fail to recognize the positive qualities in their children and communicate to their children that, whatever they do, they should do better. That type of communication sends a message to children that their accomplishments are never quite good enough. Furthermore, parents sometimes expect performance beyond the ages and abilities of their children.

Promoting Competition Between or Among Siblings
Children are discouraged when parents promote competition between or among them by praising one child's success while ignoring another child's efforts. Also, parental gestures or facial expressions can generate competition as much as parental comments. If parents practice the use of encouragement with all their children, however, competition among children decreases and cooperation increases.

Overly Ambitious Parents
Overly ambitious parents expect their children to demonstrate a high level of excellence but that parental goal actually inhibits children from boldly trying new experiences. Because they have come to understand that their parents' standards are very high regarding their accomplishments, children of overly ambitious parents might not try things unless they feel confident of their success.

The Double Standard
Some parents practice a double standard by expressing the belief that it is okay to deny their children the rights and privileges they themselves enjoy. Some ways of avoiding the double standard consist of having rules that affect all family members such as, "family members do not yell at or hit each other," or "cursing or swearing is not practiced in this house."

FIGURE 11.1   Parental Attitudes and Behaviors That Discourage Children
Source: Adapted from *Systematic Training for Effective Parenting: The Parent's Handbook* (3rd ed.), by D. Dinkmeyer and G. McKay, 1989, American Guidance Services, Circle Pines, MN.

Attitudes and Behaviors That Encourage Children.   Avoiding attitudes and behaviors that discourage children is an important first step toward the encouragement of children. The next step is for parents to develop the attitudes and behaviors of encouragement to replace discouraging patterns of interactions with their children. Attitudes and behaviors of parents that provide encouragement for children include (a) appreciating each of their children's uniqueness, (b) showing confidence in their children, (c) building on their children's strengths, (d) avoiding sending mixed messages to their children, and (e) using humor in their parent–child interactions (Popkin, 1987; see Figure 11.2).

Appreciate Each Child's Uniqueness

It is encouraging for children when their parents take an interest in each child's activities, get to know what is interesting to each child, and show an awareness of what each child thinks about things, including favorite foods, colors, etc. Examples: "Grace, we're having your favorite food tonight—spaghetti," and "Philip, you seem to enjoy that activity."

Show Confidence in Children by Giving Them Responsibility

Parents show confidence in their children when they give them responsibility. When assigning responsibilities to children, though, the parent needs to be aware of the child's level of ability and to be mindful of the goal the parent wants to accomplish in assigning the child certain responsibilities. Example: Allowing children to have a puppy, provided they assume some of the duties associated with feeding and caring for the pet.

Show Confidence in Children by Asking for Their Advice

When parents seek their children's advice, they send the message that they have assurance in their children's knowledge and judgment. Consulting children on their opinion bolsters their children's sense of self-worth and encourages them to speak up to parents regarding their ideas and beliefs. Example: "Brandon, come look at this map with us and help us decide which route would be best for us to take on our trip."

Show Confidence in Children by Avoiding Rescuing Them

It is discouraging for children when parents do things for them on a regular basis that they are capable of doing by themselves. Parents encourage their children by demonstrating confidence in their ability to complete a task. Example: "I have confidence in your ability to make that decision for yourself," or "I think you can do it on your own but if you'd like a little help, let me know."

Build on a Child's Strengths to Promote Positive Behaviors

A way to focus attention on a child's strengths is to acknowledge those things that the child does well. An example of building on the child's strengths is included in the following request: "Kenny, how about showing your brother, Todd, how to tie his Cub Scout tie." In that example, the parent fosters cooperation between the brothers while promoting the self-esteem of the older child.

Build on a Child's Strengths While Disapproving of Behaviors

Even when a child misbehaves, parents can focus on the child's strength while expressing disapproval of the child's misbehavior. Example: "Nicole, I'm glad that you want to be able to stand up for yourself; that is an important strength but hitting is not acceptable behavior. Let's talk about how you could stand up for yourself without resorting to fighting."

Avoid Sending Mixed Messages

Children receive mixed messages when parents make qualifying or moralizing comments to them, such as "So, why don't you clean your room like this all the time," or "Well, it's about time," or "See what you can do when you try." Those qualifying or demoralizing statements do not fall into the realm of encouragement and are actually discouraging to children.

Continued

> **Use Humor**
> Parents who can see things from a humorous point of view encourage children to re-
> consider rigid perceptions of themselves and other persons. The use of humor helps
> parents and children to relate to the challenges of life in a more relaxed manner.
> When humor is present in families, there are fewer catastrophes because both par-
> ents and children are aware of other ways to look at each situation.

FIGURE 11.2 Parental Attitudes and Behaviors That Encourage Children
Source: Adapted from *Systematic Training for Effective Parenting: The Parent's Handbook* (3rd ed.), by
D. Dinkmeyer and G. McKay, 1989, American Guidance Services, Circle Pines, MN; *New Beginnings:
Skills for Single Parents. Parent's Manual*, by D. Dinkmeyer, G. McKay, and J. McKay, 1987, Champaign,
IL: Research Press; and *Active Parenting: Teaching Cooperation, Courage, and Responsibility*, 1987,
San Francisco: Perennial Library.

Thinking Critically

Suppose your 4-year-old child had made his bed for the first time, and, because that was his
first time, it was not as neat as it is when you make it. How might you compose a response to
the child that represents an example of encouragement?

Research Findings Linking the Use of Encouragement to Positive Outcomes.   Harter
(1999) recommends that parents use the language of encouragement to promote children's sense of pride in their accomplishments, thereby nurturing their success. The
link between parental encouragement and children's success has been observed in
various settings. For example, when parents encourage their children's participation
in decision making, their children gain the experience needed to engage in thoughtful and responsible behaviors when interacting with their peers (Steinberg et al.,
1991). Another illustration of the link between parental encouragement and children's
attainment of success is when parents demonstrate encouragement of their children's
involvement in sports programs. The findings of Green and Chalip (1997) demonstrated that children's level of performance and feelings of success were highly correlated to their parents' satisfaction with and encouragement of their performance.

Four Pluses and a Wish—A Strategy for Motivating Children's Compliance

One of the chief complaints of parents is "How can I get my child to do a particular
thing?" From picking up toys to studying for homework, parents are highly interested in
gaining their children's cooperation. When attempting to get a child to comply with
parental requests, it is important to determine if the behavior being asked of the child is

within the child's capability to perform. It is valuable as well for parents to know how to make a request of a child that is designed to gain the child's cooperation while respecting the child's feelings. A technique developed by William Purkey (Purkey, Schmidt, & Benedict, 1990) known as **four pluses and a wish** is an excellent choice for motivating children's cooperation because it contains an affirming exchange that is far more likely to inspire cooperation than is the typical parental command (see Figure 11.3).

In using four pluses and a wish, parents should be certain that their facial expression and body language convey friendliness toward the child. They, then, must take a moment to generate a request that acknowledges and affirms the child before making their request. The effectiveness of the strategy of four pluses and a wish is that children who feel respected are far more motivated to comply with parental wishes than are children who do not feel valued. Using four pluses and a wish benefits parents by assisting in becoming aware of the ways in which their facial expressions, their body language, their tone of voice, and their verbal statements impact their children's motivation to comply with parental wishes.

Four pluses and a wish might be used to inspire the cooperation of a child in the following ways.

Plus 1—Smile
The parent approaches the child with a smiling face (Plus 1). Plus 1 might sound very elementary but it is exceedingly powerful. Children monitor facial expressions from birth and are keenly attuned to parental moods.

Plus 2—Relaxed Body Language
When making a request of a child, it is also important to use relaxed body language that minimizes the psychological distance between the parent and the child (Plus 2). Stiff body language, such as crossed arms or crossed legs, are examples of ways that parents sometimes establish barriers between themselves and their children and communicate a lack of acceptance toward the child.

Plus 3—Say the Child's Name
When making a request of a child, saying that child's name while using an approving voice tone (Plus 3) personalizes the request and conveys respect for the child.

Plus 4—Pay a Compliment to the Child
Then, before making a request from the child, it is important for parents to affirm the child by paying a compliment to the child (Plus 4). At that point, the parent might say something nice about the child or what the child is presently involved in.

The Wish
Only after providing four pluses for the child, does the parent make the request (The Wish).

FIGURE 11.3 Four Pluses and a Wish
Source: Adapted from *Invitational Learning for Counseling and Development*, by W. Purkey, J. J. Schmidt, and G. C. Benedict, 1990, Ann Arbor, MI: ERIC Counseling & Personnel Services Clearinghouse.

Three examples of the use of four pluses and a wish are as follows: Five-year-old Mario is busy playing with his toys and Dad wants him to put his toys away and get ready for bed. Commands such as "Mario, put your toys away and get ready for bed" or "Time for bed, Mario" are not likely to be highly motivating for a 5-year-old boy who is highly focused on playing with his toys. First of all, Mario is less interested in going to bed than he is in playing. Second, a transition from one activity to another is often difficult for children and particularly problematic for preschool children. Using four pluses and a wish, Dad might walk over to Mario with a smile on his face (Plus 1), stoop down (Plus 2), and (in a friendly voice) say "Hi Mario" (Plus 3). Then Dad might compliment Mario by saying "Wow, you've built a great fort; tell me about it" (Plus 4). At that point, Mario is likely to tell his Dad about his project since his Dad has shown an interest in what Mario is doing. After a friendly exchange, Dad might make the request (A Wish) as follows: "Mario, in a little while (or about 10 minutes), it will be time for you to put your toys away and start getting ready for bed. I will tell you when it is time." Although this example is of a parent and a preschool boy, the technique is effective with children of all ages.

Thinking Critically

Suppose you want your school-age children (Mark and Lora) to help you rake the leaves in the fall. Using the technique of four pluses and a wish, how might you request their assistance?

Research Findings That Demonstrate the Importance of Respectful Treatment of Children. Leaper, Anderson, and Sanders (1998) found that parents use different types of speech when interacting with their children: supportive, directive, and negative. The technique of four pluses and a wish represents supportive speech. Supportive speech consists of respectful ways of speaking to children as well as giving children the time and opportunity to reply to parental requests. One of the effects of supportive versus nonsupportive parental speech is its relation to children's social relationships. In exploring the links between communication patterns in mother–child, father–child, and child–peer interactions Black and Logan (1995) found that parents of children who are rejected by their peers make significantly more requests of their children than do parents of popular children and do not give their children time to reply to their requests.

The Concept of Belongingness and Children's Goals of Misbehavior

Children's behavior is labeled misbehavior when it is found to be unacceptable by parents or other adults. Parents and other adults, however, are more or less tolerant of a wide range of children's behavior (Heath, 1993). One parent might call the young child's inability to sit still or stand in line for an extended period of time *misbehavior.*

Another parent might realize that young children are, by nature, very active and curious and might not require the same behavior from the young child. Furthermore, parents often label noncompliance and defiance as misbehavior without regard for the child's ability or motivation to comply with stated expectations. Dreikurs (1972) provided an approach for understanding the feelings and goals that underlie children's misbehavior by emphasizing the ways in which the socialization process frequently contributes to children's misconduct. He maintained that the chief human goal is belongingness. In their efforts to achieve a sense of belongingness, children often pursue four secondary goals of misbehavior: attention, power, revenge, and a display of inadequacy (see Figure 11.4).

Goal 1—Misbehavior Designed to Gain Attention
Children feel they have a place in the family, belongingness, when they receive sufficient attention from other members of the family, especially their parents. Based on their high needs for attention, children behave in a variety of ways to gain their parents attention and much of that behavior is appropriate. When parents and/or other family members fail to provide children with sufficient attention, however, children are likely to engage in misbehavior that is designed to attract parental attention.

Goal 2—Misbehavior Designed to Gain Power
To achieve a sense of belongingness in one's family, children need to feel as if they have influence and choices regarding matters pertaining to themselves, such as what they wear, what they eat, and what behaviors they will engage in. Furthermore, children need to feel that they are able to have influence on the interactions of the family group, such as being included in activities the family is engaged in as well as having a say as to how and when those activities are carried out. When children are not consulted or given a say regarding matters that affect them directly and/or what is going on in the family, they tend to feel powerless and might misbehave to regain a sense of control.

Goal 3—Misbehavior Related to the Goal of Revenge
The goal of revenge emerges from frustrated attempts to seek attention and power. Children misbehaving with the goal of revenge are hurt due to past reactions to their behaviors seeking attention and power. Out of their hurt feelings, they engage in misbehavior clearly recognized as vengeful, because their goal is to take revenge on others who have hurt them.

Goal 4—Misbehavior That Reflects a Display of Inadequacy
Children whose behaviors reflect a display of inadequacy are those who are no longer engaging in behavior with the goals of seeking attention or power. Those children are convinced of their lack of belongingness based on their inability to get the attention and power they need in their lives. They have, therefore, given up trying to gain attention and/or power and feel powerless to seek revenge. Attitudes of despair and a stance of "What's the use?" are displayed in various areas of those children's lives. Children who exhibit a display of inadequacy are often viewed as lazy, unkempt, or unmotivated.

FIGURE 11.4   The Four Goals of Misbehavior
Source: Adapted from *Discipline without Tears,* by R. Dreikurs, 1972, New York: Hawthorne.

The Mistaken Goals of Misbehavior.   Because the child's primary goal is belonging-ness, the **four goals of misbehavior** are actually secondary goals, each of which is be-lieved to assist the child in the quest for belongingness. The belief of children that belongingness and acceptance within the family will be achieved through their mis-behavior is not realized, though, because unacceptable behavior generally alienates one from others. In recognition of that dilemma, Dreikurs and Soltz (1964) pointed out that children's four goals of misbehavior are mistaken goals whereby events are often misinterpreted, mistaken conclusions are drawn, and faulty decisions are made.

Recognizing the Underlying Goals of Children's Misbehavior.   Whereas children are generally unaware of the mistaken goals underlying their misbehavior, parents can learn to recognize those underlying goals by the effects of the misbehavior on others. As noted by Dreikurs and Soltz (1964), what a parent is inclined to do in re-sponse to a child's behavior is generally consistent with the child's goal underlying that behavior. Parental reactions that correspond to children's goals of misbehavior include giving attention, engaging in power struggles, seeking retaliation, or giving up in despair. Although the method for recognizing the goals of misbehavior is clear and simple, it requires that parents observe carefully not only their children's unde-sirable behavior but also their own responses to that behavior.

If the parent's typical response to a particular infraction is to provide attention (positive or negative), then a bid for attention is probably the underlying goal behind the child's misbehavior. If the parent becomes angry and loses control, or is inclined to become angry and lose control in relation to unacceptable behavior, the underly-ing goal of the child is most likely to gain or regain power. When a child's actions re-sult in a parent losing control, then the child gains control or power. If a parent feels hurt by a child's words or other deliberate acts designed to hurt others (such as dam-aging property), the parent's reaction reflects an attempt by the child to hurt others (revenge). The child's motivation to seek revenge is due to the child's feelings of hurt, born of a perceived lack of attention or power. When a parent sees the child as gen-erally unmotivated (not doing homework, not keeping up personal hygiene, or show-ing little interest in activities), the child is probably expressing a belief that efforts will not be noticed, appreciated, or rewarded (Dreikurs & Soltz, 1964).

Thinking Critically

Daylon and Dakota, who are brothers, generally get along pretty well. The older brother, Day-lon, has recently made the softball team, looks great in his new uniform, is playing well on the team, and has been the main topic of conversation in the family for a couple of weeks. One day, Dakota unexpectedly throws Daylon's baseball cap in the trash. Upon learning of the in-cident, the parents are disappointed with Dakota's behavior. What do you think was the goal of Dakota's misbehavior? Explain your answer.

Parental Goals for Prevention of Children's Misbehavior. After recognizing the underlying goals of children's misbehavior, parents are in the position to establish goals directed toward the prevention of children's undesirable actions. As recommended by Dreikurs and Soltz (1964), the strategy for preventing misbehavior consists of three parental objectives: (a) changing one's responses to the child's unacceptable behavior so that the action does not achieve the goal it is designed to achieve, (b) assisting the child in becoming aware of the underlying goal motivating the misbehavior, and (c) making deliberate efforts to help children who are prone to misbehavior to achieve a sense of belonging through appropriate means so that they do not resort to misconduct to achieve attention or power.

Changing One's Response to a Child's Misbehavior. To prevent their children's misbehavior, parents need to be certain that their responses to their children do not promote unacceptable behavior. Specifically, the parent (a) should not give attention to their children's misbehavior designed to attract parental attention, (b) should not react angrily or lose control in response to their children's behavior that typically contributes to parental anger or a loss of control, (c) should not focus on or expose hurt feelings in response to their children's misbehavior based on the goal of revenge, and (d) should not give up in despair when their children seem unmotivated.

Helping Children to Become Aware of Their Goals of Misbehavior. Assisting the misbehaving child in becoming aware of the underlying goal of misbehavior is sometimes accomplished by calling the child's attention to what seems to be the objective of the child's behavior. An example of that approach might be to say to the child, "Josephine, do you think you knock over Gabriel's blocks to get my attention?" When parents help children to become aware of the underlying goals of their misbehavior, they prompt them to realize why they act in ways that parents and others consider unacceptable. If the technique is to be successful, however, it must be expressed in a manner that does not communicate a value judgment of the child or sound reproachful to the child. If children are not suffering the sting of disapproval, they might be helped to understand the reasons behind their misbehavior (which typically troubles them as well as their parents). Dreikurs and Soltz (1964) referred to children's awareness of their goal of misbehavior as the **recognition reflex.** They pointed out that the tactic of helping children achieve awareness of the goals underlying their unacceptable behavior is more effective with children than with adolescents and adults, who have had more experience at building up defense mechanisms.

Helping Children to Achieve Belongingness Without Resorting to Misconduct. When parents realize that their children need to be able to get their parents' attention and to have a sense of power in order to feel that they have a place in the family, they are in a position to help their children meet those needs without resorting to misbehavior. To assist children in their quest for belongingness, parents should provide sufficient attention to their children while ensuring that children feel as if they have a say in what is happening in their lives.

Prevention of Children's Misbehavior Designed to Gain Attention.   To prevent their children's misbehavior that is designed to obtain attention, parents should look for opportunities to give their children positive attention for behaviors that meet parental standards. Sometimes, parents wait until their children behave in unacceptable ways to notice what they are saying or doing. The child thus learns that misconduct will capture the attention of the parent. Although it is beneficial when parents respond favorably to a child's appropriate behavior, it is not necessary to wait for desired behavior to occur before giving attention to the child. For some parents, whose children have gotten into a cycle of misbehavior, that could be a long wait. When providing attention to their children to prevent them from resorting to misbehavior, parents should remember that attention might be given to their children at any time those children are not misbehaving. It is important for children to know that parents are interested in them, not only when they are doing what parents expect but also just *for being*. Examples of giving attention to a child *for being* include talking with children about what they are feeling or doing and greeting children when they come into a room (Heath, 1993).

Prevention of Children's Misbehavior Designed to Gain a Sense of Power.   To prevent children's acts of misbehavior designed to achieve a sense of power, parents should provide children with experiences that endow them with a feeling of empowerment. Providing choices for children is one way in which to empower children. For small children, a parent might ask "Do you want to wear your red shirt or your yellow shirt?" For older children, a parent might solicit their input regarding what to have for dinner by saying, "What do you want for dinner tonight, chicken or spaghetti?" There are a variety of ways to empower children and every opportunity to make choices, or to be heard on their views of things, boosts their self-esteem. Empowering experiences help children to feel a sense of belongingness, thereby preventing misbehavior designed to gain power. To decrease a child's misbehavior motivated by power needs, it is useful to closely monitor the daily experiences in a child's life that might diminish that child's sense of power, while making deliberate efforts to help the child gain power through appropriate means.

Empowering Children: What the Research Shows.   Empowerment of children consists of granting them autonomy, and autonomy granting by parents has been consistently related to positive outcomes for children. It has been shown that when parents are highly supportive of their children's drives toward autonomy, their children become bolder and more competent individuals (Deater-Deckard, 2000). Parents who empower their children are not only highly supportive of their children's urge toward autonomy but also are more patient with them and tolerant of their mistakes. An example of the link between parental impatience and diminished autonomy seeking among children can be discerned in the findings of Heyman et al. (1992). Those researchers found that when asked why they had given up on assigned tasks, young children reported concerns that their parents would be mad at them or punish them for making mistakes. As a final point, parental empowerment has been linked with children's ability to regulate their behavior. For example, Clark, Novak, and Dupree (2002) found that autonomy granting by parents was negatively related to the acting out of anger by adolescents.

Finding the time to talk and listen to children is an extremely effective parenting strategy.

EFFECTIVE PARENT–CHILD COMMUNICATION AS A PARENTING STRATEGY

In addition to having a variety of strategies that are designed to motivate children toward appropriate behavior, parents are best equipped to foster the healthy development of their children when they are able to create an atmosphere of healthy dialogue. Effective parent–child communication is the basis of positive parent–child interactions and high self-esteem in children. Furthermore, effective communication between parents and children prevents problematic behavior and provides a way for children to learn how to interact effectively with others. Thomas Gordon (1975) developed a valuable model for parent–child communication that has been used in various parenting programs for over 25 years. That approach consists of the strategies of problem ownership, active listening, I-messages, and conflict negotiation. The first three approaches that focus on prevention of and discussion of problems will be presented in this part of the chapter. The fourth approach, which focuses on the resolution of conflict in the parent–child relationship, will be explained later in the chapter.

Problem Ownership

Knowing when to use the techniques of active listening or I-messages depends on the ability to sort out "who has the problem" when a problem has arisen in a relationship. The ability to identify **problem ownership** prevents parents from blaming their children for problems that have arisen in the parent–child relationship or from believing that parents must assume responsibility for solving their children's troubles. To establish who owns the problem, one needs to determine who is distressed by the situation. If the child is troubled by events that have occurred or are occurring in a relationship, the child owns the problem. If the child has the problem, it is appropriate for the parent to use the technique of active listening to respond to the child's feelings. If behaviors of the child or events in the parent–child relationship are bothersome to the parent, then the parent owns the problem. If the parent owns the problem, then the appropriate technique to use for communicating the parent's feelings to the child is a three-part I-message.

Thinking Critically

Sandy and Billy have been told that they might have no more than three friends in the house after school and that they and their friends must clean up after themselves if they have a snack. For several days in a row, their parents have come home and found that Sandy, Billy, and their friends have made snacks and left a mess in the kitchen. Their parents are feeling irritated with the situation. In this example, who do you think has the problem? Is it Sandy and Billy, their friends, or their parents? Why?

Active Listening

Active listening is a compelling communication strategy that consists of a verbal response containing no actual message of the parent but rather a mirroring back of the child's previous message. Basically, the parent listens for, paraphrases, and feeds back the child's previous message but the feedback is not merely a tape recording of actual words bouncing back. Instead, the parent listens to and reflects back (in the parent's own words) the feelings of the child as well as the content of the child's message the parent thinks is being expressed. It takes practice and commitment to be able to effectively use the skill of active listening. To actively listen to a child, a parent needs to listen carefully (actively) to the words the child is speaking while attending to the child's voice tone and body language. For example, a child might burst into a room, with tears in his eyes, and exclaim, "I hate my teacher!" Although the child's verbal statement, in that example, does not convey that he is upset or what happened with the teacher, the child's voice tone, body language, and tears, clearly express both feelings and content. A parental response that reflects having actively listened to the child might be "Something happened with Mrs. Smith that made you very upset."

There are two main challenges involved in learning to use the strategy of active listening. The first challenge is the development of an affective vocabulary, which includes a range of feeling words. "Boy, you're upset or angry" might be a helpful response to a child in some instances but a child has a large assortment of emotions that need to be responded to, for example, aggravated, irritated, embarrassed, left out, proud, happy, great, etc. The biggest hurdle to being effective in the use of active listening, however, lies in the parent's tendency to use **communication roadblocks** (see Figure 11.5) instead of active listening. Communication roadblocks stop

1. **Ordering, Directing, Commanding**
   "Stop whining"
   "Don't play with that boy anymore"

2. **Warning, Admonishing, Threatening**
   "If you can't play without arguing, you will have to be separated."

3. **Moralizing, Preaching**
   "You shouldn't complain so much."

4. **Advising, Giving Suggestions or Solutions**
   "If I were you, I would . . ."
   "Why don't you play with someone else."

5. **Teaching, Instructing**
   "Let me tell you how to handle this."

6. **Judging, Criticizing, Blaming**
   "You're being very careless."
   "What did you do to Tommy to make him mad at you?"

7. **Praising, Buttering Up**
   "You're usually very nice to your friends."
   "You're such a nice person. I'm sure you can handle this."

8. **Name Calling, Ridiculing**
   "Shame on you for being so naughty."
   "Boy, you are getting to be such a whiner."

9. **Interpreting, Diagnosing, Psychoanalyzing**
   "You're just jealous of your brother."
   "You always want to bother me when I'm tired.

10. **Reassuring, Sympathizing, Supporting**
    "Don't worry, I'm sure it's going to be alright."
    "Cheer up, why don't you. Lots of people have bigger problems than that."

11. **Probing, Questioning**
    "Where (or when) did that happen?
    "Why did your friend say that to you?

12. **Diverting, Distracting, Humoring**
    Walking away, checking the time, or changing the subject when the child is talking.

FIGURE 11.5 Roadblocks to Communication
Source: Adapted from *Parent Effectiveness Training*, by T. Gordon, 1976, New York: New American Library.

the free flow of problem sharing; whereas active listening communicates to children that the parent hears what has happened as well as how children feel about what has happened.

To develop skills in active listening, it is essential that parents become aware of communication roadblocks and avoid using them when the child is attempting to communicate a problem. The use of communication roadblocks by a parent results in the child feeling as if the parent has not heard, is not interested in hearing, does not understand what is being said, or does not care about the child's feelings. Even when the parent avoids each of the communication roadblocks and provides accurate verbal feedback related to the child's feelings and the content of the message, the child might not feel heard if the body stance and voice tone of the parent do not communicate warmth and understanding.

Using Active Listening to Respond to Nonproblematic Behavior.   Even though active listening is an effective strategy for letting children know that parents hear and care about the problems they express, the strategy is equally effective for responding to children's efforts to convey their feelings related to positive experiences in their lives. In response to the child who runs into the room and says, "Dad, I hit a home run, today!" the parent can send the following active listening response. "Wow, you're pretty excited about hitting a home run. Good for you!"

I-Messages

As previously noted, when the parent owns the problem, an "**I-message**" is used for the purpose of expressing the parent's feelings regarding the child's behavior. *I* messages are not blameful; hence, they are not *you* messages. That is the main objective of the strategy, not to blame the child for the feelings the parent is having regarding a particular action or lack of action of the child. I-messages have three parts: (a) the feelings of the sender, (b) the unacceptable behavior of the recipient, and (c) the tangible effect of the recipient's behavior on the sender. An example of an effective three-part I-message goes something like this: "Kelly, I have a problem I would like to discuss with you" (problem ownership). "When I went into the kitchen and saw the peanut butter and jelly jars with the lids off, and the bread and the milk not put away (unacceptable behavior of the recipient), I felt frustrated (feelings of the sender) because I knew that I would have to either clean up the clutter myself or ask you to do it" (tangible effect of the recipient's behavior on the sender).

Notice that the parent in this case has not sent a blameful you-message such as: "Kelly, you never clean up after yourself. Get in there and clean up that mess you made; don't expect me to do it for you." Children and adolescents are much more likely to respond favorably to a parental I-message delivered in a warm, nonthreatening manner than to an angry-sounding, blameful you-message. When children and adolescents feel parents are criticizing their personalities (you-messages), they feel put down and misunderstood by their parents. In those cases, they are likely to respond defensively. The purpose of using I-messages is to express dissatisfaction with a child's behavior, not to attack the child.

Sending a three-part I-message to inform a child of how that child's behavior affects the parent might sound as if the parent is telling the child what the child already should know. People in relationships often think that the other person ought to be more considerate without being told, should know how some behavior would affect them, and so on. Even though it would be wonderful if all family members could guess how other family members feel and act accordingly, that simply does not occur in real life. People in close relationships are continuously affected by each other's behavior and do all sorts of things without considering the ways in which their actions affect the people they care about. To develop the ability to empathize with the feelings of other family members, it is important that both parents and children learn to use effective communication skills.

Preventive I-Messages.   Gordon devised the strategy of the I-message to provide parents with an effective way to address problems that arise in the parent–child relationship since those problems are often challenging for parents and because they are sometimes handled in ways that are hurtful to both parents and their children. I-messages are useful as well for preventing difficulties in the relationship. As a prevention technique, parents can use I-messages to communicate their positive feelings regarding behaviors of the child that they appreciate.

Let us revisit 12-year-old Kelly and her Mom on the day after Mom used an effective I-message to tell Kelly how she felt about things being left out in the kitchen. The next day, Kelly is sitting in the living room eating her usual after-school peanut butter and jelly sandwich and drinking a glass of milk. Mom comes in the door and Kelly, who has a big smile on her face, says "Hi, Mom." Kelly watches as Mom goes into the kitchen, because she has cleaned up after herself and is hoping Mom will notice. When Mom enters the kitchen and sees that the bread, peanut butter, jelly, and milk have all been put away, she goes back into the living room. With a warm smile, she sends her daughter a positive three-part I-message: "Kelly, when I went into the kitchen, I noticed that you had put away all the things you used to make your snack, and that you cleaned the counter as well (behaviors on the part of the recipient that have not caused a problem), I was so pleased (feelings of the sender). I really appreciate your cleaning up after yourself because that makes things easier for me" (tangible effect of child's behavior on the mother).

As a final point, when parents use I-messages to address or prevent problems, it is important that they have a friendly-sounding voice tone and nonthreatening body language. Furthermore, it is essential that the message be specific regarding the behavior in question. Children and adolescents are often confused about what parents are trying to tell them because parents often talk in generalities to their children with statements such as "I want you to clean up after yourself," which could mean a variety of things. An effective I-message, on the other hand, does not threaten or attack the child nor does it confuse the child. In the case of the preventive I-message, the parent actually affirms the child. Even when no problem has occurred in a particular area, parents might send I-messages to prevent unacceptable behavior in the future. An example of a preventive I-message is "I like to know where you are when school is out so that I know that you are okay."

Research Findings Showing the Value of Effective Parent–Child Communication.
Effective parent–child exchanges impact the development of children in a variety of ways at all developmental levels. For instance, infants learn to trust that their needs will be met when their parents are consistently responsive to their communication

As shown in this scene, parents have many opportunities to serve as positive models for their children's behavior.

attempts (Erikson, 1963, 1982). Another example of the influence of parent–child communication patterns is that the verbal exchanges of parents and children are reflected in the dialogues their children have with siblings and friends (Woodward & Markman, 1998). Just as effective parent–child communication is related to positive child outcomes, ineffective parent–child communication is associated with problems in the parent–child relationship. For example, Arnett (2001) suggests that some of the arguments that occur between parents and their adolescent children might stem from unexpressed parental concerns.

GUIDANCE AS REINFORCEMENT AND MODELING

In addition to having strategies for encouraging and motivating children toward appropriate behavior, being able to understand the goals underlying children's misbehavior, and having effective communication skills, parents benefit as well from understanding ways in which to reinforce children for appropriate behavior and being aware of their roles as models for their children's behavior.

Reinforcement of Approved Behavior

Although there are a number of socialization techniques that take into account the child's feelings and motivation and help the child to understand the ways in which their behaviors affect themselves and others, an understanding of the role of **reinforcement** in child guidance continues to be a valuable strategy. According to Skinner (1974), any consequence that strengthens a particular behavior, thereby increasing the likelihood that the behavior will be repeated, is reinforcing. Reinforcements might include special treats or desired activities or they might include various forms of social approval. The primary value of using reinforcement as a socialization strategy is because it is far more effective to reinforce approved behavior than punishing disapproved behavior. In using the technique of reinforcement, parents need to be aware of the conditions that facilitate learning. First, the reinforcing consequences must be noticeable to the child, which requires that the child is paying attention to the reinforcement being presented. For example, if a parent uses social approval in the form of a smile and a comment after the young child has picked up her toys, it is important to stoop down in front of the child so that the child can see the parent's smiling face and hear the parent's reinforcing comment. When a parent says "Wow, nice job" to a child who is flying out the back door, the positive comment is not an effective reinforcement because it is not noticeable. Second, reinforcements of specific behaviors must be consistent to be successful. Parents who are attempting to help their children to develop the habit of wiping their feet on a mat when coming into the house should consistently reinforce their children after feet wiping (by making an approving remark) until that behavior becomes habitual. Reinforcing once or twice and then resorting to the commonly used parental phrase of "I told you to wipe your feet when you come into the house" is not nearly as effective as gentle reminders and consistent reinforcement.

Effective use of reinforcement requires that parents understand that the consequence of reinforcement always maintains or increases the frequency of the occurrence of a behavior. An example of a positive reinforcement would be Mom saying to her very young children in an approving voice, "Kenny and Christopher, I see that you are cooperating with each other by sharing your toys." The fact that the parent made the remark does not tell us if the response is reinforcing for the children. To determine if the remark was reinforcing, we need to observe its effect on the children's subsequent behavior. If, after hearing that remark, Kenny and Christopher continue to share and play even more cooperatively, the remark was a positive reinforcement.

To use reinforcement to maintain or increase desired behavior, it is important to remember that what is reinforcing varies from one individual to another and from one time to another. An example of what is reinforcing being individually determined is evident in the following example: Two young children, Jangjie and Maho are offered chocolate bars for picking up papers along the side of a street. Jangjie loves chocolate and, therefore, finds that treat reinforcing as indicated by her offering to pick up papers again the next week. Maho, however, does not particularly like sweets and definitely does not like chocolate. Maho does not offer to pick up papers again, and when it is suggested that she do so, she replies that she is too busy.

An example of how reinforcement varies from one time to another is provided by the next illustration: Twelve-year-old Abby knocks on her neighbor's door and offers to cut the neighbor's grass for $15. She does a great job, gets her $15 and comes back the following week to ask if she can cut the neighbor's grass again. That $15 is reinforcing to Abby is evident by her returning to ask to cut the grass again. A few years pass and Abby, now 16, has a part-time job and a very busy social life. The neighbor sees her on the street and offers her $15 to cut the grass. Abby answers that she is sorry but that she just does not have the time—same consequence, same girl, different time, and changed circumstances. What was reinforcing for Abby at 12-years-old is not reinforcing at 16.

In spite of the fact that what is reinforcing varies from one individual to another and from one time to another, a consequence that is reinforcing for most children, most of the time, is social approval. Social approval, which consists of providing positive attention, approval and affection, is the most effective type of reinforcement a parent might use. Guidelines for using social approval as a means of reinforcement include using eye contact, being physically close, smiling, focusing on the behavior of the child, and immediate delivery.

Research Findings Demonstrating the Effectiveness of Reinforcement.   The relation between parental reinforcement and children's behavior is seen in a number of ways in which parents might encourage young children's self-reliance. For example, Mauro and Harris (2000) found that young children's ability to delay gratification is enhanced when parents use an authoritative parenting approach. The conclusion reached by those researchers was that the behaviors associated with authoritative parenting serve as a reinforcement of children's positive behavior. The value of the use of social reinforcement in the parent–child relationship is not limited to the effects of parents on children. For example, Hyun et al. (2002) demonstrated that when family members perform helpful activities for new mothers, including assistance in child care, those behaviors serve as social reinforcement of the new mother and enhance her competence in caring for her infant.

Imitation and Modeling

We will now consider a parenting approach which involves two interrelated strategies, **imitation** and **modeling**, the two key concepts of Social Learning Theory, developed by Bandura and Walters (1963) to demonstrate that many of the behaviors children pick up daily are products of vicarious learning. By observing the consequences experienced by others around them, children selectively choose behaviors that have a higher probability of being reinforced and avoid behaviors that have a lower probability of being reinforced, or are likely to result in punishment. Of the models in their environment whose behaviors are likely to be imitated by children, parents are the most influential. Although parents are not generally aware of the ramifications of their behavioral examples on their children, the reality is that parental modeling can produce significant change in children. Then again, children's imitation of parental behavior is often considered a mixed blessing because parents attempt to have children imitate certain behaviors and discourage them from imitating others. That dilemma is expressed in the often-repeated parental lament of "Do as I say, not as I do."

What Contributes to Children's Choice of Models?   Although parents will invariably act as models of behavior for their children, becoming aware of how children choose the models whose behaviors they will imitate helps parents to become more effective models for their children. Even though parents are the primary models for their children's behaviors, other people in children's lives are chosen as models as well. By and large, children choose the models they imitate based on whether they perceive those individuals as successful in gaining reinforcement and avoiding punishment. Consequently, not all persons with whom the child interacts will be chosen as models. As observed by Bandura (1986), children select the persons in their environment to serve as models for their own behavior based on several criteria. Children are more inclined to imitate parents and others who are perceived as warm and approachable and less motivated to imitate the behaviors of those individuals who seem to be missing those qualities. The selection of a parent or another person as a model is also more likely to occur if the child considers that person to be prestigious. Having prestige, being competent, or being influential is interpreted by children as controlling resources, being able to make major decisions, and having the respect of significant others. In the case of prestige, imitation is influenced by observable consequences to the model as well as by distinctive status symbols the model represents. For example, celebrities or recognized experts are chosen as models for children's behavior more often than are persons not perceived as having status. Unfortunately, even deviant models, if seen by children as having prestige, can generate imitation of socially disapproved behavior.

Another quality that children look for in a model is that of similarity. Children who are aware that they have qualities in common with a person are more disposed to pick that person as a model of desired behavior than are children who share no common characteristics with that person. For example, a girl who is told by her father that she is athletic like her mother is more likely to think of herself as capable of playing sports. On the other hand, a father who tells his daughter that she is just like her mother, not good at sports, is unwittingly likely to discourage his daughter's athletic motivation. Although children are influenced by the behaviors of persons outside the family, the most influential models are likely to be family members (parents, brothers, and sisters). Even though individuals outside the family might possess more or less of the characteristics associated with the choice of a model, children most frequently see those characteristics in relation to their family environments. Due to close proximity and the endurance of time, family members have many more opportunities to affect each other's behavior than do people outside the family. The child is therefore continually learning who in the family is more warm and approachable, has more prestige, and is more similar.

Ways to Increase Imitation.   Children have a natural tendency to imitate, and they selectively choose the models whose behaviors they will emulate based on attributes previously explained. Furthermore, models of children's behavior are in the position to increase imitation of certain desired behaviors by understanding the circumstances that promote imitative behavior. Bandura (1977) identified the following conditions under which imitation is most likely to occur. First, the model must gain the attention of the child and the target behavior should be observable to the child. When those conditions are met, the model might increase imitation of desired behavior by using language. One of the functions of language is to call attention to the behavior being demonstrated. Using language, the parent is able to (a) explain what behavior is expected (including the various steps included in the performance of the behavior), (b) clarify instructions, and (c) reinforce the child for performance of the behavior. Children's imitation efforts might be further enhanced if they are encouraged to practice or rehearse the target behavior because children's rehearsals of learned behaviors increase the likely performance of those behaviors. Furthermore, learning new behaviors through imitation of a model is best achieved when the modeled behavior builds on behavior already learned. That is achieved by the integration of previously learned elements into new patterns. If the child already has mastered the various components of a particular activity, showing that child how to integrate those diverse pieces of behavior is likely to result in imitation.

Finally, parents who are attempting to instill certain behaviors in their children by modeling those behaviors might supplement their efforts by selectively exposing their children to other models who exhibit the desired behaviors. In spite of the fact that peers become increasingly important as models of behavior and agents of socialization as the child gets older, parents play a large role in the selection of the peers who will influence their children. First, children tend to choose peers who share the values they have learned at home and who reinforce similar standards of conduct. Next, parents have the opportunity to choose schools, neighborhoods, and places of worship (such as churches, synagogues, or mosques), as well as activities (such as scout troops, baseball teams, and dance instruction) that their children are involved in.

Parents further influence children's choice of models outside the family when parents are involved in their children's lives and when they monitor their children's activities. Parental monitoring includes frequent discussions of what their children are doing and with whom they are spending their time. Parental influence of the models their children choose to emulate is enhanced as well by parents' involvement in children's leisure activities with their friends. For instance, parents might take their children and their children's friends swimming, hiking, to the movies, or to sports activities, and have their children's friends over for get-togethers, such as for barbecues or pizza. Additionally, parents might have other adults who are suitable models over for meals and interactive activities with the family. Besides acting as models for their children and influencing their children's selection of models outside the family, parents should be aware of the ways that models in the media influence their children's behavior. It is helpful for parents to monitor the media to which their children are exposed because models portrayed on television, in films, or in music influence children's behavior. The imitation of models, therefore, should be viewed as a continuous process involving multiple models, rather than occurring only in familial relationships.

It should be noted that once children have imitated the behavior of a model, they might or might not repeat the behavior depending on whether or not those actions are reinforced. Because parental approval is typically an effective reinforcement for children, especially when the parent–child relationship is close, parental reactions to a child's behavior are a strong determinant of whether or not that behavior will be maintained.

Research Findings Demonstrating the Effectiveness of Modeling and Imitation.
Researchers have demonstrated numerous examples of the effectiveness of modeling
and imitation as parenting strategies. Parents use modeling techniques to demonstrate appropriate behaviors that range from helping their toddlers to achieve independent toileting (Spock & Rothenberg, 1985) to promoting their children's language
development and social interactions (Woodward & Markman, 1998). Furthermore,
parents serve as primary identification models for children (Facio & Batistuta, 1998).

GUIDANCE AS LIMITS, CONSEQUENCES, AND CONFLICT RESOLUTION

In this section of the chapter, we will examine strategies that parents might use for
pointing out consequences to children's behavior (induction), setting up consequences
for children that are logically related to their behavior (logical consequences), and
working with children to help them to alter future consequences by changing current
behavior patterns (reality therapy). Parents who adopt the strategies presented in the
upcoming discussion must be willing to consider the use of consequences in child
guidance as a learning process for the child rather than a mandate for punishment. Understanding that being exposed to any guidance technique is a learning experience for
the child, and that many undesirable lessons can be learned from punitive consequences, helps parents to evaluate their guidance choices. A relevant question for parents to ask themselves is: "What responses to misbehavior will be most valuable in
motivating my children to act responsibly?" In choosing the appropriate socialization
strategy, Dinkmeyer and McKay (1989) suggest that parents deal with their personal issues of control. The issue of control comes from the mistaken view that the role of the
parent is a way to be in control of others. In actuality, if child guidance is to be a valuable learning experience, it cannot be concerned primarily with control. When parents
intentionally and consistently adopt strategies that assist children in their efforts to feel
good about themselves and that increase children's self-esteem, there is less resistance
and less need for parenting strategies designed to punish and control.

Although it is generally understood that the consequences children experience
affect their future behavior, what is often overlooked is that those consequences influence as well how children feel about themselves, how they feel about their parents, and the effectiveness of the learning experience. With those concerns in mind,
the guidance techniques presented in this portion of the chapter are designed for parents who wish to help their children to understand the link between their behaviors
and the consequences of those behaviors. Those methods are valuable for assisting
parents in setting limits, establishing boundaries, and providing consequences for children. A strategy that parents and children might use for resolving conflict is presented
as well. The child socialization approaches discussed in this portion of the chapter, as
with those examined earlier, are based on values of democratic parent–child relations
that emphasize the equal worth of all family members.

This parent is taking the time and opportunity to explain to her child the behaviors that are expected of the child.

The Technique of Induction

Induction is a parenting strategy designed to promote desirable behavior and reduce undesirable behavior in children by increasing their awareness of the likely consequences of their actions for themselves as well as for others. Induction is a valuable technique for encouraging children's prosocial behavior, helping them to take responsibility for their actions, and promoting the development of their perspective-taking ability. There are two types of induction: self-oriented and other-oriented, depending on who is likely to experience consequences related to the child's behavior. Self-oriented induction involves pointing out to the child what the consequences of the child's behavior are likely to be for the child. Other-oriented induction consists of an explanation to the child regarding how the child's actions affect other persons or animals (Maccoby & Martin, 1983). An example of self-oriented induction is shown in the following example: The next example demonstrates the use of other-oriented induction: "Kenny and James, when you both forget to feed your puppy, he gets hungry." "Patty, you should walk on the sidewalk because if you run you might fall down and get hurt."

Induction Versus Producing Guilt.   The appropriate use of the induction technique is to convey to the child the probable consequences of the child's behavior, not to suggest that positive regard of the child is being withdrawn. The use of induction involves drawing generalizations from children's actions rather than blaming the child. Furthermore, parents do not have to wait until an act has occurred to use the strategy. Induction might be used in a discussion of anticipated actions of the child or through vicarious experiences whereby consequences of others' behaviors are discussed with the child (Maccoby & Martin, 1983). Examples include: "Katerina, when you want to go visit your friend, be sure to let me know. If you leave and don't tell me, I won't know where to find you." Or "Jose forgot to tell his mother that he was coming over here to play and Jose's mother was very worried about him."

The previous examples of how to use self-oriented and other-oriented induction focused on informing the child of possible negative consequences. Another benefit of the strategy is that it might be used to let children know how their positive and/or helpful behavior benefits others or brings about positive results (Maccoby & Martin, 1983). In the case of self-oriented induction, a child might be told, "If you share your toys with your sister, she will probably feel more like sharing her toys with you." In the case of other-oriented induction, the child might be informed that, "When you picked those flowers and gave them to your grandmother, she was very pleased. You put a big smile on her face."

Why Induction Is Effective. There are a number of reasons why induction is an effective parenting strategy. First, because it explains consequences of the child's behavior, induction is concerned with action and attention is directed away from a personal evaluation of the child. Second, induction teaches the child how to produce actions such as sharing or apologies. Third, induction motivates children toward more mature reasoning regarding the behavioral choices they make. Fourth, induction communicates to children that they have the ability to behave in ways that contribute to better consequences to themselves and others. Finally, induction fosters the development of empathy and understanding of others, thereby promoting children's prosocial behavior while inhibiting their antisocial behavior. The effectiveness of induction is based on the following premises: (a) children have the need to engage in prosocial behavior, (b) children are motivated toward behaving more maturely, (c) children have the ability to understand cause and effect, and (d) children have the capability of understanding others' points of view (Maccoby & Martin, 1983).

Research Findings Supporting the Use of Inductive Parenting. Recently, Barnett, Quackenbush, and Sinisi (1996) reviewed the research focused on the behavioral correlates of the parental use of induction when contrasted with parental use of power assertion. Those researchers reported that the parental use of induction is associated with children's and adolescents' heightened empathy and prosocial behavior, lower levels of antisocial behavior, more mature moral judgment, and greater popularity. The link between inductive parenting and children's prosocial behavior was demonstrated also by Krevans and Gibbs (1996) who found that children of inductive parents are more empathic and more prosocial.

Natural and Logical Consequences

In recognition that children need to be guided by warm, caring parents to make appropriate choices in their behaviors and to accept responsibility for their actions, Don Dinkmeyer and Gary McKay (1989) developed the parenting strategy known as logical consequences. That socialization technique addresses the need of parents for guidelines to: (a) develop relationships with their children that emphasize a balance between children's rights and responsibilities, (b) provide children with an opportunity to make decisions regarding their behavior and to be accountable for their choices, and (c) communicate respect for children while teaching them to respect others. Closely aligned with logical consequences are natural consequences. As will be explained, a natural consequence "occurs naturally" and as such is not a socialization technique. Dinkmeyer and McKay, nevertheless, identified the concept of natural consequences to demonstrate its cohort, logical consequences. The idea behind natural or logical consequences is that children learn from consequences when their parents allow them to experience the results of their own actions.

Natural Consequences.   **Natural consequences** occur in our everyday lives when we make hasty or naive choices and we learn from them (Dinkmeyer & McKay, 1989). A very young child who is running down the sidewalk does not usually consider the suitability of the sidewalk for running. Taking a nasty spill while running on the sidewalk and getting a scraped knee is a natural consequence of running. Taking a spill while running on the grass and discovering that it is not so bad is also a natural consequence. If parents do not interfere with their children's natural consequences, they will undoubtedly learn from those experiences. That approach to child socialization, though, would be dangerous and ill advised in many instances. Take the case of the child running down the sidewalk. Yes, the child would learn from the consequence of getting a skinned knee but that accident could be prevented by closely supervising the young child and using the technique of induction to warn the child of the problems of running on the sidewalk. Similarly, the parent might use induction to suggest that the child run on the grass instead of the sidewalk.

Logical Consequences.   Closely related to natural consequences are **logical consequences** that are appropriate choices when parents want to avoid punitive approaches to guiding their children but want their children to experience consequences that are logically related to their actions (Dinkmeyer & McKay, 1989). An example of the use of logical consequences is when a mother tells her young children that they may play outdoors, inside the fence; or that they will have to come inside to play. The mother might combine the use of logical consequences with the use of induction to explain to her children why it is important for them to play within the confined area. Children could be informed that the parent needs to keep an eye on them while they play to be sure they are all right and will not be able to do so if they go outside the fence. If, while playing inside the fence, the children see a puppy, open the gate, and start running after the puppy toward the road, the mother might bring the children inside and explain to them that they will have to play inside the house today because they went outside the fence.

In the situation just described, the children are assisted by the parent to make the connection between their actions and the consequences much better than if the parent had used a punitive consequence, such as yelling at or striking them. Another example of the use of logical consequences is when parents expect a child to get a paper towel and wipe up the milk the child has spilled. Still another example of a logical consequence is when the child is given the responsibility for paying for the replacement of a sibling's toy if the child broke the toy. In using logical consequences, parents need to use logic in assigning responsibility to the child. For example, a 4-year-old who accidentally broke a sibling's toy might not be expected to replace that toy, whereas a 12-year-old might be given that logical consequence.

Research Emphasizing the Problems Associated with Using Punishment. Parents are encouraged to use logical consequences rather than relying on punishment as a consequence of children's misbehavior due to the negative side effects associated with the use of punitive methods. First of all, attempts at punishment of an undesirable behavior might actually serve as a reinforcement of that behavior. An example of that problem is when the child is misbehaving for attention and the parent provides attention while attempting to punish the child. Even though the parental attention might be negative, some children are likely to repeat the misbehavior to gain parental attention. A second reason for parents to avoid the use of punishment is that in most cases punishment is not logically related to the child's problematic behavior. If the child who spills milk is calmly asked to get a cloth and wipe it up, the accident and the consequence are logically related. A punitive consequence of that child's behavior, on the other hand, is not a logical choice.

A side effect of the use of punishment is that punishment of the child compromises the parent–child relationship. Children who are subjected to repeated punishment from parents learn to avoid their parents, fight back, or lie about their behavior to avoid punishment. Another drawback related to the use of punishment as a child socialization technique is that children who receive frequent punishment from parents are more likely than are other children to be punitive toward others as well as toward themselves (Grusec & Goodnow, 1994). The parental use of power assertion when contrasted with parental use of induction has been shown to be associated also with children's and adolescents' lowered empathy, higher levels of antisocial behavior, less mature moral judgment, and decreased popularity with peers (Barnett et al., 1996).

Parents who rely on punishment (often because they are unaware of more appropriate strategies) are at a disadvantage when presented with a situation wherein children might benefit from experiencing consequences for their behavior. Their first thought is typically how to punish the child to regain control over the child. That choice, however, has many drawbacks since power-assertive control tactics do not motivate children to become more independent or guide them to behave more responsibly. Instead, it leaves children in a dependent or power-oriented relationship, with their parents in authority (Dinkmeyer & McKay, 1989).

It is not that the child does not learn anything from punishment and power-oriented strategies; indeed, every parent–child interaction is a learning experience. Parents who are faced with the choice of using familiar punishment and power-oriented strategies or learning other more democratic childrearing strategies might ask themselves the following questions: "What is the child learning when I am using this guidance technique?" "What kind of learning experience comes from spanking?" "What is learned when a child is told to shut up?" When children are punished, they learn to feel bad about themselves, to fear the parent, and to lie about their behavior if they think that the parent will disapprove. They learn about who has power and who does not and that those in authority can punish those with less influence. In the case of yelling and hitting, they learn that those expressions of anger are acceptable behaviors to use with others.

Glasser's Reality Therapy

Although not a part of contemporary mainstream parenting programs, the goals of William Glasser's (1965) parenting approach, known as **reality therapy**, are valuable for assisting older children and adolescents who have developed irresponsible patterns of behavior that are likely to have future negative consequences. Reality therapy provides a valuable strategy for helping children find their inner strength and realize their potential, while assisting parents with encouraging their children's development. In his work with adolescents with behavior problems, Glasser found that if children do not improve their conduct when it is below their own standards they will not fulfill their need to feel worthwhile. According to that perspective, successful parents have intense, personal involvement with their children, face reality, and reject irresponsible behavior, while assisting their children to work toward more responsible behavior.

Parental Involvement.   Understanding the importance of parental involvement is basic to comprehending the guidance strategy of reality therapy. Addressing the issue of involvement, Glasser emphasized that for reality therapy to work parents must be willing to be involved with their children, rather than remaining separate and controlling entities. Basically, all persons have basic human needs of relatedness and respect, and through involvement parents respond to those basic needs of their children.

Realism.   The concept of realism is crucial to understanding and using the reality therapy approach to child guidance. Glasser (2000) cautioned parents against pushing their children to become the people parents think they should be, which often results in alienation of children from their parents. He emphasized that children need to pursue their own goals. Although children's goals and dreams are somewhat different from their parents, it is important for parents to strive to reason and negotiate with their children as to what behaviors are realistic in helping their children meet their own goals. Once children who have adopted self-defeating behaviors are made aware of the future reality they are constructing for themselves, parents are in a position to assist them toward behaving more responsibly. The first step in that process is for parents to encourage their children to examine their actions when they find themselves in a dilemma brought about by their irresponsible behavior. The goal of having the child take a close look at the problematic situation is to attempt to discover the child's true feelings related to the quandary. After both parent and child understand the true nature of the child's predicament, the next step is taken. That move is accomplished by the parent and the child working together to discern (a) the relation between the child's behavior and the consequences the child is experiencing as a result of that behavior, and (b) the likely future consequences if the child's unproductive behavior continues.

The Development of a Plan.   After a child has been assisted by the parent to see the connection between the child's irresponsible behavior and the negative consequences the child is experiencing, the child is asked by the parent to consider what is likely to happen in the future if the child's careless behavior continues. The parent then invites the child to consider what changes in the child's current behavior need to be made to ensure that the child's goals for the future are met. At that point, the parent and the child cooperate in the development of a plan for the child to replace current self-defeating behaviors with behaviors designed to help the child achieve stated goals. During that stage, it is important that the child feels comfortable with the plan and is capable of carrying out all aspects of the agreement. The role of the parent in the negotiation process is to assist the child to keep goals realistic so that the child is not set up for failure.

A Commitment to Carrying Out the Plan.   After the parent and the child have negotiated a plan designed to assist the child in achieving stated goals, both parent and child make a commitment to carrying out the plan. The parent makes a commitment to play an active role in assisting the child to reach specified goals by various means such as a commitment of time to the child to help with homework at certain times, checking on the child's progress, and so on. The child makes a commitment to the parent by specifying exactly what behaviors the child will be responsible for and how, when, and where, those behaviors will be carried out. Moreover, the child is expected to keep the parent informed as to the progress being made. Reality therapy not only provides a strategy for children to evaluate their own behavior in terms of future goals, it also places the onus on parents to assess their own parenting objectives and willingness to make a commitment to support their children in meeting their goals (Glasser, 2000).

Sticking with the Plan.   After the plan is developed, which is typically written out and signed by both the parent and the child, the parent emphasizes to the child the importance of both the parent and the child living up to the bargain they have struck. The emphasis on sticking with the plan is an important idea in reality therapy. Parents who accept a variety of excuses, ignore reality, and allow their children to blame their problems on others, make their children feel better temporarily at the expense of having helped them escape responsibility for their behavior. Obviously, the emphasis on sticking with the plan applies equally to parents; and children should not have to listen to parents making excuses regarding why they have not lived up to the time and other commitments made to the child.

Research Findings Demonstrating the Positive Influence of Parental Involvement.
Parental involvement might be conceptualized as emotional availability which includes structuring, sensititivity, nonhostility, and nonintrusiveness, as well as responsiveness. Birengen (2000) found that parental emotional availability predicts attachment, positive child development, and the quality of the parent–child relationship. Further support of the positive influence of parental involvement was demonstrated by Wenk, Hardesty, and Morgan (1994) who found that maternal and

paternal behavioral and emotional involvement is equally important for boys and girls. Also, Juang and Silbereisen (1999) found that adolescents who report their parents as consistently more supportive have lower levels of depression, higher levels of self-efficacy, and do better in school than do children and adolescents who report that their parents are inconsistently supportive. Finally, there is evidence that parental involvement is related to children's anger regulation and coping strategies. For example, Clark and colleagues (2002) found that adolescents who perceived their parents as involved were more likely to seek diversions rather than acting out their anger.

RESOLVING PARENT–CHILD CONFLICT

Parent–child conflict is an important aspect of parent–child interactions and strategies for resolving conflict should be incorporated into the child guidance approach rather than viewed as a threat to parental authority. Parents can expect children to seek greater autonomy and increasing self-regulation at every developmental level. Conflict serves the normative functions of testing and changing (or resisting change) in the parent–child relationship. Because of physical proximity, shared tasks, and long-term commitments, parent–child conflict is both frequent and difficult to escape. Since the most significant conflict occurs near the expanding boundary between the child's autonomy and the parent's authority, parents need effective conflict negotiation skills to manage conflict in such a way as to maintain an appropriate level of parental authority while supporting children's individual needs (Emery, 1995).

Explained earlier in this chapter were ways in which parents could send I-messages to their children when they found their children's behavior unacceptable. There are times, however, when I-messages are not effective due to the child's strong desire to engage in a particular behavior even when the child knows that the parent disapproves, or the child's reluctance to participate in behaviors that the parent wishes to encourage. In that situation, a conflict exists in the relationship that calls for the employment of methods of conflict resolution. A problem associated with getting parents to consider using a conflict resolution technique is that a lot of parents are committed to either an authoritarian or permissive approach to conflict management. Many other parents are willing to adopt democratic strategies for other aspects of the parent–child relationship but not when it comes to the issue of conflict.

When parent–child conflict occurs, parents typically rely on two win–lose methods of conflict resolution: strict or lenient. Authoritarian parents believe that in the case of conflict, they should step in to regain control and exert authority over the child. In those situations, the parents win at the expense of the child. Permissive parents, on the other hand, back off from their positions when the child objects, which results in the child winning and the parent losing. In contrast to either the strict or lenient approaches, the **no-lose method of conflict resolution** that was developed by Thomas Gordon (1975) is a democratic approach to the resolution of parent–child conflict. The no-lose method of conflict resolution is a win–win approach where both parents and children win. That method consists of the six steps outlined in Figure 11.6.

Step I. Defining the problem. Mommy: "Gabriel, what's wrong? You're not eating your vegetables?" Gabriel: "Mommy, I don't wike dese widdle twees (broccoli)."

Step II. Generating possible solutions. Mommy: "Gabriel, you need to eat green vegetables to grow big and strong. Why don't I put some cheese sauce on the little trees? By the way, they are called broccoli."

Step III. Evaluating the possible solutions. "Here, I will put some cheese sauce on your broccoli and let you try it. Well, Gabriel, what do you think?"

Step IV. Deciding on the best solution. Gabriel: "Mommy, I wike bwockwey wif jees saws! Dis is weally good!"

Step V. Implementing the decision. Mommy: "Now we've worked out a great plan to help you eat your green vegetables so you will grow big and strong."

Step VI. Follow-up evaluation. Daddy: "Gabriel, I see you are eating your green vegetables and growing big and strong." Gabriel: "Yep, me and Mommy sided to put jees saws on all my gween vegdubbles. Now, dey taste weally good!"

FIGURE 11.6   A No-Lose Method of Conflict Resolution
Note: Adapted from *Parent Effectiveness Training*, by T. Gordon, 1976, New York: New American Library.

The Advantages of Using the No-Lose Method of Conflict Resolution

Accepting the idea of the no-lose method of conflict management is difficult for parents who embrace the authoritarian style of parenting. When parents are accustomed to thinking of parent–child conflict in win–lose terms, it is hard for them to comprehend that the no-lose method is not some form of permissiveness. Actually, nothing could be further from the truth because the no-lose method requires that both parent and child be satisfied with the outcome. In the example provided in Figure 11.6, the parent's goal was to have the child eat green vegetables and the child's goal was to eat food that tasted good to him. When the parent listened to and accepted the child's evaluation of the broccoli, considered a creative solution for resolving the dilemma, and invited feedback from the child, the parent and child were able to resolve their conflict with a solution that was satisfactory to both of them. Parents do not lose when they are able to work out mutually satisfactory solutions to problems they are having with their children. On the contrary, both parents and children win when they have negotiated a mutually satisfying solution to a conflict. Effective conflict resolution enhances the parent–child relationship, fosters the development of the child's self-esteem, and results in a more equitable outcome than does power-assertive techniques.

At this point, some readers might think that the example of conflict resolution illustrated in Figure 11.6 is too easy or that it would not work with older children. Even though the problem seems simple because of the child's age, many parents of young children will not take the time to attempt a creative solution to parent–child conflict, even when their children are very young. Children are often forced to eat food they do not like or do a number of other things they would prefer not to do because parents do not empathize with the child's feelings and are unaware of a better way of handing a situation like the one in Figure 11.6. The underlying problem behind the parental resistance statement of "It won't work in real life, with older kids, with my kids, etc." is due to some parents' lack of trust in their children, coupled with their reluctance to allow children to be heard when parent–child conflict emerges.

For parents invested in a strict way of handling conflict, the no-lose method seems so unfamiliar to them that they will not even try it. Another reason parents resist attempting the conflict-resolution method described in Figure 11.6 is due to the time investment. Many parents who complain that they do not have the time to work out equitable solutions to problems with their children are willing to work out creative solutions to problems with coworkers. They might use democratic methods of resolving conflict with individuals who are not their family members. Those same adults, who express satisfaction in handling situations at work in a democratic fashion, are frequently unwilling to invest the time or the patience to try those same methods with their children (Gordon, 1975).

Research Support for the Parental Use of Conflict Management. From the perspective of Emery (1995), family conflict is different from other forms of conflict in at least three respects. First, because of physical proximity, shared tasks, and long-term commitment, family conflict is both common and hard to escape. Second, because change is necessary for the development of individual family members, family relationships must be continuously reconfigured. Third, conflict in the family has added significance due to the essential social, emotional, and practical functions that families serve. According to Chapman and McBride (1995), when children encounter viewpoints different from their own, being able to discuss those differing perspectives contributes to the child's development of rational thinking. In their discussion of differing viewpoints, children's expectations are disconfirmed which often leads them to modify their expectations, thereby leading them out of an egocentric bias. Obviously, parents benefit as well from the willingness to modify their expectations and move away from an egocentric bias.

❧ SUMMARY

The parenting skills described in the first part of this chapter emphasize a prevention-of-problems approach, explain a variety of ways that parents might assist their children in meeting their goals, and show parents ways in which to motivate their children toward cooperative behavior. The techniques presented in that section of the chapter emphasize as well the significance of understanding children's feelings, the role of parents in the promotion of children's self-esteem, and the value of enhancing parental effectiveness through the development of positive communication skills. Next we examined the impact of positive reinforcement on children's behavior. That discussion was followed by an exploration of the role that parents play as models of their children's behavior. We then looked at a diversity of effective approaches for setting limits, establishing boundaries, and providing consequences for children, including the technique of induction, the strategies of natural and logical consequences, and the parenting approach known as reality therapy. The dangers of using punishment as a method of rearing children also were emphasized in that section. Finally, a method for resolving parent–child conflict was discussed. All of the socialization strategies presented in this chapter are based on values of democratic parent–child relations.

❧ KEY TERMS

- active listening
- atmosphere of psychological safety
- communication roadblocks
- encouragement
- four goals of misbehavior
- four pluses and a wish
- I-messages
- imitation
- induction

- logical consequences
- modeling
- natural consequences
- no-lose method of conflict resolution
- praise
- problem ownership
- reality therapy
- recognition reflex
- reinforcement

References

Abel, M. (1997). Low birth weight and interactions between traditional risk factors. *The Journal of Genetic Psychology, 158*, 443–456.

Ainsworth, M. D. S. (1967). *Infancy in Uganda: Infant care and the growth of love.* Baltimore: Johns Hopkins University Press.

Ainsworth, M. D. S. (1973). The development of infant–mother attachment. In B. M. Caldwell & H. N. Ricciutti (Eds.), *Review of child development research: Vol. 3. Child development and social policy* (pp. 1–94). Chicago: University of Chicago Press.

Ainsworth, M. D. S., & Bell, S. M. (1969). Some contemporary patterns of mother–infant interaction in the feeding situation. In A. Ambrose (Ed.), *Stimulation in early childhood.* London & New York: Academic Press.

Ainsworth, M. D. S., Blehar, M. C., Waters, E., & Wall, S. (1978). *Patterns of attachment.* Hillsdale, NJ: Erlbaum.

Aldous, J., Klaus, E., & Klein, D. M. (1985). The understanding heart: Aging parents and their favorite child. *Child Development, 56*, 303–316.

Allen, J., Hauser, S., Bell, K., & O'Connor, T. (1994). Longitudinal assessment of autonomy and relatedness in adolescent–family interactions as predictors of adolescent ego development and self-esteem. *Child Development, 65*, 179–194.

Allen, J., & Land, P. (1999). Attachment in adolescence. In J. Cassidy & P. R. Shaver (Eds.), *Handbook of attachment: Theory, research and clinical applications* (pp. 319–335). New York: Guilford.

Allen, J. P., & Bell, K. L. (1995, April). *Attachment and communication with parents and peers in adolescence.* Paper presented at the biennial meeting of the Society for Research in Child Development, Indianapolis, IN.

Allen, J. P., & Kuppermine, G. P. (1995, April). *Adolescence attachment, social competence and problematic behavior.* Paper presented at the biennial meeting of the Society for Research in Child Development, Indianapolis, IN.

Allen, S., & Crago, M. (1996). Early passive acquisition in Inuktitut. *Journal of Child Language, 23*, 129–155.

Alwin, D. F. (1988). From obedience to autonomy: Changes in traits desired in children, 1928–1978. *Public Opinion Quarterly, 52*, 33–52.

Amato, P., & Booth, A. (1996). A prospective study of divorce and parent–child relationships. *Journal of Marriage and the Family, 56*, 45–56.

Amato, P. R. (2000). Diversity within single-parent families. In D. H. Demo, K. R. Allen, & M. A. Fine (Eds.), *The handbook of family diversity* (pp. 149–172). New York: Oxford University Press.

Ambert, A. (1992). *The effects of children on parents.* New York: Haworth Press.

American Psychiatric Association (1987). *Diagnostic and statistical manual of mental disorders* (3rd ed., rev.). Washington, DC: Author.

Anders, T. (1994). Infant sleep, nighttime relationships, and attachment. Part of a symposium on: Relationships and development. *Psychiatry, 57*, 11–21.

Andrews, J., & Lewinsohn, R. (1992). Suicidal attempts among older adolescents: Prevalence and co-occurrence with other psychiatric disorders. *Journal of the American Academy of Child and Adolescent Psychiatry, 3*, 655–662.

Angell, G., Dennis, B., & Dumain, L. (1998). Spirituality, resilience, and narrative: Coping with parental death. *Families in Society: The Journal of Contemporary Human Services, 79*, 615–630.

Anglin, J. (1993). Vocabulary development: A morphological analysis. *Monographs of the Society for Research in Child Development, 58 (Serial No. 238), 10.*

Ansbaugh, R., & Peck, S. (1998). Treatment of sleep problems in a toddler: A replication of the faded bedtime with response cost protocol. *Journal of Applied Behavior Analysis, 31,* 127–129.

Aquilino, W. (1994). Later life parental divorce and widowhood: Impact on young adults' assessments of parent–child relations. *Journal of Marriage and the Family, 56,* 908–922.

Aquilino, W., & Supple, K. (1991). Parent–child relations and parents' satisfaction with living arrangements when adult children live at home. *Journal of Marriage and the Family, 53,* 13–27.

Aries, P. (1962). *Centuries of childhood: A social history of family life* (R. Baldick, Trans.). New York: Knopf. (Original work published 1960.)

Arlin, P. K. (1975). Cognitive development in adulthood: A fifth stage? *Developmental Psychology, 11,* 602–606.

Armstrong, N., & Welsman, J. (1997). *Young people and physical activity.* England: Oxford University Press.

Arnett, J. J. (1998). Learning to stand alone. The contemporary American transition to adulthood in cultural and historical context. *Human Development, 41,* 295–315.

Arnett, J. J. (1999). Adolescent storm and stress reconsidered. *American Psychologist, 54,* 317–326.

Arnett, J. J. (2000). Emerging adulthood: A theory of development from the late teens through the twenties. *American Psychologist, 55,* 469–480.

Arnett, J. J. (2001). *Adolescence and emerging adulthood: A cultural approach.* Upper Saddle River, NJ: Merrill/Prentice Hall.

Arroyo, C. G., & Zigler, E. (1995). Racial identity, academic achievement, and the psychological well-being of economically disadvantaged adolescents. *Journal of Personality and Social Psychology, 69,* 903–914.

Asarmov, J. R., & Horton, A. A. (1990). Coping and stress in families of child psychiatric inpatients: Parents of children with depressive and schizophrenic spectrum disorders. *Child Psychiatry and Human Development, 21,* 145–157.

Atchley, R. C. (1991). *Social forces and aging.* Belmont, CA: Wadsworth.

Aunola, K., Stattin, H., & Nurmi, J. E. (2000). Parenting styles and adolescents' achievement strategies. *Journal of Adolescence, 23,* 205–222.

Baker, J. (2000). Immunization and the American way: Childhood vaccines. *American Journal of Public Health, 90,* 199–207.

Baldwin, A. L., Baldwin, C., & Cole, R. E. (1990). Stress-resistant families and stress-resistant children. In J. Rolf, A. Masten, D. Cicchetti, K. Neuchtherlin, & S. Weintraub (Eds.), *Risk and protective factors in the development of psychopathology* (pp. 257–280). Cambridge, UK: Cambridge University Press.

Ball, H., Hooker, E., & Kelly, E. (1999). Where will the baby sleep? Attitudes and practice of new and experienced parents regarding cosleeping with their newborn infants. *American Anthropologist, 101,* 143–151.

Bamford, F. N., Bannister, R., Benjamin, C. N., Hillier, V., Ward, B., & Moore, W. (1990). Sleep in the first year of life. *Developmental and Child Neurology, 32,* 718–734.

Bandura, A. (1977). *Social learning theory.* Upper Saddle River, NJ: Merrill/Prentice Hall.

Bandura, A. (1986). *Social foundations of thought and action: A social cognitive theory.* Upper Saddle River, NJ: Merrill/Prentice Hall.

Bandura, A., & Walters, R. (1963). *Social learning and personality development.* New York: Holt, Rinehart, & Wilson.

Bankoff, E. A. (1983). Aged parents and their widowed daughters: A support relationship. *The Gerontologist, 38,* 228–230.

Bar-Haim, Y., Sutton, D. B., & Fox, N. (2000). Stability and change of attachment at 14, 24, and 58 months of age: Behavior, representation, and life events. *The Journal of Child Psychology and Psychiatry and Allied Disciplines, 41,* 381–388.

Barkley, R. A. (1990). *Attention deficit hyperactivity disorder: A handbook for diagnosis and treatment.* New York: Guilford Press.

Barnes, G. (1990). Impact of the family on adolescent drinking patterns. In R. L. Collins, K. E. Leonard, & J. S. Searles (Eds.), *Alcohol and the family: Research and clinical perspectives* (pp. 137–161). New York: Guilford Press.

Barnett, D., Kidwell, S., & Leung, K-H. (1998). Parenting and preschooler attachment among low-income urban African American families. *Child Development, 69,* 1657–1671.

Barnett, M., Quackenbush, S., & Sinisi, C. (1996). Factors affecting children's, adolescents', and young adults' perceptions of parental discipline. *Journal of Genetic Psychology, 157,* 411–424.

Barrera, M., & Stice, E. (1998). Parent–adolescent conflict in the context of parental support: Families with alcoholic and non-alcoholic fathers. *Journal of Family Psychology, 12,* 195–208.

Barrett, D., & Frank, D. (1987). *The effects of undernutrition on children's behavior.* New York: Gordon & Breach.

Barton, K., & Baglio, C. (1993). The nature of stress in child-abusing families: A factor analytic study. *Psychological Reports, 73,* 1047–1055.

Barusch, A. S., & Spaid, W. M. (1989). Gender differences in caregiving. *Gerontologist, 29,* 667–676.

Baum, A. C., Crase, S. J., & Crase, K. L. (2001). Influences on the decision to become or not to become a foster parent. *Families in Society, 82,* 202–213.

Baumrind, D. (1967). Child care practices anteceding three patterns of preschool behavior. *Genetic Psychology Monographs, 75,* 43–88.

Baumrind, D. (1968). Authoritarian vs. authoritative parental control. *Adolescence, 3,* 255–272.

Baumrind, D. (1971). Current patterns of parental authority. *Developmental Psychology Monographs, 4*(1, Pt. 2), 1–103.

Baumrind, D. (1973). The development of instrumental competence through socialization. In A. D. Pick (Ed.), *Minnesota symposium on child psychology* (Vol. 7, pp. 3–46). Minneapolis: University of Minneapolis Press.

Baumrind, D. (1980). New directions in socialization research. *Psychological Bulletin, 35,* 639–652.

Baumrind, D. (1987). A developmental perspective on adolescent risk taking in contemporary America. In C. E. Irwin, Jr. (Ed.), *Adolescent social behavior and health. New Directions for Child Development, 37,* 93–125.

Baumrind, D. (1989). Rearing competent children. In W. Damon (Ed.), *Child development today and tomorrow* (pp. 349–377). San Francisco: Jossey-Bass.

Baumrind, D. (1991a). Effective parenting during the early adolescent transition. In P. A. Cowen & E. M. Hetherington (Eds.), *Advances in family research* (Vol. 2, Family Transitions, pp. 111–163). Hillsdale, NJ: Erlbaum.

Baumrind, D. (1991b). The influence of parenting style on adolescent competence and substance abuse. *Journal of Early Adolescence, 11,* 56–95.

Baumrind, D. (1996). The discipline controversy revisited. *Family Relations, 45,* 405–414.

Bean, F., Curtis, R., & Marcum, J. (1977). Familism and marital satisfaction among Mexican-Americans: The effects of family size, wife's labor force participation, and conjugal power. *Journal of Marriage and the Family, 39,* 759–767.

Beatty, V. (2000). A Dad's diary of labor and delivery. *Baby Talk, 65,* 32–34.

Beevar, D. A., & Beevar, R. J. (1988). *Family therapy: A systemic integration.* Boston: Allyn & Bacon.

Belsky, J., & Cassidy, J. (1995). Attachment theory and evidence. In M. Rutter, D. Hay, & S. Baron-Cohen (Eds.), *Developmental principles and clinical issues in psychology and psychiatry.* Oxford, England: Blackwell.

Belsky, J., & Kelly, J. (1994). *The transition to parenthood.* New York: Dell.

Bempechat, J., Graham, S., & Jimenez, N. (1999). The socialization of achievement in poor and minority students: A comparative study. *Journal of Cross-Cultural Psychology, 30,* 139–159.

Benedikt, R., Wertheim, E. H., & Love, A. (1998). Eating disorders and weight-loss attempts in female adolescents and their mothers. *Journal of Youth and Adolescence, 27,* 43–57.

Bengston, V. L. (1979). Research perspectives on intergenerational interaction. In P. K. Ragan (Ed.), *Aging parents* (pp. 37–57). Los Angeles: University of Southern California.

Bengston, V. L. (1985). Diversity and symbolism in grandparental roles. In V. L. Bengston & J. F. Robertson (Eds.), *Grandparenthood* (pp. 11–26). Beverly Hills, CA: Sage.

Bengston, V. L., Rosenthal, C., & Burton, L. (1990). Families and aging: Heterogeneity. In R. H. Binstock & L. George (Eds.), *Handbook of aging and the social sciences* (3rd ed., pp. 263–287). San Diego: Academic Press.

Berenthal, B., & Clifton, R. (1998). Perception and action. In W. Damon, K. Kuhn, & R. S. Siegler (Eds.), *Handbook of child psychology: Cognition, perception, and language.* New York: Wiley.

Berger, K. S., & Thompson, R. A. (2001). *The developing person through the life span* (5th ed.). New York: Worth.

Berger, R. (2000). Gay stepfamilies: A triple stigmatized group. *Families in Society, 81,* 504–516.

Bigner, J. J. (1996). Working with gay fathers: Developmental, post-divorce, and therapeutic issues. In R.-J. Green & J. S. Laird (Eds.), *Lesbian and gay couple and family relationships: Therapeutic perspectives* (pp. 370–403). San Francisco: Jossey-Bass.

Bigner, J. J. (1998). *Parent–child relations: An introduction to parenting* (5th ed.). Upper Saddle River, NJ: Merrill/Prentice Hall.

Birengen, Z. (2000). Emotional availability: Conceptualization and research findings. *American Journal of Orthopsychiatry, 70,* 104–114.

Black, B., & Logan, A. (1995). Links between communication patterns in mother–child, father–child, and child–peer interactions. *Child Development, 66,* 255–270.

Black, D., & Urbanowicz, M. A. (1987). Family intervention with bereaved children. *Journal of Child Psychology and Psychiatry, 28,* 467–476.

Blenkner, M. (1965). Social work and family in later life, with some thoughts on filial maturity. In E. Shanas & G. Streib (Eds.), *Social structure and the family: Generational relations* (pp. 46–59). Upper Saddle River, NJ: Merrill/Prentice Hall.

Block, J., & Robins, R. (1993). A longitudinal study of consistency and change in self-esteem from early adolescence to early adulthood. *Child Development, 64,* 900–923.

Bloom, B., & Steinhart, D. (1993). *Why punish the children? A reappraisal of the children of incarcerated mothers in America.* San Francisco: National Council on Crime and Delinquency.

Bogenschneider, K., Wu, M., Raffaelli, M., & Tsay, J. C. (1998). Parent influences on adolescent peer orientation and substance abuse: The interface of parenting practices and values. *Child Development, 69,* 1672–1688.

Borland, M., Laybourn, A., Hill, M., & Brown, J. (1998). *Middle childhood: The perspectives of children and parents.* London: Jessica Kingsley.

Bornstein, M., & Lamb, M. (1992). *Developments in infancy* (3rd ed.). New York: McGraw-Hill.

Bottom, W., & Lancaster, J. (1981). An ecological orientation toward human abuse. *Family and Community Health, 4*, 1–10.

Bower, A., & Hayes, A. (1998). Mothering in families with and without a child with disability. *International Journal of Disability, Development, and Education, 45*, 313–322.

Bowlby, J. (1951). Maternal care and mental health. *Bulletin of the World Health Organization, 3*, 355–534.

Bowlby, J. (1958). The nature of the child's tie to his mother. *International Journal of Psychoanalysis, 39*, 350–373.

Bowlby, J. (1969). *Attachment and loss, Vol. 1. Attachment.* New York: Basic Books.

Bowlby, J. (1982). *Attachment and loss, Vol. 2. Separation.* New York: Basic Books.

Boyle, M., & Morris, D. (1999). *Community nutrition in action: An entrepreneurial approach* (2nd ed.). Belmont, CA: Wadsworth.

Brand, H., Crous, B., & Hanekom, J. (1990). Perceived parental inconsistency as a factor in the emotional development of behavior-disordered children. *Psychological Reports, 66*, 620–622.

Brandstadter, J. (1998). Action perspectives on human development. In W. Damon & R. Lerner (Eds.), *Handbook of child psychology, Vol. 1: Theoretical models of human development* (5th ed., pp. 941–973). New York: Wiley.

Braus, P. (1998). When the helpers need a hand. *American Demographics, 20*, 66–72.

Bray, J., & Kelly, J. (1998). *Stepfamilies: Love, marriage and parenting in the first decade.* New York: Broadway Books.

Bretherton, I. (1985). Attachment theory: Retrospect and prospect. In I. Bretherton & E. Waters (Eds.), *Growing points of attachment theory and research.* Monographs of the Society of Research in *Child Development, 50*, Serial No. 209.

Briggs, D. (1975). *Your child's self-esteem: The key to his life.* New York: Doubleday.

Bril, B. (1986). Motor development and cultural attitudes. In H. T. A. Whiting & M G. Wade (Eds.), *Themes in motor development.* Dordrecht, Netherlands: Martinus Nijhoff.

Brill, A. (1938). *The basic writings of Sigmund Freud.* New York: The Modern Library.

Britton, L. (1992). *Montessori, play and learn: A parent's guide to purposeful play from two to six.* New York: Crown.

Brockington, I. F. (1992). Disorders specific to the puerperium. *International Journal of Mental Health, 21*, 41–52.

Brody, G., Ge, X., & Conger, R. (2001). The influence of neighborhood disadvantage, collective socialization, and parenting on African American children's affiliation with deviant peers. *Child Development, 72*, 1231–1246.

Brody, G. H., Stoneman, Z., Flor, D., & McCrary, C. (1997). Religion's role in organizing family relationships: Family processes in rural, two-parent African-American families. *Developmental Psychology, 32*, 696–706.

Bronfenbrenner, U. (1979). *The ecology of human development.* Cambridge, UK: Cambridge University Press.

Bronfenbrenner, U. (1989). Ecological systems theory. In R. Vasta (Ed.), *Annals of child development* (Vol. 6). Greenwich, CT: JAI Press.

Brook, J. S., Brook, D. W., Gordon, A. S., & Whiteman, M. (1990). The psychosocial etiology of adolescent drug use: A family interactional approach. *Genetic, Social, and General Psychology Monographs, 116*, 111–267.

Brophy, G. (2000). Social work treatment of sleep disturbance in a 5-year-old boy: A single case evaluation. *Research in Social Work Practice, 10*, 748–758.

Brown, J., & Pollitt, E. (1996). Malnutrition, poverty, and intellectual development. *Scientific American, 274*, 38–43.

Bruer, J. (1999). *The myth of the first three years: A new understanding of early brain development and lifelong learning.* New York: Free Press.

Bryan, T. (1988). Discussion: Social skills and learning disabilities. In J. K. Kavanagh & J. Truss (Eds.), *Learning disabilities: Proceedings of the national conference.* Parkton, MD: New York Press.

Bryant, W., & Zick, C. (1996). An examination of parent–child shared time. *Journal of Marriage and the Family, 58,* 227–238.

Burnett, D. (1999). Social relationships of Latino grandparent caregivers: A role theory perspective. *Gerontologist, 39,* 49–58.

Burton, L. M., & Dilworth-Anderson, P. (1991). The intergenerational family roles of aged black Americans. *Marriage and Family Review, 16,* 116–330.

Butler, R. (1998). Age trends in the use of social and temporal comparison for self-evaluation: Examination of a novel developmental hypothesis. *Child Development, 69,* 1054–1073.

Cairns, R., Leung, M., Buchanan, L., & Cairns, B. (1995). Friendship and social networks in childhood and adolescence: Fluidity, reliability, and interrelations. *Child Development, 66,* 1330–1345.

Cantos, A., Neale, J., & O'Leary, K. (1997). Assessment of coping strategies of child-abusing mothers. *Child Abuse and Neglect, 21,* 631–636.

Carney, D. (1997). House overwhelmingly passes foster care adoption bill. *Congressional Quarterly Weekly Report, 55,* 1024.

Carton, M., & Dominguez, M. (1997). The relationship between self-actualization and parenting style. *Journal of Social Behavior and Personality, 12,* 1093–1100.

Caspar, R. C. (1992). Risk factors in the development of eating disorders. In S. C. Feinstein (Ed.), *Adolescent Psychiatry* (pp. 91–103). Chicago: University of Chicago Press.

Ceron-Mireles, P., Harlow, S., & Sanchez-Carrillo, C. (1996). The risk of prematurity and small-for-gestational-age birth in Mexico City: The effects of working conditions and antenatal leave. *American Journal of Public Health, 86,* 825–831.

Cervera, N., & Videka-Sherman, L. (1989). *Working with pregnant and parenting teenage clients.* Milwaukee, WI: Family Services America.

Chan, D. (2002). Perceptions of giftedness and self-concept among junior secondary students in Hong Kong. *Journal of Youth and Adolescence, 31,* 243–252.

Chao, R. K. (1994). Beyond parental control and authoritarian parenting styles: Understanding Chinese parenting through the cultural notion of training. *Child Development, 65,* 1111–1119.

Chapman, M., & McBride, M. (1995). The education of reason: Conflict and its role in intellectual development. In C. Shantz & W. Hartup (Eds.), *Conflict in child and adolescent development* (pp. 36–69). Cambridge, UK: Cambridge University Press.

Chase-Lansdale, P. L., Brooks-Gunn, J., & Paikoff, R. L. (1991). Research programs for adolescent mothers: Missing links and future promises. *Family Relations, 40,* 396–403.

Chase-Lansdale, P. L., Mott, F. L., & Brooks-Gunn, J. (1991). Children of the national longitudinal study of youth: A unique research opportunity. *Developmental Psychology, 27,* 918–931.

Chavira, V., Lopez, S., & Blacher, J. (2000). Latina mothers' attributions, emotions, and reactions to the problem behaviors of their children with developmental disabilities. *The Journal of Child Psychology and Psychiatry and Allied Disciplines, 41,* 245–252.

Checkovich, T., & Stern, S. (2002). Shared caregiving responsibilities of adult siblings with elderly parents. *The Journal of Human Resources, 37,* 441–478.

Chen, H., & Lan, W. (1998). Adolescents' perceptions of their parents' academic expectations: Comparisons of American, Chinese American, and Chinese high school students. *Adolescence, 33,* 385–390.

Cherlin, A. J., & Furstenberg, F. F. (1986). *The new American grandparent: A place in the family, a life apart.* New York: Basic Books.

Chin-Yee, F. (1990). Through the maze: Grief counseling through the childbearing cycle. *International Journal of Childbirth Education, 5,* 31–32.

Chirkov, V., & Ryan, R. (2001). Parent and teacher autonomy-support in Russian and U.S. adolescents: Common effects on well-being and academic achievement. *Journal of Cross-Cultural Psychology, 32,* 618–635.

Chirobogo, D. A., Yee, B. W. K., & Weiler, P. G. (1992). Stress and coping in the context of caring. In L. Montada, S. Filipp, & M. J. Lerner (Eds.), *Life Crises and experiences of loss in adulthood* (pp. 94–118). Hillsdale, NJ: Erlbaum.

Christmon, K. (1990a). Parental responsibility and self-image of African American fathers. *Families in Society, 71,* 563–567.

Christmon, K. (1990b). Parental responsibility of African-American unwed adolescent fathers. *Adolescence, 25,* 645–653.

Cicirelli, V. G. (1991). Attachment theory in old age: Protection of the attached figure. In K. Pillimer & K. McCartney (Eds.), *Parent–child relations throughout life* (pp. 25–42). Hillsdale, NJ: Erlbaum.

Clarizio, H. F. (1994). *Assessment and treatment of depression in children and adolescents.* Brandon, VT: Clinical Psychology.

Clark, R., Novak, J., & Dupree, D. (2002). Relationships to perceived parenting practices to anger regulation and coping strategies in African-American adolescents. *Journal of Adolescence, 25,* 373–384.

Clarke, E., Preston, M., & Raskin, J. (1999). Types of conflicts and tensions between older parents and adult children. *The Gerontologist, 39,* 261–270.

Cleaver, J. Y. (1999). Good old dad. *American Demographics, 32,* 58–62.

Cleverley, J., & Phillips, D. (1986). Visions of childhood: Influential models from Locke to Spock (Rev. ed). New York: Teachers College Press.

Clinton, J. F., & Kelber, S. T. (1993). Stress and coping in fathers of newborns: Comparisons of planned versus unplanned pregnancy. *International Journal of Nursing Studies, 30,* 437–443.

Clyburn, L., Stones, M., & Hadjistavropoulos, T. (2000). Predicting caregiving burden and depression in Alzheimer's disease. *Journals of Gerontology, Series B: Psychological Sciences and Social Sciences, 55B,* S2–S13.

Cohen, D. (1979). *J. B. Watson: The founder of behaviorism.* London: Routledge & Kegan Paul.

Cohen, S. E. (1995). Biosocial factors in early infancy as predictors of competence in adolescents who were born prematurely. *Journal of Developmental and Behavioral Pediatrics, 16,* 36–41.

Colarusso, C., & Nemiroff, R. (1981). *Adult development.* New York: Plenum Press.

Cole, P., Michel, M., & Teti, L. (1994). The development of emotion regulation and dysregulation: A clinical perspective. *Monographs of the Society for Research in Child Development, 59,* 73–100.

Coleman, M., Ganong, L., & Fine, L. (2000). Reinvestigating marriage: Another decade of progress. *Journal of Marriage and the Family, 62,* 1288–1307.

Collins, W., & Laursen, B. (1992). Conflict and relationships during adolescence. In C. Shantz & W. Hartup (Eds.), *Conflict in child and adolescent development* (pp. 216–241). New York: Cambridge University Press.

Committee on Nutrition, American Academy of Pediatrics. (1993). *Pediatric Nutrition Handbook,* 3rd ed., Elk Grove Village, IL: American Academy of Pediatrics, pp. 23–33.

Compas, B., Banez, G., Malcarne, V., & Worsham, N. (1991). Perceived control and coping with stress: A developmental perspective. *Journal of Social Issues, 47*, 23–34.

Conley, D., & Bennett, N. (2001). Birth weight and income: Interactions across generations. *Journal of Health and Social Behavior, 42*, 450–465.

Connolly, K. (1970). Response seed, temporal sequencing, and information processing in children. In K. Connolly (Ed.), *Mechanisms of motor skill development* (pp. 161–192). New York: Academic Press.

Conrad, M., & Hammen, C. (1993). Protective and resource factors in high- and low-risk children: A comparison of children with unipolar, bipolar, medically ill, and normal mothers. *Development and Psychopathology, 5*, 593–607.

Cook, E., Kieffer, J., & Charak, D. (1993). Autistic disorder and post-traumatic stress disorder. *Journal of the American Academy of Child and Adolescent Psychiatry, 32*, 1292–1294.

Corcoran, J. (1999). Ecological factors associated with adolescent pregnancy: A review of the literature. *Adolescence, 34*, 603–619.

Cornell, D. G. (1983). Gifted children: The impact of positive labeling on the family system. *American Journal of Orthopsychiatry, 53*, 322–334.

Cornell, D. G., & Grossberg, I. N. (1988). Family environment and personality adjustment in gifted program children. *Gifted Child Quarterly, 31*, 59–64.

Cornell, S. (2001). Governor responds as CT grapples with teen pregnancy. *Fairfield Journal, 4*, 8.

Cramer, D. W., & Roach, A. J. (1988). Coming out to Mom and Dad: A study of gay males and their relationships with their parents. *Journal of Homosexuality, 8*, 47–69.

Crisp, M. (2001, April). Growing up with a disability: What children with disabilities need from parents. *Exceptional Parent*, 74–78.

Cunningham, C., & Boyle, M. (2002). Preschoolers at risk for attention-deficit hyperactivity disorder and oppositional defiant disorder: Family, parenting, and behavioral correlates. *Journal of Abnormal Child Psychology, 30*, 555–569.

Cunningham, M. (2001). The influence of parental attitudes and behaviors on children's attitudes toward gender and household labor in early adulthood. *Journal of Marriage and the Family, 63*, 111–122.

Daly, D. I., & Dowd, T. P. (1992). Characteristics of effective, harm-free environments for children in out-of-home care. *Child Welfare, 71*, 487–496.

Daniels, D., Dunn, J., Furstenberg, F., Jr., & Plomin, R. (1985). Environmental differences within the family and adjustment differences within pairs of adolescent siblings. *Child Development, 56*, 764–774.

Dankoski, M. (2001). Pulling on the heart strings: An emotionally focused approach to family life cycle transitions. *Journal of Marriage and Family Therapy, 27*, 177–187.

Dannemiller, J., & Stephens, B. (1988). A critical test of infant pattern preference models. *Child Development, 59*, 210–216.

Davies, E., & Furnham, A. (1986). The dieting and body shape concerns of adolescent females. *Journal of Child Psychology and Psychiatry, 27*, 417–428.

Davies, P. T., & Cummings, E. M. (1994). Marital conflict and child adjustment: An emotional security hypothesis. *Psychological Bulletin, 116*, 387–411.

Dean, A., Matt, G. E., & Wood, P. (1992). The effects of widowhood on social support from significant others. *Journal of Community Psychology, 20*, 309–325.

Deater-Deckard, K. (2000). Parenting and child behavioral adjustment in early childhood: A qualitative genetic approach to studying family processes. *Child Development, 71*, 458–484.

DeCasper, A. J., & Fifer, W. P. (1980). On human bonding: Newborns prefer their mothers' voices. *Science, 208*, 1174–1176.

DeJong, L., & Cottrell, B. (1999, January). Designing infant care programs to meet the needs of children born to teenage parents. *Young Children,* 37–45.

DeMarrias, K., Nelson, P., & Baker, J. (1994). Meaning in mud: Yup'ik Eskimo girls at play. In J. Roopnarine, J. Johnson, & F. Hooper (Eds.), *Children's play in diverse cultures* (pp. 170–209). Albany, NY: SUNY Press.

DeMier, R., Hynan, M., & Hatfield, R. (2002). A measurement model of perinatal stressors: Identifying risk for postnatal emotional distress in mothers of high-risk infants. *Journal of Clinical Psychology, 56,* 89–100.

Demo, D. H. (1992). Parent–child relations: Assessing recent changes. *Journal of Marriage and the Family, 54,* 104–117.

Demo, D. H., & Acock, A. C. (1996). Family structure, family process, and adolescent well-being. *Journal of Research on Adolescence, 6,* 457–488.

Denham, S., Renwick, S., & Holt, R. (1991). Working and playing together: Prediction of preschool social–emotional competence from mother–child interaction. *Child Development, 62,* 242–249.

DePanfelis, D., & Zuravin, S. (2002). The effect of services on the recurrence of child maltreatment. *Child Abuse and Neglect, 26,* 187–205.

Dietrich, D. (1984). Psychological health of young adults who experienced early parent death: MMPI Trends. *Journal of Clinical Psychology, 40,* 901–908.

Dietz, W. (1999). Barriers to the treatment of childhood obesity: A call to action. *Journal of Pediatrics, 134,* 535–536.

DiFilippo, J. M., & Overholser, J. C. (2000). Suicidal ideation in adolescent psychiatric inpatients as associated with depression and attachment relationships. *Journal of Clinical Child Psychology, 29,* 155–166.

Dinkmeyer, D., & McKay, G. (1989). *Systematic training for effective parenting: The parent's handbook* (3rd ed.). Circle Pines, MN: American Guidance Services.

Dinkmeyer, D., McKay, G., & McKay, J. (1987). *New beginnings: Skills for single parents. Parent's manual.* Champaign, IL: Research Press.

Dori, G., & Overholser, J. C. (1999). Depression, hopelessness, and self-esteem: Accounting for suicidality in adolescent psychiatric inpatients. *Suicide and Life-Threatening Behavior, 29,* 309–318.

Dornbusch, S. M., Ritter, R., Liederman, P., Roberts, D., & Fraleigh, M. (1987). The relation of parenting style to adolescent school performance. *Child Development, 58,* 1244–1257.

Dornbusch, S. M., Ritter, R., Mont-Reynaud, R., & Chien, Z. (1990). Family decision making and academic performance in a diverse high school population. *Journal of Adolescent Research, 5,* 143–160.

Douvan, E., & Adelson, J. (1966). *The adolescent experience.* New York: Wiley.

Dreikurs, R. (1972). *Discipline without tears.* New York: Hawthorne.

Dreikurs, R., & Grey, L. (1968). *A new approach to discipline: Logical consequences.* New York: Hawthorne Books.

Dreikurs, R., & Grey, L. (1970). *A parent's guide to child discipline.* New York: Hawthorne.

Dreikurs, R., & Soltz, V. (1964). *Children: The challenge.* New York: Duell, Sloan, & Pearce.

Dryfoos, J. (1991). Preventing high-risk behavior. *American Journal of Public Health, 81,* 157–165.

Dubois, D. L., Felner, R., Brand, S., Phillip, R., & Lease, A. (1996). Early adolescent self-esteem: A developmental–ecological framework and assessment strategy. *Journal of Research on Adolescence, 6,* 543–579.

Dubois, D. L., & Tevendale, H. D. (1999). Self-esteem in childhood and adolescence: Vaccine or epiphenomenon? *Applied and Preventive Psychology, 8,* 103–117.

Dunn, J. (1992). Siblings and development. *Current Directions in Psychological Sciences, 1*, 6–9.

Dunn, M., Burbine, T., & Bowers, C. (2001). Moderators of stress in parents of children with autism. *Community Mental Health Journal, 37*, 39–52.

Durbin, D. L., Darling, N., Steinberg, L., & Brown, B. B. (1993). Parenting style and peer group membership among European-American adolescents. *Journal of Research on Adolescents, 3*, 87–100.

Eccles, J., Wigfield, A., & Harold, R. (1993). Age and gender differences in children's self- and task-perceptions during elementary school. *Child Development, 64*, 830–847.

Eckenrode, J., Laird, M., & Doris, J. (1993). School performance and disciplinary problems among abused and neglected children. *Developmental Psychology, 29*, 53–62.

Edelstein, S., & Burge, D. (2001). Helping foster parents cope with separation, loss, and grief. *Child Welfare, 80*, 5–25.

Edwards, C., & Liu, W.-L. (2002). Parenting toddlers. In M. Bornstein (Ed.), *Handbook of parenting* (2nd ed., pp. 45–71). Mahwah, NJ: Erlbaum.

Elkin, F., & Handel, G. (1989). *The child and society: The process of socialization* (5th ed.). New York: Random House.

Elkind, D. (1976). Child development and education: Piagetian perspective. New York: Oxford University Press.

Elkind, D. (2003). The overbooked child: Are we pushing our kids too hard? *Psychology Today, 36*, 64–70.

Emery, R. (1995). Family conflicts and their developmental implications: A conceptual analysis of meanings for the structure of relationships. In C. Shantz & W. Hartup (Eds.), *Conflict in child and adolescent development* (pp. 270–298). Cambridge, UK: Cambridge University Press.

Emick, M., & Hayslip, B. (1996). Custodial grandparenting: New roles for middle-aged and older adults. *International Journal of Aging and Human Development, 43*, 135–154.

Erdwins, C., Buffardi, L., & Casper, W. (2001). The relationship of women's role strain to social support, role satisfaction, and self-efficacy. *Family Relations, 50*, 230–238.

Erera, P., & Fredrickson, K. (1999). Lesbian stepfamilies: A unique family structure. *Families in Society: The Journal of Contemporary Human Services, 80*, 263–270.

Erera-Weatherly, P. (1996). On becoming a stepparent: Factors associated with the adoption of alternative stepparenting styles. *Journal of Divorce and Remarriage, 25*, 155–174.

Erikson, E. (1963). *Childhood and society.* New York: Norton.

Erikson, E. H. (1968). *Identity, Youth and Crisis.* New York: Norton.

Erikson, E. H. (1982). *The life cycle completed: A review.* New York: Norton.

Erikson, E. H., Erikson, J., & Kivnick, H. (1986). *Vital involvement in old age.* New York: Norton.

Ernst, M., Moolchan, E., & Robinson, M. (2001). Behavioral and neural consequence of prenatal exposure to nicotine. *Journal of the American Academy of Child and Adolescent Psychiatry, 40*, 630–641.

Eskenazi, B., Stapleton, A., Kharrazi, M., & Chee, W.-Y. (1999). Associations between maternal decaffeinated and caffeinated coffee consumption and fetal growth and gestational duration. *Epidemiology, 10*, 242–249.

Evans, D., Leckman, J., Carter, A., Reznick, J., Henshaw, D., & King, R., et al. (1997). Ritual, habit, and perfectionism: The prevalence and development of compulsive-like behavior in normal young children. *Child Development, 68*, 58–68.

Eveleth, P., & Tanner, J. (1991). *Worldwide variation in human growth.* Cambridge, UK: Cambridge University Press.

Facio, A., & Batistuta, M. (1998). Latins, Catholics, and from the far south: Argentenian adolescents and their parents. *Journal of Adolescence, 21,* 49–67.

Fagot, B. (1997). Attachment, parenting, and peer interactions of toddler children. *Developmental Psychology, 33,* 489–499.

Feldman, R., Greenbaum, C., & Yirmiya, N. (1999). Mother–infant affect synchrony as an antecedent of the emergence of self-control. *Developmental Psychology, 35,* 3–19.

Feldman, R., Weller, A., & Sirota, L. (2002). Skin-to-skin contact (kangaroo care) promotes self-regulation in premature infants: Sleep–wake cyclicity, arousal modulation, and sustained exploration. *Developmental Psychology, 38,* 194–207.

Fernald, A. (1993). Approval and disapproval: Infant responsiveness to vocal affect in familiar and unfamiliar languages. *Child Development, 64,* 657–674.

Fernandez, C., & Antonio, J. (1997). Youth residential independence and autonomy: A comparative study. *Journal of Family Issues, 18,* 576–607.

Fine, M. (1991). The handicapped child and the family: Implications for professionals, In M. Fine (Ed.), *Collaboration with parents of exceptional children* (pp. 3–24). Brandon, VT: Clinical Psychology.

Fingerman, K. (2001). A distant closeness: Intimacy between parents and their children in later life. *Gerontology, 25,* 26–33.

Fishman, C. (1999). The smorgasbord generation. *American Demographics, 21,* 54–60.

Flanagan, T. J., & Maguire, K. (Eds.). (1992). *Sourcebook of criminal justice statistics—1991.* Washington, DC: U.S. Department of Justice.

Flowers, P., & Buston, K. (2001). "I was terrified of being different." Exploring gay men's accounts of growing up in a heterosexual society. *Journal of Adolescence, 24,* 51–65.

Floyd, F., Stein, T., & Harter, K. (1999). Gay, lesbian, and bisexual youths: Separation–individuation, parental attitudes, identity consolidation, and well-being. *Journal of Youth and Adolescence, 28,* 719–739.

Franco, N., & Levitt, M. (1998). The social ecology of middle childhood: Family support, friendship quality and self-esteem. *Family Relations, 47,* 315–321.

Frankel, M. T., & Bates, J. E. (1990). Mother–toddler problem solving: Antecedents in attachment, home behavior, and temperament. *Child Development, 61,* 810–819.

Fredrickson, K. (1999). Family caregiving responsibilities among lesbian and gay men. *Social and Work, 44,* 142–155.

French, S., Story, M., Downes, B., Resnick, M., & Blum, R. (1995). Frequent dieting among adolescents: Psychosocial and health behavior correlates. *American Journal of Public Health, 85,* 695–701.

Freud, A. (1946). *The ego and the mechanisms of defense.* New York: International Universities Press.

Freud, S. (1961). *Civilization and its discontents* (J. Strachey, Trans.). New York: Norton. (Original work published 1931)

Frieman, B., Garon, H., & Garon, R. (2000). Parenting seminars for divorcing parents: One year later. Teaching parents to help their children cope with divorce. *Journal of Divorce and Remarriage, 33,* 129–143.

Froebel, F. (1909). *Friedrich Froebel: Pedogogies of the kindergarten, or his ideas concerning play and playthings of the child* (Josephine Jarvis, Trans.). New York: Appleton. (Original work published 1895)

Fuligni, A., & Eccles, J. (1993). Perceived parent–child relationships and early adolescents' orientation toward peers. *Developmental Psychology, 29,* 622–632.

Fuligni, A. J., Tseng, V., & Lam, M. (1999). Attitudes toward family obligations among American adolescents with Asian, Latin American and European backgrounds. *Child Development, 70,* 1030–1044.

Fuller-Thomson, E. (1999–2000). Loss of the kin-keepers: Sibling conflict following parental death. *Omega, 40*, 547–559.

Fuller-Thomson, E., & Minkler, M. (2001). American grandparents providing extensive child care to their grandchildren: Prevalence and profile. *Gerontologist, 41*, 201–209.

Fuller-Thomson, E., Minkler, M., & Driver, D. (1997). A profile of grandparents raising grandchildren in the United States. *The Gerontologist, 37*, 406–415.

Furstenberg, E. F., Jr., Brooks-Gunn, J., & Chase-Lansdale, L. (1989). Teenaged pregnancy and childbearing. *American Psychologist, 44*, 313–320.

Furstenberg, F., Hoffman, S., & Shrestha, L. (1995). The effect of divorce on intergenerational transfer: New evidence. *Demography, 32*, 319–333.

Ganong, L., Coleman, M., & Fine, M. (1999). Stepparents' affinity-seeking and affinity-maintaining strategies with stepchildren. *Journal of Family Issues, 20*, 299–327.

Garbarino, J., Kostelny, K., & Barry, F. (1997). Value transmission in an ecological context: The high-risk neighborhood. In J. Grusec & L. Kuczynski (Eds.), *Parenting and children's internalization of values: A handbook of contemporary theory.* New York: Wiley.

Gardiner, H. W., Mutter, J. D., & Kosmitzki, C. (1998). *Lives across cultures: Cross-cultural human development.* Boston: Allyn & Bacon.

Garey, A. (1995). Constructing motherhood on the night shift: Working mothers as stay-at-home moms. *Qualitative Sociology, 18*, 415–437.

Garey, A. (1999). *Weaving work and motherhood.* Philadelphia: Temple University Press.

Garmezy, N. (1993). Vulnerability and resilience. In D. Funder, R. Parke, C. Tomlinson-Keasy, & K. Widaman (Eds.), *Studying lives through time.* Washington, DC: American Psychological Association.

Garner, D. M., & Garfinkel, P. E. (1997). *Handbook of treatment for eating disorders.* New York: Plenum.

Garrity, C., & Baris, M. (1996). Bullies and victims. *Contemporary Pediatrics, 13*, 90–114.

Gaylor, E., Goodlin-Jones, B., & Anders, T. (2001). Classification of young children's sleep problems: A pilot study. *Journal of the American Academy of Child and Adolescent Psychiatry, 40*, 61–67.

Gecas, V., & Seff, M. (1990). Families and adolescents: A review of the 1980s. *Journal of Marriage and the Family, 52*, 941–958.

Gelles, R. (1989). Child abuse and violence in single-parent families: Parent absence and economic deprivation. *American Journal of Orthopsychiatry, 59*, 492–501.

Gelles, R., & Maynard, P. (1987). A structural family systems approach to intervention in cases of family violence. *Family Relations, 36*, 270–275.

Gelman, R., & Baillargeon, R. (1983). *A review of some Piagetian concepts. Handbook of child psychology: Vol. 3. Cognitive development* (4th ed., pp. 167–230). New York: Wiley.

Gibson, P. (2002). Caregiving role affects family relationships of African American grandmothers as new mothers again: A phenomenological perspective. *Journal of Marital and Family Therapy, 28*, 341–353.

Gill, V., & Maynard, D. (1995). On "labeling" in actual interaction: Delivering and receiving diagnoses of developmental disabilities. *Social Problems, 42*, 11–37.

Gillham, B., Tanner, G., & Cheyne, B. (1998). Unemployment rates, single-parent density, and indices of child poverty: Their relationships to different categories of child abuse and neglect. *Child Abuse and Neglect, 22*, 19–90.

Gindes, M. (1998). The psychological effects of relocation for children of divorce. *Journal of the American Academy of Matrimonial Lawyers, 15*, 115–148.

Ginsburg, G., & Bronstein, P. (1993). Family factors related to children's intrinsic/extrinsic motivational orientation and academic performance. *Child Development, 64*, 1461–1474.

Ginsburg, G., LaGreca, A., & Silverman, W. (1998). Social anxiety in children with anxiety disorders: Relation with social and emotional functioning. *Journal of Abnormal Child Psychology, 26,* 175–185.

Glasser, W. (1965). *Reality therapy: A new approach to psychiatry.* New York: Harper & Row.

Glasser, W. (2000). *Reality therapy in action.* New York: Harper Collins.

Gleason, J. (1967). Do children imitate? *Proceedings of the International Conference on Oral Education of the Deaf, 2,* 1441–1448.

Glenn, N. D., & Weaver, C. N. (1990). Quantitative research on marital quality in the 1980s: A critical review. *Journal of Marriage and the Family, 52,* 818–831.

Goduka, N. I., & Kunnie, J. E. (2004). Indigenous peoples' wisdom and power: Affirming our knowledge through narratives. Hampshire, UK: Ashgate.

Goldhaber, D. (2000). *Theories of human development.* Mountain View, CA: Mayfield.

Goldscheider, F. (1997). Recent changes in U.S. young adult living arrangements in comparative perspective. *Journal of Family Issues, 18,* 709–724.

Goldscheider, F., & Goldscheider, C. (1999). *The changing transition to adulthood: Leaving and returning home.* Thousand Oaks, CA: Sage.

Goldscheider, F., & Waite, L. (1991). *New families, no families: The transformation of the American home.* Berkeley: University of California Press.

Gopnik, A., Meltzoff, A., & Kuhl, P. (1999). *The scientist in the crib: Minds, brains, and how children learn.* New York: Morrow.

Gordon, T. (1975). *P.E.T.: Parent effectiveness training.* New York: New American Library.

Gordon, T. (1976). *Parent effectiveness training.* New York: New American Library.

Gortmaker, S., Must, A., Sobol, A., Peterson, K., Coditz, G., & Dietz, W. (1996). Television viewing as a cause of increasing obesity among children in the United States, 1986–1990. *Archives of Pediatrics & Adolescent Medicine, 150,* 356–362.

Grant, J. P. (1986). The state of the world's children: 1986. New York: Oxford University Press.

Green, C., & Chalip, L. (1997). Enduring involvement in youth soccer: The socialization of parent and child. *Journal of Leisure Research, 29,* 61–77.

Greene, A. L., & Boxer, A. M. (1986). Daughters and sons as young adults: Restructuring the ties that bind. In N. Datan, A. L. Greene, & H. W. Reese (Eds.), *Lifespan developmental psychology: Intergenerational relations* (pp. 125–149). Hillsdale, NJ: Erlbaum.

Gregory, A., & O'Connor, T. (2002). Sleep problems in childhood: A longitudinal study of developmental change and association with behavioral problems. *Journal of the American Academy of Child and Adolescent Psychiatry, 41,* 964–971.

Grotevant, H., & Cooper, C. (1985). Patterns of interactions in family relationships and the development of identity exploration in adolescence. *Child Development, 56,* 415–428.

Grusec, J., & Goodnow, J. (1994). Impact of parental discipline on the child's internalization of values: A reconceptualization of current points of view. *Developmental Psychology, 30,* 4–19.

Grusec, J., Hastings, P., & Mammone, N. (1994). Parenting cognitions and relationship schemes. In J. Smetana (Ed.), *Beliefs about parenting: Origins and developmental implications* (pp. 5–19). San Francisco: Jossey-Bass.

Gunnoe, M., Hetherington, E., & Reiss, D. (1999). Parental religiosity, parenting style, and adolescent responsibility. *Journal of Early Adolescence, 19,* 199–225.

Hack, M., Klein N. K., & Taylor, H. G. (1995). Long-term developmental outcomes of low birth weight infants. *The Future of Children, 5,* 176–197.

Hackel, L. S., & Ruble, D. N. (1992). Changes in the marital relationship after the first baby is born: Predicting the impact of expectancy disconfirmation. *Journal of Personality and Social Psychology, 62,* 944–957.

Hackney, H. (1981). The gifted child, the family, and the school. *Gifted Child Quarterly, 25,* 51–62.

Hafen, B., & Frandsen, K. (1986). *Youth suicide: Depression and loneliness.* Evergreen, CO: Cordillera Press.

Hagestad, G. O. (1987). Able elderly in the family context: Changes, chances and challenges. *Gerontologist, 27,* 417–428.

Haith, M. (1993). Preparing for the 21st century: Some goals and challenges for studies of infant sensory and perceptual development. *Developmental Review, 18,* 354–371.

Hall, G. S. (1904). *Adolescence: Its psychology and its relation to physiology, anthropology, sociology, sex, crime, religion, and education* (Vols. 1 & 2). Upper Saddle River, NJ: Merrill/Prentice Hall.

Hall, G. H. (1965). *Health, growth, and heredity: G. Stanley Hall on Natural Education,* Edited and with an Introduction and Notes, by Charles Strickland, and Charles Burgess. New York: Teachers College Press.

Hamilton, E., Asarnov, J., & Tompson, M. (1997). Social, academic, and behavioral competence of depressed children: Relationship to diagnostic status and family interaction style. *Journal of Youth and Adolescence, 26,* 77–89.

Hamner, T., & Turner, P. (2001). *Parenting in contemporary society.* Boston: Allyn & Bacon.

Hanna, K. (1996). Helping grieving parents explain perinatal death to children. *Journal of Perinatal Education, 5,* 45–49.

Hare, J. (1994). Concerns and issues faced by families headed by a lesbian couple. *Families in Society, 75,* 27–35.

Harris, R. L., Ellicott, A. M., & Holmes, D. S. (1986). The timing of psychological transitions and changes in women's lives: An examination of women aged 45 to 60. *Journal of Personality and Social Psychology, 51,* 409–416.

Harrison, C., & Sofronoff, K. (2002). ADHD and parental psychological distress: Role of demographics, child behavioral characteristics, and parental cognitions. *Journal of the American Academy of Child and Adolescent Psychiatry, 41,* 703–711.

Hart, B., & Risley, T. (1995). *Meaningful differences in the everyday experience of young American children.* Baltimore: Brooks.

Harter, S. (1990). Issues in the assessment of the self-concept of children and adolescents. In A. LaGreca (Ed.), *Through the eyes of a child* (pp. 292–325). Boston: Allyn & Bacon.

Harter, S. (1998). The development of self-representations. In W. Damon & N. Eisenberg (Eds.), *Handbook of child psychology: Vol. 3. Social, emotional, and personality development* (pp. 553–618). New York: Wiley.

Harter, S. (1999). *The construction of the self: A developmental perspective.* New York: Guilford Press.

Hattery, A. (2001). *Women, work, and family: Balancing and weaving.* Thousand Oaks, CA: Sage.

Havens, L. (1972). Youth, violence, and the nature of family life. *Psychiatric Annals, 2,* 18–29.

Heath, P. (1993). Misbehavior and learning. In F. N. Magill & J. Rodriquez (Eds.), *Survey of science: Applied science series (Vol. 1, Survey of social sciences: Psychology Series,* (pp. 1581–1588). Pasadena, CA: Salem Press.

Heath, P., & Camarena, P. (2002). Patterns of depressed affect in early adolescence. *Journal of Early Adolescence, 22,* 256–276.

Heath, P., & MacKinnon, C. (1988). Factors related to children's social competence following divorce. *Journal of Divorce, 11,* 67–76.

Heights, R., & Beaty, L. A. (1999). Identity development of homosexual youth and parental and familial influences on the coming out process. *Adolescence, 34,* 597–601.

Hermes, P. (1987). *A time to listen.* San Diego: Harcourt Brace Jovanovich.

Herrenkohl, E., Herrenkohl, R., & Egolf, B. (1994). Resilient early school-age children from maltreating homes: Outcomes in late adolescence. *American Journal of Orthopsychiatry, 64,* 301–309.

Herrgard, E., Luoma, L., Tuppurainen, K., Karjalainen, S., & Martikainen, A. (1993). Neurodevelopmental profile at five years of children born at < or = 32 weeks gestation. *Developmental Medicine and Child Neurology, 35,* 1083–1096.

Hetherington, E. M., & Clingempeel, W. G. (1992). Coping with marital transitions: A family systems perspective. *Monographs of the Society for Research in Child Development, 57* (Issue 2/3, Serial No. 227), 1–14.

Heyman, G., Dweck, C., & Cain, K. (1992). Young children's vulnerability to self-blame and helplessness: Relationship to beliefs about goodness. *Child Development, 63,* 401–415.

Hill, S., & Yuan, H. (1999). Family density of alcoholism and onset of adolescent drinking. *Journal of Studies on Alcohol, 60,* 7–17.

Hinton, H. C. (Ed.). (1986). *The People's Republic of China, 1979–1984: A documentary survey (Vol. II).* Wilmington, DE: Scholarly Resources.

Hirsch, B., & DuBois, D. (1991). Self-esteem in early adolescence: The identification and prediction of contrasting longitudinal trajectories. *Journal of Youth and Adolescence, 20,* 53–72.

Hobbes. (1994). *Leviathan: With selected variants from the Latin edition of 1668.* Edited, and Introduction and Notes by Edward Curley. Indianapolis/Cambridge: Hackett.

Hochschild, A. R. (1997). *The time bind: When work becomes home, and home becomes work.* New York: Metropolitan Books.

Hoff-Ginsberg, E., & Tardif, T. (1995). Socioeconomic status and parenting. In M. Bornstein (Ed.), *Handbook of parenting: Biology and ecology of parenting, Vol. 2.* (pp. 211–234). Mahwah, NJ: Erlbaum.

Hoffman, C., & Ledford, D. (1995). Adult children of divorce: Relationships with their mothers and fathers prior to and following parental separation, and currently. *Journal of Divorce and Remarriage, 24,* 41–57.

Hoffman, L. (1991). The influence of the family environment on personality: Accounting for sibling differences. *Psychological Bulletin, 110,* 187–203.

Holden, K., & Smock, P. (1991). The economic costs of marital dissolution: Why do women bear a disproportionate cost? *Annual Review of Sociology, 17,* 51–78.

Holmbeck, G. N., Paikoff, R. L., & Brooks-Gunn, J. (1995). Parenting adolescents. In M. H. Bornstein (Ed.), *Handbook of Parenting, Vol. 1. Children and parenting* (pp. 91–118). Mahwah, NJ: Erlbaum.

Houts, A., Berman, J., & Abramson, H. (1994). Effectiveness of psychological and pharmacological treatments for nocturnal emissions. *Journal of Consulting and Clinical Psychology, 62,* 737–745.

Hoyert, D. L., & Seltzer, M. M. (1992). Factors related to the well-being and life activities of family caregivers. *Family Relations, 41,* 74–81.

Hsai, H.-C., & Scanzoni, J. (1996). Rethinking the roles of Japanese women. *Journal of Comparative Family Studies, 27,* 309–329.

Hurley, D. (1987, August). A sound mind in an unsound body. *Psychology Today,* 34–43.

Hyun, O.-K., Lee, W., & Yoo, A.-J. (2002). Social support for two generations of new mothers in selected populations in Korea, Hong Kong, and the United States. *Journal of Comparative Family Studies, 33,* 515–527.

Imber-Black, E., & Roberts, J. (1993). Family change: Don't cancel holidays! Excerpts from *Rituals for our times, Psychology Today, 26,* 62–65.

Isabella, R., & Belsky, J. (1991). Interactional synchrony and the origins of infant–mother attachment: A replication study. *Child Development, 62,* 373–384.

Isolauri, E., Sutas, Y., Salo, M. K., Isosomppi, R., & Kaila, M. (1998). Elimination diet in cow's milk allergy: Risk for impaired growth in young children. *Journal of Pediatrics, 132,* 1004–1009.

Jackson, S., Thompson, R., & Christiansen, E. (1999). Predicting abuse-prone parental attitudes and discipline practices in a nationally representative sample. *Child Abuse and Neglect, 23,* 15–29.

Jacob, T. (1997). Parenting influences on the development of alcohol abuse and dependence. *Alcohol Health and Research World, 32*(3), 204–209.

Jacobs, L. (1974). *A deaf adult speaks out.* Washington, DC: Gallaudet College Press.

Jacobson, K. C., & Crockett, L. J. (2000). Parental monitoring and adolescent adjustment: An ecological perspective. *Journal of Research on Adolescence, 10,* 65–98.

Jacobson, S. W., Fein, G. G., Jacobson, J. L., Schwartz, P. M., & Dowler, J. K. (1985). Neonatal correlates of exposure to smoking, caffeine, and alcohol. *Infant and Behavior Development, 7,* 253–265.

Jaffe, J., Beebe, B., Feldstein, S., Crown, C., & Jasnow, M. (2001). Rhythms of dialogue in infancy. *Monographs of the Society for Research in Child Development, 66* (Serial No. 265).

Jerome, A., Fujiki, M., Brinton, B., & James, S. (2002). Self-esteem in children with specific language impairment. *Journal of Speech, Language and Hearing Research, 45,* 700–714.

Johnson, B. M., Shulman, S., & Collins, W. A. (1991). Systemic patterns of parenting as reported by adolescents: Developmental differences and implications for psychosocial outcomes. *Journal of Adolescent Research, 6,* 235–252.

Johnson, J., & Koegel, R. (1982). Behavioral assessment and curriculum development. In R. Koegel, A. Rincover, & A. Egel (Eds.), *Educating and understanding autistic children* (pp. 1–32). San Diego: College-Hill Press.

Johnson, L., Gallagher, R., & Montagne, M. (1994). *Meeting early intervention challenges: Issues from birth to three.* Baltimore: Paul H. Brookes.

Johnson, V., & Pandina, R. (1991). Effects of the family environment on adolescent substance abuse, delinquency, and coping styles. *American Journal of Drug and Alcohol Abuse, 17,* 71–88.

Johnston, D., & Gabel, K. (1995). Incarcerated parents. In K. Gabel & D. Johnston (Eds.), *Children of incarcerated parents* (pp. 3–20). New York: Lexington Books.

Jones, M. (1993). Decline of the American orphanage (1941–1980). *Social Service Review, 67,* 459–480.

Jones, S., Smith, L., & Landau, B. (1991). Object properties and knowledge in early lexical learning. *Child Development, 62,* 499–516.

Josselson, R. (1988). The imbedded self: I and thou revisited. In J. Adelson (Ed.), *Handbook of adolescent psychology* (pp. 185–210). New York: Wiley.

Juang, L., & Silbereisen, R. (1999). Supportive parenting and adolescent adjustment across time in former East and West Germany. *Journal of Adolescence, 22,* 719–736.

Juang, L. P., & Nguyen, H. H. (1997, April). Autonomy and connectedness: Predictors of adjustment in Vietnamese adolescents. Paper presented at the biennial meeting of the Society for Research in Child Development, Washington, DC.

Kagan, J. (1978, August). The parental love trap. *Psychology Today,* 54–61, 91.

Kahn, R. S., Wise, P. H., Kennedy, B. R., & Kawachi, I. (2000). State income inequality, household income, and maternal mental and physical health: Cross sectional national survey. *British Medical Journal, 321,* 1311–1315.

Kaplan, A. G., & Klein, R. (1985). The rational self in late adolescent women. *Works in progress* (Paper No. 17). Wellesley, MA: Stone Center Working Papers Series.

Karp, N. (1996). Legal problems of grandparents and other kinship caregivers. *Generations, 20,* 57–60.

Kashani, J., & Allan, W. (1998). *The impact of family violence on children and adolescents.* Thousand Oaks, CA: Sage.

Kashani, J. H., Daniel, A. E., Dandoy, A. C., & Holcomb, W. R. (1992). Family violence: Impact on children. *Journal of the American Academy of Child and Adolescent Psychiatry, 31,* 181–189.

Kaufman, G., & Uhlenberg, P. (1998). Effects of life course transitions on the quality of relationships between adult children and their parents. *Journal of Marriage and the Family, 60,* 924–938.

Kaufman, J., & Zigler, E. (1987). Do abused children become abusive parents? *American Journal of Orthopsychiatry, 57,* 186–192.

Kaufmann, R., & Kaufmann, F. (1980). The face schema in 3- and 4-month infants: The role of dynamic properties of the face. *Infant Behavior and Development, 3,* 331–339.

Kelly, J. (2000). Children's adjustment in conflicted marriage and divorce: A decade review of research. *Journal of the American Academy of Child and Adolescent Psychiatry, 39,* 963–973.

Kelly, J. R., Steinkamp, M. W., & Kelly, J. R. (1987). Later-life satisfaction: Does leisure contribute? *Leisure Sciences, 9,* 189–200.

Kelly, T., & Kropf, N. (1995). Stigmatized and perpetual parents: Older parents caring for children with life-long disabilities. *Journal of Gerontological Social Work, 24,* 3–16.

Kemp, V. H., Sibley, D. E., & Pond, E. F. (1990). A comparison of adolescent and adult mothers on factors affecting maternal role attainment. *Maternal Child Nursing Journal, 19,* 63–75.

Kempe, C., Silverman, F., Steele, B., Droegenmueller, W., & Silver, H. (1962). The battered child syndrome. *Journal of the American Medical Association, 181,* 17–24.

Kenny, M. (1987). The extent and function of parental attachment among first-year college students. *Journal of Youth and Adolescence, 16,* 17–29.

Kenny, M. E., & Hart, K. (1992). Relationship between parental attachment and eating disorders in an inpatient and a college sample. *Journal of Counseling Psychology, 39,* 521–526.

Keogh, J. (1977). The study of movement skill and development. *Quest (Monograph #28),* 76–80.

Kermani, H., & Brenner, M. (2000). Maternal scaffolding in the child's zone of proximal development across tasks: Cross-cultural perspectives. *Journal of Research in Childhood Education, 15,* 30–52.

Kinard, E. (2001). Perceived and actual academic competence in maltreated children. *Child Abuse and Neglect, 25,* 33–45.

Kitson, G. C. (1990). The multiple consequences of divorce: A decade review. *Journal of Marriage and the Family, 52,* 913–924.

Kivett, V. R. (1991). Centrality of the grandfather role among older rural black and white men. *Journal of Gerontology: Social Sciences, 45,* 250–258.

Kivnick, H. Q. (1982). *The meaning of grandparenthood.* Ann Arbor, MI: UMI Research.

Klerman, L. (1993). The relationship between adolescent parenthood and inadequate parenting. *Children and Youth Services, 15,* 309–320.

Klesges, R. (1993). Effects of television on metabolic rate: Potential implications for childhood obesity. *Pediatrics, 91,* 281–286.

Kluwer, E., Heesink, J., & van de Vliert, E. (2002). The division of labor in close relationships: An asymmetrical conflict issue. *Personal Relationships, 7,* 263–282.

Kooreman, P., & Kapteyn, A. (1987). A disaggregated analysis of the allocation of time within the household. *Journal of Political Economy, 95,* 223–249.

Kopp, C. B. (1982). Antecedents of self-regulation: A developmental perspective. *Developmental Psychology, 18,* 199–214.

Kornhaber, A. (1996). *Contemporary grandparenting.* Thousand Oaks, CA: Sage.

Kranzler, E. M., Shaffer, D., & Wasserman, G. (1990). Early childhood bereavement. *Journal of the American Academy of Child and Adolescent Psychiatry, 29,* 513–520.

Krevans, J., & Gibbs, J. (1996). Parents' use of inductive discipline: Relations to children's empathy and prosocial behavior. *Child Development, 67,* 3263–3277.

Kruk, E. (1994). The disengaged noncustodial father: Implications for social work practice with the divorced family. *Social Work, 39,* 15–25.

Kubler-Ross, E. (1969). *On death and dying.* New York: Macmillan.

Kuhn, B., Mayfield, J., & Kuhn, R. (1999). Clinical assessment of child and adolescent sleep disturbance. *Journal of Counseling and Development, 77,* 359–368.

Kupersmidt, J., Griesler, P., DeRosier, M., Patterson, C., & Davis, P. (1995). Childhood aggression and peer relations in the context of family and neighborhood factors. *Child Development, 66,* 360–375.

Kurdek, L. A. (1993). The allocation of household labor in gay, lesbian, and heterosexual married children. *Journal of Social Issues, 49,* 127–139.

Kurdek, L. A., Fine, M. A., & Sinclair, R. J. (1994). The relation between parenting transitions and adjustment in young adolescents: A multi-sample investigation. *Journal of Early Adolescence, 14,* 412–432.

Kurdek, L. A., Fine, M. A., & Sinclair, R. J. (1995). School adjustment in sixth graders: Parenting transitions, family climate, and peer norm effects. *Child Development, 66,* 430–445.

Lagerspetz, K., & Bjoerkqvist, K. (1994). Indirect aggression in boys and girls. In L. Rowell Huesmann (Ed.), *Aggressive behavior: Current perspectives* (pp. 131–150). New York: Plenum.

Laible, D., & Thompson, R. (2000). Mother–child discourse, attachment security, shared positive affect, and early conscience development. *Child Development, 71,* 1424–1440.

Lamb, M., & Elster, A. B. (1985). Adolescent mother–infant–father relationships. *Developmental Psychology, 21,* 768–773.

Lamb, M. E., Thompson, R. A., Gardner, W., Charnov, E. L., & Connell, J. P. (1985). Infant–mother attachment: The origins and developmental significance of individual differences in the Strange Situation: Its study and biological interpretation. *Behavioral and Brain Sciences, 7,* 127–147.

Lamborn, S. D., Mounts, N. S., Steinberg, L., & Dornbusch, S. M. (1991). Patterns of competence and adjustment among adolescents from authoritative, authoritarian, indulgent, and neglectful families. *Child Development, 62,* 1049–1065.

Landry, S., Smith, K., & Swank, P. (2001). Does early responsive parenting have a special importance for children's development or is consistency across early childhood necessary? *Developmental Psychology, 37,* 387–403.

Larson, E. (1998). Reframing the meaning of disability to families: The embrace of paradox. *Social Science and Medicine, 47,* 865–875.

Larson, R., & Richards, M. H. (1994). *Divergent realities: The emotional lives of mothers, fathers, and adolescents.* New York: Basic Books.

Larson, R., Richards, M., & Moneta, G. (1996). Changes in adolescents' interactions with their families from ages 10 to 18: Disengagement and transformation. *Developmental Psychology, 32,* 744–754.

LaSala, M. (2002). Walls and bridges: How coupled gay men and lesbians manage their inter-relationships. *Journal of Marriage and the Family, 28*, 327–339.

Laursen, B., Coy, K. C., & Collins, W. A. (1998). Reconsidering changes in parent–child conflict across adolescence: A meta-analysis. *Child Development, 69*, 817–832.

Laursen, B., & Hartup, W. (1989). The dynamics of preschool children's conflicts. *Merrill-Palmer Quarterly, 35*, 281–297.

Lawrence, R. (1998). *Breastfeeding: A guide for the medical profession* (5th ed.). St. Louis: Mosby.

Lawton, M. P., Brody, E. M., & Saperstein, A. R. (1989). A controlled study of respite service for caregivers of Alzheimer's patients. *Gerontologist, 29*, 8–16.

Leach, P. (1997). *Your baby and child: From birth to age 5.* New York: Knopf.

Leaper, C., Anderson, K., & Sanders, P. (1998). Moderators of gender effects on parents' talk to their children: A meta-analysis. *Developmental Psychology, 34*, 3–27.

Lee, C. M., & Gotlib, I. H. (1990). Family disruption, parent availability, and child adjustment. In R. Prinz (Ed.), *Advances in behavioral assessment of children and families* (Vol. 5, pp. 173–202). New York: Kingsley.

Lee, Y.-R., & Sung, K.-T. (1998). Cultural influences on caregiving burden: Cases of Koreans and Americans. *International Journal of Aging and Human Development, 46*, 125–141.

Leitch, M. L. (1998). Contextual issues in teen pregnancy: Refining our scope of inquiry. Comment on L. Blinn-Pike et al.: P. M. Camarena et al.; R. Solomon and C. P. Liefield. *Family Relations, 47*, 145–148.

Leonardari, A., & Kiosseoglou, G. (2000). The relationship of parental attachment and psychological separation to the psychological functioning of young adults. *The Journal of Social Psychology, 140*, 451–464.

Levine, R., Dixon, S., LeVine, S., Richman, A., Leiderman, P., Herbert K., et al. (1994). *Child care and culture: Lessons from Africa.* New York: Cambridge University Press.

Lewit, E., & Kerrebrock, N. (1998). Child indicators: Dental health. *The Future of Children: Protecting Children from Abuse and Neglect, 8*, 4–22.

Leyser, Y., & Heinze, T. (2001). Perspectives of parents of children who are visually impaired: Implications for the field. *RE:view, 33*, 37–48.

Lieberman, A. B. (1987). *Giving birth.* New York: St. Martin's Press.

Lieberman, A. F. (1993). *The emotional life of the toddler.* New York: Free Press.

Lindahl, K., & Malik, N. (1999). Marital conflict, family processes, and boys' externalizing behaviors in Hispanic American and European American families. *Journal of Clinical and Child Psychology, 28*, 12–24.

Lockery, S. (1991). Caregiving among racial and ethnic minority elders. *Generations, 15*, 58–62.

Logan, J., & Bian, F. (1999). Family values and coresidence with married children in urban China. *Social Forces, 77*, 1253–1282.

Love, J., Raikes, H., Paulsell, D., & Kisker, E. (2000). New directions for studying quality in programs for infants and toddlers. In D. Cryer & T. Harms (Eds.), *Infants and toddlers in out-of-home care* (pp. 117–162). Baltimore: Paul H. Brookes.

Lowenthal, B. (1999). Effects of maltreatment and ways to promote children's resiliency. *Childhood Education, 75*, 204–209.

Lubic, R. (1997). A missed opportunity. *Public Health Reports, 112*, 284–287.

Luke, B. (1993). Nutrition and prematurity. In F. Witter & L. Keith (Eds.), *Textbook of prematurity: Antecedents, treatment, and outcome* (pp. 25–38). Boston: Little, Brown.

Lynch, R., Thuli, K., & Groombridge, L. (1994). Person-first disability language: A pilot analysis of public perceptions. *Journal of Rehabilitation, 60*, 18–22.

Maccoby, E. E., & Martin, J. A. (1983). Socialization in the context of the family: Parent–child interaction. In E. M. Hetherington (Ed.), *Handbook of child psychology, Vol. 4: Socialization, personality and social development* (4th ed., pp. 1–102). New York: Wiley.

Mantzipoulos, P., & Oh-Hwang, Y. (1998). The relationship of psychosocial maturity to parenting quality and intellectual ability for American and Korean adolescents. *Contemporary Educational Psychology, 23*, 195–206.

Marano, H. (1997). Why Johnny can't play. A husband and wife team finds that kids' social skills come fundamentally from parents' everyday style of interacting with them. *Psychology Today, 30*, 22.

Marcia, J., Waterman, A., Matteson, D., Archer, S., & Orlofsky, J. (Eds.). (1993). *Ego identity: A handbook for psychosocial research.* New York: Springer-Verlag.

Margalit, M., & Almougy, K. (1991). Classroom behavior and family climate in students with learning disabilities and hyperactive behavior. *Journal of Learning Disabilities, 24*, 406–412.

Martin, M. J., & Pritchard, M. E. (1991). Factors associated with alcohol use in later adolescence. *Journal of Studies on Alcohol, 52*, 5–9.

Masahiro, Y. (2001). Parasite singles feed on family system. *Japan Quarterly, 48*, 10–16.

Maslow, A. (1970). *Motivation and Personality* (2nd ed.). New York: Harper & Row.

Masten, A., & Coatsworth, J. (1998). The development of competence in favorable and unfavorable environments: Lessons from research on successful children. *American Psychologist, 53*, 205–220.

Maurer, D., & Maurer, C. (1988). *The world of the newborn.* New York: Basic Books.

Mauro, C., & Harris, Y. (2000). The influence of maternal child-rearing attitudes and teaching behaviors on preschoolers' delay of gratification. *The Journal of Genetic Psychology, 161*, 292–306.

Mayseless, O., Daniel, R., & Sharabang, R. (1996). Adults' attachment patterns: Coping with separations. *Journal of Youth and Adolescence, 25*, 667–690.

McAdoo, H. (1995). Stress levels, family help patterns, and religiosity in middle- and working-class African American single mother households. *Journal of Black Psychology, 21*, 424–449.

McAnarna, E., & Hendee, W. (1989). Adolescent pregnancy and its consequences. *Journal of the American Medical Association, 262*, 74–77.

McCamish-Svenson, C., Samuelsson, G., & Hagberg, B. (1999). Social relationships and health as predictors of life satisfaction in old age: Results from a Swedish longitudinal study. *International Journal of Aging and Human Development, 48*, 301–324.

McCarthy, B. (1994). Youth on the street. Violent offenders and victims. In H. Coward (Ed.), *Anger in our city: Youth seeking meaning* (pp. 69–107). Victoria, British Columbia: Centre for Studies in Religion and Society.

McCarty, M., & Ashmead, D. (1999). Visual control of reaching and grabbing in infants. *Developmental Psychology, 35*, 620–631.

McClosky, L., Treviso, M., & Scionti, T. (2002). A comparative study of battered women and their children in Italy and the United States. *Journal of Family Violence, 17*, 53–74.

McCord, W., & McCord, J. (1959). *Origins of crime: A new evaluation of the Cambridge–Somerville study.* New York: Columbia University.

McDonald, M., Sigman, M., Espinosa, M., & Neumann, C. (1994). Impact of a temporary food shortage on children and their mothers. *Child Development, 65*, 404–415.

McLanahan, S., & Sandefur, G. (1994). *Growing up with a single parent: What hurts, what helps.* Cambridge, MA: Harvard University Press.

Miller, A. (1990). *For your own good: Hidden cruelty in child-rearing and the roots of violence* (H. Hannum & H. Hannum, Trans.). New York: Noonday Press.

Miller, B. D. (1995). Precepts and practices: Researching identity formation among India Hindu adolescents in the United States. *New Directions for Child Development, 67,* 71–85.

Minkler, M., & Roe, K. (1991). *Preliminary findings from the grandmother caregiver study of Oakland, California.* Berkeley: University of California Press.

Minuchin, S. (1974). *Families and family therapy.* Cambridge, MA: Harvard University Press.

Moen, P., & Yu, U. (1999). Having it all: Overall work/life success in two-earner families. In T. Parcel (Ed.), *Research in the sociology of work* (Vol. 7, pp. 109–139). Greenwich, CT: JAI Press.

Moerk, E. (2000). *The guided acquisition of first language skills.* Westport, CT: Ablex.

Mogelonsky, M. (1996). The rocky road to adulthood. Why more adults are living at home. *American Demographics, 18,* 26–29.

Monahan, D. (2001). Teen pregnancy prevention outcomes: Implications for social work practice. *Families in Society, 82,* 127–135.

Montmeyer, R. (1982). The relationship between parent–adolescent conflict and the amount of time adolescents spend alone and with parents, siblings, and peers. *Journal of Youth and Adolescence, 13,* 543–557.

Moon, S., & Hall, A. (1998). Family therapy with intellectually and creatively gifted children. *Journal of Marital and Family Therapy, 24,* 59–80.

Moore, L., Van Hasselt, V., Ammerman, R., & Hersen, M. (1994). The assessment and treatment of adolescents with visual impairments and their families. *Teaching Exceptional Children, 26,* 56–59.

Morelli, G., Rogoff, B., Oppenheim, D., & Goldsmith, D. (1992). Cultural variations in infants' sleeping arrangements. Questions of independence. *Developmental Psychology, 28,* 604–613.

Morin, S., & Welsh, L. (1996). Adolescents' perceptions and experiences of death and grieving. *Adolescence, 31,* 585–595.

Morrisette, P. (1996). Family therapist as consultant in foster care: Expanding the parameters of practice. *The American Journal of Family Therapy, 24,* 55–65.

Morrongiello, B., Fenwick, K., & Chance, G. (1998). Cross-modal learning in newborn infants: Inferences about properties of auditory–visual events. *Infant Behavior and Development, 21,* 543–553.

Munch, S., & Levick, S. (2001). "I'm special too": Promoting sibling adjustment in the neonatal intensive care unit. *Health and Social Work, 26,* 58–64.

Murphy, S. A., Johnson, C. C., Gupta, K. C., & Das, A. (1998). Broad-spectrum group treatment for parents bereaved by the violent deaths of their 12- to 28-year-old children: A randomized controlled trial. *Death Studies, 22,* 209–235.

Mussen, P. H., Conger, J. J., Kagan, J., & Huston, A. (1990). *Child development and personality* (7th ed.). New York: Harper & Row.

Myers, B., Smarsh, T., & Amlund-Hagen, K. (1999). Children of incarcerated mothers. *Journal of Child and Family Studies, 8,* 11–25.

Myers, M. G., Wagner, E. E., & Brown, S. A. (1997). Substance abuse. In V. B. Van Hasselt & M. Hersen (Eds.), *Handbook of psychological treatment proctocols for children and adolescent* (pp. 381–411). Mahwah, NJ: Erlbaum.

Nelson, J. (1998). The meaning of crying based on attachment theory. *Clinical Social Work, 26,* 9–22.

Newberger, E. (1991). Child abuse. In M. L. Rosenberg & M. A. Fenley (Eds.), *Violence in America: A public health approach* (pp. 51–78). New York: Oxford University Press.

Newman, B. S., & Muzzonigro, P. G. (1993). The effects of traditional family values on the coming out process of gay male adolescents. *Adolescence, 28,* 213–216.

Newman, K. (1988). *Falling from grace: The experience of downward mobility in the American middle class.* New York: Free Press.

Nickman, S., Silverman, P., & Normand, C. (1998). Children's construction of a deceased parent: The surviving parent's contribution. *American Journal of Psychiatry, 68,* 126–134.

Nock, S. (1998). The consequences of premarital fatherhood. *American Sociological Review, 63,* 250–263.

Noonan, A., Tennstedt, S., & Rebelsky, F. (1996). Making the best of it: Themes of meaning among informal caregivers to the elderly. *Journal of Aging Studies, 10,* 313–327.

Nydegger, C., & Mitteness, L. (1988). Etiquette and ritual in family conversation. *American Behavioral Scientist, 31,* 702–716.

Nydegger, C., & Mitteness, L. (1991). Fathers and their adult sons and daughters: *Marriage and Family Review, 16,* 3–4.

Nydegger, C., Mitteness, L., & O'Neil, J. (1983). Experiencing social generations: Phenomal dimensions. *Research on Aging, 5,* 527–546.

O'Brien Caughu, M., O'Campo, P., & Randolph, S. (2002). The influence of racial socialization on the cognitive and behavioral competence of African American preschoolers. *Child Development, 73,* 1611–1625.

O'Connor, T., Allen, J., Bell, K., & Hauser, S. (1996). Adolescent–parent relationships and leaving home in young adulthood. In J. Graber & J. Dubas (Eds.), *Leaving home: Understanding the transition to adulthood. New Directions for Child Development, 71.* San Francisco: Jossey-Bass/Pfeiffer.

Offer, D. (1969). *The psychological world of the teenager.* New York: Basic Books.

Offer, D., & Schonert-Reichl, K. A. (1992). Debunking the myths of adolescence: Findings from recent research. *Journal of the American Academy of Child and Adolescent Psychiatry, 31,* 1003–1014.

Oller, D., & Eilers, R. (1988). The role of audition in infant babbling. *Child Development, 59,* 441–449.

Orlofsky, J. (1993). Intimacy status: Theory and research. In J. E. Marcia, A. S. Waterman, D. R. Mateson, S. L. Archer, & J. L. Orlofsky (Eds.), *Ego identity: A handbook for psychosocial research* (pp. 111–133). New York: Springer-Verlag.

Orthner, D. K., & Mancini, J. A. (1990). Leisure impacts on family interaction and cohesion. *Journal of Leisure Research, 14,* 295–306.

Owusu-Bempah, J. (1995). Information about the absent parent as a factor in the well-being of children of single-parent families. *International Social Work, 38,* 253–275.

Paikoff, R. L., & Brooks-Gunn, J. (1991). Do parent–child relationships change during puberty? *Psychological Bulletin, 110,* 47–66.

Parish, T. S., & McCluskey, J. J. (1992). The relationship between parenting styles and young adults' self-concepts and evaluations of parents. *Adolescence, 27,* 915–918.

Parizkova, J. (1989). Age-dependent changes in dietary intake related to work output, physical fitness, and body composition. *American Journal of Clinical Nutrition, 49,* 962–967.

Parizkova, J. (1998). Interaction between physical activity and nutrition early in life and the impact on later development. *Nutrition Research Reviews, 11,* 71–90.

Pasztor, E. M., & Wynne, S. F. (1995). Foster parent retention and recruitment: The state of the art in practice and policy. Washington, DC: Child Welfare League of America.

Patterson, C. J. (1992). Children of lesbian and gay parents. *Child Development, 63,* 1025–1042.

Patterson, C. (1986). Performance models for antisocial boys. *American Psychologist, 41,* 432–444.

Patterson, C. J. (1995). Families of the baby boom: Parents' division of labor and children's adjustment. Special Issue: Sexual orientation and human development. *Developmental Psychology, 31*, 115–123.

Patterson, G., & Capaldi, D. (1991). Antisocial parents: Unskilled and vulnerable. In P. Cowan & E. M. Hetherington (Eds.), *Family Transitions* (pp. 195–218). Hillsdale, NJ: Erlbaum.

Patterson, G., & Dishion, T. (1985). Contributions of families and peers to delinquency. *Criminology, 23*, 63–79.

Patterson, G. R., Debaryshe, B. D., & Ramsey, E. (1989). A developmental perspective on antisocial behavior. *American Psychologist, 44*, 329–335.

Patterson, G. R., & Yoerger, K. (1997). A developmental model for late-onset delinquency. In D. W. Osgood (Ed.), *Motivation and delinquency* (pp. 119–177). Lincoln: University of Nebraska Press.

Paulson, S. E., Marchant, G. J., & Rothlisberg, B. A. (1998). Early adolescents' perceptions of patterns of parenting, teaching, and school atmosphere: Implications for achievement. *Journal of Early Adolescence, 18*, 5–26.

Paxton, W., Wertheim, E., Gibbons, D., Szmukler, G., Hillier, L., & Petrovoch, J. (1991). Body image satisfaction, dieting beliefs, and weight-loss behaviors in adolescent girls and boys. *Journal of Youth and Adolescence, 20*, 361–380.

Pears, K., & Capaldi, D. (2001). Intergenerational transmission of abuse: A two-generational prospectus study of an at-risk sample. *Child Abuse and Neglect, 25*, 1439–1461.

Perry, B. (2001). Death and loss: Helping children manage their grief. *Scholastic Early Childhood Today, 15*, 22–23.

Peters, M. F. (1985). Racial socialization of young black children. In H. P. McAdoo & J. McAdoo (Eds.), *Black children, social educational, and parental environments* (pp. 159–173). Beverly Hills: CA: Sage.

Petersen, A. (1988). Adolescent development. *Annual Review of Psychology, 39*, 583–607.

Petersen, A. C. (1987, September). Those gangly years. *Psychology Today*, 28–34.

Petersen, A. C., Compas, B. E., Brooks-Gunn, J., Stemmler, M., Ey, S., & Grant, K. E. (1993). Depression in adolescence. *American Psychologist, 48*, 155–168.

Petersen, A. C., Leffert, N., Graham, B., Alwin, J., & Ding, S. (1997). Promoting mental health during the transition into adolescence. In J. Schulenberg, J. Moggs, & K. Hurrelman (Eds.), *Health risks and developmental transitions during adolescence* (pp. 471–497). New York: Cambridge Press.

Peterson, P., Hawkins, J., Abbott, R., & Catalano, R. (1994). Disentangling the effects of parental drinking, family management, and parental alcohol norms on current drinking by Black and White adolescents. *Journal of Research on Adolescence, 4*, 203–227.

Petitto, A., & Marentette, P. (1991). Babbling in the manual mode: Evidence for the ontogeny of language. *Science, 251*, 1493–1496.

Petitto, L. A., Holowka, S., Sergio, L., & Ostry, D. (2001). Language rhythms in baby hand movements. *Nature, 413*, 35–41.

Pfeffer, C. R. (1986). *The suicidal child*. New York: Guilford Press.

Phelps, L., Johnson, L. S., Jiminez, D. P., Wilczenski, F. L., Andrea, R. K., & Healy, R. W. (1993). Figure preference, body dissatisfaction, and body distortion in adolescence. *Journal of Adolescent Research, 8*, 297–310.

Phinney, J., Romero, I., & Nava, M. (2001). The role of language, parents, and peers in ethnic identity among adolescents in immigrant families. *Journal of Youth and Adolescence, 30*, 135–153.

Phinney, J. S. (1990). Ethnic identity in adolescents and adults: A review of research. *Psychological Bulletin, 108*, 499–514.

Phua, V. C., Kaufman, G., & Park, S. (2001). Strategic adjustments of elderly Asian Americans: Living arrangements and headship. *Journal of Comparative Family Studies, 32*, 263–281.

Piaget, J., & Inhelder, B. (1958). *The growth of logical thinking from childhood to adolescence* (A. Parsona & S. Seagrin, Trans.). New York: Basic Books.

Piaget, J., & Inhelder, B. (1969). *The psychology of the child* (H. Weaver, Trans.). New York: Basic Books.

Piazza, C., & Fisher, W. (1991). A faded bedtime with response cost protocol for treatment of multiple sleep problems in children. *Journal of Applied Behavior Analysis, 24*, 129–140.

Pillemer, K., & Suitor, J. J. (1991). "Will I ever escape my child's problems?" Effects of adult children's problems on elderly parents. *Journal of Marriage and the Family, 53*, 585–594.

Planinsec, J. (2002). Relations between the motor and cognitive dimensions of preschool girls and boys. *Perceptual and Motor Skills, 94*, 415–432.

Plomin, R., & Daniels, D. (1987). Why are children in the same family so different from one another? *Behavioral and Brain Sciences, 10*, 1–60.

Podolski, C. (2001). Parent stress and coping in relation to child ADHD severity and associated child disruptive behavior problems. *Journal of Clinical Child Psychiatry, 30*, 503–513.

Pollitt, E., Golub, M., Gorman, K., Grantham-McGregor, S., Levitsky, D., Schurch, B., et al. (1996). A reconceptualization of the effects of undernutrition on children's biological, psychosocial, and behavioral development. *Social Policy Report: Society for Research in Child Development, 10*, 1–21.

Popkin, M. (1987). *Active parenting: Teaching cooperation, courage, and responsibility.* San Francisco: Perennial Library.

Pratt, C. (1970). *I learn from children.* New York: Harper & Row.

Presser, H. (1994). Employment schedules among dual-earner spouses and the division of household labor by gender. *American Sociological Review, 59*, 348–364.

Protinsky, H., & Shilts, L. (1990). Adolescent substance abuse and family cohesion. *Family Therapy, 17*, 173–175.

Pruchno, R., & Johnson, K. (1996). Research on grandparenting: Review of current studies and future needs. *Generations, 20*, 65–70.

Purkey, W., Schmidt, J. J., & Benedict, G. C. (1990). *Invitational learning for counseling and development.* Ann Arbor, MI: ERIC Counseling & Personnel Services Clearinghouse.

Radbill, S. (1974). A history of child abuse and infanticide. In R. E. Helfer & C. H. Kempe (Eds.), *The battered child* (2nd ed., pp. 3–21). Chicago: University of Chicago Press.

Ramirez, O., & Acre, C. (1981). The contemporary Chicano family: An empirically based review. In A. Baron, Jr. (Ed.), *Exploration in Chicano psychology* (pp. 3–28). New York: Praeger.

Rao, U., Weissman, M., Martin, J., & Hammond, R. (1993). Childhood depression and risk of suicide: A preliminary report of a longitudinal study. *Journal of the American Academy of Child and Adolescent Psychiatry, 32*, 21–27.

Raveis, V., Siegel, K., & Karus, D. (1999). Children's psychological distress following the death of a parent. *Journal of Youth and Adolescence, 28*, 165–180.

Raymond, J. (2000). The joy of empty nesting. *American Demographics, 22*, 48–54.

Reed, D., & Reed, E. (1997). Children of incarcerated parents. *Social Justice, 24*, 152–169.

Rice, F. P. (1997). *Child and adolescent development.* Upper Saddle River, NJ: Merrill/Prentice Hall.

Richlin-Klonsky, J., & Bengston, V. (1996). Pulling together, drifting apart: A longitudinal case study of a four-generation family. *Journal of Aging Studies, 10*, 255–279.

Riegel, K. F. (1976). The dialects of human development. *American Psychologist, 31*, 689–700.

Roan, C., & Raley, R. K. (1996). Intergenerational coresidence and contact: A longitudinal analysis of adult children's response to their mother's widowhood. *Journal of Marriage and the Family, 58*, 708–717.

Robinson, C., Wright, L., & Watson, W. (1994). A nontraditional approach to family violence. *Archives of Psychiatric Nursing, 8*, 30–37.

Robinson, L. (2000). Interpersonal relationship quality in young adulthood: A gender analysis. *Adolescence, 35*, 775–784.

Roche, T. (2000). The crisis of foster care. *Time, 156*, 74–82.

Rogoff, B. (1990). *Apprenticeship in thinking: Cognitive development in social context.* New York: Oxford University Press.

Rogoff, B., Mistry, J., Goncu, A., & Mosier, C. (1993). Guided participation in cultural activity by toddlers and caregivers. *Monographs of the Society for Research in Child Development, 58* (Serial No. 236).

Roosa, M. W., Fitzgerald, H. E., & Carlson, N. A. (1982). A comparison of teenage and older mothers: A systems analysis. *Journal of Marriage and the Family, 44*, 367–377.

Rosen, H. (1984–1985). Prohibitions against mourning in childhood sibling loss. *Omega, 15*, 307–316.

Rosen, K., & Stith, S. (1993). Intervention strategies for treating women in violent relationships. *Family Relations, 42*, 427–433.

Rosenberg, M., & Guttman, J. (2001). Structural boundaries of single-parent families and children's adjustment. *Journal of Divorce and Remarriage, 36*, 83–98.

Rosenblum, G. D., & Lewis, M. (1999). The relations between body image, physical attractiveness, and body mass in adolescence. *Child Development, 70*, 50–64.

Rosenfeld, A. A., Pilowsky, D. J., Fine, P., Thorpe, M., Fein, E., Simms, M. O., et al. (1997). Foster care: An update. *Journal of American Academy of Child and Adolescent Psychiatry, 36*, 448–457.

Rosenfield, A., & Wise, N. (2000). *The Over-Scheduled Child. How to Avoid the Hyper-Parenting Trap.* New York: St. Martin's Press.

Rosenthal, P. A. (1980). Short-term family therapy and pathological grief resolution with children and adolescents. *Family Processes, 19*, 151–159.

Rossi, A., & Rossi, P. (1990). *Of human bonding: Parent–child relations across the life course.* New York: Aldine de Gruyter.

Rothbaum, F., Pott, M., & Azuma, H. (2000). The development of close relationships in Japan and the United States: Paths of symbiotic harmony and generative tensions. *Child Development, 71*, 1121–1142.

Rotheram-Borus, M. J. (1993). Suicidal behavioral and risk factors among runaway youth. *American Journal of Psychiatry, 150*, 103–107.

Rotheram-Borus, M. J., Koopman, C., & Ehrhardt, C. (1991). Homeless youths and HIV infection. *American Psychologist, 46*, 1188–1197.

Rotheram-Borus, M., & Wyche, K. (1994). Ethnic differences in identity development in the United States. In S. L. Archer (Ed.), *Interventions for adolescent identity development.* Thousand Oaks, CA: Sage.

Ryff, C., Lee, Y., Essex, M., & Schmitte, P. (1994). My children and me: Mid-life evaluations of grown children and of self. *Psychology and Aging, 9*, 195–205.

Sagi, A., van Ijzendoorn, M., Aviezer, O., Donnell, F., & Mayseless, O. (1994). Sleeping out of the home in a kibbutz communal arrangement: It makes a difference for infant–mother attachment. *Child Development, 65*, 992–1004.

Sarigiani, P., Heath, P., & Camarena, P. (2003). The significance of parental depressed mood for young adolescents' emotional and family experiences. *Journal of Early Adolescence.*

Savin-Williams, R. C. (1989). Coming out to parents and self-esteem among gay and lesbian youths. *Journal of Homosexuality, 18*, 1–35.

Savin-Williams, R. C., & Demo, D. H. (1983). Conceiving or misconceiving the self: Issues in adolescent self-esteem. *Journal of Early Adolescence, 3*, 121–140.

Scarr, D. (1992). Developmental theories for the 1990s: Development and individual differences. *Child Development, 63*, 1–19.

Schlegel, A., & Barry, H. (1991). *Adolescence: An anthropological inquiry.* New York: Free Press.

Sedney, M., & Baker, J. (1994). "The story" of a death: Therapeutic considerations with bereaved families. *Journal of Marriage and Family Therapy, 20*, 287–296.

Seixas, J., & Youcha, G. (1985). *Children of alcoholism.* New York: Crown.

Serpell, R. (1979). How specific are perceptual skills? A cross-cultural study of pattern reproduction. *British Journal of Psychology, 70*, 365–380.

Shaffer, D., Fisher, P., & Dulcan, M. (1996). The NIMH Diagnostic Interview for Children version 2.3 (DISC-2.3): Description, acceptability, prevalence, rates, and performance in the MECA study. *Journal of the American Academy of Child and Adolescent Psychiatry, 35*, 865–877.

Shagle, S. C., & Barber, B. K. (1994, February). *Effects of parenting variables, self-derogation, and depression on adolescent suicide ideation.* Paper presented at the biennial meeting of the Society for Research on Adolescence, San Diego, CA.

Shapiro, J. (1996). Custody and conduct: How the law fails lesbian and gay parents and their children. *Indiana Law Journal, 71*, 623–671.

Shaw, J., Lewis, J., Loeb, A., Rosado, J., & Rodriquez, R. (2001). A comparison of Hispanic and African-American sexually abused girls and their families. *Child Abuse and Neglect, 25*, 1363–1379.

Shek, D. T. L., & Chen, L. K. (1999). Hong Kong Chinese parents' perceptions of the ideal child. *The Journal of Psychology, 133*, 291–302.

Shiono, P., Rauh, V., Park, M., Lederman, S., & Zuskar, D. (1997). Ethnic differences in birthweight: The role of lifestyle and other factors. *American Journal of Public Health, 87*, 787–793.

Silbereisen, R. K., Meschke, L. L., & Schwarz, B. (1996). Leaving the parental home: Predictors for young adults raised in the former East and West Germany. In J. Graber & J. Dubas (Eds.), *Leaving home: Understanding the transition to adulthood. New Directions in Child Development, 71*, 71–86.

Silverstein, M., & Bengtson, V. (1994). Does intergenerational social support influence the psychological well-being of older parents? The contingencies of declining health and widowhood. Part of a symposium on: Frailty and its consequences. *Social Science and Medicine, 38*, 943–957.

Singer, J., Fuller, B., Keiley, M., & Wolf, A. (1998). Early child care selection: Variation by geographic location, maternal characteristics, and family structure. *Developmental Psychology, 34*, 1129–1144.

Skinner, B. F. (1950). Are theories of learning necessary? *Psychological Review, 57*, 193–216.

Skinner, B. F. (1974). *About behaviorism.* New York: Knopf.

Smetana, J. (1988). Concepts of self and social convention: Adolescents' and parents' reasoning about hypothetical and actual family conflicts. In M. Gunnar & W. A. Collins (Eds.), *Minnesota Symposium on Child Psychology: Vol. 21. Development during the transitions to adolescence* (pp. 79–122). Hillsdale, NJ: Erlbaum.

Smetana, J. (1989). Adolescents' and parents' reasoning about actual family conflict. *Child Development, 59*, 1052–1067.

Smetana, J., Abernathy, A., & Harris, A. (2000). Adolescent–parent interactions in middle-class African American families: Longitudinal change and contextual variation. *Journal of Family Psychology, 14*, 458–474.

Smetana, J., & Asquith, R. (1994). Adolescents' and parents' conceptions of parental authority and personal autonomy. *Child Development, 65,* 1147–1162.

SmithBattle, L. (1996). Intergenerational ethics of caring for adolescent mothers and their children. *Family Relations, 45,* 56–64.

Spitz, R. A. (1954). Unhappy and fatal outcomes of emotional deprivation and stress in infancy. In I. Galdston (Ed.), *Beyond the germ theory.* Washington, DC Health Education Council.

Spitze, G., & Logan, J. (1992). Helping as a component of parent–adult child relations. *Research on Aging, 14,* 291–312.

Spitze, G., Logan, J., & Joseph, G. (1994). Middle generation roles and the well-being of men and women. *Journal of Gerontology, 49,* 107–116.

Spock, B. (1946). *The pocket book of baby and child care.* New York: Pocket Books.

Spock, B. (1985). *Baby and child care* (Rev. ed.). New York: Simon & Schuster.

Spock, B., & Rothenberg, M. (1985). *Baby and child care.* New York: Dutton.

Sprouse, C., Hall, C., Webster, R., & Bolen, L. (1998). Social perception in students with learning disabilities and attention deficit/hyperactivity disorder. *Journal of Nonverbal Behavior, 22,* 125–134.

Steinbeck, K. (2001). Obesity in children—The importance of physical activity—Proceedings of the Kellogg's Nutrition Symposium 2000, Sydney, Australia, 8 August 2000. *Australian Journal of Nutrition and Dietetics, 58,* 28–32.

Steinberg, L. (1990). Autonomy, conflict, and harmony in the family relationship. In S. Feldman & G. Elliott (Eds.), *At the threshold: The developing adolescent* (pp. 255–276). Cambridge, MA: Harvard University Press.

Steinberg, L. (1996). *Beyond the classroom: Why school reform has failed and what parents need to do.* New York: Simon & Schuster.

Steinberg, L. (2000, April). *We know some things: Parent–adolescent relations in retrospect and prospect.* Address presented at the biennial meeting of the Society for Research on Adolescence, Chicago.

Steinberg, L., Fletcher, A., & Darling, N. (1994). Parental monitoring and peer influences on adolescent substance abuse. *Pediatrics, 93,* 1060–1064.

Steinberg, L., & Levine, A. (1997). *You and your adolescent: A parent's guide for ages 10 to 20* (Rev. ed.). New York: Harper-Collins.

Steinberg, L., Mounts, N., Lamborn, S., & Dornbusch, S. (1991). Authoritative parenting and adolescent adjustment across various ecological niches. *Journal of Research on Adolescence, 1,* 19–36.

Steinberg, L., & Steinberg, W. (1994). *Crossing paths: How your child's adolescence triggers your own crisis.* New York: Simon & Schuster.

Stern, D. N., Beebe B., Jaffe, J., & Bennett, S. L. (1977). The infant's stimulus world during social interaction: A study of caregiver behaviors with particular reference to repetition and timing. In H. R. Schaffer (Ed.), *Studies in mother infant interaction* (pp. 177–202). London: Academic Press.

Stevens, V., Bourdeaudhuij, I., & Oost, P. (2002). Relationship of the family environment to children's involvement in bully/victim problems at school. *Journal of Youth and Adolescence, 31,* 419–428.

Stevenson, H. C. (1994). Racial socialization in African American families: The art of balancing intolerance and survival. *The Family Journal: Counseling and Therapy for Couples and Families, 2,* 190–198.

Stevenson, H. C. (1995). Relationship of adolescent perceptions of racial socialization to racial identity. *Journal of Black Psychology, 21,* 49–70.

Stevenson-Hinde, J., & Shouldice, A. (1995). Maternal interactions and self-reports related to attachment classifications at 4.5 years. *Child Development, 66,* 583–596.

Stewart, S. (1999). Nonresident mothers' and fathers' social contact with children. *Journal of Marriage and the Family, 61,* 894–907.

Stinnett, N., & DeFrain, J. (1989). The healthy family: Is it possible? In M. J. Fine (Ed.), *The second handbook on parent education* (pp. 53–71). San Francisco: Academic Press.

Stone, N. M., & Stone, S. F. (1983). The prediction of successful foster placement. *Social Casework, 64,* 11–19.

Strayhorn, J. M., Weidman, C. S., & Larson, D. (1990). A measure of religiousness and its relation to parent and child mental health variables. *Journal of Community Psychology, 18,* 34–43.

Strength, J. M. (1991). Factors influencing the mother–child relationship following the death of the father and how that relationship affects the child's functioning. *Dissertation Abstracts International, 52*(06): 3310B.

Suarez-Orozco, C., & Suarez-Orozco, M. (1996). *Transformations: Migration, family life, and achievement motivation among Latino adolescents.* Palo Alto, CA: Stanford University Press.

Suitor, J., & Pillemer, K. (1988). Explaining intergenerational conflict when adult children and elderly parents live together. *Journal of Marriage and the Family, 50,* 1037–1047.

Suitor, J., Pillemer, K., Keeton, S., & Robison, J. (1994). Aged parents and aging children: Determinants of relationship quality. In R. Blieszner & V. Bedford (Eds.), *Aging and the Family* (pp. 223–242). Westport, CT: Praeger.

Synnott, A. (1988). Little angels, little devils: A sociology of children. In G. Handel (Ed.), *Childhood socialization.* New York: Aldine De Gruyter.

Szinovacz, M., & Davey, A. (2002). Retirement effects on parent–adult contacts. *Gerontologist, 41,* 191–200.

Takas, M. (1995). Grandparents raising grandchildren: A guide to finding help and hope. New York: Brookdale Foundation.

Taylor, R. D. (1997). The effects of economic and social stressors on parenting and adolescent adjustment in African-American families. In R. D. Taylor & M. C. Wang (Eds.), *Social and emotional adjustment and family relations in ethnic minority families* (pp. 35–52). Mahwah, NJ: Erlbaum.

Taylor, R. J., Chatters, L. M., Tucker, M. B., & Lewis, E. (1990). Developments in research on black families: A decade review. *Journal of Marriage and the Family, 52,* 993–1014.

Teller, D. (1997). First glances: The vision of infants. *Investigative Ophthalmology & Visual Science, 38,* 2183–2203.

Thiruchelvam, D., Charach, A., & Schachar, R. (2001). Moderators and mediators of long-term adherence to stimulant treatment in children with ADHD. *Journal of the American Academy of Child and Adolescent Psychiatry, 40,* 922–928.

Thomas, R. M. (2000). *Comparing theories of child development* (5th ed.). Belmont, CA: Wadsworth/Thomson Learning.

Thompson, R. (1988). The effects of infant day care through the prism of attachment theory: A critical appraisal. *Early childhood research quarterly, 3,* 273–282.

Thompson, R. A., & Lamb, M. E. (1983). Security of attachment and stranger sociability in infancy. *Developmental Psychology, 19,* 184–191.

Timpka, T., & Lindqvist, K. (2001). Evidence-based prevention of acute injuries in a WHO Safe Community. *British Journal of Sports Medicine, 35,* 20–27.

Toews, M., & McHenry, P. (2001). Court-related predictors of parental cooperation and conflict after divorce. *Journal of Divorce and Remarriage, 35,* 57–73.

Tomb, D. A. (1991). The runaway adolescent. In M. Lewis (Ed.), *Child and adolescent psychiatry* (pp. 1066–1071). Baltimore: Williams & Wilkins.

Townsend, A., Noelker, L., Deimling, G., & Bass, D. (1989). Longitudinal impact of interhousehold caregiving stressors. *Psychology and Aging, 4,* 393–401.

Trawick-Smith, J. (2000). *Early childhood development.* Upper Saddle River, NJ: Merrill/Prentice Hall.

Tripp, R. (1970). *The international thesaurus of quotations.* New York: Harper & Row.

Troiano, R., Briefel, R., Carroll, M., & Bialostosky, K. (2000). Energy and fat intakes of children and adolescents in the United States: Data from the national health and nutrition examination surveys. *The American Journal of Clinical Nutrition, 72,* Suppl. 1343S–1353S.

Tse, L. (1999). Finding a place to be: Ethnic identity exploration of Asian Americans. *Adolescence, 34,* 121–138.

Umberson, D. (1992). Relationships between adult children and their parents: Psychological consequences for both generations. *Journal of Marriage and the Family, 54,* 665–674.

Umberson, D., & Chen, M. (1994). Effects of a parent's death on adult children: Relationship salience and reaction to loss. *American Sociological Review, 59,* 152–168.

UNICEF. (1995). *The state of the world's children, 1995.* New York: Oxford University Press.

UNICEF. (1998). *The state of the world's children, 1998.* New York: Oxford University Press.

U.S. Bureau of the Census. (1992). Statistical abstract of the United States, 1992 (112th ed.). Washington, DC: U.S. Department of Commerce.

U.S. Bureau of the Census. (1996). Statistical abstract of the United States, 1996 (116th ed.). Washington, DC: U.S. Department of Commerce.

U.S. Bureau of the Census. (1998). Statistical abstract of the United States, 1998 (118th ed.). Washington, DC: U.S. Department of Commerce.

U.S. Bureau of the Census. (1999). CH-7. Grandchildren living in the home of their grandparents: 1970 to present, Internet release, based on Current Population Reports Series P20-514, "Marital Status and Living Arrangements: March 1998."

U.S. Bureau of the Census. (2000). Statistical Abstracts of the U.S.: 2000: Report No. # 69. Children under 18 years old by presence of parents: 1980 to 1998.

Valenza, E., Simion, F., & Cassia, V. (1996). Face preference at birth. *Journal of Experimental Psychology. Human Perception and Performance, 22,* 892–903.

Vandell, D., & Bailey, M. (1995). Conflict between siblings. In C. Shantz & W. Hartup (Eds.), *Conflict in child and adolescent development* (pp. 242–269). New York: Cambridge University Press.

van Ijzendoorn, M. (1995). Adult attachment representations, parental responsiveness, and infant attachment: A meta-analysis. *Psychological Bulletin, 117,* 387–403.

Van Schaick, K., & Stollberg, A. (2001). The impact of parental involvement and parental divorce on young adults' intimate relationships. *Journal of Marriage and the Family, 36,* 99–121.

Verschueren, K., Alfons, M., & Schoefs, V. (1996). The internal working model of the self, attachment, and competence in five-year-olds. *Child Development, 67,* 2493–2511.

Verville, E. (1985). *Behavior problems of preschool children.* Springfield, IL: Thomas.

Visher, J. (1994). Concerns and issues faced by families headed by a lesbian couple. *Families in Society, 75,* 27–35.

Volkmar, F., Cook, E., & Pomeroy, J. (1999). Practice parameters for the assessment and treatment of children, adolescents, and adults with autism and other pervasive developmental disorders. *Journal of the American Academy of Child and Adolescent Psychiatry, 38,* 32S–54S.

Vygotsky, L. (1978). *Mind in society: The development of higher psychological processes.* Cambridge, MA: Harvard University Press.

Waldrup, D., & Weber, J. (2001). From grandparent to caregiver: The stress and satisfaction of raising grandchildren. *Families in Society, 82*, 461–462.

Walker, L., & Taylor, H. (1991). Family interactions and the development of moral reasoning. *Child Development, 62*, 264–283.

Wallerstein, J. S. (1989). Children after divorce: Wounds that don't heal. *The New York Times Magazine, 19–21*, 41–44.

Watson, J. B., & Watson, R. (1928). *The psychological care of the infant and child.* New York: Norton.

Wegscheider, S. (1989). *Another chance: Hope and health for the alcoholic family.* Palo Alto, CA: Science and Behavior Books.

Weinberg, M., & Tronick, E. (1996). Infant affective reactions to the resumption of maternal interaction after the still-face. *Child Development, 67*, 905–914.

Weinberg, M., Tronick, E., & Cohn, J. (1999). Gender differences in emotional expressivity and self-regulation during early infancy. *Developmental Psychology, 35*, 175–188.

Weinfield, N., Sroufe, L., & Egeland, B. (2000). Attachment from infancy to early adulthood in a high-risk sample: Continuity, discontinuity, and their correlates. *Child Development, 71*, 695–703.

Weisner, T. (1982). Sibling interdependence and child-caretaking: A cross-cultural view. In M. Lamb & B. Sutton-Smith (Eds.), *Sibling relationships: Their nature and significance across the life span* (pp. 307–312). Hillsdale, NJ: Erlbaum.

Wels, F., Linssen, H., & Abna, R. (2000). The parental bond and the well-being of adolescents and young adults. *Journal of Youth and Adolescence, 29*, 307–318.

Wenk, D., Hardesty, C., & Morgan, C. (1994). The influence of parental involvement on the well-being of sons and daughters. *Journal of Marriage and the Family, 56*, 229–234.

Wentzel, K. R., & Feldman, S. S. (1993). Parental predictors of boys' self-restraint and motivation to achieve at school: A longitudinal study. *Journal of Adolescence, 13*, 183–203.

Werner, E. E., & Smith, R. S. (1989). *Vulnerable but invincible: A longitudinal study of resilient children and youth.* New York: Adams, Bannister, & Cox.

Whipple, E., Fitzgerald, H., & Zucker, R. (1995). Parent–child interactions in alcoholic and nonalcoholic families. *American Journal of Orthopsychiatry, 65*, 153–159.

White, D., Saudargas, R., & Zanolli, K. (1991). LD children's regular classroom behavior before and after identification and placement. *Learning Disability Quarterly, 13*, 196–204.

White, L. (1992). The effect of parental divorce and remarriage on parental support for adult children. *Journal of Family Issues, 13*, 234–250.

Whiting, B., & Edwards, C. (1988). *Children of different worlds: The formation of social behavior.* Cambridge, MA: Harvard University Press.

Widom, C. (1989). The cycle of violence. *Science, 244*, 160–166.

Wiener, J., Harris, P., & Shirer, C. (1990). Achievement and social–behavioral correlates of peer status in LD children. *Learning Disability Quarterly, 13*, 114–127.

Wilson, M. N. (1989). Child development in the context of the black extended family. *American Psychologist, 44*, 380–383.

Windle, M. (1996). Effect of parental drinking on adolescents. *Alcohol Health and Research World, 20*, 181–184.

Wolke, D., Woods, S., & Bloomfield, L. (2000). The association between direct and relational bullying and behavior problems among primary school children. *The Journal of Child Psychology and Psychiatry and Allied Disciplines, 41*, 989–1002.

Wong, C. A. (1997, April). *What does it mean to be African-American or European-American growing up in a multi-ethnic community?* Paper presented at the biennial meeting of the Society for Research in Child Development, Washington, DC.

Wood, D., Bruner, J., & Ross, G. (1976). The role of tutoring in problem solving. *Journal of Child Psychology and Psychiatry, 17*, 89–100.

Woodward, A., & Markman, E. (1998). Early word learning. In W. Damon, D. Kuhn, & R. Siegler (Eds.), *Handbook of child psychology, Vol. 2: Cognition, perception and language* (5th ed., pp. 371–420). New York: Wiley.

Worden, J. W. (1996). *Children in grief: When a parent dies.* New York: Guilford Press.

Wyman, P., Cowen, E., Work, W., Hoyt-Meyers, L., Magnus, K., & Fagen, D. (1999). Caregiving and developmental factors differentiating young at-risk urban children showing resilient versus stress-affected outcome: A replication and extension. *Child Development, 70*, 645–659.

Yegidis, B. (1992). Family violence: Contemporary research findings and practice issues. *Community Mental Health Journal, 28*, 519–530.

Yoder, K. A., Hoyt, D. R., & Whitbeck, L. B. (1998). Suicide behavior in homeless and runaway adolescents. *Journal of Youth and Adolescence, 27*, 753–772.

Young, B., Dixon-Woods, M., Findlay, M., & Heney, D. (2002). Parenting in a crisis: Conceptualizing mothers of children with cancer. *Social Science and Medicine, 55*, 1835–1847.

Young, D., & Smith, C. (2000). When moms are incarcerated: The needs of children, mothers, and caregivers. *Families in Society, 81*, 130–141.

Zarit, S., & Eggebeen, D. (1995). Parent–child relationships in adulthood and old age. In M. Bornstein (Ed.), *Handbook of parenting, Vol. 1: Children and parenting* (pp. 119–140). Hillsdale, NJ: Erlbaum.

Zarit, S. H., Todd, P. A., & Zarit, J. M. (1986). Subjective burden of husbands as caregivers: A longitudinal study. *Gerontologist, 26*, 260–266.

Zabelski, M. (2001). Encouraging self-esteem in children: A parent's view. *RE:view, 33*, 99–101.

Zhou, M. (1997). Growing up in America: The challenge confronting immigrant children and children of immigrants. *Annual Review of Sociology, 23*, 63–95.

Zinsmeister, K. (1996). Divorce's toll on children. *The American Enterprise, 7*, 39–44.

Zupanick, C. (1994). Adult children of dysfunctional families: Treatment from a disenfranchised grief perspective. *Death Studies, 18*, 183–195.

Zuravin, S. (1988). Child maltreatment and teenage first births: A relationship mediated by chronic socio-demographic stress? *American Journal of Orthopsychiatry, 58*, 91–102.

Zuravin, S. J., & DiBlasio, F. A. (1992). Child-neglecting adolescent mothers: How do they differ from their maltreating counterparts? *Journal of Interpersonal Violence, 7*, 471–489.

Author Index

Abbott, R., 168
Abel, M., 59
Abernathy, A., 157, 158, 161
Abna, R., 176
Abramson, H., 111
Acock, A. C., 41
Acre, C., 180
Adelson, J., 157
Ainsworth, M. D. S., 8, 9, 53, 67, 68, 69, 92, 176
Aldous, J., 218
Alfons, M., 92
Allan, W., 242, 250
Allen, J. P., 150, 151, 161
Allen, S., 107
Almougy, K., 230
Alwin, D. F., 33
Alwin, J., 164
Amato, P., 202
Amato, P. R., 41
Ambert, A., 188
American Psychiatric Association, 231
Amlund-Hagen, K., 278
Ammerman, R., 238
Anders, T., 75
Anderson, K., 290
Andrea, R. K., 166
Andrews, J., 165
Angell, G., 262, 263
Anglin, J., 139
Ansbaugh, R., 112
Antonio, J., 174
Aquilino, W., 200, 201, 202
Archer, S., 152
Aries, P., 1
Arlin, P. K., 183
Armstrong, N., 128, 131, 132
Arnett, J. J., 31, 32, 148, 158, 159, 162, 300
Arroyo, C. G., 35
Asarnov, J. R., 126,164
Ashmead, D., 77
Asquith, R., 158
Atchley, R. C., 216, 221, 222

Aunola, K., 26, 27, 120, 121, 141, 247
Aviezer, O., 68
Azuma, H., 159

Baglio, C., 244
Bailey, M., 113, 114
Baillargeon, R., 136, 256
Baker, J., 74, 102, 262, 263
Baldwin, A. L., 51
Baldwin, C., 51
Ball, H., 68
Bamford, F. N., 75
Bandura, A., 14, 302, 303
Banez, G., 125, 126
Bankoff, E. A., 217
Bannister, R., 75
Bar-Haim, Y., 92
Barber, B. K., 165
Baris, M., 125
Barkley, R. A., 232
Barnes, G., 247
Barnett, D., 92, 113
Barnett, M., 307, 309
Barrera, M., 247
Barrett, D., 127
Barry, F., 128
Barry, H., 36, 113, 159, 160
Barton, K., 244
Barush, A. S., 213
Bass, D., 214
Bates, J. E., 92
Batistuta, M., 150, 305
Baum, A. C., 52
Baumrind, D., 2, 3, 4, 25, 26, 27, 28, 29, 32, 33, 34, 120, 121, 125, 145, 146, 147–148, 152, 169, 176, 248, 281
Bean, F., 180
Beatty, V., 62
Beaty, L. A., 157
Beebe, B., 82, 84
Beevar, D. A., 22, 39, 192
Beevar, R. J., 22, 39, 192

Bell, K., 150, 151, 161
Belsky, J., 65, 67, 84, 92, 195
Bempechat, J., 141
Benedict, G. C., 289
Benedikt, R., 167
Bengston, V., 181, 205
Bengston, V. L., 208, 212, 216
Benjamin, C. N., 75
Bennett, N., 58
Bennett, S. L., 82
Berenthal, B., 77
Berger, K. S., 73, 77, 99, 103, 130, 132, 135, 139, 140, 239
Berger, R., 42, 48
Berman, J., 111
Bialostosky, K., 126, 129
Bian, F., 36
Bigner, J. J., 46, 75, 96, 283
Birengen, Z., 311
Bjoerkqvist, K., 125
Blacher, J., 232
Black, B., 290
Black, D., 259
Blehar, M. C., 9, 53, 67, 176
Blenkner, M., 189, 191, 218
Block, J., 152
Bloom, B., 277
Bloomfield, L., 125
Blum, R., 166
Bogenschneider, K., 168
Bolen, L., 229, 230
Booth, A., 202
Borland, M., 125
Bornstein, M., 81
Bottom, W., 243
Bourdeauhuij, I., 125
Bower, A., 228
Bowers, C., 228, 229
Bowlby, J., 7, 8, 9, 260, 270
Boxer, A. M., 218
Boyle, M., 72, 73, 231, 232
Brand, H., 31
Brand, S., 152
Brandstadter, J., 105

Subject Index